SURVEY OF AMERICAN LAW

SURVEY OF
AMERICAN LAW

ELMER C. JOHNSON
J. D., Ph.D

An Exposition-University Book

EXPOSITION PRESS   NEW YORK

340.0973
J63s
80484
oct/1972

EXPOSITION PRESS INC.

50 Jericho Turnpike   Jericho, New York 11753

FIRST EDITION

LIBRARY OF CONGRESS CATALOG CARD NUMBER: 78-98957

EP 682–47032-5

Dedicated to

THE HONORABLE JUDGE ELMER N. HOLMGREN

of the Circuit Court of Cook County, Chicago, Illinois

and

TO MY BELOVED MOTHER

CONTENTS

PREFACE

Today, when change is in the air, there seems to be a great need among Americans for practical legal knowledge, to answer questions about the rights and duties of all citizens, whether in home, office, school, or elsewhere.

Knowledge of the law builds respect for law and order. Once you know your rights and duties as a citizen, you will have a guide to legal first aid. There is little justification for resorting to violence and destruction to secure what one thinks is one's right. Even labor unions, though by some considered militantly aggressive, usually win their reasonable requests by peaceful legal means in seeking new contracts with employers.

Because ignorance of the law is never an excuse, a broad knowledge of the law, in perspective, should be every citizen's aim. There is a real need for good "practical lawyers" who know how to keep out of trouble and can assist others in keeping out of trouble. This survey will inform readers of the ways that lead away from litigation, so that they can carry on their dealings with an intelligent awareness of their rights, duties, and limitations.

Actual cases decided in the courts furnish much of the material. These are more valuable to the average reader, as well as to the student, than purely hypothetical cases. Careful selection has been made throughout from among cases reported in the United States and England, the fruit of many years of searching for answers and precedents in the practice and part-time teaching of law.

Under twenty-five headings most of the legal problems commonly met with are taken up, and in sufficient detail to be helpful. Sometimes the different conclusions arrived at by the courts of different states are pointed out, to indicate that the law can vary with the jurisdiction.

This book should enable you to cooperate with your attorney more advantageously in preserving your rights and presenting your evidence in any litigation to which you may become a party.

–E. C. J.

INTRODUCTION

Agency of Social Control. Law is a body of rules prescribed by the state for the regulation of human conduct. Although man now comes into the world as a member of organized society, formerly he must have lived on this earth for a long time, perhaps hundreds of thousands of years, without being subject to any authority coming from the state. In this prestatal period the individual possessed every right that could be gained by physical force and violence. Authorities are divided as to the status of man in early times: some maintain that he lived in peace with his neighbors, others that there was constant conflict. Whichever it was, the individual was not under any sort of social control. Instead, he exercised every right that he was capable of defending. He bowed to no authority but his own conscience.

Origin and Function of State. The state as a distinct social institution in human affairs came into existence first for the protection of life and property—in other words, to maintain order. The functions of the modern state have been so expanded that we might think it is an agency that stands chiefly for educational opportunities, transportation facilities, welfare work, and the like; but the fact remains that the state today, as before, stands primarily for the maintenance of law and order.

Great men disagree on just how the state began. Hobbes, Locke, and other famous political speculators approved the contract theory of the origin of the state (although all organizations are based somewhat on contract). The idea that the state was first formed by private agreement presupposes a higher degree of intelligence than primitive man probably possessed.

In the medieval period religious writers promoted the theory and doctrine that the state is of holy origin. The Stuart kings of England followed the same line with their theory of the divine right of kings. But today the idea that Divine Providence created the state and endowed it with supreme power has been cast aside by all leading authorities, and it is generally admitted that the state is an institution made by man. (However, the Ten Commandments given to Moses on Mount Sinai did form a basis for guidance in human relations.)

Some writers have held that the state came about wholly as the result of force imposed by the strong upon the weak. But modern scholars do not hold that force as a single element brought the state into existence, although force always has been present, and needed by the state and its program. Now that the theory of evolution has been applied to the planets, to life on this earth, and to the soul of man, the same theory is being offered to explain almost every known condition in the material, social, and spiritual worlds. The idea that out of the family grew the clan, the tribe, and then the state thus fits in with the modern trend to explain everything in terms of evolution. It is the most orderly and reasonable explanation of the origin of the state we can think of. It assumes that the family as an institution in human society came before the state.

State and Individual. After the state was established, it proved to be a superorganization over the individual. From that time on man did not have every right; to gain the protection of the state, he had to give up certain rights to be transferred to the state. He was now a member of the social group. The state owed him the duty to protect his life and his property. Man, as a member of the social group, found it to his advantage to trade with his fellow men. Private transactions called for intercession by this superauthority. Governmental agencies, being the machinery of the state, were responsible for regulating the conduct of individuals in their dealings with one another as well as in their dealings with the government. The body of law today consists of these regulations on the part of the modern state.

Systems of Law. This brief introduction does not aim at tracing the development of law, as that would involve the history of civilization.

There are two systems of jurisprudence from which the legal systems of modern nations have developed. They are the civil, or Roman, law; and the common law. The civil law was originally the law of the city of Rome, and it spread throughout the Roman Empire. Its tenets have been preserved and come down to us through the Justinian Code. It is the basis for the legal systems of Continental Europe and the Latin-American countries of the Western world. Quebec and Louisiana inherited the Roman law.

The common law grew up in medieval England. Its principles form the basis of the legal system in all English-speaking countries throughout the world.

Development of Common Law. The common law of England is often referred to as the unwritten law. This is correct to only a limited extent: court decisions of England have been recorded and preserved for over seven hundred years. Through these records may be traced the principles of human conduct as they affect the legal relationships of English-speaking people. Before the Norman Conquest, 1066, litigation was carried on in England by a system of local courts. These courts carried on a primitive and cruel procedure. There was no trial by jury. The common method of proof was by oath or by wager of law in civil cases and by ordeal of fire in criminal actions. One charged with a crime might be thrown into a deep pool of water or be made to carry a red-hot coal a certain distance. In the ordeal of water, if he sank, he was guilty; if he did not sink, his innocence was established. In the ordeal of fire, if the hand that carried the coal showed no scar after a certain time, the accused was freed. Under such a system the courts often failed, of course, to give real justice. These local Anglo-Saxon courts were decentralized and their services limited to local communities. The Normans did not overthrow these courts, but they died out as the people became used to the more efficient royal courts.

The Normans did not bring a judicial system with them to England, but they did introduce the inquest, which was a procedure for determining the facts, and from this developed the jury system, an outstanding feature of the common law. William the Conqueror established the Curia Regis, or King's Court, and gave it legislative, executive, and judicial functions. It served as a court for wealthy and powerful litigants for the first one hundred years. During the reign of Henry II (1154-89) certain reforms were brought about, and the royal courts were thrown open to the common people. The nationalization of English law can only be given a brief summary here. It represents on a grand scale the development of a system of jurisprudence that expands and develops itself to the changing needs of society. Out of the Curia Regis gradually emerged the Court of Common Pleas, the Court of the Exchequer, and the Court of the King's Bench. Originally the first of these had jurisdiction over disputes, the second dealt with matters concerning the king's revenue, and the third had jurisdiction over criminal matters. Later, the Court of the King's Bench and the Court of the Exchequer were given jurisdiction with Common Pleas over private controversies.

Common-law procedure in the courts was very formal and technical. A particular action required the pleadings to be in a certain phraseology, another action required a slightly different one, and a pleading not in exact form would have no standing in court. Thus substance gave way to form. Today our code pleadings, by simplification of procedure, consolidation of types of action, and other reforms, have greatly expedited the administration of justice; however, the procedures and principles of common law were transplanted in America by the colonists, so that American law is an outgrowth of the common law inherited from England. The statutes have codified the great principles of human conduct that have been adapted to our own conditions.

Equity Jurisprudence. When the common-law courts in England were developed, a system of equity jurisprudence grew up. The equity courts did not cover the broad field included within the jurisdiction of the common-law courts. They modified or supplemented the activities of the latter. They did not compete with the law courts but provided a remedy when these were unable to bring about justice. For example, the common-law courts had no power to enforce contracts or to prevent the commission of an act. They could render a judgment for the possession of personal or real property and a judgment for damages, but it might be that neither of these remedies would give genuine relief to the party bringing the action. For example: A contracts to buy B's farm. B changes his mind and refuses to convey same. Under common law A had no relief except to sue for damages as a result of B's non-performance. Equity, on the other hand, would grant specific performance and thus compel B to deed over the property to A. Again, B threatens to divert a stream of water, causing it to overflow on A's land. Under common law A could not prevent this but must wait and then sue B for damages. Equity would prohibit B from this act pending adjudication of the rights of the parties in court. This developed into the modern writ of injunction. In addition the procedure of the equity courts was less formal than that of the law courts. Greater freedom was allowed in the submission of proof, and the chancellor who presided over this court was given discretion not allowed the law-court jurists.

Beginning with the chancellorship of Lord Nottingham (1673-82), who is called the father of equity, judgments of the equity courts were written out in full. Before this time each chancellor decided the controversies submitted to him on the basis of individual merit, as there was no written record from which to follow precedent. Following the practice of Lord Nottingham, equity became about as rigid in its application as had been the law courts. Equity was administered in England by separate courts until 1873, when the Judicature Act united all the higher tribunals into a Supreme Court of Judicature and provided that "it shall have jurisdiction, over all civil cases whether in law or equity." Along with the common law, we inherited equity from England. At present most of our states follow the English practice and provide for the adjudication of rights, legal or equitable, by the same court and under a single form of action.

Law Merchant. In addition to common-law courts and equity courts England developed a system of jurisprudence called the law merchant. This special law dealt with controversies among merchants and was based on customs of international usage. Courts administering these laws were called mercantile courts. They were located mostly along the seacoast. They came into existence to serve the needs of businessmen engaged in foreign commerce. These merchants were a roving class; they demanded justice in a hurry, and the law courts with their technical procedure were not adapted to serve them. Foreign merchants temporarily in England were especially handicapped, as they were utterly unfamiliar with this complicated system of jurisprudence. The mercantile courts dealt principally with matters pertaining to bills of exchange, insurance, sales, and the like. Following the appointment of Sir Edward Coke as chief justice of the Court of Common Pleas in 1606, the law courts began to draw mercantile cases. This movement was accelerated by the appointment of Lord Mansfield as chief justice in 1756; this distinguished English jurist made a special effort to learn what constituted the usages of trade. The mercantile courts were later merged with the law courts, but they made a distinct contribution to the law of business transactions. In our own country the idea of special legislation dealing with business is an outgrowth of the law merchant in England. We now have among our American states varying degrees of uniformity in such legislation as negotiable-instrument acts, sales acts, stock-transfer acts, partnership acts, and warehouse-receipt acts.

Admiralty and Ecclesiastical Courts. A separate and distinct branch of law called admiralty law is maintained in some countries. The jurisdiction of admiralty courts extends to contracts, torts, and other offenses involved in maritime transactions. In the United States there are no admiralty courts, since our Constitution, under Article III, Section 2, provides that federal courts shall have jurisdiction over maritime and admiralty cases.

Another distinct type of court is the ecclesiastical court, established in England after the Norman Conquest. Originally it had jurisdiction over civil and criminal cases involving clergymen or any spiritual matters. These courts are retained in England, but their jurisdiction has been greatly limited, and at present they deal only with purely ecclesiastical matters. Our legal system has nothing similar to these courts.

Organization of Government. Law in its broader aspect may be thought of as an expression of the people through their governmental agencies. To understand the functioning process of law one must be familiar with the organization of government through which it operates. Most of the great nations have a unitary type of government. France is an example. The central government at Paris has virtually complete sovereign power. The political subdivisions of France—departments, arrondissements, communes—possess only such powers as have been delegated to them. In contrast our government is a federation. This means that the sovereign power is divided between the states and the national government. In matters pertaining to war, defense, coinage of money, treaties, and the like, our national government has exclusive and final power to act. Likewise, in matters concerning education, roads, charity, health, and the like, the American state is absolutely sovereign in its control. Sovereignty, which is the "supreme will of the people," is not divisible; but under our plan of government the sovereign power is divisible and flows from two distinct channels, each of which is supreme in its own field. From the revolutionary period to the adoption of our Constitution, in 1789, we had a confederation. The American states were supreme, for in the last analysis they enjoyed every sovereign power. Upon adoption of the Constitution the states transferred to the national government certain powers as irrevocable powers. Our central government, then, is one of delegated powers; and our framework of government is the outstanding example in the world today of a federation.

Constitutional, or Fundamental, Law. As a result of our type of government, we have two main divisions of law, federal and state. In each classification we have constitutional, or fundamental, law and statutory law. The former is the basic, organic law. It provides for the framework or structure of government, creates the various governmental agencies, defines their powers, and prescribes whatever limitation to the exercise of these powers the people may desire. And change in constitutional law is brought about by following the amending process set out in the constitution itself.

Statutory Law. Statutory law, on the other hand, is the law enacted by legislative bodies, either the United States Congress or the state legislatures. It comprises the great body of rules setting out in detail the relationship between the individual and the state as well as the complicated legal relationships among individuals. Not only does it provide for the fundamental law, but it covers the entire field of private rights. The laws dealing with contracts, torts, crimes, and the like are within its scope, and machinery for the operation and administration of the same is prescribed in detail. For many years our state constitutions were brief documents providing for the bare framework of government. In recent years the tendency has been to lengthen these constitutions and to incorporate within their boundaries much of the law that would ordinarily be thought of as statutory law. In contrast to constitutional law, a legislative enactment may be made today and revoked tomorrow; that is, the legislative body itself can change the statutory law at will. For example: In the law of descent the surviving spouse takes only half the personal property; the legislature can change this so that the surviving spouse takes all the personal property.

Miscellaneous Classification of Law. In addition to the classification of law as federal and state, and as constitutional, or fundamental, and statutory, various classifications are frequently made on the basis of relationships involved. A few of the more important types of law frequently referred to may be summarized as follows:

International law is the system of jurisprudence that defines the rights and prescribes the duties of nations in their intercourse with one another (Kent's *Commentaries on the American Law*).

Municipal law is a rule of civil action prescribed by the supreme power of a state (Kent's *Commentaries*). In theory this law defines the rights to be observed and the wrongs to be avoided. It points out the remedies to be pursued by injured parties and contains the penalties to be imposed upon violators of the law.

Substantive law refers to the law that deals with the rights and duties of individuals or groups. It defines and limits the acts of one party in respect to those of another party.

Adjective law deals with the rules of procedure by which the rights and duties under substantive law may be enforced.

Public law deals with the legal relationships between the individual or group on the one hand and the state or government on the other.

Private law deals with the controversies or relationships between individuals. It is divided into the law of persons, the law of property, the law of damages, the law of domestic relations, and the like.

Judiciary. Under our system of government the judiciary is charged with the responsibility of enforcing and interpreting the law. The courts provide the legal machinery for this work. As noted above, our plan of government is a federation with two main bodies of law, federal and state. Space will permit only a brief summary.

A national judiciary is necessary to determine the limits within which each branch of government must move. The Constitution delegates certain powers to Congress; other grants of power are given to the President. It denies the right of the national Congress to legislate with regard to certain things. Prohibitions are also placed upon the states. In some fields both the states and the national Congress are forbidden to act, whereas in others they enjoy concurrent powers. In short, a federal type of government carries with it the need for a strong, independent national judiciary. This was recognized by the framers of our Constitution. Alexander Hamilton stated that the crowning defect of the government under the Articles of Confederation was the absence of a national judiciary. In extent of power our federal judicial system outrivals that of any other country, and critics of government point to our doctrine of "judicial supremacy" as America's most conspicuous contribution to the science of government.

Federal Courts. Our federal courts are divided into three classes: district courts, circuit courts of appeals, and the Supreme Court. Special federal courts also have been created, as the Court of Claims and the Court of Customs Appeals. The Constitution itself prescribes definitely the scope of the national judicial power as follows: The judicial power shall extend to all cases in law and equity arising under the Constitution, the laws of the United States, and treaties made, or which shall be made, under their authority; to all cases affecting ambassadors and other public ministers and consuls; to all cases of admiralty and maritime jurisdiction; to controversies to which the United States shall be a party; to controversies between two or more states, between a state and a citizen of another state, between citizens of the same state claiming lands under grants of different states, and between a state and the citizens thereof and foreign states, citizens, or subjects. The phrase "between a State and a citizen of another State" does not apply now, since the Eleventh Amendment (passed in 1798) denies to federal courts the right to take cognizance of any suit against a state by a "citizen of another State or by citizens or subjects of any foreign State." (The 11th Amendment reflects the reaction of public sentiment against the decision in Chisholm v. Georgia, 2 Dallas 419.)

It should be noted that federal judicial power extends to certain matters regardless of the character of the parties involved. Whenever a controversy hinges upon interpretation of any clause in the United States Constitution, federal statutes, or a treaty to which the United States is a party, it is within the jurisdiction of federal courts (Cableman v. Peoria R.R. Co., 179 U.S. 335). For example: The Constitution provides that no one shall be deprived of life, liberty, or property without due process of law. Any individual whose rights under this due-process clause have been violated may sue in federal courts. He may, if he prefers, sue in state courts. In most cases involving rights set out in the Constitution, suit may be brought in either state or federal courts. The exclusive jurisdiction of federal courts, as provided by Congress, is limited to all civil actions to which a state is a party except those between a state and its citizens or against a state by citizens of another state or aliens; also to the following cases arising under either the Constitution or national statutes: crime penalties and seizures, and all admiralty, maritime, patent-right, copyright, and bankruptcy cases; and further to all suits and proceedings against ambassadors and other public ministers and against consuls and vice consuls.

TRANSFER OF CASES FROM STATE COURTS. Certain actions may be started in state courts and at the request of defendants be transferred to federal courts: First, where the parties to a suit reside in different states. Such transfer is said to be by reason of "diverse citizenship" of the parties. Second, if the matter at issue rests on some right found in the Constitution, federal laws, or treaties, suit may be transferred to federal courts; removal is then said to be by reason of a "federal question" involved. Transfer of cases within either of these two fields is based on the theory that plaintiff could have chosen the federal court if he had so desired and consequently defendant should be entitled to the same choice; also on the theory that defendant can often protect himself in this way from local prejudices. Such removals are nearly always made to inferior federal courts, but they may eventually reach the Supreme Court. Appeals may, however, be made from the supreme court of a state to the Supreme Court of the United States if the decision in the state supreme court involves a right claimed under the Constitution, laws, or treaties of the United States.

U.S. DISTRICT COURTS. There are 85 United States district courts and 305 district-court judges in the United States. In each district there are a United States district attorney and a United States marshal. Each district court has attached to it a federal commissioner who conducts preliminary hearings in criminal cases and decides whether the accused shall be held for the grand jury. The jurisdiction of this court includes all federal crimes. Its civil cases include those arising out of internal-revenue, postal, copyright, patent, and bankruptcy laws, and the like. The great majority of cases that come before federal courts are entered in district courts, and most of them are settled there, very few cases going to circuit courts of appeals.

U.S. CIRCUIT COURTS OF APPEALS. There are ten circuit courts of appeals. Each one embraces three or more states and has assigned to it from two to four judges, for a total of 76 judges. The District of Columbia Circuit Court of Appeals has eight judges. These courts have appellate but not original jurisdiction, their cases being limited to those first tried in federal district courts or to a review of orders issued by certain administrators of such bodies as the Interstate Commerce Commission, the Federal Trade Commission, and the Federal Reserve Board. In many cases they exercise final authority; but when the constitutionality of an act is involved, the case may always be appealed to the Supreme Court. As the name indicates, the circuit courts of appeals were created for the purpose of relieving the Supreme Court and expediting its work.

U.S. SUPREME COURT. The Supreme Court consists of one chief justice and eight associate justices. Like all federal judges, the members of this court are appointed by the President with the consent of the Senate and hold office during good behavior. The Federal Act of 1938 permits voluntary retirement of Supreme Court justices at the age of seventy with full pay after ten years of service (28 USCA 375a). This court has original jurisdiction in but two kinds of cases: those affecting ambassadors, public ministers, and consuls; and those to which a state is a party. The great majority of its cases come up from lower federal courts, or from state supreme courts when federal questions are involved. As a matter of fact the Supreme Court never officially annuls a statute. What it does is to refuse to enforce the particular statute. The executive department of the federal government or of the state government, as the case may be, merely drops enforcement of the law, and the court below takes cognizance of the Supreme Court's decision. Federal courts will take no notice of the constitutionality of a statute except when the issue is raised in the regular course of litigation. Washington in one instance sought the advice of the Supreme Court on twenty-nine different questions; the court refused in each case on the ground that it could give opinions only in cases properly brought before it through regular judicial proceedings.

State Courts. The state judiciary differs greatly in the various states. In fact, we have fifty state judicial systems. In a very general classification the state courts fall into three groups: local courts, the general trial court, and the supreme court. The police court is also an important local court in our city centers. This court originated in England during the fourteenth century. It stands primarily for the settlement of trivial disputes, and its decisions are final in only the most petty cases. There are no clerks connected with the court, no permanent official records, and no seal. For these reasons the justice of the peace court is not a court of record. When an appeal is taken, the trial in the higher court is ordinarily a trial *de novo*—that is, the trial is conducted as if no trial had previously taken place, ignoring completely the justice of the peace trial. In addition to serving as judge of the court, the justice of the peace is authorized to issue warrants, conduct examinations, and bind the accused over to wait the action of a grand jury. He may perform marriage ceremonies and administer oaths.

COUNTY COURT. A general trial court is held in every county at least once a year. This court is called by various names, including district court, county court, and circuit court, but in all cases it serves as an intermediate court of general trial jurisdiction and equally has authority to try all cases in law or equity. This court has original jurisdiction in all criminal cases and can in all matters render a final decision concerning the facts. An appeal may be taken on points of law. In civil matters the jurisdiction of this court is not only original but also appellate from the justice of the peace court or municipal courts. In some states probate matters also come within the jurisdiction of this court; in others a separate probate court is established.

SUPREME COURT. Every state has a supreme court. In Kentucky, Maryland, and New York it is called the Court of Appeals; in New Jersey, the Court of Errors and Appeals. The term of office of state supreme court justices varies from two years in Vermont, fourteen in New York, and twenty-one in Pennsylvania to "good behavior" in Massachusetts, New Hampshire, and Rhode Island. The function of this court is to hear and decide appeals from courts of general trial jurisdiction. In a few instances it exercises original jurisdiction, but in the large majority of cases its attention is centered on appeals from lower courts dealing with questions of law. In a few states—Maine, New Hampshire, Massachusetts, Rhode Island, Florida, Missouri, Colorado, and South Dakota—the governor or the legislature may require the opinion of the supreme court on the constitutionality of an existing or proposed law, but as a general rule the decision of the court may be obtained only through regular channels of litigation.

SPECIAL STATE COURTS. In about one third of the states there are intermediate courts between the general trial court and the supreme court. There are also a variety of courts known as Court of Domestic Relations, Juvenile Court, Land Court, Municipal Court, etc. The jurisdiction and function of these various courts are governed expressly by statutory regulation. Outside of the justice of the peace court, the general trial court, and the supreme court, there is no uniformity of court structure among the states.

Court Procedure—Criminal Cases. Court procedure depends upon whether the case is a criminal or a civil action. The general principles of procedure are alike in federal and state courts. If the action is criminal, prosecution is by the state, and the purpose of the trial is punishment for the violation of law. In a civil case the injured party brings action, and the purpose of the suit is usually damages. The steps in a criminal action include arrest, bail, if the offense is bailable, accusation, either through indictment by a grand jury or information by the prosecuting attorney, arraignment before the court, and the entering of a plea by the accused of guilty or not guilty. (Accusation is by indictment in federal criminal cases.) If the plea is not guilty, the next step is the trial; this involves selection of a jury, presentation of evidence by the state and cross-examination by the defense, presentation of evidence by the accused and cross-examination by the prosecution, arguments before the jury, instructions to the jury by the court, and the verdict. Sentence is then pronounced by the court.

Civil Cases—Pleadings. In civil actions the court procedure varies greatly and requires strict compliance with statutory regulations. Some states retain many of the common-law formalities; others have limited the number of pleadings and simplified the procedure throughout. To illustrate the simplest type of civil procedure, a brief summary of the steps will be given.

A civil action is begun by the filing of a complaint. This particular pleading must conform to certain standards. It must contain a title consisting of the names of the court, the county, and the parties to the action. In addition it must contain a statement of the facts of plaintiff's case in ordinary, concise language and must contain a demand for relief. If money is demanded, the amount must be set out. To avoid multiplicity of lawsuits, the complaint may join all causes of action arising out of contract, claims for the specific recovery of real property, claims for the specific recovery of personal property, claims against a trustee by virtue of a contract or by operation of law, injuries to persons, injuries to character, and injuries to property. The complaint is filed with the clerk of the court, signed by plaintiff's attorney, verified, and served with summons on defendant.

Upon filing of the complaint, the clerk issues the summons and indorses on the complaint the year, month, day, hour, and minute when it was received. The summons is directed to defendant. It contains the names of the parties, the court, and the county, the signature of the clerk of the court, and the seal of the court. It is generally served by the sheriff, and return of the service is made by the sheriff in the form of a certificate; if the service is made by one other than the sheriff, an affidavit of the service must be filed. The court may grant permission to make service of the summons by publication, in which case the summons must contain in addition a statement of the cause of action. The need for the summons may be waived by the appearance of defendant in court or by defendant's filing an answer to the complaint. A copy of the complaint is served with the summons.

Defendant may file a demurrer, or answer to the complaint. In some states he may file a cross-complaint. A demurrer may be made on the ground that the court has no jurisdiction over the defendant or over the subject matter of the action; that plaintiff has no legal capacity; that there has been a misjoinder of parties; that there has been a misjoinder of causes; that the facts of the complaint are not sufficient to state a cause of action; that another action is pending for the same cause; that the complaint is ambiguous, unintelligible, or uncertain. The demurrer must be filed with the clerk of the court and a copy served on plaintiff or his attorney, usually within about twenty days after service of the summons; if summons is served by publication, a longer period is granted. The demurrer raises a question of law, which is to be decided by the judge. If it is sustained, defendant wins; if overruled, defendant under modern practice is usually allowed to file an answer.

The answer is filed with the clerk and a copy served on plaintiff or his attorney. It may consist of a general or a specific denial of the material allegation in the complaint. It may contain new matter consitituting a defense or counterclaim. If the complaint is verified, the answer must usually contain a specific denial to each allegation; but if it is not verified, a general denial is sufficient. In case a counterclaim is omitted, defendant cannot as a rule sue plaintiff later for this claim. Plaintiff may file a demurrer to the answer on the ground that several causes of counterclaim are improperly joined; that the answer does not state facts sufficient to constitute a defense; or that the answer is ambiguous, unintelligible, or uncertain.

Court Trial. After the pleadings have culminated in an issue, the next step is the trial. If the issue is one of law, it is decided by the judge; if it is one of fact, it rests with the jury to decide, unless the parties waive their right to a jury trial and ask the judge to pass on the facts. If it is a jury trial, the first step is the impaneling of the jury. Each party is entitled to a limited number of peremptory challenges and can also challenge for cause. Plaintiff's case is presented first and is usually opened with a brief statement to the jury by plaintiff's attorney outlining what he intends to establish and the more important parts of the evidence that he will produce. Presentation of testimony is a very technical matter. Witnesses are brought into court through a subpoena issued by the court. Leading questions are not permitted, except to a very limited extent. Each witness is subject to cross-examination by defendant on the points involved in the direct examination. When plaintiff has finished, defendant, through his attorney, makes an opening statement to the jury, and the evidence of the defense follows the same routine as that of plaintiff. This may be done immediately following the opening statement of plaintiff's attorney. Rebuttal evidence is permitted and likewise cross-examination of the same. Also, depositions may be presented by both plaintiff and defendant under certain conditions.

Following the presentation of evidence by plaintiff and defendant, the case is argued by the attorneys, the argument being opened and closed by the party having the affirmative side, which is usually plaintiff. The judge then instructs the jurors on the law which governs the issues before them. The jury then retires to a jury room and remains until a verdict is agreed upon or until it is discharged because no agreement can be reached. Upon arriving at a verdict, the jury is brought before the court, and its decision is announced by the foreman. The verdict is then made part of the court record of the case, and the jury is discharged. The court then renders a judgment on the verdict. The judgment is signed by the judge presiding at the trial and is also made a part of the court record. The case may be appealed to a higher court by following the required technical procedure. If not reversed by a higher court, it is carried into effect by a process known as an execution.

Commercial Law. Commercial law is a phrase to denote those branches of the law which relate to persons engaged in commerce and their rights to property. As the subjects with which commercial law has to deal are dispersed throughout the globe, it results that this branch of the law is local and more general in its character than any other. Many of the maxims and rules are of great antiquity and of the highest value and authority.

Statutory law takes precedence of and nullifies common law.

An illustration will more effectively point out the difference between common law and statutory law and the precedence which one takes over the other in applying the rules of commercial law. X and Y, husband and wife, sign a promissory note for $2,000. At common law the wife would not be liable on the note, because a married woman could not make herself liable on contracts: all her contractual rights were, at the time of marriage, merged into those of her husband. The legislatures of the different states have, however, passed acts (statutory law) removing the disability of coverture and empowering a married woman to make contracts, either jointly with her husband or alone, on which she can be sued.

Because of the nature of the transaction, the law which governs it is called commercial law, and it is regulated by either common law or statutory law.

Legal Maxims

1. No one is bound to do what is impossible.
2. No injury is done by things long acquiesced in.
3. Voluntary outward acts indicate the inward intent.
4. An action is not given to one who is not injured.
5. The act of God does wrong to no one.
6. Ignorance of the law is no excuse.
7. An act done by me against my will is not my act.
8. The proof lies upon him who affirms, not him who denies.
9. Let the purchaser beware.
10. That is certain which can be made certain.
11. No one is punished for his thoughts.
12. Confirmation supplies all defects.
13. When two parties are equally at fault, the claimant is always at the disadvantage, and the party in possession has the better cause.
14. Debts follow the person of the debtor.
15. The law helps persons who are deceived, not those deceiving.
16. A man's house is his castle.
17. A gift is not presumed.
18. Equity looks upon that as done which ought to be done.
19. He who comes into court must come in with clean hands.
20. Every man is presumed to intend the natural and probable consequences of his own voluntary acts.
21. A right of action cannot arise out of fraud.
22. A contract cannot arise out of an illegal act.
23. The law does not regard the fraction of a day.
24. No one shall be profited by his own wrongs.
25. Public rights are to be preferred to private rights.
26. A right cannot arise from a wrong.
27. Many promises lessen confidence.
28. No one can be punished twice for the same fault.
29. No man can contradict his own deed.
30. Things invalid from the beginning cannot be made valid by subsequent acts.
31. A thing void in the beginning does not become valid by lapse of time.
32. Ratification is equal to command.
33. A wrong is not done to one who knows and wills it.
34. If anything is due to the corporation, it is not due to the individual members of it, nor do the members individually owe what the corporation owes.
35. When the law presumes the affirmative, the negative is to be proven.

SURVEY OF AMERICAN LAW

I. CONTRACTS

Definition. A contract is an oral or written agreement, based upon legal consideration, to do or not to do some legal, possible thing, made between two or more competent parties.

Necessary Conditions. Four fundamental elements are the foundation of all contracts: (1) competent parties, (2) legal subject matter, (3) agreement, (4) consideration. In the case of some written contracts, a seal is necessary, which is said to signify consideration.

Executed and Executory Contracts. An executed contract is one in which the transaction has been performed and the terms of the agreement have been fulfilled. It is a contract that has been carried out.

An executory contract is one in which the thing agreed on has not been done.

Some contracts may be executed on one side and executory on the other; that is, one party may have performed his part of the contract, while the other party has not.

An illustration of this class of contracts is found in Andreas v. Holcombe, 22 Minn. 339, which was an action on the following agreement:

$140.   St. Paul, Minnesota, 17 June, 1874
In consideration for using a 12-inch view of Park Place Hotel to be printed in his atlas of the State of Minnesota, I promise to pay A. T. Andreas, or his order, the sum of one hundred forty dollars; payments to be made, one half on completion of design, draft, or sketch; remainder when atlas is complete. One hundred extra views given on delivery of atlas.
                          [Signed] E. V. Holcombe

Andreas had got out the book as above specified. The defense claimed that the agreement was not binding upon both parties. It was held that while the writing did not show any consideration on the part of Andreas, it was in the nature of a request to do the things specified and became a binding and valid contract when

performed on the one side, as the performance was but complying with the request.

Miller v. McKenzie, 95 N.Y. 575, was an action on a
promissory given by McKenzie. The consideration was for board
and care during illness and for future services to be rendered by
plaintiff when required. Such services were rendered by plaintiff
until McKenzie died. It was held that a promissory note given
in consideration of future services to be rendered becomes valid
upon the performance of such services in reliance thereon, even
though there was no agreement on the part of the payee at the
time of receiving the note to render them.

Formal and Simple Contracts. Contracts are again classified as formal and simple.

Formal contracts are also known as contracts under seal, and
are required to be executed in a certain way, that is, with a
seal attached. Contracts executed in this way do not require any
consideration. The seal is said to give consideration.

In Van Valkenburgh v. Smith, 60 Me. 97, defendant,
to obtain discharge of a suit pending against a railway company
and in favor of plaintiff, gave a bond to plaintiff conditioned
upon allowing a given time within which defendant would give
certain notes indorsed to plaintiff as specified. This was not
done, and the defense set up that there was no consideration
for the agreement. The court held that the bond being under
seal, the law implied a consideration from the solemnity of its
execution.

Rutherford v. Baptist Convention, 9 Ga. 54, was an action on
a written instrument given to Baptist Convention, and recited
the consideration to be "the importance of literary and religious
institutions to the wellbeing of society." The instrument was
sealed. The defense was, no consideration. The court said, "The
seal imports a consideration, and no other consideration is
necessary to give it validity."

Under English law the form of the seal was definitely
prescribed. In early times the seal was an impression on wax, but
statutes have relaxed the rigor of the rule, and now the impression may be on a wafer or on the document itself, and in some
states a scroll or mark made with the pen, or the word "seal,"
printed or written, if employed as a seal, is sufficient.

L.S. are letters commonly used to designate a seal. They are the initial letters of the Latin words *locus sigilli,* meaning the place of the seal.

In Norvell v. Walker, 9 W. Va. 447, the parties entered into a written agreement which concluded with the words "Witness the following signatures and seals." Then followed W's signature, followed by a scroll, and directly under it N's signature. It was held that one scroll was adopted as the seal of both parties and was sufficient.

Farmers and Manufacturers Bank v. Haight, 3 Hill (N.Y.) 493, is a case decided in New York in 1842. It was held that the seal of a private individual or of a religious corporation impressed directly upon paper without the use of wax or other tenacious substance is a nullity. (But this is not the express law in New York State at the present time.)

The principal requisite to the validity of a seal is that it be the intent of the parties to use the scroll or mark as such, and this is usually expressed by the words "In witness whereof we have hereunto set our hands and seals," with the day and year first above written, or some analogous form.

A seal is not now given the prominence it formerly had, and in some jurisdictions it is regarded as merely presumption of consideration. The contracts usually required to be sealed are deeds, bonds, and mortgages, and some other important instruments.

The simple contract known as a parol contract is one that depends for its validity on the presence of consideration. It may be a contract required by law to be in some particular form other than under seal, as contracts which by law are required to be in writing. It may also be a contract of which no particular form is required by law, as one that is valid whether written or oral, for instance a contract of employment.

Oral and Written Contracts. As just indicated, contracts may be either oral or written. All contracts under seal must be in writing, and some simple contracts as well, but most contracts in business are oral. You hire a man to do a day's work for you. He agrees. This is an oral contract.

Express and Implied Contracts. There are also express and implied contracts. The former are those in which the agreement on each side is expressly stated, and the latter those in which the terms are understood from acts or words.

Blackstone (II, 443), says, "When the terms of the agreement are openly uttered and avowed at the time of the making, as to deliver an ox or ten loads of timber, or to pay a stated price for certain goods, it is an express contract. Implied are such as reason and justice dictate and which therefore the law presumes that every man undertakes to perform; as, if I employ a person to do any business for me or perform any work, the law implies that I undertake, or contract, to pay as much to him as his labor deserves."

PARTIES

Two or More Persons Necessary. We have learned that a contract is an agreement between two or more persons. There arises the question what persons can be parties to a contract.

Our definition says that there must be two or more persons. A man cannot contract with himself; that is, a man as trustee or agent cannot in such capacity deal with himself in his individual capacity.

In Bain v. Brown, 56 N.Y. 285, Brown was the agent for Bain and was authorized to sell certain real estate for $17,000. He contracted to sell at this figure and so advised Bain. Next day he negotiated to sell the property to other parties for $26,000 and signed a contract in his own name. He then secured an assignment of the first contract and had Bain deed direct to the second purchasers. An action was brought to recover the difference between $17,000 and $26,000. It was held that assuming the first sale to have been made in good faith, the agent could not appropriate the advances but that the principal was entitled to the benefit.

In White v. Ward, 26 Ark. 445, it was held that the purchase by a trustee or an agent of property of which he has the sale carries fraud on the face of it. It is an abuse of confidence, and any title or benefit derived therefrom enures to the benefit of the principal.

There are disqualifying circumstances or conditions, necessary for us to consider, which render a person incompetent to enter into a contract with another.

INFANCY

Infancy Defined. By common law all persons under the age of twenty-one years are infants; and this is the law in all states, excepting that in a few states females are by statute declared of age at eighteen, and either males or females upon marriage at any age.

Infancy is a period in the life of every person during which, because of his tender years, he is incapable of doing business for himself, when he is not of sufficient maturity to bind himself by agreement. But as the child increases in age, his mental capacity grows and strengthens, and he arrives at a time when he is fully qualified to care for himself and to make agreements that will bind him.

The exact age when this condition begins differs with the person, but the law has decided that twenty-one is an average age. It is then that a person, in the eyes of the law, attains full mental capacity.

Law Protects Infants. Until this age arrives, the law puts many safeguards around the infant so that he will not be imposed upon. In general it may be said that any contract made by an infant is in law voidable; that is, the infant on coming of age can repudiate it and demand that any consideration he may have paid be returned to him.

In Spencer v. Carr, 45 N.Y. 406, the parents of an infant six years of age deeded real estate to her. Subsequently the parents deeded the same property in trust to another, and the infant, at the mother's request, signed the mother's name to the deed. It was held that the infant could claim title under the original deed to her.

In Carpenter v. Carpenter, 45 Ind. 142, plaintiff, an infant, had traded horses. He tired of his bargain, and having tendered back the horse he received, demanded his original horse. It was refused. The court held that he could recover his horse, and do so even if he could not tender back the horse he had got in the trade and even if it was injured or dead. It is not necessary for disaffirmance to put the other party in status quo, unless it is possible for the infant to do so. This case also holds that the infant's falsely representing himself to be of age did not prevent his avoiding the contract.

Contract of Infant Is Voidable and Not Void. No one but the infant himself, his legal representatives after his death, or those entitled to his estate can, if the contract is avoided, disaffirm it. The contract is said to be held in abeyance during the infancy, and upon the infant's becoming of age, he may either affirm or disaffirm. When a contract with an infant is made by a person of full age, the infant alone has the right to disaffirm; the other party cannot repudiate it. The privilege is also personal to the infant; neither his guardian during his minority nor his creditors after he has become of age can disaffirm his contracts.

In Kendall v. Lawrence, 22 Pick (Mass.) 540, an infant deeded certain land to another, and after becoming of age, neither avoided nor confirmed the deed. After he became of age, the creditors of the infant tried to set aside the sale or take the land on attachment. It was held that the deed was valid as to third parties. The deed of a minor is voidable, and the right to avoid it is a personal privilege to the minor and his heirs.

Affirmance of Executed Contracts. The question at once arises, Must the infant, upon becoming of age, disaffirm to avoid the contract, or will it be considered to be avoided unless he actually affirms it? The answer depends entirely on the nature of the contract. The rule varies in its application to executed and executory contracts. In the case of an executed contract the benefit which the infant seeks to bestow is given to the other party and is good until it is disaffirmed, and the disaffirmance must be by express words or by some distinct and positive act which leaves no doubt of intent.

In Towle v. Dresser, 73 Me. 252, plaintiff, an infant, sold a horse to defendant and took two notes in payment. Later he tendered back the notes, rescinded the contract, and sued for possession of the horse. It was held that he could recover the horse. This, it will be seen, is a case in which express disaffirmance is necessary. The case also holds that the disaffirmance can be made during the infancy; this suit was brought by plaintiff, through his father, while he was yet an infant.

Silence for a reasonable time after majority will be construed, in many cases of this kind, as an affirmance, if it is coupled with retention of the benefits.

Affirmance of Executory Contracts. On the other hand, if the contract is executory, it is necessary for the infant to affirm upon becoming of age, or the contract is avoided. In such an agreement infancy is a defense if sued upon, unless it can be shown that the contract was affirmed after maturity.

Eureka Co. v. Edwards, 71 Ala. 248, was an action to cancel a deed executed by minors. It was held that if an infant executes a deed to lands, a binding satisfaction of the contract after he becomes of age requires that there be some positive act on his part either affirming the conveyance or making it inconsistent with the right to repudiate it.

An infant can generally disaffirm his contracts before as well as after becoming of age.

In Childs v. Dobbins, 55 Iowa 205, plaintiff, a minor, entered into a contract with defendant for the purchase of some trees and shrubbery amounting to $500, which he paid. About five days thereafter and while still a minor he tendered back the stock and demanded the consideration paid. It was held that an infant can disaffirm a contract at any time during minority or within a reasonable time thereafter.

The rule is well established that the infant cannot avoid a part and affirm the rest. He cannot affirm as to part and disaffirm as to the balance.

Heath v. West, 28 N.H. 101, is a case in which plaintiff purchased a horse, paying $75 in cash and giving his note secured by a mortgage on the horse for the balance. Plaintiff refused to pay the mortgage, and when the horse was sold to satisfy the same, brought an action to recover it. It was held that he could not repudiate the mortgage and hold the horse. It was all one transaction, and he could not avoid a part and affirm the rest. He must take the benefits with the detriments.

In rescinding an executed contract the infant must restore the property he has received if he has it, and he is liable to an action at law for its recovery; still, the right of an infant to disaffirm is superior to this right, and although the consideration the infant has received may have disappeared, yet the infant may disaffirm, even if he cannot return the thing received or its equivalent.

In Green v. Green, 69 N.Y. 553, defendant, a minor, sold certain land to his father for $400. After arriving at his majority, he re-entered upon the land and disaffirmed his contract. An action for trespass was brought by the father. The son did not offer to restore the $400, and it was shown he had used up, lost, or squandered the money, and had no part of it when he became of age. It was held that he had the right to disaffirm the deed without restoring the consideration. The right to rescind is a protection for the infant and is not contingent on an impossibility, and it might be impossible for him to restore the consideration if he did not have it.

There is a particular class of infant's contracts that are always void and therefore have no effect. This class is the power of attorney under seal, which is in no case valid. Many jurisdictions extend the rule to every appointment of an agent in any case, except where such appointment is necessary. When, however, the welfare of the infant requires the employment by him of others to perform services in his behalf, appointment of an agent under such circumstances will be valid for necessaries.

In Trueblood v. Trueblood, 8 Ind. 195, a bond was given by an infant and his father that the infant would, upon becoming of age, convey a certain piece of property, and action was brought for the transfer. It was proved that after becoming of age, the boy ratified the act of his father in giving the bond as his agent. He later repudiated it and sold it to another. The court held that an infant cannot appoint an agent. Such an act is void, and ratification after becoming of age cannot make it of any effect.

Contracts for Necessaries. But there exist a number of cases in which an infant will be absolutely bound by his contracts, the principal illustration being his contracts for necessaries.

If the law did not give protection to parties furnishing the necessaries of life to an infant, many cases would arise, we can see, in which the infant might suffer. Therefore the law says that where an infant is not supplied with necessaries by his parents or guardian or others whom he may look to, he may contract for them himself. The law creates a promise on the part of the infant to pay what they are reasonably worth. This does not mean that the tradesman can charge what he pleases; so, it will be seen, the infant is still protected.

In Hyman v. Cain, 48 N.C. 111, defendant, an orphan about nine years of age, boarded with plaintiff for about two years. An action was brought for his board. The court held that the law implies a promise on the part of the infant to pay a reasonable price for necessaries furnished to him.

Morton v. Steward, 5 Bradwell (Ill.) 533, was an action on a note given by an infant, and it was proved that the consideration was necessaries furnished the infant. But the court held that an infant is incapable of starting an account or binding himself by a note to pay a particular price or sum for necessaries, although he is liable for the reasonable value of the necessaries furnished. The protection of an infant requires that the price charged be inquired into.

Necessaries Defined. The question of what necessaries are is often in dispute. The rule generally laid down is that they are any things required by the particular person for his reasonable comfort, subsistence, and education, regard being had to his means, occupation, and standing in society.

Peters v. Fleming, 6 M & W 41, was an action in an English court for a bill of goods sold to defendant. The goods consisted of four finger rings, a watch chain, some pins, etc., amounting to over 8 pounds. Plaintiff sought to hold defendant for necessaries. It appeared that defendant was a student at the University of Cambridge and that his father was a gentleman of fortune and a member of Parliament. The court held that it was a question for the jury whether the articles were such as a person of his station in life would reasonably require, and that necessaries included articles useful and suitable to the state and condition of the party.

In Strong v. Foote, 42 Conn. 203, defendant, a minor fifteen years of age and owner of a large fortune, had his teeth filled by plaintiff, a dentist. The bill rendered amounted to $93. It was proved that the teeth were decayed and pained the defendant. It was held that the work was for necessaries.

In Werner's Appeal, 10 Norris (Pa.) 222, it was held that a bill of $45 for nursing a person through his last illness and preparing the body for burial was a necessary and proper charge against his estate.

An infant is liable for necessaries supplied to his wife the same as if he were an adult.

A tradesman who furnishes an infant with supplies is bound to show that they are necessaries; and if they are necessaries,

but if the infant already has a sufficient supply, he cannot recover.
Barnes v. Toye, 13 Q.B.D. (Eng.) 410, was an action for the
price of necessaries furnished an infant. The defense was that the
infant was already sufficiently with goods of the same class and
not in want of these. The court held that defendant could
show that the goods were not necessaries, as he was already
supplied with sufficient goods of a similar description, and it was
immaterial whether plaintiff did or did not know of the existing
supply.

INSANITY

General Rule. Since a contract requires a meeting of the
minds of the contracting parties, it is evident that a person lacking the mental capacity cannot make a valid contract. Some
insane persons appear perfectly rational, and others have rational
periods. It is difficult, therefore, to determine the mental condition
of such parties, and one may deal with them in ignorance of
their insanity.

The rule is generally adopted in this country that if the insanity of a person has been decreed by the courts, and a party
dealing with him is ignorant of the insanity, and the contract has
been so far executed that the parties cannot be put in their original condition, the insane party is held.

Gribben v. Maxwell, 34 Kan. 8, was an action to set aside a
conveyance of real property executed by Olive Gribben, a lunatic. The purchaser did not know of her insanity and paid a
fair price for the property. The court held that where the purchaser of the real estate was made and the conveyance obtained
in good faith prior to an inquisition and finding of lunacy, and
for a fair and reasonable price, without knowledge of the
insanity, no advantage being taken of the insane person, the
conveyance cannot be avoided, if the consideration has not
been returned to the purchaser and no offer has been made to
return it.

But if the lunatic has been declared by the courts to be
insane, or if the party dealing with him knew of his insanity, the
contract is void.

In Carter v. Beckwith, 128 N.Y. 312, plaintiff, an attorney, upon the request of B, who had legally been declared insane, instituted proceedings to have him adjudged sane and to have control of his property restored to him. In this proceeding it was determined that he was still insane, and the application was refused. After B's death plaintiff presented his claim for services. It was held that he could not recover on the ground of a contract with B, as any contract entered into with a person judicially declared insane is absolutely void. The court, however, in its discretion allowed reasonable costs.

If the lunatic afterward becomes sane, he may then ratify or disaffirm all his voidable contracts, the same as an infant upon attaining his majority.

In Arnold v. Richmond Iron Works, 1 Gray (Mass.) 434, an insane person deeded away some land and after becoming of sound mind and knowing that the grantees were in possession, did not re-enter or disaffirm the conveyance, but received payments on the notes given for the purchase price. It was held that from this act his intention to ratify the deed might be inferred, although he did not know at the time that he had the power to avoid the deed. The deed was not void but voidable, and in order to avoid such a deed before affirmance, the consideration for it must be restored.

A lunatic, like an infant, is liable for necessaries.

Sawyer v. Lufkin, 56 Me. 308, was an action for services in caring for defendant, who was an insane person and incapable of caring for herself. The court held that if necessaries are furnished an insane person in good faith and under justifiable circumstances, the person furnishing them may recover of the insane person. The judge said, "If the law were not so, the insane might perish if guardians having means should neglect or refuse to furnish the supplies needed. They stand in the same position as a minor, and are liable for necessaries."

During a lucid interval, the lunatic being sane, his contracts are binding on him unless he has been declared legally insane.

Drunkenness May Render Contract Voidable. If a man enters into a contract while drunk, he may afterwards affirm or disaffirm it, unless he has been judicially declared a habitual drunkard, in which case his contracts are void.

In Carpenter v. Rodgers, 61 Mich. 384, plaintiff traded a good team of horses worth $150 to $200 with defendant, a horse dealer, for a team worth about $75. It was shown that plaintiff was of feeble mind and scarcely able to do business and that when the deal was made he was intoxicated to such a degree that he did not know what he was doing. There was, however, no rescission on the part of plaintiff, nor offer to return the team. It was held that a contract entered into by a party so drunk as not to know what he is doing is voidable and not void and may therefore be ratified or rescinded when he becomes sober. Not having been rescinded, the contract was binding.

In Bush v. Breinig, 113 Pa. St. 310, Breinig attended a public sale of real property, and he having made the highest bid, the property was struck off to him. Afterwards, while so drunk as to be deprived of reason and understanding, he executed a written contract of purchase and paid part of the purchase price. Thereafter he sought to avoid the contract and brought action to recover the money paid. The court allowed him to rescind the contract and to recover his money.

To affect his contract it is necessary that a person's reason be so impared by intoxication for the time being as to render him incompetent to comprehend the consequences of his own acts.

In Johns v. Fritchey, 39 Md. 258, a party sought to avoid a power of attorney given by him, on the ground that he was intoxicated. The court held that to avoid the contract on such ground, it was incumbent on him to produce clear and satisfactory proof that he was in such a state of drunkenness at the time as to be unable to know what he was doing or to judge of the consequence of his own acts.

Cummings v. Henry, 10 Ind. 109, was an action to recover on a note given for the purchase price of a horse. It was proved that defendant was intoxicated at the time and had afterwards offered to return the horse and asked for a rescission of the contract. It was held that the party might rescind if he was so far intoxicated as to be incompetent to contract.

MARRIED WOMEN

Under common law, from the earliest times, the husband was the head of the family. At marriage a life interest in his wife's real estate and absolute title to her personal property vested in him. The wife could not sue or be sued without her husband's joining or being joined as a party; her earnings became his; and in fact the identity of the married woman was lost, and she could not in her own name make a contract.

This is now so completely changed by statute throughout our own country and in England that is scarcely worth our notice except as an illustration of the changes which our laws undergo with the progress of time. Now we find that by the statute the married woman can conduct her own separate business and can contract independently of her husband; and in fact in most states she has the same legal rights and powers as an unmarried woman.

OFFER AND ACCEPTANCE

Foundation of Contract. Traced back to its origin, a contract amounts to this: The first party says, "I will take a certain sum for this article;" to this the second party answers, "I will accept your offer and give you the specified sum."

You enter a furniture store. The tradesman exhibiting his wares virtually says he will take the stated price for such articles. You say you will take a certain chair, marked $20. Here we have an offer and an acceptance.

The offer must be clearly stated. If A says, "I may take $100 for this desk when I get ready to sell," this is not an offer which B can accept and thereby create a contract.

The acceptance must be absolute and on the exact terms contained in the offer. If A offers to sell a box of oranges for $10, and B says he will give $9 for it, no contract is made, because there is no acceptance of the offer.

In Minneapolis & St. Louis v. Columbus Rolling Mill, 119 U.S. 149, plaintiff asked defendants the price on iron rails. On December 8 defendant offered to sell plaintiff from 2,000 to 5,000 tons of iron rails at a certain price, and added, "If accepted, we shall expect to be notified prior to December 20." On December 16 plaintiff wired, "Please enter our order for 1200 tons as per your favor of the 8th." December 18 defendant wired, "We can not book your order at that price." On December 19 plaintiff wired, "Enter our order for 2000 tons as per your letter of the 8th." Defendant refused to furnish the rails, and an action was brought for breach of contract. The court held that the telegram of the 16th was not an acceptance, as it was different in terms from the offer, and that this order amounted to a rejection of the offer and left it no longer open, as the telegram of the 19th was of no effect.

There Must Be No Qualification in Acceptance. If A offers to sell his automobile to B for $900, and B accepts it if A will take $300 down and his note for the balance at 30 days, the acceptance is qualified and does not constitute a contract.

In Baker v. Holt, 56 Wis. 100, defendant in Connecticut wrote to plaintiff in Wisconsin, offering to sell him certain land at a stated price payable at a specified time but said nothing about place of payment or delivery of the deed. Plaintiff replied that he would take the land on the terms mentioned, and added, "You may make out the deed, leaving the name of the grantee blank, and forward the same to I. L. Mosher at Grand Rapids, Wisconsin or to your agent, if you have one here, to hand to me on the payment of $200 and the delivery of the necessary security." It was held that the acceptance was not good, as it was based on the conditions that the deed be executed in blank and that payment be made in Wisconsin.

In Honeyman v. Marryatt, 6 H.L.C. (Eng.) 112, an estate was advertised for sale on certain terms. A authorized his solicitor to make an offer. B's agent in reply wrote: "Mr. B has authorized me to accept the offer subject to the terms of a contract being arranged between his solicitor and yourself. Mr. B requires a deposit from 1200 pounds to 1500 pounds and the completion of the purchase at Midsummerday next." There was no reply to this letter. It was held that the acceptance was conditional and so formed no complete contract.

Offer and Acceptance Must Pertain to Same Object. A may offer to sell his black dog for $100. B says, "I will give you that amount for your brown." There is no contract, because the minds of the parties have not met.

Offer Must Be Communicated to Party Accepting It. If the offer is not communicated, it cannot be said that the minds of the parties have met. If A says to B, "I will sell my car to X for $100 if he will give that amount," that does not constitute an offer to X about it, as it cannot be said to have been communicated by A.

In some states it is held that one who gives information concerning the parties to a crime without any knowledge of the reward which has been offered cannot claim the reward, as the offer has not really been communicated to him. Other states hold that he can recover, as the reward is a public offer and when acted upon binds the offeror. The weight of authority seems to be in favor of denying the right of plaintiff to recover when he had no knowledge of the reward prior to giving the information.

When a man works for another without his request or knowledge, there is no contract, and he cannot recover.

In Bartholomew v. Jackson, 20 Johns (N.Y.) 28, Jackson owned a field in which Bartholomew had a stack of wheat which he had promised to move in time for plowing. Notice having been given, he promised that it would be moved at 10 A.M. Relying on this promise, Jackson, shortly after 10 A.M., set fire to the stubble in a distant part of the field, but later he found that the stack had not been removed, so he removed it himself to save the grain, and then he sued Bartholomew for the work. It was held that the services were rendered without request and with no promise express or implied to pay for them, and there could be no recovery. The judge said, "If a man humanely bestows his labor, and even risks his life, in voluntarily aiding to preserve his neighbor's house from destruction by fire, the law consider the services rendered gratuitous."

Acceptance Must Be Communicated. Not only must the offer be communicated, but the acceptance must also be communicated, and whether it reaches the offeror or not, it must be something more than mere mental assent.

Stensgaard v. Smith, 43 Minn. 11, is a case in which plaintiff received from defendant a letter or statement setting forth that in consideration of plaintiff's agreement to act as agent for the sale of certain land, defendant gave to plaintiff the exclusive right of such sale for three months and promised to pay a stated commission on the sales. Plaintiff, a real-estate broker, took immediate steps to advertise and post notices for the sale of the premises, but one month thereafter defendant sold to another. Action was brought for damages for breach of contract. It was held that there was no contract. The instrument conferred authority on plaintiff to sell, and if he did sell, promised a commission. There was no mutuality of obligation. Plaintiff did not bind himself to do anything. If plaintiff, acting under this authority, had sold before revocation, the sale would have completed the contract, and the commission would have been earned.

Acceptance Is Binding as Soon as Made.—As we have seen, the offer must be communicated to the party before it is effectual, while an acceptance is binding as soon as made, even though it has not come to the knowledge of the offeror. The acceptance must be made in the way prescribed or in the way that would be naturally expected. If the offeror requires or suggests a mode of acceptance, he takes the risk of acceptance reaching him. A common illustration of this is the case of an offer made through the post office; here it may be assumed that the acceptance is to be made in the same way unless otherwise expressly stated. When made in the required way, it is held that as soon as the acceptance is sent the contract is made. And completion of the agreement dates from the time of mailing the letter (or sending the telegram), and not from the time of receiving it.

Taylor v. Merchants' Fire Insurance Co., 9 How. (U.S.) 390, is a case in which, after some correspondence, defendant insurance company wrote that it would insure plaintiff's house for $57. This letter was received December 21, and on that day plaintiff accepted the offer and sent his letter of acceptance with check enclosed. On December 22, and before plaintiff's letter of acceptance and check had reached the defendant, the house burned down. It was held that the contract was complete when the letter of acceptance was mailed and that therefore the company was liable.

In Trevor v. Wood, 36 N.Y. 307, plaintiff, living in New York, telegraphed defendant in New Orleans, asking the price of Mexican dollars delivered. On January 31 defendant answered by telegraph, giving price on 50,000, and on the same day plaintiff telegraphed and accepted the offer. The telegraph lines became disabled, and the message was not received until defendant had wired that the dollars had been sold to other parties. It was held that the contract was closed as soon as the acceptance was sent. As the offer was by telegraph, it was sufficient to accept in the same manner, and the offeror was bound irrespective of the time the acceptance was actually received.

Acceptance Must Be Made as Prescribed. But the preceding rule does not hold good if the offeror prescribes a particular way in which the acceptance must be made. For example, if the offer is made by mail and expressly requires that the acceptance be telegraphed back, it will not be sufficient to send the acceptance by mail. The offer may be withdrawn any time before acceptance, but the notice of withdrawal dates from the time it reaches the party to whom it is sent. The offer is made irrevocable only by acceptance.

In White v. Corlies, 46 N.Y. 467, plaintiff, a builder, received a note from defendant, which said, "Upon an agreement to finish the fitting up of offices at 57 Broadway in two weeks from date, you can commence at once." No reply was sent, but plaintiff bought lumber and prepared to begin work. Next day defendant withdrew the offer. It was held that there was no agreement. The mere buying of lumber was not an act sufficient to notify defendant of the acceptance. A mere mental determination to accept was not sufficient to give notice to defendant.

In Boston & Maine Ry. v. Bartlett, 3 Cush. (Mass.) 224, defendant made a proposition in writing to plaintiff to accept a certain price for some land if taken within thirty days. Plaintiff accepted the proposition before the thirty days expired. It was held that it was a continuous offer that might be withdrawn at any time before acceptance, but its acceptance within the given time, and before being withdrawn, constituted a valid contract that could be enforced.

Offer May Lapse. The lapse of an offer may be caused by the death of either party before acceptance.

Pratt v. Trustees, 93 Ill. 475, was an action on a note given by Pratt to the trustees of a church as a subscriber to enable them to procure a bell. Pratt died before the bell was purchased. It was held that the note was an offer and could be revoked until acted upon by purchasing the bell. The death of the offeror revoked the offer, and the note could not be collected.

Parties May Fix Time During Which Offer Will Remain Open. If it is not accepted within such time, the offer lapses. In the absence of an express limitation of time the offer is construed to be open for a reasonable time. What constitutes a reasonable time depends entirely on the circumstances, the relations of the parties, and other facts which would tend to determine what would be fair and just. It might be a few days or a number of months.

In Stone v. Harmon, 31 Minn. 512, there was a written offer to
sell certain real estate, and no time was stated for its acceptance.
The court held that the offer remained open for a reasonable
time and that acceptance after nearly a year was not within a
reasonable time.

CONSIDERATION

Consideration in Executory Contract. Another element to
support an executory contract is what we term consideration.
There must be some value received to make a contract enforceable, unless its terms are fully carried out or executed.
Therefore there must be consideration in every executory contract.

A contract under seal is in a way, under common law, an
exception, for the seal is said to import a consideration, and the
instrument being sealed, no other evidence of consideration is
required. Now, however, in a few states the seal is by statute
regarded only as a presumption of consideration in an executory
contract and is not sufficient without some actual consideration.
But if the seal is used on a gratuitous promise for the purpose of
creating a consideration, the effect is the same as at common law.

In Aller v. Aller, 40 N.J.L. 446, a father gave his daughter a
written instrument under seal by which he promised to pay her
$312. This was understood to be part of the money which the
father had owed his wife, now deceased, and he felt that it
should go to the daughter, although there was no legal obligation.
The defense to this promise was want of consideration. It was
held that as the promise was intended to be a gratuitous one, the
seal imported sufficient consideration.

Consideration in Executed Contract. A contract that has
been executed will not be set aside because of lack of consideration; we shall therefore limit ourselves to those contracts which
have not yet been carried out.

In Matthews v. Smith, 67 N.C. 374, plaintiff purchased of
defendant a quantity of fertilizer and gave his note for it. When
the note became due, he said the fertilizer was not good and had
injured his land; still he paid the note, and then he brought suit
to recover the money paid. It was held that as he had paid the

money with full knowledge of the facts, he could not maintain his action.

Consideration for Gift. An example of lack of consideration is the case of a gift. A mere promise to give a present is void for want of consideration, but when the promise is executory by delivery of the gift the defect is remedied, and the gift cannot be reclaimed.

In Brewer v. Harvey, 72 N.C. 176, plaintiff's father pointed out a colt to her when she was twelve years old and said, "This is your property; I give it to you." It was known to the family as her colt, but the father kept possession of it until he died. Plaintiff brought an action to recover the horse. It was held that it being a gift, there was no valuable consideration. To make agreement valid, there must have been a delivery. There having been no delivery, title did not pass to the daughter.

In Camp's Appeal, 36 Conn. 88, N handed C some money to put in a savings bank for him, and when the books were brought back he said, "I give you these bank books." C kept them, and in an action by N's administrator to recover the books it was held that this was a good delivery, sufficient to constitute a complete gift.

Consideration Must Have Value. As consideration a benefit must accrue to the party promising or a loss to the party to whom the promise is made.

It is not necessary that the consideration be adequate in value to the thing promised, but it must be of some value in the eyes of the law. It will be seen that it would be impossible for the courts to require an adequate full consideration, as they would then have to determine the merits of every bargain.

In Hamer v. Sidway, 124 N.Y. 538, one Story promised his nephew, William, that if he would refrain from drinking liquor, using tobacco, swearing, and playing cards or billiards for money until he became twenty-one years of age, Story would pay him $5,000. William lived up to his part of the agreement and upon becoming of age asked his uncle for payment. His uncle said he had set apart the money for him in the bank. The court held that the promise to pay this money was founded on a good consideration, as it was enough that something had been done or forborne by the party to whom the promise was made. He had the legal right to do the things his uncle objected to if he wished; the sus-

pension or forbearance of that right sustained the agreement.
Bainbridge v. Firmstone, 8 A & E. (Eng.) 743, is a case
in which defendant obtained plaintiff's consent to let him weigh
two boilers belonging to plaintiff and promised to place them
back in the shape he found them in. Defendant took the boilers
apart and weighed them and then refused to put them together
again, claiming that there was no consideration for his promise
to put them back. It was held that plaintiff had given up the right
he had to refuse to let the boilers be weighed; there was a detriment to plaintiff in parting with possession of them for even so
short a time. This constituted a sufficient consideration, and
defendant was obliged to replace the boilers.

Wolford v. Powers, 85 Ind. 294, was an action on a note given
in consideration of a parent's naming a child after the maker of
a note. The court held that this was based on a sufficient consideration; the parent had surrendered his right to name the
child.

Promise May Be Sufficient Consideration. The consideration
must come from the promisee, and it may consist of a present act
or a promise. It may be to give or to do something, or to refrain
from doing something which the promisee has a legal right to do.
As illustration a promise to forbear suit and extend the time of
payment of a claim is held to be a good consideration.

In Flanigan v. Kilcome, 58 N.H. 443, defendant promised to
pay plaintiffs a certain sum if they would drop a lawsuit which
they had commenced against her. This was done, but she did
not pay, and suit was brought. It was held that there was a
valuable consideration for the promise, even though it be shown
that she would have succeeded if the suit had come to trial.
Plaintiffs had surrendered their right to have it tried.

In Pennsylvania Coal Co. v. Blake, 85 N.Y. 226, the firm of
C. A. Blake & Co. was indebted to plaintiff. Plaintiff agreed to
extend the time of payment upon receiving as collateral security
a mortgage upon land owned by Elizabeth Blake, wife of C. A.
Blake, who had no interest in the firm. This was an action
brought to foreclose that mortgage. The court held that it was
made for a good consideration, the consideration being the
agreement on the part of plaintiff to grant a longer time to C.A.
Blake & Co. and to forbear to sue said firm.

Consideration for Discharge of Debt. But payment of a

smaller sum of money in satisfaction of a larger one is not a valuable consideration for discharge of a debt, since it is in fact doing no more than the party is already legally bound to do. This is one case in which the court will look into the amount of the consideration and determine whether it is adequate.

In Ayres v. C.R.I. & P.R. Co., 52 Iowa 478, one Q entered into a contract to build a certain section of road for defendant. After building a part, Q informed defendant that he owed for supplies and could not go on at the contract price. Defendant told him to go on and his actual expenditures would be met and his creditors paid. It was held that the agreement was without consideration, as it simply bound Q to do what he was already under a legal obligation to do.

If something else than money is taken in part satisfaction of the debt, the rule is different.

This is seen in Jaffray v. Davis, 124 N.Y. 164, in which defendant, who owed plaintiff a certain amount on an open account, gave plaintiff his promissory note for one half the amount, secured by a chattel mortgage under an agreement that it would be accepted as payment in full. It was held that this was a valid agreement upon sufficient consideration and that action could not be brought for the balance. Here defendant gave extra security and deprived himself of legal title to the goods mortgaged.

In Wharton v. Anderson, 28 Minn. 301, defendant leased premises of plaintiff for five years at $250 per month. Thereafter plaintiff agreed to a certain reduction for defendant's paying promptly. It was held that the promise to take less was without consideration and could not be enforced.

But if the amount due is in dispute, the promise to pay any sum in settlement of the disputed claim is valid, even if such sum is less than actually due. Liquidation of the claim constitutes a good consideration.

Riley v. Kershaw, 52 Mo. 224, was an action to recover rent and taxes alleged to be due. The defense was that a new agreement had been entered into between the parties by which, in consideration of the defendant's paying the rent monthly instead of quarterly, a smaller sum was stipulated to be paid, and that this smaller sum was actually paid in full satisfaction of all claims. It was held that payment of part of the debt is no satisfaction of the whole debt, even though agreed to be taken as such. But in case of a dispute a compromise fairly made and faithfully carried out will be upheld.

In Lee v. Timken, 23 App. Div. (N.Y.) 349, plaintiff's husband before his death transferred to plaintiff certain real estate which was subject to a mortgage of $10,000 and gave other property to defendant. His widow sued for $6,000, which she claimed to be due under the agreement, and alleged that only $4,000 had been paid. The defense was accord and satisfaction —that this $4,000 had been paid and accepted in full satisfaction of the daughter's obligations. The court held that the defense, if true, was a good answer to the complaint, as the payment direct to the mother instead of applying it on the mortgage was a sufficient consideration to support the agreement to accept it as full payment. So accord and satisfaction, if proved, was a good defense.

Settlement to Avoid Litigation. A settlement to avoid litigation where the party forbears to sue or consents to drop a pending suit is a good consideration, and the promise made for this consideration can be enforced.

In Parker v. Enslow, 102 Ill. 272, plaintiff had been in the habit of going into defendant's store and filling his pipe from tobacco left on the counter for use of the public. Defendant, for a joke, mixed gunpowder with the tobacco, and when plaintiff lit it an explosion followed that injured his eyesight. Plaintiff threatened, and was intending, to sue defendant. As a compromise and settlement of this cause of action defendant gave plaintiff the promissory note here sued upon. The court held that the note was given as settlement of a threatened suit; if the payee supposed or believed that he had a cause of action and the note was given and accepted in good faith as a compromise, it was supported by a sufficient consideration and could be enforced.

Compromise With Creditors. If several creditors of a party agree with each other and with the debtor to accept a part of what he owes each of them in discharge of the whole debt, the forbearance of each one is the consideration to the others, who might otherwise lose the whole. A compromise with creditors is therefore held to be for a good consideration, and such an agreement can be enforced.

In Pierce v. Jones, 8 S.C. 273, Jones & Co., an insolvent

firm, entered into a written agreement with its creditors whereby they were to accept 25 cents on the dollar in payment of their several claims and give receipts in full, provided all the creditors assented to the agreement. It was held that this was a valid agreement and that the firm complying therewith was discharged from the balance of the indebtedness.

Consideration for Extension of Time. But a promise to extend the time of payment of a debt already due is void for want of consideration unless the debtor makes some concession; as by giving some security, paying interest in advance, or doing something that will form a consideration for the promise to extend the time.

Warner v. Campbell, 26 Ill. 282, held that an agreement to extend the time of payment of a promissory note upon payment of the interest in advance is valid, as it is founded on a valuable consideration.

Moral Obligations. A distinction is sometimes made between "good" consideration and "valuable" consideration. Blackstone says, "Good consideration is such as that of blood, or of natural love and affection; when a man grants an estate to a near relative; being founded on motives of generosity, prudence, and natural duty; a valuable consideration is such as money, marriage, or the like, which the law esteems as equivalent given for the grant: and is therefore founded on motives of justice."

Accordingly it was held by some old authority that a moral obligation was a sufficient consideration to make a promise valid.

But the courts are now practically united on the point that neither a moral obligation nor a "good" consideration is sufficient to make a promise valid and enforceable at law.

In McElven v. Sloan, 56 Ga. 208, Sloan & Co. sued McElven Bros. on a promissory note given to them, consideration for which was payment of a note against their father, who was dead. Before his death the father had become insolvent and had gone through bankruptcy. It was held that this claim against their father did not impose such an obligation on them as to constitute a valuable consideration to support the new note given.

Consideration Must Be Legal. Doing or promising to do an illegal act is not sufficient consideration to support an agreement.

In McBratney v. Chandler, 22 Kan. 692, plaintiff sued for services in presenting a claim of the Miami Indians at Washington. It was contended that the services were those of a lobbyist and illegal. The court held that it was for the jury to decide whether the services were those of an attorney in drawing papers and making agreements, or of a lobbyist in influencing the legislators. If the former, he could recover; if the latter, the consideration was illegal and void, and he could not recover. If both, the illegal part of the consideration vitiated and avoided the whole contract.

Consideration Must Be Possible. A promise to do an impossible act is never a sufficient consideration to support an agreement. This means not a mere pecuniary impossibility but an obvious physical impossibility. The non-existence of the thing given as consideration would render the consideration void and a promise made thereon invalid.

Gibson v. Pelkie, 37 Mich. 380, was an action on an agreement concerning judgment which plaintiff was to collect, retaining one half for his services. It appeared that no such judgment existed. It was held that as the subject matter of the contract was not in existence, there was no valid contract.

In Rogers v. Walsh, 12 Neb. 28, plaintiff bought of defendant what she supposed were, and what appeared to be, tax warrants of York County, but which being issued by the county commissioners without authority, were void. There was an action to recover the price paid. It was held that she might recover, for while the articles she bought resembled county bonds, they were really worthless paper, as the tax warrants did not exist. The agreement was therefore void for want of consideration.

Consideration Must Be Present or Future. A past consideration is no consideration at all, for it confers no value. It is simply some act of forbearance in time past which has been conferred without incurring any legal liability. If afterwards from a feeling of thankfulness or good will a promise is made to the person by whose acts or forbearance the promisee has been benefited, such promise is gratuitous and cannot be enforced.

In Summers v. Vaughan, 35 Ind. 323, plaintiff sold defendant an engine and machinery and took a note for the same. This action was to recover on the note. Defendant claimed that after the sale plaintiff had warranted the machinery, whereas in fact it was defective. The court refused to consider such a warranty because, being made after completion of the contract of sale, which was in writing, it was without consideration and void.

In Dearborn v. Bowman 3 Met. (Mass.) 155, Bowman was nominated for senator. Plaintiff rendered services and furnished literature to advance defendant's cause but without any solicitation on defendant's part. After the election defendant gave plaintiff his note for $60 for such services. The court held that the note was void for want of consideration. Past performance of services constitutes no consideration for an express promise, unless the services were performed at the express or implied request of defendant.

But if there has been, either expressly or impliedly, a request for the act of forbearance beforehand, the consideration for a promise to pay afterwards will be valid, because it is then evident that the service was not intended to be a gratuity, and the whole is but one transaction.

REALITY OF CONSENT—MISTAKE

Mistake. After the parties have entered into the apparent agreement, the questions arise whether the minds of the parties have met on the same thing for the same sense and whether the consent of both parties was given under such circumstances as to make it a real expression of intention.

The parties may have not meant the same thing. It may not have been the intent of one or both of two parties to make a contract in which they have been brought by the misrepresentations of a third party. Should such a condition be occasioned by the carelessness of either party, he is not excused, as when, able to read, he signs a contract thinking it is something different from what it really is.

Walker v. Ebert, 29 Wis. 194, was an action on a promissory note. Defendant proved that at the time he signed the note he was unable to read or write the English language and that the note was represented to him as, and he believed it to be, an agreement in reference to a patented machine about which the party to whom he gave the note had been talking with him. It was held that the note having been procured by false representations as to the character of the instrument itself, and the maker being ignorant of its character and having no intention of signing such a paper, the note was void.

The mistake as to the nature of the transaction must be mutual and must arise from some detail which ordinary diligence could not foresee or from some accident which ordinary diligence could not avert.

Nevius v. Dunlap, 33 N.Y. 676, was an action brought to reform a bond. The court held that to entitle plaintiff to a decree re-forming a written instrument he must show that the part omitted from or inserted in the instrument was omitted or inserted contrary to the intent of both parties and under a mutual mistake.

Again, the mistake may be in the identity of the one with whom the party deals. A may enter into a contract, thinking and intending to contract with B, when in fact he has been dealing with C. There is no meeting of their minds, for A never contemplated dealing with C.

Boston Ice. Co. v. Potter, 123 Mass. 28, was an action for the price of ice furnished to defendant from April 1, 1874, to April, 1875. Defendant was supplied with ice by plaintiff in 1873, and becoming dissatisfied, terminated his contract and made a new one with Citizens Ice Co. Just before April, 1874, Citizens Ice sold out to plaintiff. The court found that defendant had had no notice of the change. It held that plaintiff could not recover, as there was no meeting of the minds of these parties to this action. A man has the right to select and determine the persons he will deal with and cannot have others thrust upon him without his consent.

There may be a mistake as to the subject matter of the thing contracted for, as where one party contracts expecting to receive one article and the other party thinks that the agreement refers to another. The parties clearly have not agreed on the same thing, and the agreement is void.

Kyle v. Kavanagh, 103 Mass. 356, was an action to recover the purchase price of land. It transpired that defendant was negotiating for one piece of land and plaintiff was selling another. It was held by the court that as their minds had not met on the subject matter, they could not be said to have entered into a contract, and although there was no fraud on the part of plaintiff, the mistake alone was a good defense.

The mistake may be as to the existence of the thing contracted for.

In Thwing v. Hall, 40 Minn. 184, plaintiff made a contract to sell certain timber lands to defendant, thinking they contained seven million feet of fine lumber, defendant also believing there was good lumber there. The fact was that unknown to either party, the land had been practically stripped of good lumber. Defendant had sent a man who mistook the location and reported good lumber. It was held a mutual mistake, which was a sufficient cause for the court to cancel the contract.

There may be a mistake by one party as to the intention of the other. It appears that if the second party knows that the first party is mistaken in his intention, the contract is void.

In Parrish v. Thurston, 87 Ind. 437, plaintiff sold defendant a buggy and harness and received a promissory note signed "E. K. Parrish." There was a man by that name living near Shelbyville, the place where the sale was made, who was wealthy and was known to both parties. The note was really made by E. K. Parrish of Hamilton County, a man entirely unknown to plaintiff. Plaintiff supposed he was getting a note signed by the man from Shelbyville, and defendant knew that plaintiff believed this. As plaintiff learned the truth he tendered back the note and sought to rescind the contract. It was held that the contract could be rescinded, as the silence of defendant, when honesty required him to correct plaintiff's mistake, amounted to fraud.

The cases make the following distinction: If the second party knows that the first party is under a misapprehension as to what the first party is getting, the contract is not voided, but if the first party is under a misapprehension as to what is promised by the second party, and the second party knows of the misapprehension, the contract is void.

In Smith v. Hughes, L.R.6 Q.B. (Eng.) 597, plaintiff offered to sell defendant some oats and showed a sample. Defendant wrote the next day that he would take them at the price named. He afterwards refused to take the oats on the ground that they were new oats and he thought he was buying old oats. Nothing has been said at the time of the sale about their being old oats, but the price was high for new oats. It was held that in order to relieve defendant from liability it was necessary to show not only that plaintiff believed defendant thought he was buying old oats but that plaintiff believed defendant thought plaintiff was contracting to sell old oats.

Misrepresentation. Misrepresentation is defined as an innocent misstatement of fact as distinguished from fraud or a willful misstatement, and as thus defined it is almost, if not entirely, identical with mistake.

REALITY OF CONSENT—FRAUD

Fraud Defined. Fraud is a willful misrepresentation of fact, made either with a knowledge of its falsity or recklessly, without belief in its truth, with the intention of having it acted upon by the complaining party and actually inducing him to act upon it. Aside from vitiating the contract, fraud is an actionable wrong, and the party guilty of fraud is liable for deceit.

Fraud May Be Actual. In Holmes's Appeal, 77 Pa. St. 50, a party about to purchase a farm asked the owner whether the neighborhood was sickly and declined to purchase it if it was. The owner assured him it was free from sickness, whereas fever and ague were prevalent. The court held that the agreement to purchase could not be enforced, it having been induced by the vendor's misrepresentation.

Fraud may also arise where there is active or artful concealment.

Jones v. Edwards, 1 Neb. 170, was an action brought for damages because of alleged fraud in the sale of a horse. Jones bought the horse when it had a sweeny (stiffness in the neck) and other ailments. He cut the cords in its neck and doctored it up. Later Edwards came and wanted to buy a farm team. Jones said he had what he wanted and showed him this and another horse, saying they were sound so far as he knew but that he never warranted a horse. He did not say a word about the former ailments. It was held that it was fraud on the part of Jones not to acquaint defendant, Edwards, with conditions affecting the value of the horse which if known would have prevented him from buying.

One who conceals a fact which he ought, as a legal duty, to disclose is guilty of fraud.

Smith v. Aetna Life Insurance Co., 49 N.Y. 211, was an action upon a life-insurance policy. The defense was fraud in obtaining it. In the physician's examination it was asked whether the insurance applicant had cough, occasional or habitual expectoration, or difficulty in breathing. The answer was, "No cough; walking fast upstairs or uphill produced difficulty in breathing." The fact was that he had raised blood for two and a half years. He died three months after the policy was issued. It was held that there was a fraudulent concealment and misrepresentation which would avoid the policy.

False representation may arise from suppression of the truth amounting to suggestion of a falsehood.

In Grigsby v. Stapleton, 94 Mo. 423, plaintiff sold defendant a herd of cattle at the ordinary market price, knowing they had Texas fever, a disease not easily detected by one having no experience with it. He did not disclose this to defendant. It was held that plaintiff was guilty of a fraudulent concealment, for which he was liable.

Caveat Emptor. In a sale of goods in which the buyer can inspect them the rule of caveat emptor is said to apply. The term means "Let the buyer beware," and its application denotes that a vendor is under no obligation to communicate the existence of even latent defects in his wares, unless, by act or implication, he represents that such defects do not exist.

In Lucas v. Coulter, 104 Ind. 81, defendant leased certain premises for one year and defended an action for rent on the ground that they became unfit for his business. It appeared that the woodwork shrank and cracked the plaster, causing dust to fall on the musical instruments which defendant kept in stock. Plaintiff had made no representations or warranties. It was held that there was no implied warranty and that the tenant must determine for himself, before engaging the premises, their safety and fitness for his business.

Effect of Non-Disclosure. Mere non-disclosure does not vitiate a contract unless the parties stand in a relation of confidence to each other and one party has the means of knowing facts that are inaccessible to the other. He is then bound to tell everything that is likely to affect the other party's judgment. Such contracts are said to be *uberrima fides* contracts, that is, they require the "utmost good faith," such as contracts of fire and life insurance and for the sale of land.

In King v. Knapp, 59 N.Y. 462, plaintiff purchased of defendant at an auction sale a lot in New York City, paying 10 per cent down. Printed handbills were circulated containing a diagram of the lot which represented it to be 25 by 100 feet, the handbill also stating this to be the size. Relying on the description, plaintiff purchased the premises without inspection. As a matter of fact a building on the adjoining lot, which had stood there for over twenty-five years, encroached on the premises. This was known to defendant, but there was no mention of it in the handbills or at the sale. Plaintiff refused to complete the sale and brought this action to recover the amount paid. It was held that plaintiff had bought under the suppression of a material fact and that the contract could not be upheld.

It is held also in contracts for the sale of shares of stock in a company that the utmost candor and fullness of statement are required of the promoter and of those who make statements on the strength of which purchasers subscribe.

In Brewster v. Hatch, 122 N.Y. 349, defendants acquired options on certain mining land. A prospectus was then issued describing the property and setting forth the terms and conditions on which a company was to be organized. The proposed capital stock was $1,500,000, divided into shares of $10 each. Plaintiff and others subscribed for about 61,000 shares, and the company was organized and completed the purchase of the land. After the cost and other expenses had been paid, there remained on hand 58,235 shares of stock, which were divided among defendants, as previously agreed, and for which they paid nothing. When plaintiffs subscribed, they did not know that defendants were to receive any stock without paying for it. This was an action to recover for the benefit of the corporation the value of the shares so distributed. It was held that plaintiffs had been led to believe that defendants were acting in the interest of all the investors and that defendants knew that plaintiffs so believed; that the relations of the parties were those of trust and confidence, binding defendants to the exercise of good faith and requiring them to disclose the information they possessed affecting the value of the property.

Statement Must Be Misrepresentation of Fact. A mere expression of opinion which turns out to be without foundation or a statement of intention which is not carried out will not invalidate the contract.

In Gordon v. Butler, 105 U.S. 553, defendant borrowed money of plaintiff and gave as security a mortgage on real estate containing some sandstone which had not been sufficiently worked to show its value. Defendants furnished the certifications of two persons, saying they had lived near the place for twenty years and giving the value of the property in their best judgment to be an amount 150 per cent more than the loan. Upon sale under foreclosure the land brought one-sixth of the loan amount. Plaintiff sued, charging fraud. It was held that he could not recover—that an action will not lie for an expression of opinion, however inaccurate, in regard to the value of property which depends on contingencies that may never happen.

The representation must be a statement of something that exists or has happened; for instance, that a car cost $500 and not that the car is worth $500, which would be a statement of opinion; or that if you buy this car you can sell it again in the spring for $500, as this is merely a prediction.

The law tolerates considerable prevaricating by the tradesman in puffing his goods or wares, provided the thing bargained is open to the buyer's inspection.

Poland v. Brownell, 131 Mass. 138, is a case in which plaintiff bought out a half interest in defendant's stock of goods and business. He looked over the stock and books and had ample opportunity to investigate. It was held that he had no right to hold seller on his representations of the value of the goods or the amount of business he had previously done; the judge said, "It is everywhere understood that such statements and commendations are to be received with great allowance and distrust." (Case also illustrates rule of caveat emptor.)

The representation, if it is to render the contract void because of fraud, must be made with a knowledge of its falsity or without belief in its truth.

Cowley v. Dobbins, 136 Mass. 401, was an action for fraud in that defendant represented to plaintiff that Dobbins left an estate of $40,000 above all liabilities, whereas in truth he was insolvent. The evidence showed that defendant believed her representations to be true. It was held that no action would lie against her.

If a man makes a false statement while honestly believing it to be true, he is not liable for fraud. He can be held only when he knows the statement to be false or has no knowledge of either its truth or its falsity. The false statement must be made with the intention of its being acted upon. It need not be intended that the party to whom it is made shall act upon it but that he shall lead someone to act.

In Eaton v. Avery, 83 N.Y. 31, defendant made false representation to a mercantile agency as to the financial responsibility of the firm of Avery & Reggins, of which he was a member. This firm asked credit of plaintiff. Plaintiff went to the mercantile agency and obtained the information given by defendant, and relying on this, extended the firm credit. In an action for fraud it was held that the purpose for which such information is given to mercantile agencies is to enable them to furnish it to their subscribers for guidance in extending credit; and that defendant would therefore be liable, as the case justified the finding that the false statements were made with intent to defraud any person who might inquire of the agency.

Sheldon v. Davidson, 85 Wis. 138, was an action for deceit in which it was claimed that defendant, in order to induce plaintiff to lease certain premises, concealed the fact that a barn thereon did not belong to him; but it was not shown that this concealment induced plaintiff to lease the premises, and for this reason it was held that an action did not lie.

The false representation, therefore, must actually deceive, as in the case of Eaton v. Avery. If Eaton had not been deceived by the information, he could not have succeeded in his suit.

The effect of fraud on a contract is to give the injured party grounds for an action for damages for deceit. And the person who has been led into a contract by means of fraudulent misrepresentations may either affirm the contract and compel its fulfillment or avoid it, provided he signifies his intention to do so as soon as he becomes aware of the fraud. If he accepts any benefits under the contract after he learns of the fraud, the contract is affirmed.

Crooks v. Nippolt, 44 Minn. 239, was an action brought to recover the amount paid by plaintiff on a contract to buy a certain piece of real estate, on the ground that defendant's agent in making the sale showed plaintiff another and more valuable lot instead of the one sold. It appeared that after plaintiff learned of this, he applied to defendant twice for an extension of time within which to carry out his contract as to another payment. He also endeavored to have the contract acknowledged so that it might be recorded. It was held that he should have rescinded upon discovery of the fraud, and that his acts after knowledge of the fraud amounted to an affirmance and terminated the right to rescind.

Duress. Duress is defined as unlawful constraint exercised on a man whereby he is forced to do some act against his will.

A contract entered into by a party under duress is voidable at his option. The duress must be inflicted or threatened by a party to the contract or one acting for him and with his knowledge, and the subject of the duress must be the contradicting party himself or his wife, parent, or child.

In Morrill v. Nightingale, 93 Cal. 452, plaintiff procured several promissory notes to be executed by defendant under coercion and intimidation, caused by threats of arrest, and he also had a warrant of arrest issued by a justice of the peace, not for the purpose of punishing defendant for a crime but to compel him to pay the money or execute the notes. It was held that this constituted duress and was a good defense to the action to recover the notes.

Wrongful detention of goods or damage to them does not constitute duress, nor does threatened arrest in lawful prosecution.

Undue Influence. In the creating of a contract undue influence arises where the parties are not on an equality as to knowledge or capacity.

A promise made by a child to its parent, a client to his attorney, a patient to his physician, a ward to his guardian, or a person to his spiritual adviser will not necessarily be set aside by the court, but such relations call for clear evidence that the party benefited did not take advantage of his position.

Hall v. Perkins, 3 Wend. (N.Y.) 626, is a case in which a simple-minded, ignorant young man was induced by his uncle, a justice-court lawyer, to accept a conveyance of land worth $240 in satisfaction of a claim of $500. The uncle was one of the execu-

tors of the estate which owed plaintiff. It was held that from the
nature of the transaction, the inadequacy of the consideration,
the relative character and capacity of the parties, and the connection, fraud and imposition might well be presumed.

Bainbrigge v. Browne, 18 Ch. Div. (Eng.) 188, was an action
to set aside a deed given by children, who were of age, to their
father. The court held that the father must show that the deed
was executed with full knowledge of its contents and with the
free intention of giving the benefit conferred.

Undue influence, like duress, renders the contract voidable,
at the instance of the injured party.

SUBJECT MATTER

Object of Contract Must Not Be Illegal. The object of
a contract must not be contrary to law. Certain things are forbidden by law, and if these things are in the contemplation of
the parties at the time the contract is entered into, the contract
is not enforceable; otherwise the law would be aiding in an
indirect way what it expressly forbids.

Wells v. The People, 71 Ill. 532, is a case in which the school
law provided that a teacher should have certain certificates of
qualification. The school directors employed plaintiff to teach
school for six months at $45 per month. He had no certificate but
obtained one after he had taught three months. He then learned
that he could not collect his pay, as he had not qualified, so he
canceled his contract with the consent of the directors, and they
hired him under a new contract for the remaining three months
at $90 per month. It seemed clear that the intent was to recom-
pense him for the time already taught. It was held that the
first contract was void and that by the second there was an
attempt to do indirectly what the directors could not do directly,
which rendered the second contract void. But plaintiff could
recover reasonable pay for his services for the last three months.

This principle applies only to executory contracts, for if the
contract has been voluntarily executed by the parties, it is binding, as the law will not compel the return of anything acquired
under such a contract any more than it will compel performance. The rule is that if parties have voluntarily completed a

contract illegal as to subject matter, the law will leave them where they are.

Illegal Objects. The object of the contract may be illegal by express statutory enactment or because of rules of common law. The statutes declare some contracts illegal and void, and impose a penalty for the making of some others without rendering the contracts void. A statute requiring a lawyer or a physician to be licensed renders a contract made without compliance with it void.

In Gardner v. Tatum, 81 Cal. 370, plaintiff, a physician, was called by defendant on March 8, 1883, and continued to visit the patient until October 2, 1883. Plaintiff's application for a certificate to practice medicine was granted March 12 of the same year. It was held that he could not recover any compensation for the services rendered before the procuring of the certificate upon any contract, express or implied, such contract being illegal and against public policy.

In Buckley v. Humason, 50 Minn. 195, plaintiff, acting as a real-estate broker in Chicago, purchased certain property for defendant. An ordinance of Chicago requires that all real-estate brokers be licensed and fixes the license fee at $25, providing a penalty for violation. Plaintiff at this time had no license. In an action for his commissions it was held that he could get nothing for his services. Business transacted in violation of the law cannot be the foundation of a valid contract.

A law requiring weights and measures to be sealed as a condition precedent to a sale of goods by a merchant renders a contract made in violation thereof void.

In Eaton v. Kegan, 114 Mass. 433, a statute provided that all oats and meal should be bargained for and sold by the bushel. It was held that plaintiff could not recover the price of meal and oats sold by the bag.

Sometimes a statute simply imposes a penalty and does not invalidate the contract.

Pangborn v. Westlake, 36 Iowa 546, was an action to compel payment of a note given in purchase of a city lot. A statute existed that provided a penalty of $50 for selling any lot in a town before the plat thereof was recorded. The court held that as a general rule a penalty prescribed by statute for the doing of an act implies a prohibition which will render the act void. This is not always so, however, as the court will look to the language and subject matter of the statute and the purpose sought to be accomplished, and if from this it is manifest that it is not the intent to render the prohibited act void, it will be so construed. It was therefore held that the note was valid.

Statutes against wagers or bets have been passed in most of our states, and all wagers are now practically declared contrary to public policy and void.

In Love v. Harvey, 114 Mass. 80, plaintiff made a wager of $20 with defendant that the body of one Dr. Cahill was buried on a certain side of the main avenue in Hollywood Cemetery. The stakeholder, although forbidden to do so, paid the $40 left with him to defendant. It was held that all wagers were unlawful. The party receiving the money from the stakeholder after being forbidden to receive it was liable to the other for return of the money even though he was the winner of the wager.

Statutes in many states prohibit desecration of the Sabbath day, and any contracting done on that day contrary to the statutes is void.

Handy v. St. Paul Globe Publishing Co., 41 Minn. 188, was an action brought for breach of contract. Plaintiff was employed by defendant to take charge of the real-estate advertising in the daily, Sunday, and weekly editions of defendant's paper. A statute of the state forbade any work on Sunday except that "of necessity and charity." The court held that issuing and publishing a paper on Sunday was unlawful. The contract was for illegal work in part and was therefore void.

Clough v. Goggins, 40 Iowa 325, was an action on a promissory note made on Sunday. The court held that contracts made on Sunday were void and that a promissory note made on that day would not support an action.

In some states it is illegal for one to follow his "ordinary calling" or to work on others to make any contracts, etc. The different statutes differ so materially that no general rule can be laid down as to what acts are prohibited.

Aside from the contracts declared to be unlawful and void by statute, there are contracts that are illegal at common law. The courts will not enforce an agreement to commit a crime or to do a civil wrong.

White v. Kuntz, 107 N.Y. 518, held that in a composition of a debtor with his creditors, any contract with one of them whereby he is to receive more than his pro rata share is void, and any security given upon such a promise is void.

CONTRACTS AGAINST PUBLIC POLICY. All contracts which if enforced would be contrary to the good of the public or opposed to the welfare of the community are said to be against public policy and are therefore void. Those contracts which tend to injure the government in its relations with other countries, those with alien enemies which involve any communication over the border line, and those in restraint of trade are illustrations of this kind of contract.

In United States v. Grossmayer, 9 Wall (U.S.) 72, Ernslein, a resident of Macon, Georgia, was indebted to Grossmayer of New York when the Civil War broke out. Through an agent Grossmayer took cotton in payment and had it stored in Savannah. The government confiscated it, and Grossmayer made claim against the government. It was held that all intercourse with an enemy was unlawful, and notwithstanding that the parties sustained the relation of debtor and creditor, the plaintiff above did not present a valid claim.

All agreements looking to the aid of hostile actions against a friendly state are unlawful as being contrary to public policy. A contract to raise funds to aid an insurrection in a friendly state is such an agreement.

In Kennett v. Chambers, 14 How. (U.S.) 38, a contract was made in Cincinnati, after Texas had declared itself independent of the United States, whereby plaintiff agreed to, and did, furnish money to a Texas general to enable him to raise and equip troops to fight against Mexico. It was held that such a contract was void.

A contract to break a law of a sister state is also against public policy.

Graves v. Johnson, 156 Mass. 211, was an action for the price of intoxicating liquors sold and delivered by plaintiff in Massachusetts to a Maine hotelkeeper with a view to their being resold by defendant in Maine, contrary to the laws of that state. It was held that because the contract had in view the breaking of the laws of Maine, it could not be maintained.

Agreements to prevent or hinder the course of justice are illegal, as to agree to cancel a crime of which one has knowledge, to refrain for a certain consideration from prosecuting a criminal, to agree not to testify as a witness to influence a witness's testimony, or to bribe a juror.

Partridge v. Hood, 120 Mass. 403, held that a contract to deed a certain piece of property where the real consideration was an agreement to drop a criminal prosecution against the grantor's son was void as against public policy.

A contract tending to injure the public service is contrary to public policy and therefore void. Such an agreement is a contract by a public officer to assign his salary to a creditor or an understanding to influence the action of a legislature by lobbying or an agreement to hinder or prevent competition for public contracts.

Agreements which tend to promote and encourage litigation are also void; that is, it is not legal to speculate in lawsuits. X may have a cause of action against Y, but it is not lawful for Z to buy the action for the purpose of instituting suit. The rule was formerly more strict than now. The holding in most states at present is that an attorney can institute a suit for a "contingent fee," which means that he is to receive for his services a percentage of what he recovers. In earlier days this was forbidden.

AGREEMENTS CONTRARY TO GOOD MORALS. So also are contracts which affect the freedom or security of marriage, as an agreement not to marry, a contract made in consideration of the procuring or bringing about of a marriage, or a mutual agreement to obtain a divorce.

Sterling v. Sinnickson, N.J.L. 756, was an action on a written instrument promising to pay plaintiff $1,000 provided he was not married within six months. It was held that the contract was void as against public policy.

In Cross v. Cross, 58 N.H. 373, plaintiff, wife of defendant, received from him certain notes secured by mortgage and in return she deeded to him the land covered by the mortgage. The transaction was part of an agreement between the parties to separate. It was further agreed that plaintiff was to obtain a divorce on certain grounds and defendant was to allow the papers in the action to be served on him and make no defense; also that the children were to be divided between them, etc. It was held that the whole transaction was illegal and void, and that the law would not aid either party in enforcing their unlawful contract.

RESTRAINT OF TRADE. Contracts in restraint of trade are prohibited by law as against public policy. The good of the community and the welfare of the individual require that competition in trade should exist and that every man should be free to engage in the occupation or vocation he prefers. Still, it is but fair that a man in selling out his business shall include with it the good will and refrain from opening up a like business next door or on the same street. The rule is, therefore, that if the restraint imposed on the one party is not greater than the protection the other party requires, the contract is valid.

In Hereshoff v. Boutineau, 17 R.I. 3, plaintiff hired defendant as a teacher of languages for six months, and defendant covenanted not to teach French or German anywhere within the state of Rhode Island for one year thereafter. It was held that this covenant was unreasonable and void; the restriction extended beyond what was apparently necessary for plaintiff's protection.

In National Benefit Co. v. Union Hospital Co., 45 Minn. 272, the parties thereto were two companies engaged in issuing benefit certificates entitling the holders to care and medical treatment in case of sickness or injury. Plaintiff had acquired a good business in Minnesota, Wisconsin, and northern Michigan, and entered into a contract with defendant agreeing for a certain consideration to refrain for three years from doing business in that territory except with railway employees. It was held that the contract was valid and not void as being in restraint of trade. The question of the reasonableness of the restraint depends on whether it is such as to afford fair protection to the party in whose favor it is made.

From the nature of the case it will be seen that a covenant to refrain from engaging in the same business within the same city might be reasonable in a grocery business, while in another business the limitation of the whole state would be only just, as in the case of a manufacturer of heavy machinery requiring a wider territory for his sales.

In Perkins v. Clay, 54 N.H. 518, defendant sold his butcher business for $90 and promised that he would not carry on the same route for two years. Included in the sale was his cart. It was held that this agreement was reasonable and valid.

In Guerand v. Dandelot, 32 Md. 561, defendant sold his dyeing and scouring establishment and leased the premises to plain-

tiff, entering into a covenant that he would not at any time thereafter engage in a like business in the city of Baltimore. It was held
that this covenant was valid, as it was not too comprehensive in
its restriction.

In Diamond Match Co. v. Roeber, 106 N.Y. 473, defendant,
who was engaged in the manufacture and sale of matches
throughout the United States, sold his stock of machinery and
good will to plaintiff. He covenanted that he would not at any
time within ninety-nine years engage in such business in any of
the states or territories except Nevada and Montana. It was
held that the covenant was valid, as the restraint was coexten-
sive only with the interest to be protected.

OPERATION OF CONTRACT

Parties Acquiring Rights Under Contracts. Now arises the
question of the extent and limitation of the rights conferred and
of the obligations incurred.

As a general principle only the parties to a contract acquire
any rights under it. It is clear that a contract cannot impose
liabilities on anyone not a party to it. A man cannot voluntarily
and without being asked to do so pay another man's debts and
then seek to establish himself as a creditor. There is an apparent
exception to this rule in the case of anyone interfering with
master and servant and inducing the servant to break his contract of employment. Some authorities hold that a party so
interfering is liable for damages, and some hold that unjustifi-
ably to induce one to break any contract is actionable.

In Walker v. Cronin, 107 Mass. 555, plaintiff conducted a
shoe factory employing a large number of people. Defendant,
with intent to injure plaintiff's business, induced a number of the
employees to leave. The court held that plaintiff could recover
damages.

It is held by some courts that a man cannot acquire rights
under a contract to which he is not a party, such as for X and Y
to enter into a contract, the consideration being that X shall confer some benefit upon C, a third party. Does C acquire the right
under such an agreement to institute an action against X if the
contract is not executed? English courts say no. Massachusetts

and Michigan courts hold with English courts that no action can be maintained by one not a party to the agreement for whose benefit a promise is made.

In Linneman v. Moross, 98 Mich. 178, a father agreed with his son that he would revoke a provision in his will in favor of his daughter and devise the same property to his son in consideration of the son's paying the daughter $10 a month as long as she might live. The daughter was not a party to the agreement. It was held that the father could not enforce it.

The New York courts in the celebrated case of Lawrence v. Fox, 20 N.Y. 268, held that X, the third person, for whose benefit a promise was made by A on consideration from B, the promisee, might maintain an action on the promise, provided he was the person directly intended to be benefited and provided that B was at the time under an obligation to X, which he sought to discharge by giving X the benefit of A's promise. The facts in this case were that one Holly, at the request of defendant, loaned him $300. Holly stated at the time that he owed that sum to plaintiff and had agreed to pay him this amount the next day. Defendant, in consideration of the loan, promised Holly that he would pay the sum to plaintiff the next day. Plaintiff sued defendant on this promise, and the court held that he could recover on the promise, although he was not a party to it.

This rule as applied in New York State has been largely adopted throughout the United States.

In Dean v. Walker, 107 Ill. 540, X sold certain real property to defendant, the property being mortgaged to plaintiff. As part of the purchase price defendant agreed with X to assume the mortgage and pay the amount named therein to plaintiff. It was held that plaintiff, who was not a party to the agreement, could claim the benefits thereof and maintain an action to recover the amount of the mortgage from defendant.

Assignment of Rights. Now that we know upon whom rights and liabilities fall, we must ascertain how and when other persons may take their places and succeed to their rights, if at all. It is well established that the promisor cannot assign his liabilities under the contract; that is, the promisee cannot be compelled to accept performance from any but the promisor. This is only fair and just, for if C contracts with D to have him do a certain thing for him, C is entitled to know whom he is dealing with, as he may have taken into consideration D's particular fitness to do the work.

This rule is qualified if D undertakes to do certain work for C in which no particular knowledge or skill is required. He can then have the work done by another; but still D is responsible for the work's being done well.

In LaRue v. Groezinger, 84 Calif. 281, one H agreed to sell to defendant all the grapes he might raise in a certain vineyard during a period of ten years, and defendant agreed to pay therefor $25 per ton. At the end of five years H sold the vineyard and assigned the contract to plaintiff. Defendant refused to accept grapes from plaintiff, saying he had no contract with him. It was held that the contract could be assigned, as it was not for services of a personal nature.

The "ice case," Boston Ice Co. v. Potter, 123 Mass. 28, held that plaintiff could not recover, as there was no meeting of the minds of the parties to the action. A man has the right to select and determine the persons he will deal with and cannot have others thrust upon him. This seems almost to be in conflict with the LaRue v. Groezinger decision, and in most cases the holding seems to be that the promisor cannot assign his liability unless the agreement contemplates that someone else is to do the work or aid in it. This is true in the case of a contractor agreeing to build a house, as it is plainly within the contemplation of the parties that he will employ men to do part or all of the work.

As to the rights of the parties under a contract, we find that at common law the only way such rights can be transferred to a third party is by a new agreement between all the parties. The equity courts, however, permit an assignment in many cases under which the assignee can enforce the contract, but the party liable must be given notice of the assignment. In such cases the assignee takes no better title than his assignor has; the assignment carries with it all its defenses. Rights under contracts are assignable by statute in most states, and the assignee can enforce them in his own name. The above rule does not apply to negotiable instruments, which will be described later.

Aside from assignment of rights under a contract by the voluntary acts of the parties, rights may be transferred by operation of law. In the assignment of a lease of land, certain covenants in the lease which are said to concern the demised premises pass to the assignee, such as covenants to repair and to pay rent.

In Salisbury v. Shirley, 60 Cal. 223, it was held that the person who takes an assignment of a lease is liable on the covenant to pay rent and taxes the same as the original lessee.

By the death of a person all his rights under his contracts pass to his executor if he has left a will, or to his administrator if he has not. This is not the rule if the contract depends on his performing some acts of personal service or skill; the contract then dies with him.

In Lacy v. Getman, 119 N.Y. 109, plaintiff contracted with M to work upon his farm as an ordinary farm laborer for one year from March 1. In July, M died. It was held that his death terminated the contract.

By the bankruptcy of a party all his property, as well as his rights under his contracts, passes to the trustee.

STATUTE OF FRAUDS

Outline. In 1676 a law was passed in England entitled "An act for the prevention of frauds and perjuries." This statute required that written evidence be supplied in proving certain contracts.

The statute commonly called "the fourth section of the statute of frauds" provides as follows: "No action shall be brought whereby to charge

"1. Any executor or administrator upon any special promise to answer damages out of his own estate;

"2. Or whereby to charge the defendant upon any special promise to answer for the debt, default, or miscarriage of another person;

"3. Or to charge any person upon any agreement made in consideration of marriage;

"4. Or upon any contract for sale of lands, tenements, or hereditaments or any interest in or concerning them;

"5. Or upon any agreement that is not to be performed within the space of one year from the making thereof unless the agreement of such action shall be brought or some memorandum or note thereof shall be in writing and signed by the party to be charged therewith or some person thereunto by him lawfully authorized."

Object. The object of the statute was to lessen perjury in the testimony of witnesses, especially in important cases, and it therefore required that the contracts be evidenced in writing. In nearly all states this statute has been re-enacted in somewhat the same form, although the language of the different statutes varies. The statute does not render oral contracts void but says that no action shall be brought on them. It takes away the remedy. When action is brought in court on such contracts, it is necessary to show the written agreement. The oral agreement is valid, and after it is made, a sufficient writing may be given.

Bird v. Munroe, 66 Me. 337, is a case in which a verbal contract was made. The contract belonged to the class required by the statute of frauds to be in writing. It was broken, and the parties afterwards entered into a written agreement containing the terms of the oral contract. After the writing was signed, another was brought for breach of the contract which occurred before the written agreement was executed. It was held that the contract was sufficient to satisfy the statute. The writing was not the contract itself but the evidence necessary to prove it.

The statute of frauds is a defense solely, and the party availing himself of it must set it up, otherwise it is waived.

When Memorandum Is Sufficient. The writing need not be a formal contract. A memorandum or note containing the terms of the agreement, if signed by the party to be charged or his authorized agent, is sufficient.

Hurley v. Brown, 98 Mass. 545, was an action to compel defendants to perform their part of the following contract and to convey the land to plaintiff:

$50.   Lynn, April 14, 1866
     Received of John and Michael Hurley the sum of fifty dollars in part payment of a house and lot of land situated on Amity Street, Lynn, Mass. The full amount is $1700. The bargain is to be closed within ten days of the date hereof.

This was signed by the parties. The defense claimed that the writing was not sufficient, as there were several houses and lots on the street. It was shown that defendant owned no other house and lot on the same street. The court held that the writing was sufficient and that evidence could be given as to the particular house meant.

The memorandum or note required to be in writing need merely contain the agreement and may consist of several writings or a number of letters and memorandums.

Promise of Executor or Administrator. The promise of an executor or administrator to answer damages out of his own estate, that is, to render himself personally liable for the debts of the deceased, must be in writing. But the writing does not impart any consideration, and there must be a consideration to this as to any contract.

In Smithwick v. Shepherd, 4 Jones (N.C.) 196, Shepherd, who owed plaintiff for board, died. Defendant, his administrator, in a conversation with plaintiff stated that he would "see it paid" or that "it should be paid." It was held that the promise was not enforceable, because it was not in writing.

Promise to Answer for Debts of Another. In the case of a promise to answer for the debt, default, or miscarriage of another, there must be three parties: the debtor, the creditor, and the person who guarantees the debtor's account. To bring the case under the rule requiring a writing there must be not an absolute promise to pay but a promise to pay if the other defaults.

To illustrate, X goes to the grocery with Y and says, "Give Y a bill of groceries, and if he fails to pay for them, I will." Such a promise is under the statute and must be in writing, but if X says, "Give Y the bill of goods and I will pay for them," or "I will see that you are paid," this is an independent promise, making X the principal debtor, and is not within the statute.

In Boston v. Farr, 148 Pa. St. 220, plaintiff, a physician, brought suit to recover for services rendered defendant's stepson. Defendant said to plaintiff, "Go and get a surgeon and do all you can for the boy; I will see that you get your pay." It was held the jury was justified in finding that it was an original promise on the part of defendant by which he charged himself with the bill, and did not come within the statute.

The test seems to be whether the party for whose debt the promise is made continues to be liable; if so, the promise is within the statutes.

Agreement in Consideration of Marriage. The agreement

here meant is not the promise to marry but the promise to settle property or to make payment of money in consideration of, or conditioned upon, a marriage.

In McAnnulty v. McAnnulty, 120 Ill. 26, it was held that a verbal agreement made by the woman before marriage whereby she released and renounced all interest in her proposed husband's estate after his death was valid under the statute of frauds.

Contracts for Sale of Lands or Hereditaments, or Any Interest in or Concerning Them. This section does not apply to the deed of conveyance of land, as that must be written and sealed without statutory requirement. The statute here refers to any agreement to buy or sell land or to any interest in or concerning lands, such as a grant of a right of way over one's land, which is an interest concerning the realty and within the statute. Here the question often arises whether trees, crop grass, and ore are real or personal property. If the former, all contracts concerning them are within the statute. The distinction seems to be that before they are severed from the land, natural products, such as trees and grass, which grow without cultivation and the labor of man are parts of the realty, and if sold standing, the buyer to cut them, the contract is within the statute.

Powers v. Clarkson, 17 Kan. 218, held that wild grass growing on uncultivated land is a part of the realty and that an attempted transfer of such grass by parol is void.

Harrell v. Miller, 35 Miss. 700, held that the term "land" embraces not only the soil but the natural products growing upon and affixed to it. Therefore a sale of growing timber is within the statute of frauds and void unless in writing.

But if the owner of the land is to cut the natural products, the sale is not completed until they are severed, therefore is not a sale of a part of the realty and so is not within the statute.

In Killmore v. Howlett, 48 N.Y. 569, defendant, owner of some woodland, entered into a parol agreement with plaintiff by which defendant agreed to cut cordwood and deliver it to plaintiff at Syracuse for $5 per cord. Defendant performed part of the agreement, and then, as the price of wood went up, refused to deliver more, claiming that the contract was void under the statute of frauds, as being for the sale of an interest in real estate. It was held that as it was a sale of the trees when severed, and as plaintiff was not to have any property in the trees until they were severed, the contract was not for the sale of an interest in real estate and so was not within the statute.

The same rule applies to coal and ore.

Riddle v. Brown, 20 Ala. 412, held that a contract granting the right to dig and carry away ore from a mine is for the sale of an interest in real estate and must be in writing.

But if the products are growing crops which are harvested annually, and planted and cared for by the labor of man, the general rule is that they are personal property, even when attached to the soil.

Marshall v. Ferguson, 23 Cal. 65, was an action on an oral contract for the sale of wheat and barley which was not yet cut. The defense was that since it was an interest in real estate, the agreements must be in writing. It was held that since it was a sale of growing crop, the product of periodical planting and cultivation, it did not come within the provisions of the statute and was valid if made orally.

Agreements Not to Be Performed Within One Year. The mere fact that the contract may or may not be completed within one year is not sufficient to bring it within the statute. It must be the plain intent and purpose of the contract that it is not to be performed within that time, to bring it within the statute. If its performance depends on a contingency that may or may not happen within the year, no writing is necessary.

Kent v. Kent, 62 N.Y. 560, was an action on a contract whereby plaintiff agreed to work on K's farm and to receive his pay after K's death. Plaintiff entered upon such employment, and K died five years thereafter. It was held that the contract of employment was not within the statute, as the time was uncertain, and might have been less than one year, depending as it did on the length of K's life.

Wahl v. Barnum, 116 N.Y. 87, held that a contract of partnership to continue for three years was void under the statute of frauds unless in writing.

An agreement to support a person during his lifetime is not within the statute, as he may die within the year.

In McCormick v. Drummett, 9 Neb. 384, Z gave D, his step-son, the use of the farm during Z's lifetime in consideration of D's supporting Z and his wife during their lives. It was held that such an agreement is not within the statute.

But a contract for a year's service to be entered upon in the future, even the next day, must be in writing under the statute.

In Oddy v. James, 48 N.Y. 685, about the middle of March the parties thereto entered into a verbal agreement by which defendant employed plaintiff to superintend his cement works for one year from April 1 next. Plaintiff worked until August 3, when defendant discharged him. Plaintiff sued, and defendant set up that the agreement was void under the statute of frauds. The court held for defendant. The contract was not to be performed within one year, so it must be in writing.

A lease of land in New York State is expressly regulated by statute and is an exception to the above rule. A lease for one year or less need not be in writing, and this is true although the lease is not to commence until a future date. In other states all leases are required by statute to be in writing. By common law it was not required that any lease be written, but this was changed in England as well as in the different states by the statute of frauds.

SALE OF GOODS ACT

Conditions. Section 17 of the English statute of frauds provides: "No contract for the sale of goods, wares, and merchandise, for the price of ten pounds sterling or upwards shall be allowed to be good except

"1. The buyer shall accept part of the goods so sold, and actually receive the same; or

"2. Give something in earnest to bind the bargain, or in part payment;

"3. Or, that some note or memorandum or writing of the said bargain be made and signed by the parties to be charged by such contract or their agents thereunto lawfully authorized."

This section is re-enacted in most states. The amount involved necessary to bring the contract within the statute varies in the different states. It will be seen that the statute includes most of the articles regarded as personal property under the terms "goods, wares, and merchandise." A close question comes up when the goods are in process of manufacture. It is held that it is a sale of labor, and of material to be made up; it is not a sale of goods, wares, and merchandise, but a contract for work, labor, and services, and does not come within the statute. In England the test is that if at the time of delivery the subject matter of the transaction is a sale of goods, wares, or merchandise, it is within the statute; and the rule has been followed in Minnesota, Missouri, and other states.

Brown v. Sanborn, 21 Minn. 402, held that an agreement to purchase at $5 per ton the flax straw to be raised from 45 bushels of flaxseed, it "appearing from 20 to 50 tons were raised," was within the statute of frauds as a contract for the sale of goods and chattels. The court said, "It is essentially a contract for straw and not for labor and skill in producing the straw."

In Burrell v. Highleyman, 33 Mo. App. 183, the agreement was for three pieces of furniture, which were to be finished up and covered according to defendant's express order. The consideration of the transaction was over $50. It was held that when the subject matter of a contract is a chattel to be afterwards delivered, it is a sale of goods and not a contract for work, labor, and services, although work is to be done on such chattel before delivery.

In New York the rule is that if the article is in existence at the time of the agreement, it is within the statute, although some work is to be done on it before delivery, but it is not within the statute if the article is not in existence at the time of formation of the contract, as flour to be ground from wheat or nails to be made from iron.

Parsons v. Loucks, 48 N.Y. 17, was an action to recover damages for breach of contract. It was a parol contract that defendants should manufacture and deliver to plaintiff at New York City 10 tons of book paper of a certain quality, plaintiff to pay 13 cents a pound therefor. It was held that the contract was valid, and not within the statute. The court said that the distinction was between the sale of goods in existence at the time of making the contract, which was within the statute, and an agreement to manufacture goods, which was for work and labor and not within the statute.

In Massachusetts a different rule has existed: if the contract is for articles in existence, or the kind the vendor makes in the ordinary course of his business, even though not at the time in existence, it is within the statute; but if the articles are to be manufactured especially for the purchaser and not for the general market, it is not.

In Goddard v. Binney, 115 Mass. 450, defendant went to plaintiff's shop and gave his verbal order for a buggy to be made for him according to specific directions and marked with his monogram. The price was $675. After the buggy had been finished and the bill had been presented several times, plaintiff's shop burned and the buggy was destroyed. It was held that the contract was not within the statute applying to the sale of goods and that title to the buggy was in defendant, as this article was to be manufactured especially for the purchaser and on his special order and not for the general market. It was not in existence at the time of the contract, nor was it such an article as plaintiff in the ordinary course of his business manufactured for the general market.

One of Three Conditions Necessary. Of those contracts which are within the statute the law requires one of the three following conditions: that there be a part payment on account (to bind the bargain); or receipt and acceptance by the buyer of at least part of the goods; or if neither of the above provisions is complied with, a written note or memorandum of the contract signed by the party to be charged. This memorandum must contain all the essential terms of the sale.

Stone v. Browning, 68 N.Y. 598, held that a writing simply acknowledging the purchase of goods, without stating the price or terms of the contract of sale, is not a sufficient memorandum of the contract to satisfy the statute of frauds. All the essential parts of the contract must be evidenced by the writing.

DISCHARGE OF CONTRACT

Discharge by Agreement. As the contract is created by agreement of the parties, so the parties may, if they choose, terminate and discharge it in like manner. This may be termed a waiver or rescission of the contract. If the contract is executory, each party may waive his rights under it, and waiver of the rights of one is the consideration for waiver of the rights of the other. It is virtually a new contract; the subject matter, which is the waiver of the old contract, and all the elements of a contract are necessary to constitute a valid waiver. If one party has performed his part of the contract, there must be some consideration for release of the other party.

In Collyer v. Moulton, 9 R.I. 90, Moulton and Bromley, co-partners, entered into a contract with plaintiff, who agreed to build them a wire-bending machine. Moulton and Bromley dissolved, and Moulton withdrew from the firm, after which plaintiff agreed to release him from the agreement and look to Bromley. It was held that the release of Moulton was not binding, as it was without consideration. If Bromley had agreed to pay plaintiff the full amount if plaintiff would release Moulton, this promise would have been a valuable consideration for the release.

A waiver may be effected by substitution of a new contract which so changes the terms of the old one that it either expressly or impliedly waives the old agreement; but the intention to discharge the old contract must be clear.

The contract may by express terms provide for its own discharge, for instance a stipulation that one party may terminate it upon giving certain notice or performing certain conditions.

Moore v. Phoenix Insurance Co., 62 N.H. 240, was an action on a policy of insurance. The policy provided that if the premises should become vacant and remain unoccupied for a period of more than ten days without the assent of the company endorsed on the policy, the policy would become void. The premises became vacant and remained so for over three months. They were then occupied and thereafter burned. It was held that by the terms of the policy it was terminated and discharged by the vacancy, and subsequent occupation did not revive it.

Discharge by Performance. This is the termination of the contract contemplated by the parties when it was made. The terms having been carried out and the conditions performed, the contract is satisfied and discharged. This requires performance on both sides. If but one party has performed, he alone is discharged and not the contract, for it remains in force until all its provisions are carried out. If the contract is for the sale of a car for $2,200, the contract is discharged when the car is delivered and the money paid. If the car is delivered but payment not made, it is discharged as to the seller but not as to the purchaser.

To constitute a performance the terms of the contract must

be carried out as to time, place, and conditions. Although a substantial performance is held good, the party will be liable for damages caused by his deviation from the exact terms of the contract.

Nolan v. Whitney, 88 N.Y. 648, was an action to recover on a contract for building defendant a house. The court found that plaintiff had endeavored to live up to the agreement, and acting in good faith, had substantially performed his part. He could therefore recover, notwithstanding some slight defects in the plastering, for which compensation would be made to defendant.

Gillespie Tool Co. v. Wilson, 123 Pa. 19, was an action to recover the contract price for drilling a gas well. The contract called for a certain depth and diameter. Plaintiff had drilled to the required depth, but the diameter of part of the well was less than the contract specified. The only excuse for this was the saving of time and expense. It was held that this was not a substantial compliance and he could not recover, although the well answered every purpose a larger one would.

When the contract calls for payment of money, the party to whom the payment is to be made need not accept a note or check. But if payment is accepted, the question arises whether this discharges the original contract or whether the note or check is to be regarded as a conditional payment. If it is but a conditional payment, the contract is not discharged until payment is positive. It is the intent of the parties that governs here, but in the absence of any proof of intent to the contrary the presumption is, in most states, that it is taken conditionally.

Stone & Gravel Co. v. Gates Iron Works, 124 Ill. 623, held that the taking of a note for a pre-existing debt was no payment unless the creditor expressly agreed to take the note as payment and to run the risk of its being paid. The giving of a receipt of the amount is not sufficient to establish such a positive agreement.

In some states the courts hold exactly the contrary view as to the taking of the notes.

Dodge v. Emerson, 131 Mass. 467, held that the giving and acceptance of a promissory note for a pre-existing debt is presumptive evidence of payment.

A contract in which the performance of one party is to be satisfactory to the other gives rise to the question: Can the whims and personal taste of the party for whom the work is done prevent fulfillment of the agreement when the performance is to all intents and purposes well accomplished? The answer seems to be that if it is a matter of personal taste, as a contract for painting a portrait or a contract for the sale of goods where the parties can be put in statu quo (i.e., the same condition in which they originally stood), the agreement will be strictly construed and the buyer will be the sole judge.

In Brown v. Foster, 113 Mass. 136, plaintiff expressly agreed to make a suit of clothes for defendant that would be satisfactory to him. The clothes were made and delivered, but defendant declined to accept them. Plaintiff proved they could easily be altered and made to fit, but the court held that under the agreement it was for defendant alone to decide whether he would accept the clothes. It was plaintiff's fault if he entered into a contract that made his compensation dependent on the judgment and caprice of another.

But if it is a contract for work or labor which does not involve the question of personal taste, as for machinery or masonry, the courts hold that the party for whom the work is performed must be satisfied when in justice and reason he ought to be satisfied.

In Hawkins v. Graham, 149 Mass. 284, plaintiff agreed with defendant in writing to furnish and set up a heating system in defendant's mill according to certain specifications, and he was to be paid upon its satisfactory completion. If the system was not satisfactory, he was to remove it at his own expense. It was held that the question whether the system was satisfactory was to be determined not by the particular taste and liking of the mill owner but by the judgment of a reasonable man.

Legal Tender. Payment of money must be made in what is termed legal tender, unless the creditor consents to accept something else. Legal tender is money which Congress has declared must be accepted if offered in payment of an undisputed debt. The tender of counterfeit does not constitute payment, and it can be returned within a reasonable time and good money demanded in its place.

Sufficient Tender. The creditor may refuse to accept the money which the debtor claims is due him. If the debtor makes a sufficient tender of the amount, he will be relieved of paying any costs in a suit against him for the debt. To constitute a sufficient tender the exact amount of money must be produced and offered and the offer must be made unconditionally, that is, without any reservation. Even the offer to pay on condition that the creditor give a receipt for the money is not good legal tender. Unless the contract provides a place of payment, the tender must be made to the creditor personally if he is within the state.

Impossibility of Performance. When the act to be performed is an impossibility on the face of it, no contract exists, as such an act is not a valid consideration. But if the question of impossibility arises after formation of the contract, the rule then is that it does not excuse non-performance.

In Anderson v. May, 50 Minn. 280, plaintiff contracted in March to raise and deliver to defendant 591 bushels of beans. Plaintiff delivered only 152 bushels, because most of his crop had been destroyed by early and unusual frost. It was held that this did not excuse his non-performance. When such causes may intervene, they should be guarded against in the contract.

But if the promisor makes his promise conditional on an event the happening of which makes performance impossible, this excuses him, as where a clause is inserted providing for the contingency of fire or floods. If the promise is made unconditionally, the promisor takes all the risk.

Contingencies may arise, however, which the courts hold are sufficient excuse for not fulfilling the contract. Among these are impossiblities arising from a change in the law of one's country.

In Cordes v. Miller, 39 Mich. 581, Miller leased from Cordes a wooden building in Grand Rapids for ten years. The lease contained the covenant, "If said building burns down during this lease, said Cordes agrees to rebuild the same in a suitable time, for said Miller." Miller occupied the premises for two years, when it was destroyed by fire. About the time of the fire an ordinance was passed prohibiting the erection of wooden buildings within certain limits which embraced this site. It was held that the covenant was released by the ordinance making its fulfillment unlawful.

Another contingency which will excuse failure to fulfill is that the continued existence of a specific thing is necessary to performance of the contract: the destruction of that thing through no fault of either party discharges the contract.

Walker v. Tucker, 70 Ill. 527, is a case in which the lessee of a coal mine covenanted in his lease to work the mine during the continuance of his lease in a good and workmanlike manner. The court held that he was excused from further performance when the mine became exhausted.

Cleary v. Sohier, 120 Mass. 210, is a case in which plaintiff entered into a contract with defendant to lath and plaster a certain building. After he had partly completed his part of the contract, the building burned. It was held that plaintiff was excused thereby from fulfilling the remainder of his contract and could recover a reasonable amount for the work already done.

A contract for the rendering of personal services is discharged by the death or illness of the promisor.

In Spaulding v. Rosa, 71 N.Y. 40, defendants contracted with plaintiffs, proprietors of a theater, to furnish an opera troupe to give a certain number of performances. The leader and chief attraction of the company became ill and unable to sing, and defendants did not appear. In an action to recover damages for the breach it was held that as the illness of the chief singer made it practically undesirable and impossible to appear with him, and as it was caused by circumstances beyond his control, it constituted a valid excuse for non-performance.

Discharge by Operation of Law. Where security of a higher nature is substituted for inferior security, a merger of the lesser into the higher takes place. The common illustration of the rule is the case of a judgment taken on a simple contract, the amount owing on the contract being merged in the judgment.

Another illustration is the case of a contract under seal made by the same parties and containing the same subject matter as a simple contract then existing. The simple contract is merged into the specialty.

Clifton v. Jackson Iron Co., 74 Mich. 183, is a case in which the owner of land, on contracting for its sale, reserved the timber, with the right of removal for a specified time. Before expiration of this time he conveyed the land to the purchaser by warranty deed under seal without any such reservation. It was held that the contract became merged into the deed and discharged by it, and the timber passed to the purchaser.

Discharge by Alteration of Written Instrument. If a written instrument is altered or erased in a material part by a party to the contract, or by a stranger while the instrument is in possession of the party to it and with said party's consent and without consent of the other party to the instrument, the contract will be discharged if the alteration is made with intent to defraud; but if innocently made, there can be recovery on the original consideration.

Wood v. Steel, 6 Wall (U.S.) 80, was an action on a promissory note dated October 11, 1858, made by Steele and Newson, payable to their own order one year from date. It was indorsed from them to Wood, the plaintiff. "September" had been stricken out and "October" put in as the date. The change was made after Steele had signed the note as surety and without his knowledge or consent. It was held that it was a material alteration and extinguished Steele's liability.

But if the alteration is without intent to defraud, there can be recovery on the original contract.

In Owen v. Hall, 70 Md. 97, at the maturity of a joint promissory note a renewal note was given which was invalidated as to one of the makers on account of a material alteration made after he had signed. The alteration was the insertion of the words "with interest" without his knowledge or consent. It was held that recovery could be had against him on the original cause of action, as there was no fraudulent intent in the alteration.

Discharge by Bankruptcy. In 1867 there was enacted by Congress a United States Bankruptcy Law. This enactment was repealed in 1878, and in 1898 a new national bankruptcy law went into effect.

VOLUNTARY AND INVOLUNTARY BANKRUPTCY. The act provides: "Any person owing debts, except a corporation, shall be entitled to file a voluntary petition in bankruptcy.

"Any natural person except a wage earner, or a person engaged chiefly in farming or the tillage of the soil, any unincorporated company, and any corporation engaged principally in manufacturing, trading, printing, publishing, mining, or mercantile pursuits, owing debts to the amount of one thousand dollars or over, may be adjudged an involuntary bankrupt upon default or an impartial trial, and shall be subject to the provisions and entitled to the benefits of this act. Private bankers, but not national banks or banks incorporated under state of territorial laws, may be adjudged involuntary bankrupts."

If there have been any recent changes in the bankruptcy laws, you will find them in the state or federal statutes, which should also be consulted for further details.

DUTIES OF BANKRUPT. As soon as the voluntary petition is filed or after the hearing of the involuntary petition, if allowed, the party is a bankrupt, and it is then his duty to attend the first meeting of his creditors, if directed by a court or a judge of the court, and also upon the hearing of his application for discharge. He must comply with the lawful orders of the court; examine the proofs of claims filed against his estate; execute such papers as shall be ordered by the court; execute to his trustee a transfer of all his property in foreign countries; inform his trustee of any attempts of his creditors to evade the provisions of the bankruptcy law, coming to his knowledge, or of any attempt of the creditors to prove false claims; prepare, make oath to, and file in court within ten days, unless further time is granted, after the adjudication if an involuntary bankrupt, and with the petition if a voluntary bankrupt, a schedule of his property, showing the amount and kind of his property, the location thereof, its money value in detail, and a list of his creditors, showing their residences, if known (if unknown, that fact to be stated), the amounts due each of them, the consideration thereof, the security held by them, if any, and a claim for such exemptions as he may be entitled to, all in triplicate, one copy for the clerk, one for the referee, and one for the trustee; and when present at the first meeting of his creditors and at such other times as the court shall order, submit to an examination concerning the conduct of his business, the cause of his bankruptcy, his dealings with his creditors and other persons, the amount, kind, and whereabouts of his property, and in addition, all matters which may affect the administration and settlement of his estate; but no testimony given by him shall be offered in evidence against him in any criminal proceedings.

The bankrupt is entitled to the same exemptions as are allowed any debtor by the laws of the state in which he resides.

ACTS OF BANKRUPTCY. Certain acts of a person are called acts of bankruptcy and render him liable to be adjudged an involuntary bankrupt upon petition of his creditors. The law provides that these acts of bankruptcy by a person "shall consist of his having conveyed, transferred, concealed or removed, part of his property with intent to hinder, delay, or defraud his creditors, or any of them; or transferred while insolvent, any portion of his property to one or more of his creditors with intent to prefer such creditors over his other creditors; or suffered or permitted, while insolvent, any creditor to obtain a preference through legal proceedings, and not having at least five days before a sale or final disposition of any property affected by such preference vacated or discharged such preference; or made a general assignment for the benefit of his creditors, or being insolvent, applied for a receiver or trustee for his property, or because of insolvency a receiver or trustee has been put in charge of his property under the laws of a state, or a territory, or of the United States; or admitted in writing his inability to pay his debts and his willingness to be adjudged a bankrupt on that ground."

The petition can be filed at any time within four months after the act of bankruptcy has been committed.

TRUSTEE AND HIS CREDITORS. As soon as a person is adjudged a bankrupt, a meeting of his creditors is called at which they can examine the bankrupt, elect a trustee, and do any other proper business. As soon as the trustee is elected and has filed his bond, he becomes vested by operation of law with title of the bankrupt to all his property except that exempt by law, to all property transferred in fraud of creditors, and to all rights arising from his contracts and agreements. It is then the duty of the trustee to collect the assets and divide them among the creditors whose claims have been accepted.

DISCHARGE IN BANKRUPTCY. The bankrupt, after one month and within twelve months after being so declared, may file an application for discharge in the court of bankruptcy, and the judge shall grant the discharge unless at the hearing held thereon it appears that the bankrupt has "committed an offense punishable by imprisonment as herein provided; or with intent to conceal his financial condition, destroyed, concealed, or failed to keep books of account or records from which such condition might be ascertained; or obtained property on credit from any person upon a materially false statement in writing made to such a person for the purpose of obtaining such property on credit;

or at any time subsequent to the first day of four months immediately preceding the filing of the petition, transferred, removed, destroyed or concealed, any of the property, with intent to hinder, delay, or defraud his creditors; or in voluntary proceedings been granted a discharge in bankruptcy within six years; or in the course of the proceedings in bankruptcy refused to obey any lawful order of, or to answer any material question approved by, the court."

Discharge of the bankrupt acts as a discharge of all his debts and contracts at the time of filing the petition, except a certain class of debts which are tinged with wrong or fraud, debts due the government, and debts due creditors who have not been duly notified of the proceedings.

Discharge by Breach. A discharge may be made by failure or refusal of one or both of the parties to fulfill the agreement. When the terms of the agreement have been broken, there arises in place of the contract a new obligation under which the party in default is placed. That obligation is to pay to the other party the damage arising therefrom. The injured party acquires a new right of action.

The contract may be broken in any one of three ways. A party may renounce his liability thereunder; or he may by his own acts make it impossible for him to fulfill; or he may wholly or partially fail to perform what he promised.

BREACH BY RENOUNCING LIABILITY. When one party to the contract renounces his liability thereunder before performance is due and declares that he will not perform, a breach of contract arises, and the injured party may at once institute an action for damages.

Windmuller v. Pope, 107 N.Y. 674, was an action to recover damages for breach of contract. The parties entered into a contract whereby plaintiff sold to defendant 1,200 tons of old iron to be delivered at a certain time. Before the time expired, defendant notified plaintiff that he would not receive or pay for any of the iron. Plaintiff thereupon sold the iron elsewhere. It was held that plaintiff was justified in treating the contract as broken at that time and was entitled to bring action immediately without tendering delivery or waiting expiration of the time fixed for the performance.

If during the course of the performance one of the parties

clearly refuses to continue with his part, the contract is broken, and the other party is excused from further performance; in fact, he must not go on if his continuing would increase the damage.

In Clark v. Marsiglia, 1 Denio (N.Y.) 317, defendant delivered to plaintiff a number of pictures to be cleaned and repaired. After he had commenced, defendant gave him orders to stop, as he had decided not to have the work done. Plaintiff, however, finished the work and claimed the whole amount of the contract. It was held that he had no right to increase the amount of damages by going on with the work. When the contract was broken, he was entitled to just compensation for the injury he had sustained by breach of the agreement.

BREACH BY MAKING PERFORMANCE IMPOSSIBLE. If one of the parties puts it out of his power to perform before performance is due, the other party need not wait but may consider the contract broken.

In Wolf v. Marsh, 54 Cal. 228, Marsh promised in writing to pay Wolf a certain sum of money. The note contained the following condition: "This note is made with the express understanding that if the coal mine in the Marsh Ranch yield no profit to me this note is not to be paid and the obligation herein expressed shall be null and void." Thereafter and before the mines had yielded anything, defendant sold them. It was held that although the yielding of profit by the mines was a condition precedent to payment of the note, Marsh had rendered the happening of that condition impossible by selling the mines, and the obligation became absolute.

And this is true if the impossibility is created after the contract is performed in part.

In Woodberry v. Warner, 53 Ark. 488, Woodberry, owner of a steamboat, employed Warner, a pilot, at a salary of $720 a year with the further agreement that as soon as net earnings of the boat should amount to $8,000, he would become owner of a fourth interest. In about two years Woodberry sold the boat. It was held that as he had put it out of his power to fulfill the contract, he was liable to Warner for the value of his services over and above his regular wages.

In order that one party may recover damages for a breach of contract on the part of the other, the first party must show that the second party's promise was not dependent on the acts of the first party; for example, if X is to draw a ton of coal for Y for $15, X cannot sue Y for payment until he has performed his own part.

In Weber v. Clark, 24 Minn. 354, defendant owned a farm of 200 acres and agreed to pay plaintiff $100 if he would find a purchaser for it. Plaintiff found a man who bought part of it, and then sued for the $100. It was held that he could not recover, as he was not entitled to the money until he had performed his part of the contract and found a purchaser for the whole farm.

This rule does not apply to contracts in which the promises are independent of each other. Here a breach by one does not discharge the other.

Tracy v. Albany Exchange Co., 7 N.Y. 472, was an action for breach of covenant in a lease which provided that plaintiff might, at the expiration of the lease, have refusal of the premises for three years longer. When the lease expired, defendant refused to renew it at the same rate but asked $200 per year more. Plaintiff was somewhat in arrears of rent at the expiration of the first lease. It was held that payment of the rent was not a condition precedent to the right of plaintiff to renewal of the lease, the covenant to renew and the covenant to pay rent being independent promises. Plaintiff could bring his action for breach of the contract to renew even though he was guilty of default in payment of his rent.

BREACH BY FAILURE TO PERFORM. When one party wholly fails in the act which was the entire consideration for the second party's promise and which must be done before the second party can be required to perform his part, the second party will be excused. But certain cases come up in which one party has done part of what he promised, or a part of the contract been carried out, and we have to consider whether the whole contract has failed therefor. In other words, is it an entire or a divisible contract? A common case under which this question arises is an agreement to deliver and pay for goods in installments at different times.

The English rule, which holds all contracts of this class as divisible, is followed in Myer v. Wheeler, 65 Iowa 390, in which plaintiff sold defendant ten carloads of barley, like sample, to be delivered from time to time on the railroad tracks at Calmar, Iowa, and defendant was to pay 70 cents per bushel for each carload when delivered. After the first car was delivered, defendant refused to allow more than 65 cents, saying that the barley was not equal to sample, but urged plaintiff to ship balance. Plaintiff refused. It was held that the contract was severable and that refusal to pay for the first carload did not entitle plaintiff to rescind and refuse to deliver the other carloads; that plaintiff could recover the accrual value of the car delivered and defendant could recover damages for the failure to deliver the other nine cars.

But the courts of this country generally seem to hold the contrary view and to make the test the real intent of the parties. If it was intended to be all one contract, the courts do not make it divisible because it is to be executed or carried out at stated periods.

In Norrington v. Wright, 115 U.S. 188, plaintiff made a contract of sale to defendant of 5,000 tons of iron rails for shipment from a European port at the rate of 1,000 tons per month beginning in February, the whole contract to be shipped before August. Plaintiff shipped only 400 tons in February and 885 tons in March. As soon as defendant learned of plaintiff's failure to ship as agreed, he refused to accept and pay for what was shipped and sought to rescind the whole contract for the failure to ship 1,000 tons per month. The contract was held to be entire and not divisible, and defendant had the right to rescind the whole contract.

Representation and Condition. Certain failures to perform are not considered sufficiently important to invalidate the contract, but merely give a right of action for damages caused. If one of the terms of the contract is but subsidiary and does not defeat the main object of the contract, breach of such term does not discharge the contract. Such a term is styled a representation and not a condition. A statement descriptive of the subject matter or of some material incident, such as time or place of shipment, is generally regarded as a condition.

In Filley v. Pope, 115 U.S. 213, a contract provided for the sale of iron to be shipped from Glasgow as soon as possible. It was shipped from Leith. It was held that the buyer might refuse to accept. The place of shipment was a material incident and a warranty or condition precedent, upon failure of which the other party might repudiate the whole contract.

A representation is a separate stipulation and neither suspends nor defeats the agreement.

In Davis v. Meeker, 5 Johns (N.Y.) 354, defendant sold plaintiff a wagon for $50 and represented at the time of the sale that he had been offered $50 for it by different persons. The wagon was not really worth over $25. It was held that this was not a warranty and constituted no grounds for an action.

DAMAGES

Nature and Extent. The party who is guilty of a breach in the performance of his part of the contract may be compelled by the courts to make good the loss incurred by the other party. If the contract is discharged by the breach, the party not in default is released from further performance. He may also recover a pro rata amount on the part performed if he has done anything under the contract. In certain cases there is also provided the extraordinary relief of an injunction or a specific performance.

If the action brought by the party not in default is for money damages, the amount allowed will be the loss or injury caused as the natural result of the breach or that would ordinarily be within the contemplation of the parties. The object is to compensate the party injured and not to punish the party in default.

In Beeman v. Banta, 118 N.Y. 538, defendant contracted to construct a refrigerator for plaintiff, who was engaged in preparing poultry for market, and with the knowledge that plaintiff intended to make use of it at once for freezing and keeping chickens for the May market, expressly warranted that the freezer would keep them in perfect condition. This it failed to do, and as a consequence a large number of chickens spoiled. It was held that plaintiff, in an action on the warranty, could recover as damages the difference in the value of the refrigerator as constructed and its value as it would have been if made according to contract and that he could also recover the market value of the chickens lost, less the cost of getting them to market and selling them.

Specific Performance and Injunction. The special relief of specific performance and injunction is granted only when money damages do not constitute an adequate remedy, as in a contract calling for the conveyance of land. The particular place could not be duplicated elsewhere, and it might have a special value to the purchaser for which the money would but poorly compensate him. Specific performance would therefore be decreed at the same instance of the purchaser compelling the vendor to convey, but it would not be decreed against the purchaser to compel him to accept the property, because there would be an adequate remedy at law in the way of damages, as the owner could sell to someone else, and the difference between what the purchaser had agreed to pay and what he could get for the land after the breach would be the amount of his damages.

The remedy of injunction is used only in special cases in which damages would not afford adequate relief to the injured party.

In Court v. Lassard, 18 Ore. 221, plaintiff, a theatrical manager, sought to restrain defendants, who were acrobats, from performing at a rival theater in the same place. Defendants had agreed to perform for plaintiff exclusively for six weeks, and plaintiff alleged that he had prepared for them and advertised them and that he would lose a large profit, as they were unique attractions. It was held that when a contract stipulates special, unique or extraordinary personal services, involving special merit and skill or knowledge, so that in case of default the same services could not be easily obtained elsewhere nor be compensated by an action at law, a court of equity will be warranted in applying its preventive remedy of injunction.

DISCHARGE OF RIGHT OF ACTION

As a breach of contract gives rise to a right of action for the damages suffered, we have to determine how this right may be discharged, and we find there are three ways.

By Mutual Agreement. The parties may discharge the right by mutual agreement if a valuable consideration is given as payment in satisfaction of the damages, or an instrument under seal.

In Hale v. Spalding, 145 Mass. 482, defendant agreed in writing to pay plaintiff six-sevenths of any loss he might be subjected to as the endorser of a certain note. Thereafter plaintiff executed under seal a receipt "in full satisfaction of defendant's liability on the document." This discharged the right of action on the original agreement.

By Judgment. The party may prosecute the right of action in the courts and obtain a judgment, the right of action being then merged in the judgment.

By Statute of Limitations. If the right of action is not merged in a judgment or discharged by consent within a given time, the law will refuse to enforce it by reason of the lapse of time under what is termed the statute of limitations.

This statute, first enacted in England, provided that all actions on account, and some others, should be commenced and sued within six years. Like the statute of frauds it had for its object the discouraging of litigation and the suppression of perjury, as the lapse of time made the proof less certain and resurrection of old and stale claims would be a fruitful field for fraud and perjury. A provision analogous to the English statute has been enacted in all states. In New York and most other states the period is six years on contracts not under seal and twenty years on sealed instruments or judgments of the court duly recorded. Certain other actions are barred in three years, two years, and one year. Your latest state statute should be consulted.

The statutes vary in the different states, and in a number of them negotiable instruments are not barred for a longer time than simple contracts. In most states real-property actions are given a longer period to run.

WHEN TIME UNDER STATUTE BEGINS. The time begins to run from the day the injured party would be entitled to bring suit for the claim.

Sturgis v. Preston, 134 Mass. 372, was an action to recover money paid under mistake. It was held that it was barred unless the action was brought within six years from the date of payment of the money, because the right of action accrued on that day.

Most statutes provide that the absence of defendant from the state at the time the cause of action arises will postpone the running of the statute until his return.

In Engel v. Fischer, 15 Abb (N.Y.) 72, it was held that a person who comes within the state for the purpose of continuing therein, concealed under a fictitious name to avoid pursuit by his creditors, is not to be regarded as having come within the state within the meaning of the statute until the day he is discovered.

If plaintiff is under a disability, such as infancy, insanity, or imprisonment, at the time the right of action arises, the time will be extended. But the disability must exist at the time the statute begins to run or it will have no effect.

New Promise. The promise or right of action may be renewed, either by a new agreement, which by some statutes must be in writing, or by a payment on account. The statute then begins to run under the new promise or after the new payment.

In Blaskower v. Steel, 23 Ore. 106, plaintiff, between the years 1878 and 1885, sold to H a quantity of cigars. On May 18, 1885, there was a credit on the account. The court held that the credit revived the whole account for a further statutory period, and the claim would not outlaw until six years after the payment.

II. QUASI-CONTRACTS

DEFINITION—ILLUSTRATION

A quasi-contract possesses part of the essentials of a true contract. The word quasi means "in a sense, seeming, resembling"; so the term quasi-contract means a kind of contract, yet not a true contract. In every quasi-contract, to make it a complete contract, the law implies certain things in relation to the parties to the agreement. For example: If Paul owns a house and Peter comes by and sees the walks covered with snow and begins shoveling the snow off, and Paul stands by watching him doing this work and says nothing, Peter may collect from Paul a reasonable sum of money for his services. A quasi-contract was entered into: Paul saw Peter doing the work and stood silently by and made no protest; and the law presumes that Paul will pay Peter a reasonable sum for the work performed. In other words, in quasi-contracts the law steps in and establishes an obligation and a duty.

Another example of quasi-contract arises when the government levies a tax on a person's property. Clearly the tax is levied without the property owner's consent; but the law presumes that the owner agrees to the tax, and further it establishes his duty, obligation, and responsibility to pay it.

UNJUST ENRICHMENT

The law enforces quasi-contracts on the theory that it will not permit unjust enrichment. It would not be equitable to permit one man to stand by and watch another create wealth for him without allowing reasonable compensation to that other who creates the wealth.

TROVER FOR UNJUST CONVERSION—
WAIVER OF TORT-ASSUMPSIT

Suppose Paul gets possession of Peter's automobile without Peter's knowledge and consent, sells it and keeps the money. Paul will have committed a tort in converting the car. Peter can bring suit against Paul in trover, and Paul will be compelled to pay whatever damage Peter has suffered from the tort. We find that Peter has suffered the loss of his car and that Paul has been unjustly enriched to the extent of the money he received from the sale—all at Peter's expense. This is contrary to the principle of quasi-contracts, and the court will hold that Paul has to pay Peter for the car; in an action for tort Peter will receive the amount of money by which Paul unjustly enriched himself.

Then again, Peter may waive the tort action for conversion of his car and bring suit against Paul in assumpsit. This procedure is called waiver of tort. Suppose Paul takes Peter's car, which cost Peter $1,000, and sells it for $1,500. If Peter brings suit against Paul in trover for conversion, the court will allow Peter $1,000 damages; but if Peter waives the tort action and proceeds in assumpsit for money had and received by Paul, the court will allow him $1,500 damages—all the money that Paul received from the sale. The court will base this ruling on the principle that Paul unjustly enriched himself at Peter's expense. So, you will notice, in bringing an action in tort for conversion, Peter receives only the market value of his property, whereas if he instead brings suit in assumpsit, he will be awarded damages to whatever money Paul received for the car, no matter whether more or less than the market price. Therefore, in selecting the more advantageous action to bring, Paul should ascertain whether Paul received more than the market price or less.

We have seen that where Paul takes Peter's car without Peter's consent and sells it, Peter can bring a tort action against Paul immediately. Peter cannot, however, bring an action in assumpsit for money had and received until Paul has actually received the money for the car. The action in assumpsit can be brought at any time after that. Note that the statute of limitations will begin to run as soon as Paul has received the money from sale of the car and that if the full length of time allowable under the statute has expired before Peter attempts to bring his action in assumpsit, the court will hold that Peter can no longer bring action, and the car will then belong to Paul. Paul may then sell the car as his own property, and no quasi-contract will arise in Peter's behalf.

Suppose Paul takes Peter's car without Peter's consent, and instead of selling it, trades it for a house and lot. Paul will have received no money, and since an action in assumpsit for money had and received will not lie, Peter as a result cannot bring suit in quasi-contract. Nevertheless, Paul has unjustly enriched himself at Peter's expense; and to rectify this injustice, Peter can bring suit in equity. The equity court will hold that Paul is trustee for Peter of the house and lot and will compel him to turn these over to Peter.

Suppose Paul takes Peter's car without Peter's consent and keeps it for his personal use. A quasi-contractual relationship is thus established between them, and if Peter brings suit against Paul in quasi-contract, the court will hold that Paul took Peter's car and perfected a sale to himself; as a result Paul will be considered to hold money had and received to the extent of the market value of the car in trust for Peter, and the court will give Peter a judgment on the principle that a demand for the money had and received by Paul is presumed to have been made by Peter, and further, on the theory that Paul unjustly enriched himself at Peter's expense.

Suppose Paul borrows Peter's lawnmower and does not return it within a reasonable time. If Peter then brings suit against Paul in quasi-contract, the court will hold that Peter can recover a reasonable amount of money for Paul's use of the mower, on the theory that Paul unjustly enriched himself at Peter's expense.

Suppose Paul borrows $1,000 from Peter and gives his note for it and the note draws interest at the rate of 18 per cent per annum. Now, suppose the state statute defines the legal rate of interest as not to exceed 10 per cent per annum. The note falls due, and Peter brings suit against Paul on it. The court will hold that the contract is a usurious one and that Paul cannot collect interest above 10 per cent. Now, in the same case, suppose Peter takes out the interest in advance, and when the note falls due, brings suit against Paul. The court will hold that a quasi-contract arises between the parties in regard to the excess interest charged, above the legal 10 per cent, and Peter will be considered to hold this excess interest in trust for Paul, and will be ordered to pay it back to Paul. The judgment given Peter will be for $1,000 minus the usurious excess interest charged.

Suppose Paul borrows Peter's car, and when Peter asks him to return it, Paul refuses, saying that he will hold it until Peter pays him a certain amount of money which, he claims, Peter owes him but which according to law cannot be collected. If Peter does not want to waste time in getting back his car, he may pay Paul the money which Paul demands, and after he has gotten his car, bring an action in quasi-contract against Paul for having secured the money from him under duress. The court will hold that a quasi-contract was established between Paul and Peter when Peter paid the money over to Paul, and that Paul holds the money in trust for Peter. Judgment will be given Peter against Paul for the money paid.

Suppose the city of Jamestown levies a tax against Paul's property unlawfully, and the authorities prepare to sell the property for the tax. Paul may make a formal protest against the tax levy, pay the money to the city and afterward bring suit in quasi-contract. The court will hold that Paul can recover the tax money on the ground of a quasi-contract and that the city unjustly enriched itself at Paul's expense.

Suppose Paul delivers a box of merchandise to an express company to deliver to Peter, but the company delivers it to Harry instead. Peter brings suit against the company and recovers damages to the value of the box of merchandise. The express company in turn may bring suit against Harry on the ground of a quasi-contract, and the court will hold that Harry must pay the company the money which it was compelled to pay to Peter. Judgment is given the express company because Harry, the wrong consignee, was unjustly enriched to the extent of the box of merchandise which he received and accepted from the express company at the company's expense.

MASTER AND SERVANT— ENDORSERS—UNJUST ENRICHMENT

Suppose Paul is employed by Peter as a mechanic in the construction of a building. While Paul is working within the scope of his authority as a mechanic for Peter, he drops a hammer, and it falls on a pedestrian who happens to be walking by, and without any negligence on the part of this third party, injures him. Peter is the master, and Paul is the servant, and both Peter and Paul are liable in an action in tort by the third party. While Peter and Paul are not equally guilty of the tort, they nevertheless are equally liable for damages sustained by the injured party. This is another illustration of quasi-contracts in application of the master-servant doctrine.

Suppose Paul assigns a bond to Peter, and two parties endorse the bond for Paul. The bond comes due, and Paul is unable to pay it to Peter on demand. Peter then sues one of the endorsers and collects the face value of the bond. The endorser then brings suit against the other endorser for half the money he paid Peter, on the ground of contribution between the two endorsers. The court will hold that a quasi-contract exists between the two endorsers and that the law presumes that the first endorser, when he paid over the entire amount of the bond, paid the other endorser's half. The first endorser will be given a judgment against the second for half the money paid, on the theory of unjust enrichment and also on the basis of a quasi-contractual relationship existing between the two endorsers.

REPLEVIN

Suppose Paul has a launch tied up on a lake, and Peter has a boathouse nearby. A severe storm comes up, and to save Paul's launch from destruction, Peter takes it and puts it into his boathouse. Paul never requested Peter to perform this act, nor was Peter under any obligation to save the launch; hence Peter can secure no remuneration from Paul. Suppose, now, Paul goes to Peter and asks to have his launch, and Peter refuses to give it up unless Paul reimburses him for his services. Paul may then bring suit to replevin the launch, and the court will hold that he is entitled to it and that Peter can receive no reimbursement for his services and will have no lien against the launch for any money he might have expended in saving it, because his service was gratuitous.

Suppose Peter is Paul's father. Paul takes Peter's launch

and has a third party repair it. After the repairs have been made, Paul refuses to pay for them, and the third party brings suit against Peter for services and moneys expended. The court will hold that the third party cannot recover from Peter, because Peter did not request him to repair the launch, and even though Paul did so request him and refuses to pay.

MISTAKE OF FACT

Suppose Paul builds a boathouse on a lake lot which he thinks is his own but which as a matter of fact belongs to Peter. Peter brings a suit in ejectment against Paul. In accordance with a law of real estate, the boathouse will have become a part of the real estate, because it is attached thereto, and will thereby have become Peter's property. But when the matter comes up in a court of equity, Peter will be required to pay Paul reasonable value for the boathouse built on Peter's lot, because Paul built the house in good faith, thinking it was on his own lot, and the law of quasi-contracts will apply, because Peter was unjustly enriched at Paul's expense under a mistake of fact.

ABSOLUTE AND RELATIVE RIGHTS

As citizen of a community or a state each person has certain rights that must be respected by every other citizen and certain duties that he must perform. Laws are enacted to protect these rights and to enforce these duties, and when we have a certain series of facts regarding a case, certain rules of law may be utilized to give justice, according to the facts. In the United States, under our constitutional form of government, as citizens of the United States and as citizens of any individual state we have two kinds of rights: one, absolute rights, such as the right of personal freedom, guaranteed by the Constitution; and second, relative rights, or such rights as accrue to a person by virtue of some contract, either written or unwritten or implied, to which he is party.

MISTAKE OF LAW—UNJUST ENRICHMENT— MISTAKE OF FACT

If Paul under a mistake of fact pays some money that he thinks he owes Peter, Paul will be permitted to recover the money so paid in a suit against Peter in quasi-contract, on the theory that Peter holds the money in trust for Paul and that Peter was unjustly enriched at Paul's expense. Now, suppose Paul pays Peter some money while laboring under a mistake of the law concerning the transaction, and Paul afterward brings suit against Peter to recover this money. The court will hold that if the subject matter of the contract is lawful, Paul cannot recover the money under a mistake of law, because ignorance of the law excuses no man, whereas Paul will be permitted to recover money paid Peter under a mistake of fact.

Suppose Paul pays Peter some money under the mistake of fact that Paul thinks he and Peter have entered into a contract, but that legally there is no contract. Paul can bring suit against Peter in assumpsit, in quasi-contract, and the court will give Paul judgment against Peter for money had and received and held in trust by Peter for Paul, according to the theory of unjust enrichment under a mistake of fact.

Suppose Paul buys some horses of Peter and gives him the money for the horses but that the horses do not in fact exist. The court will hold that a quasi-contract exists between Paul and Peter; and in a suit against Peter, Paul will be permitted to recover the money paid to Peter, because of a mistake of fact and on the further principle of unjust enrichment.

Suppose Paul sells an automobile to Peter, and Peter gives Paul the money for it. A little later a third party, who really owns the car and has title to it, comes to Peter and takes his property. Peter then brings suit against Paul in quasi-contract, on the ground of unjust enrichment. Under modern law Peter will secure judgment against Paul for money had and received by Paul in trust for Peter, which Peter paid under a mistake of fact. In old times Peter would not have been permitted to recover, because of the law of personal property, in which the doctrine of caveat emptor used to apply, which meant that the party who bought a chattel had to take the risk of the seller's having legal title to it. But today, under this same series of facts, Peter can recover on the ground, stated above, of a quasi-contract existing between Paul and Peter for money had and received by Paul in trust for Peter, and further on the ground of unjust enrichment.

Suppose Paul sells Peter a ranch to which Paul does not have title. Peter pays the money, but does not receive title to the property, because all real-estate transfers take place either by a warranty deed or by a quitclaim deed. Peter cannot bring suit in quasi-contract against Paul for money had and received; he will have to bring an ordinary suit for damages on the warranty, because Paul warranted title to Peter.

Suppose Paul enters into a contract with Peter to make a suit of clothes, and Paul through his own willful neglect or default so miscuts the pattern that he cannot proceed further in making a satisfactory suit and thus complete the contract. In an action brought against Peter for money and time expended in performing part of the contract, the court will hold that Paul cannot recover, because he of his own neglect performed the contract to his own detriment, and Peter will not be compelled to pay Paul any money for the suit on the ground of unjust enrichment.

GOOD FAITH—IMPOSSIBILITY WITHOUT NEGLIGENCE—PART PERFORMANCE

Suppose Paul enters into a contract with Peter to plow Peter's farm. Paul works conscientiously and in good faith, performing the plowing in a manner which he thinks is according to the contract; but as a matter of fact he does not plow as deep by three inches as the contract calls for. Paul demands to be paid for his work. Peter refuses to pay him because, he contends, the land was not plowed according to contract. Paul brings suit for work and service rendered under the contract. The court will hold that Paul is entitled to be paid according to the contract, less whatever damage Peter may have sustained because the land was not plowed deep enough. This decision is based on the theory of quasi-contract, for if Peter does not pay Paul, Peter will be unjustly enriched at Paul's expense, for Paul performed the contract in good faith according to his interpretation of the contract.

Suppose Paul enters into a contract with Peter to build a bridge across a river. Paul starts the work and gets the bridge half completed. Suddenly, because of the effect of some dynamiting on the other side of the river by some third parties, the river bed is so fractured that it becomes absolutely impossible to finish building the bridge. Peter brings suit against Paul for non-completion of the contract. The court will hold that when the performance of any act becomes impossible through no negligence on the part of either party to the contract, the contractor is released from carrying out the contract.

Now, suppose, in this same case, Paul enters into a contract with Peter to build the bridge, and when the bridge is half completed, Paul is suddenly taken sick and is unable to complete the contract, and Paul could not have foretold at the time he entered into the contract that he would be taken ill. The court will hold that Paul can recover pay according to the contract for the work he has already performed.

Suppose, in the first part of this case, where Paul built half the bridge, and through an impossibility not due to his own negligence nor to that of the other contracting party, could not complete the contract, that Paul sues Peter on a quasi-contract for his money according to contract, for completing half the bridge. The court will allow Paul to collect this money on the ground of quasi-contract and unjust enrichment, in that Paul rendered certain benefits to Peter in building the bridge according to the terms of the contract up to the time when it became impossible to proceed further.

ILLEGAL CONTRACTS

Suppose Paul enters into a contract with Peter, and the contract is illegal. After Paul has completed a portion of the work, he sues Peter on the ground of quasi-contract and unjust enrichment. His complaint alleges that the contract is illegal. The court will not sustain Paul in his action, because both parties entered into an illegal contract, and the law will not assist either party in adjusting their affairs where the contract is illegal.

INFANTS—INSANE PERSONS—
NECESSARIES OF LIFE

Suppose Paul is a minor. He goes to a hotel and enters into an agreement with the proprietor to take board and room at a specified monthly price. After the month has expired, the proprietor brings suit against Paul for board and room at the agreed price. The court will hold that the proprietor cannot collect the agreed price for board and room according to the contract, but will hold that since Paul was an infant and the hotel man supplied him with the necessaries of life, a quasi-contract existed between Paul and the proprietor. The court will therefore give the proprietor judgment against Paul for necessaries of life furnished him, not at the agreed price but only at a reasonable price. The court's decision is based on quasi-contract and on the principle of unjust enrichment.

Suppose Paul loses his mental faculties, and Peter furnishes him with board and room for thirty days at an agreed price. Peter brings suit in assumpsit against Paul for the necessaries of life furnished him. The court will hold that Peter cannot recover according to the agreed price but only at a reasonable price for the necessaries furnished. The court bases its decision on quasi-contract and on unjust enrichment.

The same legal principle holds good in case a married man does not support his wife, or a father does not support his son. Where third persons furnish the dependents with the necessaries of life, the husband and the father will in each case be presumed to have entered into a quasi-contract with the third party, because the law compels a man to support his wife and children.

III. SALES OF PERSONAL PROPERTY

IN GENERAL

Sale and Barter. A sale is a contract between parties to give and to pass rights of property for money which the buyer pays or promises to pay the seller for the thing bought. As a sale is a contract, it is subject to all the requirements of a valid contract. The parties must be competent to enter into a binding contract; there must be mutual assent between buyer and seller; and there must be a consideration. If consideration is absent, the transfer is a gift. The price or consideration must be paid or promised in money. This distinguishes sale from barter, which is the exchange of one article of personal property for another.

In Commonwealth v. Packard, 5 Gray (Mass.) 101, defendant was tried for the unlawful sale of intoxicating liquor. It was proved by a witness that he called for intoxicating liquor at defendant's hotel, that a waiter by defendant's order gave it to him, and that he offered to pay, but defendant would not take anything. It was held it was not a sale but a mere gratuity or gift, and defendant was discharged.

As a general rule the same things apply to a barter as to a sale, and we can consider that the law applicable to barters is practically the same as to sales. It seems, however, that the power of authority vested in an agent to sell does not give authority to barter.

In Edwards v. Cottrell, 43 Iowa 194, it was held that the mortgage of a chattel with power of sale by the mortgagee upon default in payment confers on him no right to barter the mortgaged property or to dispose of it otherwise than for cash.

Transfer of Right of Property. There must be a transfer of the right of property, that is, a transfer of the absolute property in the thing sold, in order to constitute a sale. Absolute property is a term used in distinction from special property, or right in personal property. For instance, when property is pledged, the special property passes to the pledgee and the general title remains in the owner. Transfer of special property in a chattel constitutes bailment (and will be considered later).

Sale and Bailment. The rule is that if the identical thing is to be returned, even though in a different form, as wheat ground into flour, it is a bailment, but if the identical thing is not to be returned, it is a barter or a sale.

In Hyde v. Cookson, 21 Barb. (N.Y.) 92, plaintiff and one Osborn entered into an agreement whereby plaintiff furnished certain hides to Osborn, who took them to his tannery and manufactured them into sole leather and was to return them to plaintiff in New York. Plaintiff was then to sell them at his discretion, and when they had been sold, the net proceeds—less costs, commissions of plaintiff, expenses, etc.—were to go to Osborn for tanning. If there was any loss, Osborn was to stand it. Osborn failed before the contract was completed and assigned to defendant. Defendant refused to deliver the hides to plaintiff, claiming it was a sale and title was in Osborn. It was held that it was not a contract of sale but a bailment, the right of property remaining unchanged and that plaintiff was entitled to the hides.

It is held that the delivery of logs to be sawed into boards is not a sale but a bailment. The importance of the distinction is realized when we perceive that if the transaction is a bailment, title does not pass from the original owner by the delivery, but if it is a sale title does pass. The question often arises when the stock or material delivered is destroyed by fire or otherwise and it must be determined on whom the loss shall fall. An exception to the rule is the case of a warehouseman who receives grain and mixes it with like grain in the same storage. Here there is evidently no intention to return the identical grain, but some of the same kind. Still, some cases hold that this transaction is one of bailment in which title does not pass; but others follow the general rule and hold it is a sale under which title passes to the warehouseman.

FIXTURES

Personal and Real Property. It is generally known that real property is land and rights issuing out of and concerning it. As distinguished from this, personal property is property of a personal or removable nature and includes all property rights not included in real property. Personal property is also called chattels.

Many times we find it hard to distinguish between the two classes of property. It is plain that a house and lot is real property, and it is equally plain that a car or a suit of clothes is personal property. However, certain articles known as fixtures are less clearly defined. In early English law any interest in land less than the absolute title or freehold was called personal property, but in the United States this is not the rule. The only interest in land that can be classed as personal property now is the lease.

In Taylor v. Taylor, 47 Md. 295, A at the time of his death left a will giving his real estate to a certain party and his personal estate to his son absolutely. A owned a number of leases of real property, some of which were to run for ninety-nine years. It was held that these leases passed as personal property to his son.

Fixtures Are Chattels. Fixtures are chattels either actually or constructively affixed to the land. Under some conditions they cannot be removed and are considered part of and pass with the land, while under other conditions they may be separated from the realty and do not pass with it. The early common law was most favorable to the landowner, regarding anything attached to the realty as his property; but the rule was relaxed, at first in favor of the tenant who erected fixtures for use in his trade or business, which were held to be removable. Now the question arises not only between landlord and tenant but also between mortgagor and mortgagee, and vendor and vendee. A person selling his farm must know what he can remove and what he has sold with the land. The tenant must determine what he can take with him and what passes to the landlord because of its attachment to the realty. Different rules have been laid down by different courts.

One of the tests often applied is the intention of the party annexing the chattel to the land. This intention is inferred from

the nature of the article affixed, the relation of the party making
the annexation with the owner of the land, the structure and
mode of annexation, and the purpose for which it is to be used.

In Hinkley v. Black, 70 Me. 473, plaintiffs entered into possession of a tract of land for its purchase, and erected large
and substantial buildings with engines and machinery for
manufacturing an extract of bark for tanning purposes. Plaintiffs
failed to pay for the land, so never acquired title. In an action
to recover the machinery and engines it was held that these were
a part of the realty and could not be sold as personal property as
against the owners of the land.

In Ottumwa Woolen Mill Co. v. Hawley, 44 Iowa 57, it was
held that the machinery of a woolen mill, consisting of looms, carders, breakers, condensers, etc., was part of the realty. The looms
were fastened to the floor by screws and the carders were kept in
position by their own weight, one weighing 3,000 pounds. The
spinning jacks were fastened by cleats nailed to the floor. The
question in this case arose between the purchaser under a
mortgage and the owner. The court said that of the three requisites generally considered necessary to constitute a chattel a part
of the realty, the first, physical attachment, is very uncertain,
and the only value to be given to it is in determining the intention
of the owner in making the annexation. The second, application to the use or purpose to which that part of the realty with
which it is connected is appropriated, is met in this case by the
use of the machinery in the mill. The third requisite, the intention of the party making the annexation, was held by the court to
be the controlling consideration in determining the whole question.

It seems that other tests have to be applied in connection with
intent, to determine whether the chattel is part of the realty. One
is the mode and degree of the annexation. That is, if the chattel
is so firmly and securely affixed to, and incorporated into, the
building that it cannot be removed without injury to itself and
the building, it generally is not removable. Under common law
the mode and degree of annexation was practically the controlling
question.

In Murdoch v. Gifford, 18 N.Y. 28, contrary to the ruling in
Ottumwa Woolen Co. v. Hawley, it was held that looms in a
woolen factory, connected with the motive power by leather

bands and so attached to the building by screws holding them to the floor that they could be removed without injury to themselves or the building, were chattels. The question arose between mortgagor and mortgagee.

In Despatch v. Bellamy, 12 N.H. 205, it was held that an engine used in a building and so placed that it cannot be removed without taking down part of the building is a fixture; while loose removable machinery not attached to the building was not regarded as part of the real estate. The engine in this case could not be removed without taking the boards off the side of the building, and the boilers were set in brick, requiring the wall to be torn down to remove them. The question arose between grantor and purchaser.

A person may not intend to make a permanent improvement, but the chattel may be so firmly annexed that the law will not permit him to carry out his intention of removing it. Damage to the realty must be very pronounced to constitute the chattel a part of the real property if it is the expressed intent of the party that the chattel shall remain personalty.

Hendy v. Dinkerhoff, 57 Cal. 3, was an action to recover possession of a steam engine and boiler. One Lampson was in possession of lands under a contract to purchase from defendant, the contract providing that in case of failure to purchase, all tools should belong to defendant. Plaintiff later leased an engine and boiler to Lampson, and the agreement was that if Lampson failed to pay, plaintiff might retake them. The engine was built into the masonry so that it could not be removed without destroying the masonry and the wall to which it was affixed, but it was held that even as against defendant, the owner of the land, the chattel remained the property of plaintiff.

On the other hand, the fact that the fixture may be removed without such injury does not necessarily make it personalty.

Goodrich v. Jones, 2 Hill (N.Y.) 142, held that fencing material that has been used as part of the fences on a farm but is temporarily detached without any intent to divert it from such use is part of the realty and passes by conveyance of the farm to a purchaser.

Gas and water pipes running under floors and between walls are not removable fixtures, but gas fixtures, chandeliers, and water faucets screwed in through holes in walls or floors are re-

movable when erected by a tenant. Stoves and furnaces put
up in the usual way by a tenant are treated as furniture and are
removable, but if built into brickwork they are non-removable
fixtures.

In McKeage v. Hanover Ins. Co., 81 N.Y. 38, it was held that
gas fixtures simply screwed on to gas pipes and mirrors which
are not set into the wall but put up afterwards and supported
by hooks so driven into the wall that they can be removed without
injuring the wall form no part of the realty and do not pass by
deed or mortgage of the premises.

In Towne v. Fiske, 127 Mass. 125, it was held that a portable
hot-air furnace resting by its own weight on the ground, put
into a house by a person in possession under agreement for a
deed to the premises to be given him, does not become part of
the realty, although connected with the house by a cold-air box
and pipes and registers in the usual way. So gas fixtures in a house,
although attached by screws to pipes, are not part of the realty.

Another test is the appropriation of the chattel to the use or
purpose of that part of the realty to which it is connected. It
seems that an article which is essential to the use for which the
building or land is designed, or which it is especially adapted to
the place where it is erected, is regarded as a non-removable
fixture, although it is only slightly connected with the realty. This
rule is followed in Attumwa Woolen Mill Co. v. Hawley, 44 Iowa
57.

In Dudley v. Hurst, 67 Md. 44, it was held that machinery
used in the canning business, part of which is attached to the soil
and part of which is necessary to the use of the part so attached,
is a fixture that will pass to the mortgagee. When the principal
part of the machinery is a fixture by actual annexation, such part
of it as may not be so physically annexed but which if removed
would leave the principal part unfit for use and would not of
itself, standing alone, be well adapted for general use elsewhere is considered constructively annexed.

Bishop v. Bishop, 11 N.Y. 123, held that poles used necessarily in cultivating hops but which taken down for the purpose of gathering the crop and piled in the yard with the intention
of being replaced in season next year, are part of the realty.

In McRea v. Central Bank, 66 N.Y. 489, plaintiff as mortgagee claimed the machinery in a building erected expressly for use

as a twine factory. The machinery was heavy and was fastened to the floor by bolts, nails, and cleats and was attached to the gearing. Most of the machinery could have been removed without material injury to the building and used elsewhere. It was proved that the machinery was put in the building for permanent use. It was held that the evidence was sufficient to find an intent to make the machinery part of the realty. The court said that the criterion of a fixture is the union of three requisites: (1) actual annexation to the realty or something appurtenant thereto; (2) application to the use or purpose to which that part of the realty to which it is connected is appropriated; (3) intention of the party making the annexation to make a permanent annexation to the freehold. In such cases, the court said, the purpose of the annexation and the intent with which it is made are the most important considerations.

This last rule in the case of McRea v. Central Bank does not apply between landlord and tenant, as it is held that the tenant cannot intend articles for permanent use on land that does not belong to him. This rule inaugurates the theory of constructive annexation and is contrary to common law, which requires actual annexation to the realty.

Snedeker v. Warring, 12 N.Y. 170, is a case in which the owner of realty, after giving a mortgage, placed on the ground in front of his house a statue of Washington, made by himself and weighing about three tons. It was on a base three feet high. This base rested on a foundation built of mortar and stone. The statue was not fastened to the base, nor the base to the foundation. It was held that the statue was part of the realty, that it was as firmly attached to the soil by its own weight as it could have been by clamps and screws. A sundial, similarly placed, was also held to be realty.

Rogers v. Crow, 40 Mo. 91, is a case in which the builders of a church left a recess in which an organ was to be placed. The organ was required to complete the design and finish of the building and was attached to the floor and intended to be permanent. It was held that the organ was part of the realty and passed to the purchaser of the land.

Force pumps, pipes, and shafting and machinery attached by spikes, nails, and butts, are part of the realty.

Symonds v. Harris, 51 Me. 14, held that machinery used in a

sash factory and attached to the mill by spikes, bolts, and screws and operated by belts running from the permanent shafting driven by a water wheel under the mill was part of the realty.

Under the rule of constructive annexation some cases hold that machinery permanent in character and essential for the purposes of the building becomes realty, although not actually attached to it. In this class of fixtures are ponderous machinery kept in place by its own weight, cotton gins, and duplicate rollers for a rolling mill; all are held to pass with the realty.

Deal v. Palmer, 72 N.C. 582, held that a carding machine not fastened to a house but requiring several men to move it is a fixture and passes with the land to a purchaser.

Other cases hold that machinery is personal property unless actually annexed. Such cases hold that heavy machinery in a factory screwed to the floor but removable without injury is not realty.

In Hubbel v. Savings Bank, 132 Mass. 447, it was held that a mortgage of land does not cover machinery on the floor of a building on the land, supported by iron legs fastened to the floor by screws, only for the purpose of steadying it and which, although of great weight, and adapted for use in the business carried on in the building, can be removed without injury to the building and used elsewhere. The machinery in dispute consisted of a large engine lathe, an iron planer, and an upright drill.

Relation of Parties. The relation of the parties has some weight in determining the character of the fixtures. As between landlord and tenant the presumption is that a tenant does not intend improvements to be additions to the realty, and he therefore is allowed greater rights in removing the chattels than is a person of any other class . For the encouragement and promotion of industry the rule has been established that trade fixtures erected by a tenant are removables. A carpenter shop, a ballroom, and a bowling alley erected on blocks or posts have all been held to be removable.

Holmes v. Tremper, 20 Johns (N.Y.) 29 held that a cider mill and press erected by a tenant, holding from year to year at his own expense and for his own use in making cider on the farm, are not fixtures that pass with the realty.

In Conrad v. Saginaw Mining Co., 54 Mich. 249, it was held

that as between landlord and tenant under a mining lease, engines and boilers erected by the tenant on brick and stone foundation, bolted down solidly to the ground and walled in with brick arches, and also dwelling houses erected by the tenant for miners to live in, standing on posts or dry stone walls, where the intent was not to make them part of the realty but was merely to use them in the mining operations, are to be regarded as "trade fixtures" and may be removed by the tenant at or before termination of the lease.

Carlin v. Ritter, 68 Md. 478, held that as between landlord and tenant, wooden structures and buildings resting by their own weight on flat stones laid on the surface of the ground without other foundation are not part of the realty. But if the building is a permanent structure on a foundation, it becomes part of the real estate.

The tenant must exercise his right to remove fixtures before expiration of the term. If he does not remove them before he surrenders the premises, he cannot re-enter and claim them.

In Dostal v. McCaddon, 35 Iowa 318, defendant, after his lease had expired, entered upon plaintiff's premises to remove a vault and safe he had constructed, and this action was to restrain him from removing them. It was held that the tenant could not exercise his right of removing trade fixtures after he had surrendered possession of the premises.

When the question arises between vendor and vendee or between mortgagor and mortgagee, the presumption is stronger against the vendor or mortgagor; as owners of the realty they are supposed to have intended the improvements to be permanent. The parties may agree that the chattels annexed are to remain as personalty, and effect will be given to the agreement.

In Smith v. Whitney, 147 Mass. 479, the tenant's lease provided that he might erect buildings for manufacturing purposes and remove them within the limit of his lease. He erected a brick engine house complete in itself. The engine and boiler were on a solid foundation of masonry. It was held that the tenant has a right to remove the house, and the engine and boiler as well.

The question comes up whether trees, grass, and growing crops are realty or personal property. That was discussed when we learned that before they are severed from the land, natural products, such as trees and grass, which grow without cultivation and the labor of man are parts of the realty, and if sold standing, the buyer to cut them, the contract is within the statute of frauds. If the products are growing crops which are harvested annually and planted and cared for by the labor of man, the general rule is that they are personal property, even when attached to the soil.

PARTIES TO SALE

Seller and Purchaser. The parties to a sale are the seller, or vendor, and the purchaser, or vendee. The general rule is that no man can sell goods and convey good title unless he is the owner or the owner's duly authorized agent. Possession is not an essential to the right to sell, ownership being enough, and the rightful owner can sell what is wrongfully held by another.

Webber v. Davis, 44 Me. 147, was an action to recover the value of a horse once owned by defendant and which was stolen from him. After the horse was stolen, plaintiff paid defendant $20 for it and agreed to run his own risk of finding it. The horse was worth $60, but if it was not found, plaintiff was to lose his $20. A few weeks after, plaintiff located the horse, but defendant got possession first. It was held that plaintiff could recover on the ground that title would pass by a sale without delivery from the true owner, although at the time of the sale the goods were in the wrongful possession of a third person.

Seller Must Have Good Title. The principle of a holder in good faith which is spoken of in the negotiable-instrument law does not apply in the sale of personal property, the general rule being that one cannot give better title than he himself has.

In Williams v. Merle, 11 Wend. (N.Y.) 80, the master of a boat took four barrels of potash from plaintiff's warehouse and turned them over to the clerk of his principal, the boat owner, who sold them to defendant, a broker, who paid a reasonable price for them. In an action to recover them it was held that a purchaser of personal property is not protected against the claim of the true owner, although he purchases in good faith and for a valuable consideration, if the vendor has no title or authority to sell.

In Moody v. Blake, 117 Mass. 23, A, falsely representing himself to be a member of a firm, bought goods in its name from plaintiff, who sent them to the firm. On refusal of the firm to receive them A got possession of the goods from the carrier and sold them to defendant, who bought them for value and in good faith. It was held that plaintiff could recover the goods of defendant. Defendant has no better title than his vendor.

However innocent the person may be who buys property from one not the owner, he obtains no title whatever, except in a few special cases, for instance negotiable instruments. It follows, then, that a person buying goods that were either lost or stolen has no claim on them as against the true owner.

Hoffman v. Carow, 20 Wend. (N.Y.) 21, held that an auctioneer who sold stolen goods was liable to the owner, notwithstanding that the goods were sold and the proceeds turned over to the thief without knowledge that the goods were stolen.

A thief acquires no title and can convey none, and no matter how many sales or transfers of the property there may have been after the thief disposed of it before it came into possession of the holder, the true owner can recover. It makes no difference that the purchase was made in good faith and for full value.

In Breckenridge v. McAfee, 54 Ind. 141, plaintiff brought an action for the value of wheat which his hired man had stolen and sold to defendant. It was held that a thief acquires no title to property stolen and can confer none on a person to whom he sells the same and that such person is liable to the owner for the value of the property without regard to his innocence or good faith in making the purchase.

Pledgee May Sell. An exception to the rule that a person not the owner cannot sell personal property is the case of a pledgee, or one with whom chattels are left as security for money loaned, as he can sell after default in payment by the owner. So also the master of a vessel can sell the cargo in cases of absolute necessity; actual necessity must exist or the purchaser gets no title.

Factor May Sell. A factor, or commission merchant, is a person to whom goods are shipped or consigned for purpose of sale. A sale by him conveys good title and binds the original owner under statutes passed in most states, even though he goes beyond his authority and sells when he is not authorized to do so by the owner; but the factor, or commission merchant, must have actual possession or he will not give good title if he exceeds his authority. This statute is limited to mercantile transactions and applies only to factors, or commission merchants.

If the owner of goods entrusts possession of them to another, thereby enabling the other party to hold himself out to the public as having not only the possession but also the ownership of the goods, a sale by such party to a person without notice who acts on the strength of such apparent ownership will bind the true owner, if the person having possession is one who from the nature of his employment might ordinarily be taken to have the right to sell.

In Nixon v. Brown, 57 N.H. 34, plaintiff employed one M to purchase a horse for him. M bought the horse, paid for it with plaintiff's money, and took the bill of sale in his own name. He afterwards informed plaintiff of what he had done and showed him the bill of sale, but plaintiff allowed him to go away with the horse and the bill of sale. M went to defendant, who had no knowledge of the agency, showed him the bill of sale and sold him the horse. The court held that he could not recover the horse from defendant.

The purchaser must be a party competent to contract except in case of necessaries.

CONTRACT OF SALE

Contract May Be Executory or Executed. The contract of sale, like other contracts, may be executed or executory. In the executory contract of sale title has not passed to the purchaser. It is simply an agreement to make a transfer at some future time. In the executed contract title has passed, and the sale is complete. At the time of the sale the subject matter or thing sold must be in existence. If it has ceased to exist, the sale is void.

Dexter v. Norton, 47 N.Y. 62, was an action to recover damages for breach of a contract by defendant to sell and deliver to plaintiff 621 bales of cotton bearing certain marks and numbers specified in the contract at a certain price. After defendant had delivered 460 bales, the remaining 161 bales were destroyed by fire, without fault or negligence of defendant. The court held that where a contract is made for the sale of certain specified articles of personal property under such conditions that title does not vest in the vendee, if the property is destroyed by accident without fault of the vendor so that delivery becomes impossible, the vendor is excused from delivery.

Potential Existence. Regarding the sale of things not yet in existence, if they are such as the natural products or expected increase of what is already owned, they are said to have a "potential existence" and may be sold. Therefore a man may sell a crop of hay to be grown on his fields, wool to be clipped from his sheep, or wine to be produced from his vineyard.

Rochester Distilling Co. v. Rasey, 142 N.Y. 570, was an action based on the following facts: In February, 1890, Rochester Distilling Co. recovered a judgment against one Lovell. In April, 1890, Lovell, a tenant on a certain farm, gave one Page, whom he owed, a chattel mortgage on all the crops which were already sown and those which were yet to be sown. Very little seed was in the ground at that time. On July 5, Rochester Distilling Co. levied upon the growing crops and later at public sale purchased them. On July 15, Page foreclosed his mortgage and sold the growing crops to Rasey, defendant in the case. Rochester Distilling Co. brought suit against Rasey for recovery of title to the crops. It was held by the Court of Appeals that an unplanted crop is not in potential existence and therefore cannot be the subject of either mortgage or sale.

But when the subject of the contract is to be acquired afterward, as the land from which one expects to raise hay or grain, or the sheep from which one expects to clip wool, the article cannot be sold. A valid agreement may be made to sell it, that is, an executory contract to sell it can be entered into. The question whether the contract of sale is executed or executory is important when the property is lost or destroyed, for if it is an executed contract, the vendee loses, and if it is executory, the vendor loses.

When Title Passes. Title rests in the vendee immediately upon completion of the contract of sale without regard to whether or not the goods are delivered.

In Terry v. Wheeler, 25 N.Y. 520, there was a sale of lumber in the vendor's yard. The pieces sold were designated, and the price was paid by the purchaser. The vendor agreed to deliver the lumber at the railroad station. The lumber was destroyed before such delivery. It was held that it was an executed contract of sale. Title had passed, and the loss fell on the purchaser. In an executory contract, it being but a promise to sell, title does not pass until the sale is completed.

In Fitch v. Beach, 15 Wend. (N.Y.) 221, there was an agreement for the sale of a boatload of lumber, part of which was landed and the unloading of the remainder of which was suspended until an inspector could be procured to measure it. After waiting a day, the vendor reloaded the lumber landed and went away. In an action for wrongfully taking the lumber it was held that title had not passed, as something remained to be done between vendor and vendee, namely, the measuring and sorting of the lumber. The only remedy would be damages for breach of contract.

It is hard to determine whether the parties have entered into a contract of sale or simply into an agreement to sell. The intention of the parties in this respect is controlling.

In Callaghan v. Myers, 89 Ill. 566, it was held that an agreement to purchase a lot of books, if part of the price is paid, possession given, and the amount to be paid if the books should prove to be as represented is fixed, title will pass as against the creditor of the vendor. Whether the sale is complete and title passes depends on the intention of the parties.

Intention. When the intention of the parties is not clear, certain rules are observed in determining it. If the chattels in contention are not agreed upon, or are not separated from a larger number or quantity, it is clear that the parties intended only an executory contract. For example, if X buys 10 cars out of a lot of 50, there is no complete contract until the particular 10 cars out of a group of 50 have been designated or separated from the rest. If the articles are not ready for delivery, or there is still something to be done on them, it is but an executory agreement.

McConike v. New York & Erie R.R., 20 N.Y. 495, was an action to recover damages upon a contract under which plaintiff was to furnish material and build 15 lumber cars for defendant at $475 per car, to be paid six months from date of delivery; defendants were to furnish iron boxes for the cars of a model made by them. When the cars were completed, excepting the part prevented by default of defendants in not furnishing the boxes, they were destroyed by fire while in possession of plaintiff and without his fault. It was held that title to the cars was still in plaintiff and that he could not recover for labor and material.

But if it is the sale of an article in bulk, title passes, although it has not been measured, if it is the apparent intent that it shall pass; and in cases in which it is the sale of part of a bulk or mass, all of the same quality, it is not necessary to have the part sold separated in order for title to pass.

In Chapman v. Shepard, 39 Conn. 413, A sold B a quantity of bags of meal on board ship at a certain price per bag. B, without paying A, and before the bags were counted, sold 500 bags to C, who gave his promissory note. Thereafter C informed A of his purchase and was told he could remove the bags when he pleased, but after he had removed part, A refused to let him remove the remainder. It was held that title had passed to B, as it was the evident intent of the parties that it should, and it had also passed from B to C. Upon sale of a number of articles from a mass of the same quality and value, separation of the part sold is not necessary to pass title; but the ruling is otherwise when the articles composing the mass are of different qualities and values, making not only separation, but selection, necessary.

Contracts in Writing. By the statute of frauds certain contracts of sale should be in writing. To satisfy the statute, the writing need not be on any particular form, but it must contain a description of the property purchased and other elements of the agreement, signed by the purchaser or party to be charged. In sales of any importance it is customary to execute a formal bill of sale and deliver it with the property.

It is a safe plan to require a bill of sale, as the buyer then has a warranty of title from the vendor as well as a formal certificate that he is the purchaser and owner of the property mentioned.

CONDITIONAL SALE

Installment Sales. In these sales the passing of title is conditioned upon certain acts which may or may not be performed. It is common in business for certain articles, such as pianos, sewing machines, cars, and automatic washers and dryers, to be sold conditionally, title to remain in the vendor until the purchase price is fully paid. This kind of sale is used by all installment dealers who sell goods on weekly or monthly payments. Pay-

ment of the last installment is a condition precedent to the passing
of title to the purchaser. As between the original parties, a
conditional sale is valid, and title does not pass until the condition is fulfilled, even though the property is given into possession of the vendee at the time the parties enter into the contract.

McRea v. Merrifield, 48 Ark. 160, was an action to recover
an engine, a sawmill, and a lot of tools sold by plaintiff under a
contract of sale which expressly agreed that title should remain
in the vendor until the purchase price was fully paid. Payment
was never fully made. It was held that title did not pass to the
purchaser until payment was made. The contract constituted
a conditional sale, and the vendor could recover the property.

If the party in possession, that is, the vendee, is enabled to
present every appearance of ownership when the title does not
rest in him, fraud many enter in. A third party who purchases of
him without notice of title in the vendor may easily be imposed upon and defrauded. The general rule is that in the absence
of any fraud in the conditional sale, the sale is valid against third
persons. The seller can give no better title than he possesses.

McIntosh v. Beam, 47 Ark. 363, was an action to recover a
mule sold conditionally by plaintiff to a third party, title to remain in the vendor until the animal was paid for. The mule
was sold by this third party to defendant, who bought it in good
faith for a valuable consideration and without notice of the conditional sale. It was held that plaintiff could recover. The purchaser acquires no better title than his vendor.

Filing Conditional Contracts. Statutes have been passed in
many states requiring every such contract of sale to be filed; if it
is not, the condition is void as to persons who buy of the party
in possession without notice of the conditional contract. In New
York, in a few special cases, delivery to the vendee of a copy of
the contract takes the place of filing.

In Moyer v. McIntyre, 43 Hun (N.Y.) 58, plaintiff on August
5, 1885, sold a wagon to one Smith for $72.50. Five dollars was to
be paid in cash, and a note for the balance was given by Smith
to plaintiff. The note provided that title to the wagon was to remain in plaintiff until the note was paid and that plaintiff might
take possession of the wagon whenever he felt insecure. After
Smith had been in possession of the wagon about eight weeks,

he sold it to defendant, who took it without notice of plaintiff's claim, paying for it $10 in cash and applying $55 on an old debt owed him by Smith. Plaintiff tendered defendant $10 and demanded the wagon. Upon being refused, he brought this action to recover it. It was held that by the laws of 1884 this contract must have been filed, and as that was not done, the conditions in the note were void as to defendant, who purchased in good faith and without notice.

Sale on Trial. Sale on trial or on approval is another form of conditional sale, the goods being delivered subject to approval of the intended purchaser, and if not found satisfactory or as represented, they are to be returned. If they are returnable within a given time and are retained beyond that time, it will be presumed that the purchaser has approved, and the sale is absolute. If no time for the trial or examination is agreed upon, it must be within a reasonable time, and if the purchaser does not accept or return the goods within a reasonable time, he will be deemed to have approved and the sale to be consummated.

When anything is yet to be done to the goods to put them in deliverable shape, in the absence of a contrary intention the performance of these things is a condition precedent to the passing of title.

Butler v. Lawshe, 74 Ga. 352, held that if there was an agreement by which an iron press was to be sold by the pound and was to be weighed, the contract was executory until it was weighed, but if the price was fixed, the contract was executed on delivery. The press was sent by the vendor to the vendee by a drayman, and the vendee gave instructions as to where it was to be delivered. The jury found that it was not to be weighed; therefore title had passed.

In Cornell v. Clark, 104 N.Y. 451, a railroad company entered into a contract to purchase 20,000 ties at 55 cents each for first-class ties and 35 cents for what should be adjudged second-class. They were to be delivered by the vendor and counted and inspected by a person named. The company advanced 15 cents each as they were delivered. The ties were never inspected or classified. The company failed, and it was held that title to the ties had not passed to the company, the ties requiring yet to be counted and classified.

Chattel Mortgage. The chattel mortgage is another form of

conditional sale. It consists in the sale of certain chattels or goods, subject to defeat upon payment by the vendor or mortgagor of a certain debt or performance of a certain obligation. It differs from a conditional sale in that title passes to the purchaser at once, but it is liable to be defeated upon the fulfilling of certain conditions, while in a conditional sale title does not pass until the conditions are fulfilled.

McCoy v. Lassiter, 95 N.C. 88, held that the difference between a pledge and a chattel mortgage is that in the former title is retained by the pledgor, while in the latter it passes to the mortgagee.

Delivery to the pledgee is essential, but in a chattel mortgage it is not necessary as between the parties, and by statute filing or registration is substituted for delivery so as to make it effective as against third parties, such as purchasers or creditors.

Tannahill v. Tuttle, 3 Mich. 104, held that by the mortgage of chattels whole legal title to the property passed to the mortgagee conditionally.

The chattel mortgage is a means often employed by a borrower of money to secure the loan. The goods may remain in possession of either party, but if they are allowed to remain in the mortgagor's possession, the statutes of nearly all the states require that the mortgage shall be filed with some public officer, where it may be open to the inspection of the public. It is usually required to be filed with the town clerk, county clerk, or registrar of deeds, if it is to be binding against third parties who may buy the mortgaged property in good faith and without notice of the mortgage. As between the parties themselves the mortgage is valid without being filed, and is in fact without being executed in any formal way.

The subject of chattel mortgages is regulated by statute in the various states, and it is now almost a universal rule that the mortgagor keeps possession of the goods mortgaged, the filing of the mortgage taking the place of change of possession.

Requirements of Mortgage. The mortgage is required by statute to be in writing and to contain the names of the parties and a description of the property covered. The filing of the mortgage is notice to all the world, and anyone buying the property thereafter is supposed to have notice of it. In New York and in some other states it is necessary to file a renewal of the mortgage each year, and failure to file a renewal at the expiration of the year renders the mortgage of no more effect than if it never had been filed.

Foreclosure. After default in payment of the mortgage, the mortgagee must foreclose the mortgage in order to cut off all the rights of the mortgagor. The procedure differs under the statutes of the different states. It consists in giving notice to the mortgagor and selling the property at public sale. The mortgage itself may contain provisions for the foreclosure. The mortgagor is usually allowed time until the date of the sale in which to pay the amount due and redeem the property mortgaged.

WARRANTIES

Classification. A condition in a contract of a sale which is required to be performed before the contract is completed will defeat the sale if it is not carried out. A condition is one of the essential elements of such a contract. Aside from this there are certain warranties which are collateral undertakings on the part of the seller to be responsible in damages if certain conditions as to quality, amount, or title of the article are not as represented. The warranty is a separate contract, and if made at a different time from the contract of sale, it must be supported by a separate consideration. If made at the same time, the consideration of the sale will also operate as a consideration for the warranty.

There are two classes of warranty, express and implied.

Express Warranty. The express warranty is an express undertaking or agreement made by the seller. No special form or words are necessary to create a warranty. Any statement framed with the intention of making a warranty will be so construed. It must be distinguished from a mere expression of opinion on points regarding the chattel, of which the seller had no special knowledge and on which the buyer may be expected to exercise his own judgment. A warranty is an assertion of a fact of which the buyer is ignorant.

In Hunter v. McLaughlin, 43 Ind. 38, the vendor, in selling a patent right in a ditching machine, exhibited the letters patent and the model and stated that if properly constructed, the machine would work well. It was claimed that the machine was properly constructed, yet did not work well. It was not shown that the vendor had ever made or used a machine constructed after this model or that he represented that he had made and used one. The court held that the statements were nothing more than mere expressions of opinion, which for aught that appeared the vendor might honestly have believed.

Stroud v. Pierce, 6 Allen (Mass.) 413, held that a statement by a piano agent that the instrument is "well made and will stand up to concert pitch" is a warranty, it being a representation of fact.

If the representation is a warranty, the contract will not be broken by a breach, but an action for damages will arise. If it is a mere expression of opinion, there is no remedy if it turns out to be unfounded.

In Anthony v. Halstead, 37 LTNS (Eng.) 433, the following memorandum was given: "Received from C. Anthony Esq., 60 pounds for a black horse, rising five years, quiet to ride and drive, and warranted sound up to this date, or subject to the examination of a veterinary surgeon." It was held to be a warranty of soundness and not a warranty that the horse was quiet to ride and drive.

Burge v. Stroberg, 42 Ga. 88, held that a statement that a horse is fourteen years old is a warranty that he is no older.

Pritchard v. Fox, 4 Jones (N.C.) 140, held that a warranty that a soda fountain is in good condition is broken if, from inherent defects in construction existing at the time of sale, it was liable to get out of order from time to time.

A general warranty is held not to include defects apparent on simple inspection and requiring no skill to discover them, nor defects known to the buyer.

In Dean v. Morey, 33 Iowa 120, defendant sold plaintiff a horse that was a cribber. It was held that he was not bound to disclose this fact to plaintiff, as the horse was subject to the buyer's inspection, and a simple examination of the horse's mouth would have shown the defect.

An express warranty must be distinguished from the mere praising or puffing of his goods by an owner, as the statement by an agent that he has the best plow on the market or by a driver that his team is the best in the city.

Implied Warranty. Implied warranty differs from express warranty in that although it exists in the contract of sale, it is not mentioned or stated in express words. In every contract of sale there is an implied warranty of title when the goods sold are in possession of the vendor at the time of sale, unless there is an express agreement to the contrary; but in cases in which the goods are in possession of a third party, there is no such implied warranty, and the purchaser buys at his peril.

In Huntington v. Hall, 36 Me. 501, defendant sold plaintiff a small house which was on another man's land and not occupied by defendant. There was no express warranty of title, as defendant did not own the house. It was held that there was no implied warranty. The implied warranty arises when the vendor himself possesses the chattel, but when the chattel is in possession of another, the purchaser buys at his peril.

Long v. Hickingbottom, 28 Miss. 772, held that in the sale of a chattel, if possession at the time is in another and there is no covenant of warranty, the rule of caveat emptor applies, and the party buys at his peril. But if the seller has possession of the article sold and he sells it as his own and for a fair price, he warrants title.

As to the implied warranty of quality, we find the maxim caveat emptor, meaning "let the buyer beware," to be the general rule of our law. When there has been a sale of specific goods which the buyer has an opportunity to inspect, he buys at his own risk as to quality, unless there is an express warranty. There is no implied warranty of the quality.

In Frazier v. Harvey, 34 Conn. 469, defendant sold plaintiff some hogs, which, unknown to both parties, had a disease, of which they died later. This was an action on the implied warranty of soundness of the hogs. It was held that there was no express warranty and no fraud in the sale of the personal property; the purchaser took the risk of its quality and condition.

But when the chattel is to be made or supplied to the order of the purchaser, there is an implied warranty that it is reasonably fit for the purpose intended, if that purpose is made known and told to the seller.

Tabor v. Peters, 74 Ala. 90, held that the vendor of a patent churn, being himself the manufacturer and contracting to furnish the purchaser with a quantity of churns, must be held to have warranted that they are useful and reasonably suitable for the intended purpose; and if they prove to be worthless, there will be a breach of the implied warranty which will be a good defense against an action for the purchase price.

If the sale is by sample, there is an implied warranty that the quality of the bulk is equal to that of the sample.

In Myer v. Wheeler, 65 Iowa 390, plaintiff sold defendant 10 carloads of barley like sample, to be delivered from time to time. Defendants had never seen the barley. It was held that there was a warranty that the barley would be equal to the sample.

In Graff v. Foster, 67 Mo. 512, defendant bought some oranges of plaintiff. In an action for the purchase price, defendant claimed that the oranges were greatly inferior in quality to sample and set up the breach of the implied warranty. It was held that it is not necessary that the word warranty shall be used. It is sufficient if the seller undertakes that the goods shall be as represented. So if the seller exhibits samples as fair specimens of the stock and agrees to deliver goods equal in quality to samples, and the purchaser buys, relying on this promise, it is a warranty.

To constitute a sale by sample it must appear that the contract of the parties was made solely with reference to the sample exhibited.

In Day v. Raguet, 14 Minn. 273, plaintiff sold defendant whiskey which was to be 5 per cent better than a sample shown. It was held that that was not a sale case by sample.

In a sale by description there is an implied warranty that the goods shall be salable or merchantable, aside from the fact that a condition precedent to the sale is that the goods shall answer the description. The buyer having no opportunity to inspect the goods, the rule of caveat emptor does not apply, and the buyer has the right to expect that he is getting a salable article answering the description in the contract, and not an article that is worthless.

In Weiger v. Gould, 86 Ill. 180, plaintiff sold defendant oats and represented them to be a good grade of white oats, such as defendant was purchasing at forty cents. It was held that he must deliver merchantable oats and could not deliver wet oats.

When a person buys of a manufacturer an article made for a particular purpose, there is an implied warranty that it is fit for the desired purpose; also that it is free from latent defects arising from the process of manufacture and unknown to the purchaser which render the article unfit for the purpose intended.

In Rodgers v. Niles, 11 Ohio St. 48, defendant agreed with plaintiff that he would deliver to him at a future time three steam boilers with which to run the engines in his roller mill. It was held that there was an implied warranty that the boilers should be free from all such defects in material or workmanship, latent or otherwise, as would render them unfit for the usual purposes of such boilers.

Delivery and Payment. To complete the sale it is necessary for the seller to deliver the goods and for the purchaser to pay for them; and unless there is an express agreement to the contrary, these acts are concurrent. Delivery in this sense does not necessarily mean the passing of the article itself but rather the passing of ownership or title. That is to say, the delivery need not be actual; it may be constructive. It is actual when the article itself is handed over. It is constructive when a bill of sale or a receipt is handed over instead.

REMEDIES FOR BREACH

Rights of Vendor. The parties may not fulfill their contract of sale, and then arises the question of their respective rights. The vendee may refuse to complete the contract of sale by declining to accept the goods, or after accepting and retaining the goods, he may refuse to pay the purchase price. If the goods have not been delivered and title has not passed to the purchaser, the vendor may elect to avail himself of any one of three remedies: First, he may resell the goods, after having tendered them and had been refused, and recover damages for the loss, if any. Second, he may hold the goods for the vendee and sue for the entire purchase price. Or as his third remedy, he may keep the goods and sue for damages, which will be the difference between the contract price and the market price at the time and place of delivery.

Dustan v. McAndrew, 44 N.Y. 72, was an action brought on a contract for the sale of certain hops, which defendant had refused to take. Plaintiff placed them in the hands of a broker who sold them for a fair price, and then he brought this action for the difference between the contract price and the price for which the hops were sold. The court held for plaintiff, and said that on failure of the purchaser to perform, the vendor as a general rule has his choice of three remedies: (1) Hold the property for the purchaser and recover of him the entire purchases money. (2) Sell it after notice to the purchaser, as agent for that purpose, and recover the difference between the contract price and the price realized at the sale. (3) Retain it as his own and recover the difference between the contract price and the market price at the time and place of delivery.

Bagley v. Findlay, 82 Ill. 524, is a case in which the purchaser refused to take goods for which he had contracted; the court said: "When the vendee of specific goods refuses to take and pay for them, the vendor may store them for the vendee, giving him notice he has done so, and then recover the full contract price; or he may keep the goods and recover the excess of the contract price over and above the market price of the goods at the time and place of delivery; or he may upon notice to the vendee, proceed to sell the goods to the best advantage and recover of the vendee the loss if they fail to bring the contract price."

Some cases do not allow the first remedy mentioned in Dustan v. McAndrew, 44 N.Y. 72, and hold that the vendor can either retain the goods and sue for the difference between the contract price and the market value or resell the goods and sue for the loss. But in a resale the vendor must be fair and obtain the reasonable value of the article; otherwise the price received will be disregarded, and the difference between the market price and the contract price will rule.

If title and possession have passed to the purchaser, the only remedy is an action against the purchaser for the contract price, or if not for the contract price, for the reasonable value of the goods.

Stoppage in Transitu. There is another class of remedy by which the seller may obtain the purchase price if title has passed to the buyer but physical possession is in the vendor, and that arises from his lien on the goods. As soon as the goods are in actual possession of the vendee, the lien is lost. After title may have passed to the purchaser, still actual possession or custody may yet be in the vendor; or the goods may be in transit, that is, on the road to delivery, in possession of the railroad or express company. When the goods are in custody of the seller, he may hold them under his lien for the purchase price, and when they are in transit the law gives the unpaid vendor the right to intercept them, if he can, and thereby prevent them from reaching the purchaser. This right, called stoppage in transitu, exists when the purchaser becomes insolvent after the sale or was insolvent when the sale was made, though the fact was unknown to the vendor. The right of stoppage in transitu extends not only to the vendor himself but to an agent who, on order of his principal, has purchased goods and paid for them with his own money. So also, a third person who advances the money for the purchase and takes an assignment of the bill of lading can exercise the right of stoppage in transitu.

In Gossler v. Schepeler, 5 Daly (N.Y.) 476, plaintiff advanced the money on a cargo of iron for defendant and received the bill of lading as security for the advance. Plaintiff sent the bill of lading to defendant, who became insolvent before he received the goods. It was held that plaintiff could stop the goods in transit and retake them and compel defendant to deliver to him the bill of lading.

This right can be exercised only against an insolvent or bankrupt person. By an insolvent is meant one unable to pay his debts in the usual course of his business.

In O'Brien v. Norris, 16 Md. 122, it was held that the right of stoppage in transitu was not defeated by showing that the vendee was actually insolvent at the time of the purchase, unless it was shown that such insolvency was known to the vendee, when of course he would be held to have contracted with that in mind. Technical insolvency, such as bankruptcy, is not necessary, and suspending payment is sufficient to justify a vendor in exercising the right of stoppage in transitu.

If the vendor stops the goods when the vendee is solvent, he does so at his peril and will be obliged to deliver the goods in addition to becoming liable for damages to the vendee. In order to exercise the right the goods must be in transit. It is held that transit begins when the seller has delivered custody of the goods to the carrier and extends to the time when actual possession and custody of the goods are acquired by the purchaser. In other words, the goods are liable to stoppage in transitu as long as they are in the carrier's possession, and as soon as delivered to the buyer or his agent, the right ceases. No particular form is necessary in order to exercise this right. It is simply required that notice be given to the carrier not to deliver the goods and that it be given in time for the carrier or transportation company, by using reasonable diligence, to notify its agents to hold them. The usual mode is a notice to the carrier stating the vendor's claim and forbidding delivery to the vendee or requiring that the goods be held subject to the vendor's orders.

In Durgy Cement Co. v. O'Brien, 123 Mass. 12, it was held that the fact that the vendee's notes went to protest because of his inability to pay them in the regular course of business was sufficient to justify plaintiff in exercising the right of stoppage in transitu.

In Jones v. Earl, 37 Cal. 630, the vendor delivered to the agent of a carrier in possession of the goods a letter to the effect that the vendee had been served with an attachment and that the vendor desired to save the goods. He gave the agent a bill of particulars of the goods and directed him to deliver them to no one but the vendor's agent, who would be there to look after them. It was held to be a sufficient notice to stop delivery of the goods.

In Mottram v. Heyer, 5 Denio (N.Y.) 629, plaintiff made demand of defendants when the goods were in the custom-house and after the bills of lading and freight receipts had been given to defendants. Defendants were insolvent. It was held that this demand was not sufficient. It must be made of the carrier in whose custody the goods are, under such circumstances that the carrier may prevent their delivery to the vendee. The vendor's right of stoppage in transitu ceases not upon arrival of the goods at the point of delivery but when they come into the vendee's actual or constructive possession.

The right of stoppage in transitu is defeated in case the bill of lading is in the hands of the vendee and he transfers it to a third person who in good faith pays value for it. The third party can hold the goods.

Rights of Vendee. There are also certain rights that the buyer has which it is necessary to consider. The vendor may fail to deliver the goods, or there may be some defect in the goods delivered. When the vendor refuses to deliver the goods and title to them has not passed to the buyer, the buyer's remedy is to sue for damages for breach of contract. If the purchase price is unpaid, the damages will be the difference between the contract price and the market price of the goods at the time and place of delivery, but if the purchase price has been paid, this sum should be added to the amount that may be recovered.

In Harralson v. Stein, 50 Ala. 347, it was held that a purchaser can recover as damages from a vendor who refuses or fails to deliver the goods bought the difference between the agreed price and the market price at the time they ought to have been delivered, that is, the loss which the vendee would suffer if he had to go out and buy the articles in the market.

Specific Performance. Another remedy is offered the buyer in a few certain cases, and that is specific performance. Generally the damages for breach are an adequate remedy, but when, because of the peculiar nature of the property and the difficulty of obtaining it elsewhere, specific performance alone can compensate the vendee, it will be granted by a court of equity.

Treasurer v. Commercial Mining Co., 23 Cal. 390, was an action to compel defendant to issue to plaintiff 46 shares of capital stock of the company. It was shown that the stock had no fixed market value, that it was fluctuating and uncertain in value and that therefore the damages arising from a breach of the contract to deliver such stock could not be ascertained. It was held that specific performance would be allowed, because damages would not afford a full and adequate remedy.

When the goods delivered do not correspond to the articles sold, the buyer may rescind the contract and sue for damages. Also, if some warranty has been violated, he can recover damages, although he will not be allowed to return the goods if title has passed to him; but the contrary is the rule when title has not passed.

IV. NEGOTIABLE INSTRUMENTS

GENERAL

Definition. A negotiable instrument is a written instrument or evidence of a debt which may be transferred from one person to another by endorsement and delivery, or by delivery only so that legal title becomes vested in the transferee. The principal forms of negotiable instruments are promissory notes, bills of exchange, and checks.

Negotiable instruments, in a sense, serve as a substitute for money. As a means of transferring funds and paying debts the check is as common among business houses as money itself, while the promissory note is an equally important factor of our business system. The note is taken to the bank when the borrower wishes to have money advanced to him by that institution. It is given to close a business transaction when so agreed when the date of payment is a day in the future; and as a large part of business today is transacted on credit, we can see the great usefulness of the promissory note as a transferable evidence of debt.

The term "negotiable" is applied to these instruments because they pass freely from hand to hand; by their terms they provide for such transfer.

Basis of Negotiable-Instrument Law. It is a common statement that the negotiable-instrument law is based on, and derived from, the customs of merchants. In early law there was but little mention of commercial questions, any dispute arising between merchant and customer being decided on the spot by a special court or committee that sat to administer speedy justice to the merchants at the markets or great fairs. These markets or fairs were held from time to time in the different cities in which the mercantile pursuits were largely carried on by merchants of different nations. The disputes were determined not by fixed law but by the customs of merchants. In old English law books it was said that justice should be administered "while the dust fell from the feet," so quickly was the court supposed to act. This practice finally developed into certain rules which were taken up and enforced by the courts and became the basis of our mercantile laws.

As the merchants dealt between different countries, it is easy to understand that the customs of the different nations came to be much the same and that the law founded on these customs had much similarity. Consequently the negotiable-instrument law, which is based more directly on these customs than is any other branch of the law, does not materially vary in different jurisdictions.

Statute Law. It is very important that contracts which are to pass from hand to hand and from state to state with almost the freedom of money should be subject to practically the same laws and rules, and to this end a statute law covering the principal questions concerning negotiable instruments has been adopted in most states, giving a uniformity that renders these instruments more freely negotiable than they would otherwise be. We speak of negotiable instruments as contracts, and in reality they are written contracts, possessing special characteristics which give them privileges and qualities different from those in ordinary contracts.

Principal Characteristics. The principal characteristic of a negotiable instrument, and that which makes it pass freely as a substitute for money, is that in the hands of a third party who purchases it in good faith and for value before it is due, it is enforceable, while the original holder could not perhaps enforce it, for the reason that the party who made the instrument has a good defense or counterclaim. As soon, however, as the purchaser of an instrument comes into possession of it for value, he cannot be prevented from collecting because of any defenses existing between the original parties. In other contracts the purchaser acquires only the rights of the party from whom he buys, but in the case of negotiable paper he may acquire better title than the original holder.

Essential Conditions. In general no exact form need to be followed, although the custom has prescribed forms that are very generally used; but it is required that a negotiable instrument be (1) in writing; (2) properly signed; (3) negotiable in form; (4) payable in money only; (5) payable in a certain amount; (6) payable absolutely; (7) payable to the order of a designated payee or bearer; (8) payable at a certain time.

INSTRUMENT MUST BE IN WRITING. The first requirement is that the instrument be in writing. No oral contract can be negotiable. By a written contract we mean one in either writing or printing, and the writing may be executed with any substance, as ink or pencil.

The whole instrument must be written. No essential part, as the names of the parties, or the amount, can be omitted from the writing.

In Currier v. Lockwood, 40 Conn. 349, it was held that the following instrument was not a promissory note:

$17.14   Bridgeport, Connecticut, Jan. 22, 1863

Due Currier & Barker seventeen dollars and fourteen cents, value received.

Frederick Lockwood

This is merely a due bill. It does not contain a promise to pay. Bare acknowledgment of a debt does not in legal construction import an express promise to pay.

INSTRUMENT MUST BE SIGNED BY PARTY EXECUTING IT. It is usual that the signature be made by writing the name of the signer; or he may affix his mark or any other character intended to be a signature.

In Brown v. Butchers' & Drovers' Bank, 6 Hill (N.Y.) 443, the bank sued Brown as the endorser of a bill of exchange. The endorsement was made with a lead pencil and in figures, thus: "1. 2. 3.," no name being written. It was known that they were in Brown's handwriting and that he meant them as his endorsement. It also appeared that he could write. The court charged the jury that if they believed the figures were made by Brown as a substitute for his proper name with the intention of binding himself as an endorser, he was liable. Judgment was for plaintiff. This was held to be correct. A person may be bound by any mark or designation he thinks proper to adopt, provided he uses it as a substitute for his name and intends to bind himself.

It is usual to place the signature at the close of the instrument, but if it is shown that it is meant for a signature, it may be placed on any other part except where the statute requires that the name be subscribed.

Taylor v. Dobbins, Strange (Eng.) 399, is an English case decided in 1720 which holds that it is sufficient if the maker writes the note with his own hand, and there need be no subscription in that case, for it is sufficient if his name is in any part of it.

INSTRUMENT MUST BE NEGOTIABLE IN FORM. The instrument must be payable to "order" or "bearer." If made payable to a particular person or persons only, it is not a negotiable instrument, and falls under the rules governing a simple contract. In other words, the intent of the party making the instrument to execute a negotiable paper must appear by some express words showing such a purpose.

Chamberlain v. Young, 1893, 2 Q.B. (Eng.) 206, was an action on the following instrument:

Five months after date pay to .... or order, the sum of one hundred and fifty pounds, for value received.

[Signed] E. Malcolm Tower

To Mr. A. J. Young.

The defense claimed it was not a bill of exchange. The court held it was a bill of exchange payable to order and was valid. It virtually said pay to the order of the drawer.

INSTRUMENT MUST BE PAYABLE IN MONEY, AND AMOUNT MUST BE DEFINITE AND CERTAIN. The very reason it must be payable in money is that if it were payable in any other commodity, the value could not be definite and certain. If payable in a given number of bushels of wheat, the person taking it would be obliged to determine the value of wheat at that place; the value at another place might be materially different. By the term "money" is meant the legal tender of the country; for example, a note payable in Spanish money is not a negotiable instrument in the United States.

Thompson v. Sloane, 23 Wend. (N.Y.) 71, was a suit on a note made and dated at Buffalo, N.Y., for $2,500, payable twelve months after date at the Commercial Bank of Buffalo in Canadian money. It was held that it was not a negotiable note. A promissory note in order to be negotiable within the meaning of the law merchant must be payable in current money and not in the money of some other country.

The sum payable is considered fixed and certain if it is a given amount with interest, or payable in stated installments or with exchange (the banks' charges), or with the costs of collection in case payment is not made at maturity.

Dodge v. Emerson, 34 Me. 96, was an action on a note "payable to the Protection Insurance Company, or order, for $271.25, with such additional premium as may arise on policy No. 50, issued at the Calais Agency." It was held that the instrument was not a negotiable instrument, the amount payable being indefinite and uncertain.

Lent v. Hodgman, 15 Barb. (N.Y.) 274, held an instrument not negotiable, as uncertain, which provided: "Pay A.B. 68 bushels of wheat in store, at three cents below first quality wheat."

In Fralick v. Norton, 2 Mich. 130, a note for $60, but $50 if paid by January 1, was held not negotiable, as uncertain.

In Parson v. Jackson, 99 U.S. 434, certain bonds certified "that the Vicksburg, Shreveport & Texas Railroad Co. are indebted to John Roy, or bearer, for value received, in the sum of either 225 pounds sterling or $1,000 lawful money of the United States of America; to wit, if the principal and interest are payable in New York or New Orleans." It was held that in the absence of an express designation as to the place the bonds were to be paid, the instruments were not negotiable, since the amount to be paid was uncertain. The judge said, "One of the first rules in regard to negotiable paper is that the amount to be paid must be certain, and not to depend on a contingency."

INSTRUMENT MUST DESIGNATE PAYEE. There must be no uncertainty as to the person to whom the money is to be paid. The instrument must be paid to a certain person or his order, or to the bearer. It need not name the payee, but it must be payable to a person or persons who can be definitely ascertained at the time of payment. If payable to X or to Y, it is not a negotiable instrument under the law merchant, but it has so been rendered by statute in some states.

Smith v. Wilding (Wisconsin case) was an action on a written instrument drawn as follows:

$2500. La Crosse, Wisconsin, September 2, 1897

Four months after date I promise to pay to the order of twenty-five hundred dollars. Value received.

John Wilding

It was held that it was not a negotiable instrument, as it neither designated the payee nor left a blank space for the payee's name.

Shaw v. Smith, 150 Mass. 166, was an action by the administrator of the estate of F. B. Bridgman on the following instrument:

$126. Belchertown, July 19, 1873

For value received I promise to pay F. B. Bridgman's estate, or order, one hundred twenty-six dollars on demand, with interest annually.

[Signed] Eugene Bridgman

It was contended that this was not a promissory note because there was no definite payee, but the court held that as the promise was to pay F. B. Bridgman's estate and he was dead and administrators had been appointed, the payees were in existence and ascertainable. They were therefore designated with sufficient definiteness, and the instrument was negotiable.

Musselman v. Oakes, 19 Ill. 81, was an action on an instrument purporting to be a promissory note, payable to "Olive Fletcher or R. H. Oakes." It was held that the instrument was not negotiable, as it was not payable to a certain person. It was payable to Fletcher or to Oakes, but to which was not certain.

Noxon v. Smith, 127 Mass. 485, was an action on a note payable to "The Trustees of the Methodist Episcopal Church or their collector." It was held to be a negotiable instrument, as it was not payable to different persons in the alternative but to a certain designated payee, the trustees of the church, their collector being but their agent, and payment to him would be payment to them.

INSTRUMENT MUST BE PAYABLE ABSOLUTELY AND UNCONDITIONALLY. If the instrument is so drawn that any condition may arise which would render it of no effect, it is not a negotiable paper. Consequently a promise to pay a certain sum out of a designated fund is not negotiable, and this is the case even though the fund exists at the time or the condition that would nullify the contract never arises.

In Richardson v. Carpenter, 46 N.Y. 660, an instrument in the following form was held not to be a negotiable instrument, as the money was payable out of a particular fund: "Please pay A, or order, $500 for value received out of the proceeds of the claims against the Peabody Estate, now in the hands for collection, when the same shall have been collected by you."

Blake v. Coleman, 22 Wis. 415, was an action on a promissory note in the usual form; on the back was endorsed: "The conditions of the within note are as follows: L. S. Blake or bearer is not to ask, or expect payment of said note until his, Coleman's old mill is sold for a fair price." It was shown that this endorsement was made at the time the note was given. The note was given for a new fanning mill, and defendant still had his old one on hand. It was held that this endorsement qualified the note and made it a mere agreement, and not being a negotiable instrument, it could not be collected upon until the agreement was fulfilled.

Worden v. Dodge, 4 Denis (N.Y.) 159, was an action on an agreement in which defendants promised to pay to plaintiff or order $250 with interest, payable one half in two years and the other half in three years "out of the net proceeds, after paying the cost and expenses of ore to be raised and sold from the bed of the lot this day conveyed by Edward Madden and Edwin Dodge, which bed is to be opened and the ore disposed of as soon as conveniently may be." It was held that payment of the amount depended on a contingency; so the agreement was not a promissory note. A promissory note must be payable absolutely, and not dependent on some contingency or event. Here the fund might not be adequate.

But the promise is not made conditional by designating a place of payment in the instrument.

TIME MUST BE CERTAIN. The time of payment must be definite and fixed; that is, the date of payment must be definitely stated, or it must be on or before a certain definite date, or at a certain time after the happening of an event that is sure to occur, or on demand. A note payable a certain number of days after the death of a person is negotiable, the date being certain because the time is sure to arrive.

Shaw v. Camp, 160 Ill. 425, held that the following was a negotiable instrument, as the meaning was that it should be payable after the death of the maker. "After my death date I promise to pay Hanson Camp, on order the sum of $750 without interest."

But the contingent event must be certain to occur or the promise will not be absolute.

Kelley v. Hemmingway, 13 Ill. 604, was an action on an instrument in the following form:

Castleton, April 27, 1844

Due Henry D. Kelley fifty-three dollars, when he is twenty-one years old, with interest.

[Signed] David Kelley

Plaintiff proved that Henry D. Kelley had become of age before the action was commenced. The court held that the instrument was not negotiable, as payment was contingent on an event that might or might not happen. The money was therefore not payable "absolutely and at all events," and the paper lacked one of the necessary elements of a negotiable instrument.

Duffield v. Johnston, 96 N.Y. 369, was an action to recover the last two payments on the following instrument:

Thomas Johnston

Dear Sir: (1) Please pay to J. J. Duffield or order, the sum six hundred and sixty-six dollars when the brown stone work of your eight houses situated on the south side of East One Hundred and Fifth Street, between Second and Third Avenues, city is topped out. (2) The sum of four hundred dollars when the stoops of said houses are set. (3) The sum of three hundred seventy-five dollars when the brown stone work, of the said eight houses is completed; and charge the same to me, and oblige yours, etc.,

[Signed] Wm. Chave

It was held that it was not a bill of exchange because not payable absolutely. It was payable on condition that the work be done as specified, and might never become payable.

The law simply requires that the time of payment be sure to arrive.

PROMISSORY NOTES

Definition. A promissory note is an unconditional written promise made by one or more persons to pay to another or his order or bearer a certain sum of money at a specified time.

The party who makes the note and whose promise is contained therein is called the maker, and the party to whom the promise is made is called the payee.

Form. There is no exact form of note required by law in ordinary business. It may or may not draw interest, but will not unless provided for in the note. The following form is a common one:

$200.   Chicago, Illinois, July 1, 1966

    Two months after date I promise to pay to Arthur Anderson
. . . . Two Hundred no/100 . . . . . Dollars
. . . . . . at the First National Bank of Chicago . . .
Value received.

No. 1 Due September 1, 1966   [Signed] Carl Carlson

If the note is to be without interest, the words "with interest" are omitted. In this note Carlson is the maker and Anderson is the payee. If Anderson wishes to obtain the money before the note matures, he endorses it by writing his name on the back, and then he is also called the endorser, the person to whom he transfers it being called the holder or endorsee.

The above note is an illustration of a several note, as there is but one maker. There may also be a joint note and a joint and several note.

In a joint note there are two or more makers and the obligation to pay rests on the makers jointly, and they must be sued together; if one is released the others cannot be held.

In King v. Hoare, 13 M & W. (Eng.) 494, it was held that a judgment against one or two joint debtors is a bar to an action against the other on the same debt.

When two or more persons make a note and agree to pay jointly and severally, the form is substantially as follows:

$500.00   Moline, Illinois, February 10, 1966

One month after date, (without grace) value received, we jointly and severally promise to pay the Moline Trust & Savings Bank or order Five Hundred no/100 . . . Dollars at the office of the bank.

Witness:

A. B. Chase

[Signature] Henry Hanson, Principal
[Signature] Roy Redfield ⎱ Securities
[Signature] E. E. Ellis ⎰

Moline Trust and Savings Bank Moline, Illinois

On this note the makers may be sued together, or either one can be held severally for the full amount.

If the last note should be drawn in the form of the several note but be signed by Hanson and also by one or more sureties, it would be construed by law to be a joint and several note.

Dart v. Sherwood, 7 Wis. 523, was an action against the signers of the following promissory note as joint makers:

$400.   Ripon, Wisconsin, Nov. 4, 1856

Thirty days after date, for value received, I promise to pay Putnam C. Dart, or order, four hundred dollars with interest, at the rate of twelve per cent per annum.

J. C. Sherwood [Signature]
Wm. C. Sherwood, Surety [Signature]

It was held by the court to be a joint and several note—joint because signed by both parties and several because each defendant promised severally.

In Ely v. Clute, 19 Hun. (N.Y.) 35, the following note was held to be joint and several, and separate judgments might be rendered against the two makers:

$270.   Stockton, March 14, 1875

One day after date I promise to pay Lorenzo Ely, or bearer, two hundred seventy dollars at the Post Office in Stockton. Value received with use.

Thomas W. Clute [Signature]
J. B. Clute [Signature]

In a few states the distinction between joint notes and several notes has been abolished, and all notes signed by two or more parties have been declared to be joint and several.

Signature. The construction of a signature may to a certain extent be ambiguous, and it will be well to note the effect of an original which is apparently intended to be made by an agent or attorney to bind his principal.

It is plain that if the maker or any other party signing executes the signature in any of the following forms, the principal alone is bound, provided the agent acts within his authority: Arthur Anderson by his agent, Bert Boyd; Arthur Anderson by Bert Boyd, agent; or Bert Boyd, agent for Arthur Anderson, or Bert Boyd for Arthur Anderson.

Long v. Colburn, 11 Mass. 97, is a case that held that the signature "Pro William Gill—J. S. Colburn" on a promissory note was the signature of the principal William Gill and that he was bound by it.

On the other hand, we find the courts holding that the agent alone is bound by such signatures as the following: Bert Boyd, Agent; Bert Boyd, Agent for Arthur Anderson; Bert Boyd, president or treasurer, etc., or Bert Boyd, president Illinois Electric Co.

Davis v. England, 141 Mass. 587, was an action on a promissory note in the form "I promise to pay," and signed "W. H. England President and treasurer Chelsea Iron and Foundry Co." It was held that the signature made the note of England and not of the company.

McClellan v. Robe, 93 Ind. 298, held that a note in the usual form in which several persons signed and after their names added "trustees of the G. Lodge, etc." rendered the signers individually liable, the words added being but descriptive of the parties.

When the signature to the instrument is made by the agent writing the name of the principal, followed by the agent's name, the courts differ on the effect given. Such a signature as Arthur Anderson, Bert Boyd, Agent, or General Gas Co., Bert Boyd, President, is held by some courts to be the principal's signature, and he alone is bound.

Liebscher v. Kraus, 74 Wis. 387, was an action brought on the following promissory note:

$637.40

Ninety days after date we promise to pay Leo Liebscher, or order, the sum of six hundred and thirty-seven dollars and forty cents, value received. San Pedro Mining & Milling Co.

[Signed] F. Kraus, President

Plaintiff demanded judgment against the corporation and Kraus as joint makers. The court held that it was the note of the company alone and that Kraus signed for the company as its president. The signature alone showed plainly enough that Kraus was acting as officer or agent of the company.

Other courts hold that it is the signature of both the principal and the agent and that both are liable.

Matthews & Co. v. Mattress Co., 87 Iowa 246, was an action on a promissory note against Dubuque Mattress Co. and John Kapp. The note read, "we promise to pay" and was signed "Dubuque Mattress Co., John Kapp Pt." It was held that Kapp was personally liable. Where a person signs a note and adds his name of office, and there is nothing on the face of the instrument to show he does not intend to be bound, he is personally liable, because the name of the office is merely descriptive of the person.

Other courts hold the signature to be ambiguous and allow evidence to explain it.

Bean v. Pioneer Mining Co., 66 Cal. 451, was an action on a promissory note reading "we promise to pay" and signed "Pioneer Mining Company, John Mason, Supt." It was held that the signature was ambiguous and that parol evidence was admissible to show that it was understood by the payee to be the note of the company and that the consideration for which it was given passed to the company.

The body of the instruments may contain statements that will explain the instrument, but the printed heading of the paper does not necessarily prove agency.

Casco National Bank v. Clark, 139 N.Y. 307, was an action against Clark and Close on the following promissory note:

$7500.   Brooklyn, N. Y., Aug. 2, 1890

Ridgewood Ice Co.   Three months after date, we promise to pay to the order
Clark and Chaplin Ice Company, seventy-five hundred dol-
lars at Mechanic's Bank, value received.

[Signed] John Clark, Pres.
[Signed] E. H. Close, Treas.

Defendants claimed they had signed as officers of the Ridgewood Ice Co. and had not become personally liable on the note.
But the court held that the name of the company printed on the
margin of the paper did not create any presumption that the
note was made by the company and that the officers of the company had a right to obligate themselves.

Discharge. The agreement of the maker of a note or of the
acceptor of a bill of exchange is that on the date of maturity of
the note or bill he will pay absolutely the amount named therein
to the payee designated therein or to his order.

His promise is absolute, and it can be discharged only in one
of the ways in which a contract can be discharged—by payment,
lapse of time, etc.

The only condition he can require is that the holder surrender
the note or bill, and the maker is not obliged to pay without
receiving the instrument, as otherwise, if it were lost, it might
be presented by a person purchasing of the finder might be
compelled the second time. Relief in such a case is generally
given the payee, however, by compelling the maker to pay upon
being furnished a bond to indemnify him against any loss because of reappearance of the note.

BILLS OF EXCHANGE

Definition. A bill of exchange, or draft, is a written order
from one person to another to pay to a third party or his order
a certain amount of money at a specified time.

A common form of bill of exchange is:

$600.   Chicago, Ill., Aug. 10, 1966

NO PROTEST
Please take this off
before presenting if not
paid at maturity. Return
at once stating reason—

At sight pay to the order of The First National
Bank of Chicago Six hundred no/100 . . . . .
Dollars. Value received and charge to the account of
To Elmer Eaton
Rock Island, Illinois

Carlton Press, Inc.
by M. U. Sheldon, Treasurer
[Signature]

Specimen

In this bill of exchange Carlton Press, Inc., is the drawer, First
National Bank of Chicago is the payee, and Elmer Eaton is
the drawee. After Elmer Eaton has accepted the bill, he is called
the acceptor.

Bank Draft. When the drawer and drawee are banks, the bill
of exchange is known as a bank draft, and it constitutes a common
method of paying the debts of parties residing in different
localities. The form is:

NORTHERN TRUST COMPANY OF CHICAGO
Chicago, Ill., October 20, 1966 No. 112289

Pay to the order of Charles Carlson $500.00
Five Hundred and no/100   . . . . . .   Dollars
To the
Bank of America
Los Angeles, California

[Signature]
John Andrews, Cashier

Carlson owes Anderson of Los Angeles $500 and wishes to pay
him; therefore he goes to his bank in Chicago and purchases a
draft on a Los Angeles bank and sends it to Anderson. This draft
he has made payable to himself, and on the back he endorses
"Pay to the order of John Anderson" and signs "Charles Carlson."
The draft might have been payable to John Anderson on its face,
but the advantage of the other form is that when the draft is
returned to Northern Trust Co., having been endorsed by

Charles Carlson, it contains a complete record of the transaction, and in case of a dispute is a receipt which Carlson can procure for use in evidence. The banks have an arrangement among themselves, through the clearing house and their correspondents in the large financial centers like New York and Chicago, by reason of which they can issue these drafts. The New York or Chicago draft is as readily accepted as the money itself and is unhesitatingly cashed by banks anywhere. Here it may be seen how the bill of exchange or bank draft acts as a convenient transfer of obligation without the necessity of conveying money between distant points.

The bill of exchange and the promissory note, like the bank draft, may be transferred by the payee, and so may pass from hand to hand and thus take the place of money.

Bills of Exchange May Be Either Foreign or Inland. A foreign bill of exchange is a bill drawn in one state or country and payable in another. An inland bill of exchange is one made payable in the same state in which it is drawn. The last illustration is a foreign bill. A foreign bill is sometimes draw in duplicate or triplicate, and upon payment of one copy any others become void. The several copies are called a set, the object in having them so drawn being that if one is lost, the other, or others, will reach their destination. In earlier times the custom was to send each copy by a different route and thus ensure safety and dispatch. The first copy presented was the one paid. A common form for a foreign bill is:

No. 126   The First National Bank
                                          Chicago, Ill., Aug. 1, 1967

Exch. £ 100XX

Ten days . . . . . after sight of this . . .
First of Exchange Second unpaid payable to the order of
. . . . Charles Carlson . . . . . .
One hundred pounds sterling . . . . Value received and charge the same to the account of this bank
To Union Bank of London
London, England

Countersigned
Arthur E. Jones
Cashier

                                          [Signature]
                                          E. V. Prochnow
                                          Vice President

But the custom of issuing bills in a set is fast becoming obsolete, and the practice between the states is to draw foreign bills in the same form as inland bills.

Time and Sight Drafts. Drafts are also drawn as either time or sight drafts. The following is a sight draft; that is, it is payable on presentation. A time draft is payable at a given time after demand or sight or date.

$227.50   Los Angeles, California
                             December 27, 1966

NO PROTEST—Please take this off before presenting if not paid at maturity return at once stating reason

At sight pay to the order of Bank of America of California Two hundred twenty-seven . . . . . 50/100 Dollars . . . . . Value received and charge to the account of

To Arnold Anderson
Oxnard, California

                        Carlton Press
                        by M. U. Sherman, Treasurer
                        [Signature]

The draft is a means commonly used by business houses to collect debts due them from parties residing in other places. The creditor draws on the debtor, naming a bank as payee for the purpose of making the collection.

Acceptance. A bill of exchange being an order on the drawee to pay a certain amount of money to a third party, it is not binding on the drawee until he has accepted it. The acceptance is signified, if a sight draft, by payment; if a time draft, by the drawee's writing the word "accepted" across the face of the draft and signing his name. After he has accepted the bill, he becomes the acceptor, and his obligation is then fixed and absolute and can be enforced against him, his position becoming much the same as that of a maker of a note. According to the law merchant, the acceptance could be either oral or written, but by statute in most states it must be in writing. Barring the case of acceptance honor, the only person who can accept a bill is the drawee.

In Cook v. Baldwin, 120 Mass. 317, it was held that the words "I take notice of the above, Henry Baldwin" written on a bill of exchange do not necessarily import an acceptance, and parol evidence of a refusal can be shown. The court said a bill of exchange by an oral promise to pay as well as by a written one, or by such language and conduct on the part of the drawee, when the bill is presented to him, as justify the payee in believing he consents to pay it.

National Park Bank v. Ninth National Bank, 46 N.Y. 77, was an action to recover the money paid on a forged draft which plaintiff had accepted and paid. The court held that plaintiff could not recover. It is a well-settled rule that it is incumbent on the drawee of a bill to be satisfied that the signature of the drawer of the bill is genuine, that he is presumed to know the handwriting of such drawer, and that if he accepts or pays a bill to which the drawer's name has been forged, he is bound by the act and can neither repudiate the acceptance nor recover the money paid.

Bill Must Be Presented to Drawee for Acceptance or Payment. Until the bill is accepted, the drawer is the party liable to the payee. He agrees that the drawee will accept it or that he himself will pay it if proper presentment and demand are made on the drawee and notice of dishonor is given him. If the bill is payable a certain length of time after sight or on demand, it must be presented to the drawee for acceptance and the acceptance secured before the time will begin to run. The acceptor should always include the date in his acceptance on this kind of draft. If the bill is payable at sight or on demand, it must be presented to the drawee for payment within a reasonable time. If the drawee refuses to accept, the drawer must be duly notified, and he thereupon becomes liable for the bill. But if the bill is payable a certain number of days after date or on demand or on a day specified, it need not be presented for acceptance, presentment for payment being sufficient. Still, it should be presented for the purpose of securing the drawee's acceptance and thus making him liable on the instrument and at the same time giving him an opportunity to prepare to pay the bill.

In Chambers v. Hill, 26 Tex. 472, a bill of exchange dated December 18, 1851, was not presented for payment until two years and nine months thereafter. The draft contained no specific date for payment. It was held that the draft was payable on demand and must be presented for payment within a reasonable time to hold the drawer and endorser, and that an unexplained delay of two years and nine months is unreasonable and the drawer and endorser are released.

In Wallace v. Awry, 4 Mason (U.S.) 336, a bill drawn June 18 at Havana, Cuba, on Williams in London, payable sixty days after sight and presented in London on October 31, having been kept by the holder in Boston from July 6 to September 29, was found to have been presented within a reasonable time under the circumstances.

When the drawee refuses to accept, the bill is said to be dishonored.

Aymar v. Beers, 7 Cowen (N.Y.) 705, held that a bill drawn on December 12 in New York "three days after sight" and presented January 10 in Richmond, Va., having been in the payee's hands during that time, was presented within a reasonable time under the circumstances.

ACCEPTANCE FOR HONOR. This is also known as acceptance supra protest. When the bill has been presented and protested, a third party, who may or may not be the drawer, accepts it to protect the drawer or any of the other parties to the instrument. The obligation of such an acceptor is to pay the bill if upon further presentation of it to the drawee for payment at maturity, it is again dishonored and duly protested and due notice is given to the acceptor.

VIRTUAL ACCEPTANCE. There is another mode of acceptance, known as virtual acceptance, which is practically a promise to accept. If the virtual acceptance consists of a written unconditional promise to accept a bill already drawn or one to be drawn in the future, it is binding in favor of one who has taken it with knowledge of the acceptance and in reliance thereon. The promise must clearly describe the bill and must be absolute in its terms.

CHECKS

Definition. A check is a draft or order drawn on a bank or banker directing payment on demand by the bank to a third party or his order, or to bearer, of a certain sum of money. A common form of check is:

Chicago, Ill.   January 3, 1967   No. 645

THE FIRST NATIONAL BANK OF CHICAGO

Pay to the order of Bert Boyd $500.00
        Five Hundred no/100 . . . . Dollars

                                         [Signed] Edward Epperson

A check is drawn by a party having money on deposit in the
bank, and as shown in the definition, is a special form of bill of
exchange, with the bank as drawee. In the above check Edward
Epperson is the maker or drawer, First National Bank of
Chicago is the drawee, and Bert Boyd is the payee. A check is
intended for immediate payment upon presentation, and the
implied contract of the drawer is that the bank will pay the
check. If it does not, the drawer is liable absolutely, and no notice
of dishonor is necessary.

Harrison v. Nicollett National Bank, 41 Minn. 448, was an
action for damages for protesting the following instrument before it was due.

                    45 Washington Avenue South,
                        Harrison The Tailor,

                        Minneapolis, Minn., March 27, 1888

$199.92
        On April 14 pay to the order of E. Harrison . . . .
one hundred ninety-nine 92/100 . . . Dollars . . .

To Citizens' Bank,
Minneapolis, Minn.

                                         [Signature]
                                         J. T. Harrison

Payment was demanded and the instrument protested on April
14. Plaintiff contended that it was a bill of exchange and entitled
to days of grace, while defendant claimed it was a check and not
entitled to grace. It was held that one of the essentials of a check
is that it be payable on demand, and as this was payable in the
future, it was not a check but a bill of exchange and entitled to
grace.

Check Must Be Presented Without Delay. But the payee
of a check must present it for payment within a reasonable time,

or the drawer will be discharged from loss occasioned by his delay. What a reasonable time is will depend on circumstances, but it is generally considered that the check should be presented within a day after its receipt.

Granger v. Reigh, 93 Wis. 552, was an action against the drawer of a check. After banking hours on July 20 defendant drew and delivered to plaintiff in Milwaukee, where plaintiff resided, a check for $1,211 upon the South Side Savings Bank of that city. The check was not presented on July 21, although the bank was open and would have paid it at any time during the banking hours of that day. The bank failed, and did not open after that date. The court held that the party receiving a check must present it for payment within a reasonable time in order to preserve his right of recourse on the drawer in case of nonpayment; and when such party resides and receives the check at the place in which the bank is located, a reasonable time for such presentation reaches, at the latest, only to the close of banking hours on the succeeding day. Defendant in this case is therefore discharged from liability.

In Mohawk Bank v. Broderick, 13 Wend. (N.Y.) 133, a check drawn on the Mechanics & Farmers Bank of Albany was transferred by defendant to Meyers and by him deposited in the Mohawk Bank of Schenectady. This bank retained the check 23 days before presentment, although a daily mail passed between Schenectady and Albany, a distance of 16 miles. When the check was presented, payment was refused. It was held that the holders had not used due diligence in making presentment and were not entitled to maintain an action against the payee who had negotiated the check.

Certified Checks. A check purports to be drawn on a deposit made by the drawer in the bank on which it is drawn, and although in fact there may be no such deposit, it is still a check.

Checks pass freely between parties as money, yet unless the drawer is known to have on deposit in the bank funds sufficient to meet the check, or unless his solvency is known, a person is not safe in accepting the check. It is therefore common in such cases to have the bank certify the check; that is, the cashier or teller stamps the word "certified" and the date with his signature on the face of the check, and the bank then takes the amount from the drawer's deposit and puts it in a separate account. The check is thereafter the check of the bank rather than of the drawer, and it is good as long as the bank is solvent. When the holder has the check certified, the bank by so certifying becomes the only principal and only debtor, and the holder by accepting the certified check discharges the drawer. But if the drawer secures certification before delivering the check, he is not released from further liability.

Minot v. Russ, and Head v. Hornblower, 156 Mass. 458, are two cases arising from failure of the Maverick National Bank and decided together by the court. In the first case defendant, on October 29, 1891, drew a check on the Maverick National Bank payable to plaintiff, who informed him that the check must be certified by the bank before it would be received. On the same day defendant presented it to the bank for certification. The bank complied by writing on the face of it "Maverick National Bank. Pay only through clearing house. J. W. Work, Cashier. A. C. J. Paying Teller." After the check was certified, defendant, on October 31, 1891, delivered it to plaintiff for a valuable consideration. The bank stopped payment Monday morning, November 2, 1891.

In the second case, on Saturday, October 31, 1891, defendants drew their check on the Maverick National Bank payable to plaintiffs and delivered it to them. As the check was received too late to be deposited by plaintiffs for collection in time to go through the clearing house that day, plaintiffs secured certification of the check by the bank during banking hours in the following form: "Maverick National Bank. Certified. Pay only through clearing house. C. C. Domett. A., Cashier." At the time defendants in both cases had on deposit sufficient funds to pay the checks and the bank on certification charged to the defendants' accounts the amounts of the checks, which they credited to a ledger account called certified checks. It was held that in the first case defendant was not released by the certificate, as he had procured it himself, and in the second case he was released, as the payee obtained a certification in his own behalf instead of getting the check paid.

In Boyd v. Nasmith, 17 Ont. (Can.) 40, the payees of a check took it to the bank on which it was drawn on the afternoon of the day they received it from the drawer and had it marked "good." The amount was charged to the drawer's account. Payment was not demanded of the bank, and it suspended payment that evening. It was held that the drawer of the check was discharged from all liability thereon.

NEGOTIATION

Definition. Negotiation is the transfer of a negotiable instrument from one person to another in such a way that the transferee becomes the legal holder thereof. Almost all other claims and contracts can be assigned, although that was not the rule at common law. A negotiable instrument is particularly intended to be readily transferred. To aid the freedom with which it may pass from one to another, it has the distinctive feature of being collectible in the hands of a third party, even though it is subject to certain defenses in the hands of the original payee.

Endorsement. Negotiable paper is transferred by endorsement and delivery, that is, by the payee's signing his name on the back with directions as to the party to whom payment shall be made and handing it over to the transferee. When an instrument is made payable to a certain person or bearer, an endorsement is not necessary to give a good title to the transferee, delivery being sufficient, but if it is payable to a certain person or order, the endorsement is necessary to give good title.

BLANK AND FULL ENDORSEMENT. For the purpose of transfer, the endorsement must be made by the party to whom the instrument is payable. In the note on page 118, *supra*, Arthur Anderson may owe Bert Boyd, and if he hands him Carl Carlson's note in payment, he may write on the back "Pay to the order of Bert Boyd," and sign "Arthur Anderson." This would be called an endorsement in full, or special endorsement, and if Bert Boyd wishes to transfer, he must again endorse to his transferee.

RESTRICTIVE ENDORSEMENT. By this form of endorsement the endorsee is made the agent of the endorser. The form might be:

Pay John Jones, or order
for collection and credit,
to my account.
                    Jack Smith

OBLIGATION OF ENDORSER AND DRAWER. The obligation of an endorser to a transferee, like that of the drawer of a bill, is that the endorser will pay the instrument provided the maker does not, and also provided it is duly presented for payment and upon refusal is duly protested and notice of protest given the endorser. In domestic and notes the protest may be omitted and notice of non-payment may be given the endorser. It will be seen that the contract of the maker of a note or the acceptor of a bill is absolute; each is liable in any event. But the contract of the endorser and of the drawer of a bill is conditional on failure of the maker or acceptor to pay upon protest and notice to him.

ENDORSEMENT WITHOUT RECOURSE. If the endorser of the Carlson note wished to avoid any personal liability, he would endorse "without recourse" and sign "Arthur Anderson." By "without recourse" the endorser expressly stipulates that he will not be liable if the maker does not pay, but he is held to impliedly warrant that the signatures of the maker and all prior endorsers are genuine, that is, not forgeries. The intent and purpose of such endorsement is to pass title to the instrument.

In Lomax v. Picot, 2 Rudolph (Va.) 247, the court said: "An endorsement without recourse is not out of the due course of trade. The security continues negotiable, notwithstanding such an endorsement nor does such an endorsement indicate that the parties to it are conscious of any defect in the security, or that the endorser does not take it on the credit of the other party or parties to the note. On the contrary, he takes it solely on their credit, and the endorser only shows thereby that he is unwilling to make himself responsible for the payment."

ENDORSEMENT—HOW MADE. The endorsement must be on the instrument itself or on a paper attached to it. The endorsement must relate to the entire instrument; a part cannot be transferred by endorsement, or a part to one party and the remainder to another.

Hughes v. Kiddell, 2 Bay (S.C.) 324, was an action against the endorser of a note. The note was given by one David Bush to defendant, Kiddell, for 473 pounds sterling. Kiddell afterwards made the following endorsement: "I assign over to Hudson Hughes the sum of $1930.50 as part of this note of hand. "Benjamin Kiddell."

Afterward he made another endorsement and assigned the

residue to Hughes. The court held that each endorsement was bad, as it affected only part of the note, and two bad endorsements did not constitute one good one.

Any writing intended to transfer title to the instrument will be construed as an endorsement.

Adams v. Blethen, 66 Me. 19, was an action against the endorser of the following note:

Linneus, May 30, 1873

I promise to pay James H. Blethen, or order, $137.50 at ten per cent interest, on demand.

Ebenezer Tozier

On the back of this note was written:

I this day sold and delivered to Catherine M. Adams, the within note.

James H. Blethen

It was held that defendant assumed all the liability of an ordinary endorser. This endorsement but expressly stated what every endorsement impliedly states, a sale or transfer of the note. The liability of an endorser can be limited or qualified only by express terms.

Where the name of the payee or endorsee is wrongfully designed or misspelled, he may on the instrument as therein described add his proper signature.

Presentment and Demand. To fix the liability of the drawer or endorser, the first step is presentment to the drawee or maker and demand. Bills of exchange payable a certain time after sight are presented for acceptance; notes, checks, and bills payable on demand or sight are presented for payment. Presentment consists in showing the instrument to the payer or handing it to him, while demand is a request to either accept or pay as the case may be. If the paper is payable at a bank, the mere fact that at the time of maturity the paper is at the bank at which it is payable is sufficient presentment and demand, provided the bank has knowledge of the fact.

Presentment and demand must always be made at the place designated in the instrument. Promissory notes are often drawn in the following form, designating the place of payment:

$100.00   Chicago, Illinois, May 15, 1966

One month after date we promise to pay to the order of
Arthur Anderson . . . .
One hundred no/100 . . . . Dollars
at the First National Bank of Chicago . . . . . .
Value received.

No. 1 Due . . . . [Signature]
                                                     E. C. Johnson & Co.

This is called a bank note, but the place of payment designated
may be some other place than a bank.

In Brooks v. Higby, 11 Hun. (N.Y.) 235, a bill was drawn on
N. F. Mills, 114 S. Main St., St. Louis, and by him accepted. The
notary's certificate stated that the bill was presented for payment "at the place of business of N. F. Mills, St. Louis." It appeared that Mills had two places of business in St. Louis. The
court held that the certificate was insufficient, as it did not show
at which place presentment was made. The bill was addressed
to Mills at a particular place and by him accepted at that place,
making it the place of payment, and due presentment and
demand of payment at that place was necessary in order to
charge the endorser.

If there is no designated place of payment, it is said that
the paper is payable generally. This means that it is payable at
the place of business or residence of the maker of the note or
acceptor of the draft, and when he has a known place of business,
that should have preference over his residence.

Barnes v. Vaughan, 6 R.I. 259, was an action against the
endorser of a note which was not made payable at any particular
place but was left with plaintiff at the Mount Vernon Bank in
Foster for collection. The only demand made on the maker,
Northrup, was that the usual printed bank notice was mailed
to him by the cashier and directed to Providence, where he
lived in the early part of the month in which the notes became
due. The court held that there was no legal and proper demand
made on the maker, and therefore the endorser was discharged.
The rule is that in order to charge the endorser, payment must be
demanded upon the maker on the day the note becomes due,
unless the note is made payable at a designated place, as at a bank
named, when it is only necessary to make the demand at that

place; but if no place of payment is named in the note, it is necessary to present it to the maker personally or at his place of business or abode; otherwise the endorser cannot be charged.

In Taylor v. Snyder, 3 Denio (N.Y.) 145, the note was dated at Troy, N.Y. The maker then and afterwards resided in Florida to the knowledge of the holder and endorsers, but presentment was made at Troy, though not personally on the maker or at his residence. It was held to be insufficient; the court said, "When no change has taken place in the residence of the maker between the making of the note and the time of its payment, the intervention of a state does not dispose with the necessity of making due demand of payment."

If the maker or acceptor has neither a known residence nor a place of business, the holder need only be present with the paper and ready to receive payment at the place where the contract was made.

Malden Bank v. Baldwin, 13 Gray (Mass.) 154, held that a presentment for payment at any bank in Boston, of a note payable "at bank in Boston" or "at either bank in Boston" was a sufficient demand on the maker to charge the endorser.

TIME. Presentment for payment must be made on the day the instrument falls due, unless some "inevitable accident" or other legal obstacle prevents such presentment. The fact that both the holder and the endorser know that the note will not be paid when due and that the maker is dead and the estate insolvent does not relieve the holder from his obligation to make presentment and give notice of dishonor.

DAYS OF GRACE. Drafts, bills of exchange, and promissory notes formerly had three days of grace, that is, three days were added to the time stated in which the instrument should become due. The purpose of this was to give the payer in the early days of slow transportation an opportunity to arrange for payment. A note at thirty days drawn April 10 would not be payable until May 13; but days of grace have been abolished by statute in most states, so that an instrument matures on the date fixed. If given a number of days after date, the day on which the instrument is drawn is excluded; thus a note dated January 10 payable thirty days after date is due February 9. If the date of maturity is Sunday or a legal holiday, the instrument is payable on the next business day.

Salter v. Burt, 20 Wend. (N.Y.) 205, was an action on a check drawn on August 9 but postdated August 21, and as checks are payable without grace, the date on which it became due fell on Sunday. It was presented for payment, and notice of non-payment was given on Saturday, August 20. The court held that it was presented before it became due. If a negotiable instrument which does not have grace falls due on Sunday, it becomes due and payable on Monday, but when grace is allowed the rule is different, and Saturday is the day it becomes due.

In the states in which days of grace are yet allowed, if the last day of grace is a holiday or Sunday, the instrument is payable on the preceding day.

Johnson v. Haight, 13 Johns (N.Y.) 470, is a case in which the third day of grace fell on Sunday, November 29, and payment was not demanded of the maker until November 30. It was held that the law is well settled that demand must be made on the third day of grace unless that falls on Sunday, and then payment must be demanded on the second day of grace. Therefore in this case the endorser was discharged.

But when the time is reckoned by the month, as it is when the instrument is made payable one or two months after date, the note falls due on the corresponding date of the month in which it is due. Thus a note dated January 31, 1967, due two months after date, would mature March 31; it would be due March 31.

Roekner v. Knickerbocker Insurance Co., 63 N.Y. 160, held that a note without grace dated December 11, payable four months after date, is due and payable April 11.

Not only must the presentment be made on the right day, but it must be at a reasonable time on that day. If presented at a bank, it must be during banking hours. In other cases the time must be at a reasonable hour.

Dana v. Sawyer, 22 Me. 244, is a case in which presentment for payment was made at the maker's house between eleven and twelve o'clock at night, the maker being called up from bed for that purpose. It was held that presentment was made at an unreasonable hour and that the demand was not sufficient.

Farnsworth v. Allen, 4 Gray (Mass.) 453, was an action against the endorser of a note, and the defense was insufficient presentment and demand for payment. The holder did not know the maker's place of residence. He gave it to a notary, who

arrived at the maker's house at nine in the evening. The maker
and his family had retired for the night, but the maker answered
the bell, and upon the note's being presented, refused payment.
It was held to be sufficient presentment; the rule is that the note
must be presented at such a time, regard being had to the habits
and usages of the community where the maker resides, that
he reasonably be expected to be in condition to attend to ordinary
business.

Newark Indiana Rubber Mfg. Co. v. Bishop, 3 E. D. Smith
(N.Y.) 48, is a case in which a note payable at a bank was presented after banking hours and the clerk still there refused payment, although funds had been left with the regular teller to pay
it. It was held that the presentment and demand were not sufficient.

The presentment must be made by the holder or his duly
authorized agent upon the proper person, who is the maker or
acceptor, or if he is dead, his personal representative.

Stinson v. Lee, 68 Miss. 113, was an action against an endorser. The note was signed "A. G. Cunningham, Agent."
Nothing appeared on the face of the note showing for whom he
professed to act. Presentment and demand of payment was made
on S. A. Cunningham, wife of A. G. Cunningham. It was held
that the demand was insufficient. By the signature the note was
made by A. G. Cunningham, and the demand to bind the endorser must be made on him.

Toby v. Maurian, 7 La. 493, was an action against the endorser
of a note. The defense was want of due presentation. The maker
died on the last day of grace. The notary called with the note and
found no one but a mulatto woman, who informed him of the
maker's death. The note was then protested without any inquiry
or demand being made of any heirs or representatives of deceased. It was held that demand must be made on the heirs or
legal representatives, unless the impossibility of such demand is
shown.

Notice of Dishonor. After payment has been refused and the
instrument dishonored, notice of such dishonor must be given to
the drawer of a bill of exchange and to each endorser if a bill or
note, and any drawer or endorser to whom such notice is not
given is discharged.

This notice under the law merchant must be given within

a reasonable time, but by the negotiable-instrument law adopted in many states it is expressly stipulated when the notice is to be given. If the parties reside in the same place, it must be given the following day. If they reside in different places and notice is sent by mail, it must be deposited in the post office so as to go the day following the dishonor; if given otherwise than through the mail, it must be done in time to be received as soon as the mailed notice would have been.

In Simpson v. Turney, 5 Humph. (Tenn.) 419, a bank was the holder of a promissory note, payable at the bank, made by James H. Jenkins, to Anthony Dibrell, and endorsed: "A. Dibrell, S. Turney, and John W. Simpson." Turney's residence was within one mile of the bank. The note was due on February 1 and was protested on that day. On February 3 notice was sent Turney from the bank. Simpson, the next endorser, gave him no notice. The court held that the notice was not given in time. If it had been given by Simpson on the 3rd, it would have been good, as each endorser is given a day to notify his prior endorser, but this was not done. The notice given was not valid as to the bank, so could not be to anyone to whose benefit it would enure.

Smith v. Poillon, 87 N.Y. 590, is a case which the holder notified the third endorser by mail and enclosed notices for the second and first endorsers. The third endorser notified the second and enclosed notice for the first. The second endorser received the notice on the 6th, and mailed notice to the first endorser on the 7th, in time to go on the second mail closing at 1:30 P.M. The first mail closed at 9:30 A.M., and defendant contended that notice should have been sent by that mail. The court held that the notice was sufficient and that plaintiff had used due diligence in giving notice.

The notice may be given by the holder or his agent or by any party who may have to pay the debt and who is entitled to be reimbursed.

In Stafford v. Yates, 18 Johns (N.Y.), a note with two endorsers was dishonored and notice given by the holder to both endorsers. The second endorser sued the first, and it was held that the notice was sufficient—that it was not necessary for the second endorser to give notice to the first. It was sufficient that notice was given him and that notice of the holder enures to the benefit of any endorser.

Notice to Endorsers. When there are several endorsers, the last endorser can look to the previous one, or in fact to anyone who has endorsed before him, as well as to the maker or acceptor. Therefore it often happens that the holder on dishonor of the instrument gives notice to the last endorser, and he in turn gives notice to the prior endorser, to whom he will look to be reimbursed in case he is obliged to pay the instrument.

The notice of dishonor may be oral or written, and can either be delivered personally or be sent through the mail. Some cases hold that the postal service cannot be used when the parties reside in the same town, but by statute in New York State the post office can be used even then.

In Hobbs v. Straine, 149 Mass. 212, plaintiff took a written notice of dishonor to defendant's office, and finding no one there, left it. The court instructed the jury that if they determined that the notice was left in a conspicuous place, it was sufficient. It was held that this was correct. It is sufficient to charge the endorser if the notice is delivered personally, left at the endorser's place of residence or place of business, or deposited in the post office addressed to him at his residence or place of business with postage prepaid.

WAIVER. Notice may be waived, and frequently the endorser adds "protest waived," the effect of this being to waive presentment and notice of dishonor as well as formal protest.

PROTEST. Protest is a formal declaration in writing and under seal of an officer called a notary public, certifying to the demand and dishonor. When it is impossible to command the services of a notary, protest may be made by two respectable citizens who sign as witnesses of the act of presenting. Protest of foreign bills of exchange is necessary, but it is not required in the case of notes, checks, and inland bills, although it is often employed in giving notice of their dishonor. The notary makes the presentment and demand, and upon refusal issues a certificate like the following:

State of Illinois } ss
County of Cook }

I, Bert Boyd, one of the Notaries Public in and for the County aforesaid, Do hereby Certify, that on the 27th day of June in the year One Thousand Nineteen Hundred Six at the request of

First National Bank of Chicago, Illinois . . . .
I did present the original bill which is hereunto annexed, to
Edward Emerson . . . .
at Chicago, Illinois, and demanded payment thereof . . . .
. . . . , which was refused . . . .

Whereupon I, the said Notary, did Protest, and by these
presents do publicly and solemnly Protest, as well against the
maker and endorser of the said bill . . . . as against all
others whom it doth or may concern, for exchange, re-
exchange, and all costs, damages and interest, already incurred or
to be hereafter incurred by reason of the non-payment . . . of the
said bill.

And I do further Certify, that on the same day and year
above written, due notice of the foregoing demand, non-payment
. . . . . and Protest (by notice partly printed and
partly written, signed by me) was given to the drawer and the
several endorsers thereon by depositing notices at post office on
Van Buren Street, Chicago, Illinois, postage fully paid, directed
as follows:

> To Edwin Ehlers   at Chicago, Illinois
> To John Joseph   at Chicago, Illinois
>
> To Fred Fearn   at Chicago, Illinois
> To Thomas Telleen   at Chicago, Illinois

each of the above named places being the reputed place of residence of the person to whom the notice was directed, and the
post office nearest thereto.

This done and Protested in the City of Chicago, Illinois,
the day and year first above written
I have hereunto set my hand and

[SEAL]   In Testimony Whereof
affixed my official seal

> [Signature]
> Elmer Edwards
> Notary Public

After attaching the instrument to this certificate, the notary
mails a notice after the following form to all endorsers:

Chicago, Illinois, June 27, 1966

Please to take Notice, That a certain bill of exchange drawn on
and accepted by Edward Emerson for Two Hundred no/100 .

. . . . . . Dollars dated June 1st, 1966 payable Chicago, Illinois, endorsed by you, is Protested for non-payment, and the holders look to you for the payment thereof.

To Edwin Ehlers
    Chicago, Illinois

              Your obedient servant,
              [Signature]
              Elmer Edwards, Notary Public

Irregular Endorser. Often there appears on the back of a bill or note the name of a person who is not a party to it and to whom it was never endorsed. Such a person is known as an irregular, or anomalous, endorser. The object of such an endorsement is to give additional security to the payee. Under the law merchant different states held differently as to the liability of such party, some holding him to be a joint maker, others an endorser, and still others whatever he can prove that he intended to be. Under the negotiable-instrument statute he is held to be an ordinary endorser.

Coulter v. Richmond, 59 N.Y. 478, was an action on a promissory note made by Anson and endorsed by defendant, payable to the order of plaintiff. The note was endorsed at the request of the maker before delivery to the payee, to enable the maker to purchase bonds of the payee. The court said: "In some states such an endorser is regarded as a guarantor, in others an endorser, and in others a joint maker; but it is well settled in this state that a person making such an endorsement is presumed to have intended to become liable as second endorser, and on the face of the paper without explanation he is to be regarded as second endorser, and, of course, not liable upon the note to the payee, who is supposed to be the first endorser; but it is competent by proof to show that the endorsement was made to give the maker credit with the payee and others, to hold him as first endorser." In this case the latter was found to be the intention, and the endorser was held as first endorser.

Such endorsements are often used when the payee of a note wishes to get it discounted at a bank, that is, to get the money on it. The bank requires an endorser, and the payee gets a friend to endorse the note. The irregular endorser is liable to the bank the same as any other endorser.

Accommodation Paper. This is an instance of the drawer or

endorser of a bill and the endorser of a note becoming liable without notice of dishonor. Accommodation paper is the term used to denote negotiable instruments that have been executed without consideration and for the purpose of lending the name of the maker, endorser, or acceptor. For example, X may desire a loan, so he goes to Y and asks the favor. Y gives him a note which X endorses and discounts at the bank. If Y refuses payment at maturity because it is really X's debt, the bank can of course proceed against Y, as his name is on the paper, but it can also proceed against X without the formality of demand and notice. The reason is apparent: X being the real debtor, it cannot be supposed that he expects Y to pay; rather, he considers himself the principal debtor.

American National Bank v. Junk Bros., 94 Tenn. 624, was an action against the endorser of some notes. The defense was that notice of dishonor had not been given. It was shown that the notes were given for defendant's accommodation and then endorsed by him to plaintiff. Such being the case, it was the endorser's duty to provide funds to meet them at maturity, and he was therefore bound, without presentment, protest, and notice.

Holder or Payee. Whether he is the original payee or an endorsee, he is the party in whose hands the instrument rests and who has the right to the money which it represents. We have learned that negotiable instruments possess a distinguishing characteristic that no other contracts have: that when they have passed into certain parties' hands under particular conditions, they are valid and enforceable, although not valid between the original parties to them. The general rule is said to be that a negotiable instrument in the hands of an innocent purchaser for value and before maturity is not subject to any of the defenses that might be interposed to it between the original parties, but this is not true of certain absolute defenses which affect the very existence of the contract. They will be considered later.

To bring the instrument under the rule, the holder must be an innocent purchaser for value, or a "bona fide holder" or a "holder in due course." The term bona fide holder means a holder who has acquired the instrument in good faith, without knowledge or notice of any defenses or defects that could be set up against any prior holder. To constitute notice, the holder must have had actual knowledge of the defect, or his carelessness must have been so great as to amount to "bad faith."

In Hotchkiss v. National Bank, 21 Wallace (U.S.) 354, the court said: "A party who takes negotiable paper before it is due for a valuable consideration, without knowledge of any defect of title in good faith, can hold it against all the world. A suspicion that there is a defect of title in the holder, or a knowledge of circumstances that might excite such suspicion in the mind of a cautious person, or even gross negligence at the time, will not defeat the title of the purchaser. That result can only be produced by bad faith, which implies guilty knowledge or willful ignorance."

The instrument must be complete and regular on its face.

Davis Sewing Machine Co. v. Best 105 N.Y. 59, was an action to recover the value of certain notes diverted by plaintiff's president. When defendant purchased the notes, they were complete and regular and signed by plaintiff's treasurer, but they were not signed by the president, although a blank ruled space with the title of his office printed thereunder was left at the foot of the instrument. It was conceded that plaintiff was entitled to the notes unless defendant was a bona fide holder thereof. The court held that anyone buying commercial paper which remains incomplete and imperfect in some essential particular does not acquire the character of a bona fide holder.

He must be a holder "for value." This means that he must have given a valuable consideration for it, and it is not enough that it be a gift.

In DeWitt v. Perkins, 22 Wis. 473, plaintiff, being acquainted with defendant and knowing that he was responsible, purchased shortly before maturity a promissory note against defendant for $300, paying therefor $5. As between the original parties the note was invalid for want of consideration. It was held that plaintiff was not a bona fide holder for value. The consideration paid by him was nominal. It was on the face of it either merely a gift or a subterfuge to get the note into other hands to cut off the defense of want of consideration.

Under Contracts, what is necessary to constitute valuable consideration was discussed.

The purchaser of a negotiable instrument must take it before maturity, and if it is a bill of exchange that has been dishonored, without notice of previous dishonor. The mere fact that a note or bill is past due is considered sufficient notice of defect to put the purchaser on his guard, and a party buying past due paper cannot be said to be a bona fide holder. If, therefore, in the case of a bill of exchange that has been presented for acceptance and dishonored, this fact is brought to the notice of the purchaser, he is not a bona fide holder.

Continental National Bank v. Townsend, 87 N.Y. 8, was an action of endorser against maker. The defense was a set-off against the original payee. On the last day of grace the note was endorsed to plaintiff. The question was whether or not the transfer was made before maturity. The court held that it was and that the plaintiff was a bona fide holder. The maker has the whole of the last day to pay, so it was not past due until the close of that day.

O'Callaghan v. Sawyer, 5 Johns (N.Y.) 118, was an action by endorser against maker. Defendant offered to prove a set-off. At the time of transfer of the note to plaintiff it was overdue. The court held that the set-off should be allowed. The note had been long overdue and dishonored when it was endorsed, and the point is well settled that the endorser took the note subject to all the equities and to every defense which existed against it in the hands of the original payee.

DEFENSES

General Statement. It is a general proposition that a bona fide purchaser before maturity and for value takes title free from all defects and defenses, or, as is often stated, "free from all equities" except such as affect the very existence of the instrument and as are said to constitute absolute defenses.

The absolute defenses are cases in which either no valid contract ever existed or contract is declared illegal and void by statute.

No Delivery. The instrument may never have been delivered. It is considered by the law merchant to be a sufficient delivery to hold the maker or acceptor if it is handed over by the party himself or his agent either with or without authority, or if it gets into circulation through negligence of the maker. The question is, Did the maker deliver the instrument, or was his act or representation for its coming into the hands of bona fide holders? If this is true, he must suffer, although it was not his intention to deliver the instrument. On the other hand, if he has been deprived of possession of the paper by fraud or theft, he cannot be compelled to pay the amount named to anyone, as in this case the instrument was never delivered and no contract existed.

In Chapman v. Rose, 56 N.Y. 137, defendant entered into a contract with one Miller to act as agent for the sale of a patent hay fork. Another paper was then presented to defendant which Miller said was a duplicate of the order. Defendant signed it without reading or examining it. It was the note in suit, and plaintiff purchased it in good faith for value and before maturity. It was held that when one has the opportunity and the power to ascertain the exact character of the obligation, and he assumes and takes the word of another instead, he cannot claim that he intended to sign a different instrument, to defeat a bona fide holder. To avoid liability he must show that he was guilty of no negligence or carelessness in signing.

If in the making of an instrument there was such a fraud as would vitiate a contract, then no contract exists and the maker or acceptor cannot be held.

Walker v. Ebert, 29 Wis. 194, was an action against the maker of a promissory note by the holder, who claimed to have purchased for value before maturity. The defense was that defendant was a German and unable to read and write English and that the payee fraudulently induced him to sign an instrument represented to him to be a contract of agency, which was in fact a promissory note. It was held that it was a good defense. The instrument never, in the contemplation of the law, existed as a negotiable instrument. The party not having been guilty of any negligence in signing, and his signature having been obtained by fraud, he was no more bound than if his signature were a forgery.

Alteration or Forgery. A failure of contract arises when there has been a material alteration or forgery, for in these instances the minds of the parties have not met in the contract. When the instrument has been materially altered and is in the hands of a holder in due course not a party to the alteration, he may enforce payment thereof according to its original tenor.

Horn & Long v. Newton City Bank, 32 Kan. 518, was an action against Horn & Long, makers of a promissory note. The note was given for a threshing machine, and was originally drawn payable to "H. C. Pitts Sons Manufacturing Company," and after delivery to the company it was altered by substituting the name "O. B. Hildreth" as payee. The alteration was made without the knowledge or consent of Long, and he never ratified the change. The court held that this was a material alteration and released Long, although the bank was a bona fide holder for value.

Draper v. Wood, 112 Mass. 315, was an action against Wood and Higgins as makers of the following promissory note:

$1000.   North Hadley, Mar. 31, 1868

For value received, we promise to pay L. Draper, or order . . . . One Thousand dollars on demand, with interest at 12 per cent.

[Signed] George A. Wood
[Signed] H. S. Higgins

Higgins defended on the ground that the note he signed had been changed by substituting "we" for "I" and adding the words, "at 12 per cent." It was shown that Wood made the changes in good faith, but without consulting Higgins. It was held that the note was void as against Higgins.

Any alteration of a negotiable instrument which changes its legal effect is a material alteration.

Sullivan v. Rudisill, 63 Iowa 158, was an action on a note. After the note was given by defendant, with Fuller as surety, plaintiff innocently procured R to sign as surety. The court held the note void, but allowed recovery on the original consideration. When a promissory note has been innocently altered without any fraudulent purpose, the payee may recover in an action on the original consideration. It was also held that the signing by a party as a joint maker after execution by the original maker and without his knowledge and consent is a material alteration.

There must be an intent to make the alteration, and it must be made, of course, without consent of the maker or acceptor of the instrument. The alteration must also be made by a party to the instrument or one in lawful possession of it. The holder cannot be prejudiced or injured by the act of a stranger without his consent.

In Langenburger v. Kroeger, 48 Cal. 147, a person not a party to the instrument, without authority wrote across the face of a draft the words, "payable in United States gold coin." It was held that the alteration was not such as to vitiate the draft, although it is punished in some of the states if the alteration had been made by the payee or his instruction, the bill would have been invalidated, as the change was evidently material.

It will be seen from the foregoing that when a signature to a negotiable instrument is forged, the party whose name is used cannot be held.

Want of Capacity to Contract. The contract represented by the instrument may not be binding for the reason that the party or parties did not have the capacity to contract; as, the note or bill of an infant or lunatic. Still if a valid negotiable instrument comes into the hands of an infant, he may, if of full mental capacity, transfer it to another.

The mere fact that a contract is illegal is not an absolute defense to a negotiable instrument in the hands of a bona fide holder; but if the contract is expressly made illegal and void by statute, an absolute defense is created.

Equities. Other defenses than absolute defenses are called equities and are valid defenses between the original parties to the instruments, but they cannot be set up against bona fide holders. Lack of consideration is a good defense as between the original parties, but not as against a bona fide holder for value. It is an equity and not an absolute defense.

The fact that there is an absolute defense to an instrument does not discharge all the parties to it or through whose hands it has passed. Such defense exonerates the maker or acceptor of a negotiable instrument, but it does not relieve the liability of the endorser, because every person who negotiates such an instrument warrants that it is genuine, that he has good title to it, and that all prior parties have capacity to contract.

In Williams v. Tishomingo Savings Inst., 57 Miss. 633, defendants endorsed a bill of exchange to which they claimed title through a forged endorsement. The court held that the endorser warranted the genuineness of the prior endorsements on the bill and also his title to the paper. Should it be ascertained even after payment of the bill that any of the endorsements were forged, the drawee can recover the amount of the bill from the party to whom he paid it, and each preceding endorser may recover from the party who endorsed the bill to him.

DISCHARGE

Payment. Negotiable instruments, like other contracts, are discharged by payment. Payment by the maker or acceptor to the holder, and surrender of the instrument to him, ends the transaction and releases all parties to the paper.

Slade v. Mutrie, 156 Mass. 19, was an action to recover the balance of a promissory note. Defendant paid plaintiff $125 and received the note and a receipt in full settlement of all accounts to date. The jury found that plaintiff intended to receive the amount in full payment. The court said that delivery of a promissory note by the holder to the maker, with the intention of transferring to him title of the note, was an extinguishment of the note and a discharge of the obligation to pay it.

Payment Before Maturity. But if payment is made before maturity and the paper again gets into circulation, it will be valid in the hands of a bona fide holder who acquires it before maturity.

Stoddard v. Burton, 41 Iowa 582, was an action against the maker of a lost or stolen promissory note made January 5, 1866, payable to A or bearer on or before January 6, 1868. The defense was that it had been paid to Thompson, a holder on October 11, 1866. The court held that the note by its terms was payable at any time within two years after its date at the option of the maker. So it could not be said to be out of the ordinary course of business for him to pay it at any time, as that express provision was incorporated in the instrument, and the note not having been paid before maturity, plaintiff was not a bona fide holder.

Payment by Endorser. Payment by one of the endorsers after the instrument has been dishonored does not discharge it, as the prior endorsers and the maker or acceptor are still liable. Payment to extinguish the instrument must be made by or for the party primarily liable.

The instrument may also be discharged by the intentional cancellation thereof by the holder or by any other act that would discharge a simple contract.

In Larkin v. Hardenbrook, 90 N.Y. 333, Loper executed a deed of certain premises to defendant, and in consideration thereof the note in suit was executed and delivered to the grantor, who thereafter intentionally canceled and destroyed it and surrendered it to defendant. The court said: "The rule is well settled that when the payee delivers up the obligation which he holds against another with the intent and for the purpose of discharging the debt, in the absence of fraud, such surrender operates as a release and discharge of the obligation."

Discharge of Endorser. An endorser or drawer is discharged by an act that discharges the instrument or that discharges a prior party. Thus the third endorser of a promissory note would be discharged by any act that would discharge either the maker (which would cancel the instrument) or the first and second endorsers. Any agreement on the part of the holder of a negotiable instrument to extend the time of payment, unless with assent of the endorsers, discharges the endorsers' liability.

INTEREST AND USURY

Definition. Since the question of interest often arises in connection with negotiable instruments, it should be considered here. Interest is compensation paid for the use of money. The amount on which the interest is reckoned is called the principal.

In most states the rate of interest is set by statute and is known as legal interest, and when no rate is designated by the parties, this rate will prevail. In some states the legal rate is fixed at 6 per cent, in others at 7 per cent (see current tables). The statutes of the different states also determine whether a higher rate may be agreed on between the parties and, in most cases, say how high a rate may be charged by agreement.

The taking of a higher rate than that allowed by statute is called usury and in some states it is punished by forfeiture of all the interest; in others, as it was in New York State, by forfeiture of both principal and interest. Where such statutes exist, a person agreeing to accept usurious interest cannot collect either the money due or the interest.

Originally the word usury was identical in meaning with interest, and meant any compensation taken for the loan or use of money, but now, as will be seen, it is entirely different.

Claims on Which Interest Can Be Collected. Interest can be collected on all claims or amounts where it is mutually agreed by the parties that it is to be paid, as in a promissory note which contains the words "with interest" or "with use" or words to the same effect. It can also, without stipulation in the agreement, be collected on debts from the time they become due until they are paid; in other words, all overdue debts draw interest. An illustration is a promissory note containing no provision for interest, as such a note draws interest from the date it becomes due until it is paid but does not draw interest before maturity.

In the matter of Trustees, etc., 137 N.Y. 95, the court held that interest may not be allowed in any case unless by virtue of some contract, express or implied, or of some statute or on account of default of the party, when it is allowed as damages for the default.

But when the amount of the debt is not determined and is uncertain, or when the debt consists of a running account with payments at different periods, it is held that interest does not attach.

In Wood v. Hickok, 2 Wend (N.Y.) 501, plaintiffs were wholesale grocers and defendants country merchants. Defendants purchased different bill of goods of plaintiffs between February, 1824, and November, 1825, amounting in all to $1,190.62, and made various payments, amounting in June, 1827, to $1,191.25. In the suit plaintiffs charged interest amounting to $64.87. No mention had been made of interest until 1827, when an account was transmitted in which there was a barrel of brandy in dispute. Plaintiffs claimed that it was the custom among grocers to charge interest after 90 days. It was held that the account was not liquidated, and an unliquidated running account does not carry interest unless there is an agreement between the parties that interest shall be allowed.

Compound Interest. Interest on interest cannot be collected in the absence of a special agreement, and some jurisdictions do not allow it then.

V. SURETYSHIP AND GUARANTYSHIP

DEFINITION

Suretyship is an undertaking to answer for the debt, default, or miscarriage of another, by which the surety becomes bound as the principal or original debtor is bound. Suretyship adds security to the original contract or enables the original debtor to obtain credit.

This is a contract that requires the elements of any contract. So there must be a meeting of the minds of the contracting parties as to consideration, etc. If X buys goods from Y, agreeing to pay $500 for them, X's obligation to pay $500 is a primary one from a simple contract. If X buys goods from Y agreeing to pay $500 for them, and Z, as a part of the same transaction, makes a promise in writing to pay the $500 if X does not pay, Z's obligation is one of suretyship. His contract is to pay the debt of another: he has agreed to pay X's debt if X fails to pay it.

In insurance the underwriter takes all the risk, while in suretyship the company that insures the honesty and faithfulness of an employee takes little or no risk. No surety bond is issued unless the principal is found upon investigation to be of good character and as a rule good to the amount of the liability taken by the company, the company often requiring collateral security enough to cover all loss.

ILLUSTRATION

A contract of surety makes one unconditionally liable to answer for the debt or obligation of another, such as this:

Evanston, Illinois
April 22, 1938

Sixty days after date I promise to pay to the order of Y Six
Hundred Dollars ($600.)

[Signed] - - X
[Signed] - - Z, Surety

In the above note X is the principal and Z is surety. Z's
obligation is the same as that of X, his principal. Z does not
obligate himself to pay on condition that X does not or cannot
pay the note when due but obligates himself to pay the note when
due. His obligation is the same as X's liability. His obligation is
not conditioned on X's failure to pay. When the note is due, Y, the
creditor, may bring suit against Z, without making any demand of,
the surety, payment of X or without receiving X's refusal to pay.
If the note is signed by Z as above, without the word "surety"
after his name, it may be shown by oral testimony that Z signed
as surety, if this is the fact.

PRIMARY OBLIGATION

Suretyship is an accessory promise by which a person binds
himself for another already bound and agrees with the creditor
to satisfy the obligation if the debtor does not (43 La. Ann. 738).
It differs from guarantyship in this, that suretyship is a primary
obligation to see that the debt is paid, while guaranty is a
collateral undertaking, essentially in the alternative, to pay the
debt if the debtor does not pay it (24 Pick. 252). Accordingly a
surety may be sued as a promise to pay the debt specifically on
his contract (8 Pick. 423).

CLASSES OF SECONDARY OBLIGATION

These secondary undertakings may be divided into three
classes: (1) Cases in which the promise is collateral to the principal contract but is made at the same time and becomes an essential ground of the credit given to the principal or direct debtor.

Here there is not, and need not be, any other consideration than that moving between creditor and original debtor. (2) Cases in which the collateral undertaking is subsequent to creation of the debt and was not the inducement to it, though the subsisting liability is the ground of the promise without any distinct and unconnected inducement. Here there must be some further consideration shown, having an immediate respect to such liability; for the consideration for the original debt will not attach to this subsequent promise. (3) When the promise to pay the debt of another arises out of some new and original consideration of benefit or harm moving between the newly contracting parties. The two first classes of cases are within the statute of frauds; the last is not (8 Johns 29). This classification has been reviewed and affirmed in many cases (21 N.Y. 415; 15 Pick. 159).

DOES STATUTE OF FRAUDS APPLY?

The rule that the statute does not apply to class three has, however, been doubted; and it appears to be admitted that the principle is there inaccurately stated. The true test is the nature of the promise, not of the consideration (50 Pa. 39; 94 E.C.L.R. 885).

SIMPLE DIVISION INTO TWO CLASSES

A simpler division is into two classes: (1) Where the principal obligation exists before the collateral undertaking is made. (2) Where there is no principal obligation prior in time to the collateral undertaking. In the second class the principal obligation may be contemporaneous with or after the collateral undertaking. The first class includes the above second and third classes; the second includes the first class, to which must be added cases where the guaranty referring to a present or future principal obligation does not share the consideration thereof but proceeds on a distinct consideration. Moreover, there are other

original undertakings out of the statute of frauds and valid
though by parol, besides the third class. These are where the
credit is given exclusively to the promisor, though the goods or
consideration pass to another. Under this division, undertakings of
the first class are original (1) When the principal obligation is
thereby abrogated. (2) When without such abrogation the promisor for his own advantage apparent on the bargain undertakes
for some new consideration moving to him from the promisee.
(3) Where the promise is in consideration of some loss or
disadvantage to the promisee. (4) Where the promise is made to
the principal debtor on a consideration moving from debtor to
promisor (Theob. Sur. 37, 49). The cases under these heads will
be considered separately.

IS PROMISE ORIGINAL OR COLLATERAL?

First, where the principal obligation is pre-existent, there must
be a new consideration to support the promise; and where this
consideration is discharge of the principal debtor, the promise is
original and not collateral, as the first requisite of a collateral
promise is the existence of a principal obligation. This has been
held in many cases. The discharge may be by agreement, by
novation, or substitution, by discharge under final process, or by
forbearance under certain circumstances (4 B & P 24; 21 N.Y.
412; 8 Gray 233).

But the converse of this proposition, that where the principal
obligation remains, the promise is collateral, cannot be sustained,
though there have been repeated dicta to that effect (Browne
Stat. Fr. 193; 2 Johns, 291; denied in 21 N.Y. 415; 7 Ala. N.S. 54;
33 Vt. 132).

The main question arising in cases under this head is whether
the debtor is discharged; and this is largely a question for
the jury. But if in fact the principal debt is discharged by
agreement and the new promise is made on this consideration,
then the promise is original, and not collateral (1 Allen 405).

But where there is an existing debt for which a third party
is liable to the promisee, and the promisor undertakes to be responsible for it, still the contract need not be in writing if its

terms are such that it effects an extinguishment of the original liability (160 Mass. 225).

Discharge of the debtor from custody, or surrender of property taken on an execution, is a good discharge of the debt (11 M & W 857; 9 Vt. 137; 4 Dev. 261; 21 N.Y. 415; 35 Barb. 97).

Where the transaction amounts to a sale of the principal debt in consideration of the new promise, the debtor is discharged and the promise is original (3 B & C 855). So where a purchaser of goods transfers them to another, who promises the vendor to pay for them, this is a substitution and an original promise (5 Taunt. 450; 9 Cow. 266; 11 Ired. 298; 21 Me. 545).

A mere forbearance to press the principal debt is not such a discharge of the debtor as will make the promise original (1 Sm. L.C. 387; 21 N.Y. 412; 13 B Monr. 356); but where the forbearance is so protracted as to discharge the debtor it may be questioned whether the promise does not become original (33 Vt. 132).

Second, the promise will be original if made in consideration of some new benefit moving from the promisee to the promisor (3 Dutch. 371; 4 Cow. 432; Bull N.P. 281).

Third, the promise is original where the consideration is some loss to the promisee or principal creditor; but it is held in many such cases that the loss must also work some benefit to the promisor (6 Ad. & E 564; 3 Strobbs. Eq. 177; 20 N.Y. 268). As to merely refraining from giving an execution to the sheriff, see 14 Me. 140.

There have been decisions which hold that mere relinquishment of a lien by plaintiff takes the case out of the statute (7 Johns 464; 1 McCord 575). It would seem that mere surrender of a lien is not sufficient consideration (3 Metc. 396); it must appear that the surrender is in some way beneficial to the promisor, as when he has an interest in the property released (77 N.Y. 91; 43 Ind. 180; 5 Cush. 488).

The rule is well settled that when the leading object of a promisor is to induce a promisee to forego some lien, interest, or advantage and thereby to confer on the promisor a privilege or benefit which he would not otherwise possess or enjoy, an agreement made under such circumstances and on such a consideration is a new, original, and binding contract, although the effect of it may be to assume the debt and discharge the liability

of another (6 Maule & S. 204; 1 Gray 391). The advantage relinquished by the promisee must directly enure to the benefit of
the promisor, so as in effect to make it purchase by the promisor
(5 Cush. 488; 12 Johns 291). It is stated in many cases (under
classes third and fourth above) that the promise is original where
the consideration moves to the promisor. The true test, however,
must be found not in the consideration but in the nature of the
promise. Wherever the new promisor undertakes for his own
default; where his promise is virtually to pay his own debt in a
peculiar way, or if, by paying the debt, he is really discharging a
liability of his own, his promise is original. The only case is which
consideration can affect the terms of the promise is where the consideration of the promise is extinguishment of the original liability
(17 Mass. 229; 18 Tex. 446; 22 How. 28).

Fourth, the promise is original if made on a consideration
moving from debtor to promisor (10 Johns 412; 9 Cal. 92; 30 Ala.
N. S. 599; 5 Me. 31; 1 Gray 391; 22 How. U.S. 28; 32 Neb. 269).

For the rule in a class of cases quite analogous, see 9 Ill. 40; 3
Conn. 272. Where the guaranty relates to a contemporaneous or
future obligation, the promise is original, and not suretyship:
(a) if credit is given exclusively to the promisor, (b) if the
promise is merely to indemnify.

In the first of these cases the question to whom credit
was given must be ultimately for the jury. If there is any
primary liability, and the creditor resorts to the principal debtor
first, the promise is collateral. Thus if the promisor says, "Deliver
goods to A, and I will pay you," there is no primary obligation on
the part of A, and the promise is original (3 Metc. 396). But if he
says, "I will see you paid" or "I promise you that he will pay," the
promise is collateral (1 H Bla. 120; 7 Fed. Rep. 477; 3 Col. 176; 13
Gray 613; 148 Pa. 220 [where it was left to the jury to decide
whether it was an original undertaking]).

A promise to indemnify merely against contingent loss from
another's default is original (15 Johns 425). A doubt is expressed
by Browne Stat. of Frauds @ 158 whether the fact that mere
indemnity is intended makes the promise original, because in
many cases—those where the indemnity is against the default of
a third person—there is an implied liability of that person, and
the promise is collateral thereto. Now there are three classes

of cases. First: It is clear that where the indemnity is against the promisor's default or debt, he is already liable without his promise; and to use this as a defense and make the promise collateral thereto would be using the law as a cover to a fraud (1 Conn. 519; 46 Me. 41; 6 Bingh. 506; 10 Johns 42; 17 Pick. 538).

Second: So where the only debt against which indemnity is promised is the promisee's, this being not the debt of another but of the promisee, the case is clearly not within the statute, but the promise is original. And even if the execution of such a promise would discharge incidentally some other liability, this fact does not make the promise collateral (13 M & W 561; 1 Gray 391; 25 Wend. 243; 10 Gill & J 404; 31 Vt. 142).

Third: But where there is a liability implied in another person, and the promise refers to his liability or default and if executed will discharge such liability or default, the promise would seem on reason to be collateral and binding like a suretyship for future advances—that is, when accepted (9 Ired. 10; 1 Ala. 1; 1 Gill & J 424; 10 Ad. & E 453; 4 Barb. 131). But in many cases the rule is broadly stated that a promise merely to indemnify is original (8 B & C 728 [overruled, 10 Ad. & E 453]; 1 Gray 391; 10 Johns 242 [overruled, 4 Barb. 131]; 1 Ga. 294; 10 N.H. 175; 1 Conn. 519; 5 Me. 504). In other cases the distinction is made to rest on the fact that the engagement is made to the debtor (9 Gray 76; 11 Ad. & E. 438); and in other cases on the futurity of the risk or liability (12 Mass. 297).

The last ground is untenable; future guarantees are binding when accepted or acted upon, and those against torts are expressly to the contrary. The first ground is too broad, as shown above; and the second seems to ignore the clear primary liability of the principal debtor.

It is said that "a mere promise of indemnity which is not collateral to any liability on the part of another, either express or implied, is not within the statute and such a case illustrates the rule when there is no principal the promise need not be in writing. On the other hand, when the promise to indemnify is in fact a promise to pay the debt of another, then clearly such promise is within the statute and the fact that it is in form a promise to indemnify will make no difference." (Brandt Sur. & Guar. @ 59; see 4 B & S. 414.)

ORIGINAL PROMISE

When the principal obligation is void, voidable, not enforceable, or unascertained, the promise is original, there being in this case no principal obligation to sustain the promise as collateral; (Browne Stat. Fr. @ 156). It may be questionable, however, whether the promise will in such case be original unless the promisor knows the principal liability to be void or voidable (Burge, Surety 6); but this question may be settled by the principle that where credit is given to the principal notwithstanding that his obligation is void or voidable, the promise of the surety is collateral (4 Bingh. 470; 7 N. H. 368); but if no such credit is given or implied, the promise is collateral (15 N.Y. 576; 33 Ala. N. S. 106; 6 Gray 90). Such would be the guaranty of an infant's promise (7 N. H. 368); and this is accordingly so held (20 Pick. 467 [but see 11 Allen 365, contra, as to the promise of a father to pay the debt of a minor son]; 4 Me. 521); though a distinction has been made in the case of a married woman (4 Bingh. 470; 84 Pa. 135; 43 Ind. 103); but the promise is collateral where the married woman has separated property which she can charge with payment of her debts, and the credit is given exclusively to her (6 Ga. 14).

Where the liability is unascertained at the time of the promise, the promise is original, as the liabilities must concur at the time of the undertaking to make a guaranty (Browne Stat. Fr. @ 196; 1 Salk, 27; contra, Ambl. 330). Under this head would come a promise to pay damages for a tort, there being no principal liability until judgment (1 Wils. 305); or where the liability rests on a future award (2 Allen 417); and liability on indefinite executory contracts in general. It is, however, said that the liability may be prospective at the time the promise is made.

The promise is clearly original where the promisor undertakes for his own debt. The rule is that unless the promisor himself or his property is ultimately to be made liable in default of the principal debtor, the statute does not apply (Browne Stat. Fr. @ 177). Thus an engagement by one who owes the principal debtor to retain the principal debt, so that it may be attached by trustee or garnishee process, is not a collateral promise (9 Pick. 306; 63 Barb. 321; 50 Ia. 310).

So an agreement by a purchaser to pay part of the purchase money to a creditor of the vendor is an agreement to pay his own debt (55 Miss. 365; 2 Lea 543; 49 Ia. 574; 58 Ill. 232); or to pay a debt due a promise by a third person out of the moneys owing by a promisor to such third person (32 Ohio 415; 9 Cow. 266; 58 Ill. 232); or for the application of a fund due a promisor by a third party (86 Pa. 147; 18 How. 31). Such an agreement is a trust, or an original promise.

GUARANTY AND SURETY CONTRACTS MUST BE IN WRITING

Under Statute of Frauds. At common law a contract of guarantyship or suretyship could be made by parol; but by the statute of frauds (29 Cur. II c 3) "No action shall be brought whereby to charge the defendant upon any special promise to answer for the debt, default, or miscarriage of another person. . . . unless the agreement upon which such action shall be brought or some memorandum or note thereof, shall be in writing and signed by the party to be charged therewith, or by some person thereunto lawfully authorized," so that under the statute all contracts of guarantyship and suretyship must be in writing and signed. The words "debt" and "default" in the statute refer to contracts (2 East. 325); and debt includes only pre-existing liability (12 Mass. 297); miscarriage refers to torts (2B & Ald. 613). Torts are accordingly within the statute, and may be guaranteed against (2 B & Ald. 613; 2 Day 457); though this has been doubted in regard to future torts (1 Wils. 305). Perhaps a guaranty against future torts might be open to objection on the ground of public policy. But the unchallenged contracts of modern indemnity companies seem to show that such an objection would not prevail. A guaranty of indemnity to a surety is within the statute of frauds (45 Ill. App. 155).

The doctrine that a future contingent liability on the part of the principal is not within the statute (1 Salk. 27; 12 Mass. 297) is not tenable; and it is clear, both by analogy and on authority, that such a liability may support a guaranty, although such cases must be confined within very narrow limits, and the mere fact of the contingency is a very strong presumption that the promise is original (Browne Stat. Fr. @ 196; 6 Vt. 668; 88 Ill. 561). Where the promise is made to the debtor, it is not within the statute (Reed. Stat. Fr. 76; 7 Halst. 188; 2 Den. 162). "We are of opinion that the statute applies to promises made to the person to whom another is answerable" (11 Ad. & E. 446; 1 Gray 391). The word "another" in the statute must be understood as referring to a third person, and not to a debt due from either of the contracting parties (6 Cush. 562). False and deceitful representations of the credit or solvency of third persons are not within the statute (Browne Stat. Fr. @ 181; 4 Camp. 1). The English rule required the consideration to be expressed (5 East 10); it could not be proved by parol (4 B & Ald. 595). But by 19 and 20 Vict. no such promise shall be deemed invalid by reason only that the consideration does not appear in writing or by necessary inference from a written instrument (7 C.B. N.S. 361). The rule varies in different states, and in some states is settled by statute (see Brandt Sur. & Guar @ 82). In some states there are statutes similar to the English statutes. In other states the consideration is required by statutes to be expressed. Of states where statutes are silent, some have accepted and some rejected the English construction of statutes of frauds in Wain v. Walters, 5 East 10, *supra*.....

The courts lay hold of any language which implies a consideration (21 N.Y. 31). So where the guaranty and the matter guaranteed are one simultaneous transaction, both will be construed in connection and the consideration expressed in the latter applied to the sort of the former, if these are words of reference in the guaranty (36 N. H. 73).

FORMATION OF OBLIGATION

In construing the language of the contract to decide whether it constitutes an original promise or a guaranty, it is difficult to lay down a general rule; the circumstances of particular cases vary widely (1 Q. B. 288). "One test is if the promisor is totally unconnected with the transaction except by means of his promise to pay the loss, the contract is a guarantee; if he is to derive some benefit from it, his contract is an indemnity." The word guaranty or surety may or may not indicate the contract correctly, and the circumstances of the case may make an endorser liable as a guarantor or surety without any words to indicate the obligation (24 Wend. 456). In general if a promissory note is signed or endorsed when made by a stranger to the note he becomes a joint promisor and liable on the note (44 Me. 433; 9 Cush. 104; 14 Tex. 275; 20 Mo. 571); and this will be true if the note is endorsed after delivery to the payee in pursuance of an agreement made before the delivery (7 Gray 284); but parol evidence may be introduced to show he is a surety or guarantor (23 Ga. 368; 89 Ill. 550). If the third party endorses after delivery to the payee without any previous agreement, he is merely a second endorser (11 Pa. 466; 82 N.C. 313); and he is liable as a maker to an innocent holder (20 Mo. 591). But it was held otherwise where the signature was on the face of the note (19 N.H. 572); and the same is held where he signs at inception of the note, in pursuance of a custom, leaving a blank for the payee's signature above his name (12 La. Ann. 517). In Connecticut such an endorser is held to guaranty that the note will be collectible when due (46 Conn. 410). The time of signing may be shown by parol evidence (9 Ohio 139).

A payee or subsequent party who executes a guarantee on a bill or note is not liable as an endorser (3 Stew. 319; 19 Me. 359; 2 Const. 225; contra, 31 Ga. 210; 20 Vt. 499).

It has been held that a third person endorsing a blank at the making of a note may show his intention by parol (11 Mass. 436); but not if he describes himself as guarantor or if the law fixes a precise liability to endorsements in blank (2 Hill N.Y. 80). But this has been doubted (33 E. L. & E. 282). In New York the cases seem to take the broad ground that an endorser in blank, under all circumstances, is an endorser merely and cannot be made a guarantor or surety (1 N.Y. 324; see 95 U.S. 90).

The consideration to support a parol promise to pay the debt of another must be such as would be good relating to the payment of that particular debt or of any other of equal amount (33 Md. 373). It need not necessarily be a consideration distinct from that of the principal contract. An executed or past consideration (121 Mass. 116; 51 Miss. 482).

The giving of new credit where a debt already exists has been held a sufficient consideration to support a guaranty of old and of new debt (15 Pick. 159; 15 Ga. 321); but the weight of authority seems to require that there be some further consideration (Reed Stat. Fr. 70; 1 Pet. 476; 3 Johns 211; 7 Harr. & J. 457). A consideration that will take a case out of the statute of frauds must be such as will make the collateral debt agreed to be paid the debt of the promisor. It must be an original undertaking (45 Ill. App. 155).

Forbearance to sue the debtor is a good consideration if definite in time (92 Ind. 337; 45 Wis. 466; 1 Kebl. 114); or even if of considerable (Cro. Jac. 683); or reasonable time (Bulstr. 206; 4 Wash. 148). But there must be an actual forbearance, and the creditor must have had a power of enforcement (4 East 465). But the fact that it is doubtful whether such a power exists does not injure the consideration (5 B & Ad. 123). Forbearance has been held sufficient consideration even where there was no well-grounded claim (18 L.J.C.P. 222; 34 Pa. 60; contra, 3 Pick. 83). A short forbearance, or the deferment of a remedy, such as postponement of a trial or of arrest, may be a good consideration; and perhaps an agreement to defer indefinitely may support a guaranty (4 Johns 257; 6 Conn. 81). A mere agreement not to push an execution is too vague to be a consideration (4 McCord 409); and postponement of a remedy must be made by agreement as well as in fact (3 Cush. 85; 6 Conn. 81; 11 C.B. 172).

The contract of suretyship may be entered into absolutely and without conditions, or its formation may be made to depend on certain conditions precedent. But there are some conditions implied in every contract of this kind, however absolute on its face. In the case of bonds, as of other contracts of suretyship, it is essential that there be a principal, and a bond executed by the surety is not valid until executed by the principal also. One case, 10 Co. 100b, sometimes cited to the contrary, is not clear on the point. The argument that the surety is bound by his recital under seal fails, especially on all statute bonds where one important requisite of the statute, that the bond be executed by the principal, fails (2 Pick. 24; 4 Beav. 383).

Where the surety's undertaking is conditional on others joining, and this condition is known to the creditor, he is not ordinarily liable until they do so (4 B & Ad. 440; 53 Ind. 321; 4 Biss. 283; 35 Miss. 518; 124 Ill. 200); contra, if the obligee is ignorant of the condition (2 Metc. Ky. 608; 16 Wall 1; 61 Me.

505). So the surety is not bound if the signatures of his co-sureties are forged, although he has not made his signature expressly conditional on theirs (2 Am. L. Reg 349; but see 8 id. N.S. 665). Where a bond to a sheriff (1 La. 41); or an administration bond (119 Ind. 503); was signed in expectation of the party signing that other sureties would sign, and the bond was delivered without such other signatures, the surety was held liable. If a condition on which a surety signs is known to the creditor and is not complied with, the surety is not liable.

Acceptance of the contract by the promisee by words or by acts under it is often made a condition precedent to attaching the liability of the surety. The general rule is that where a future guaranty is given, absolute and definite in amount, no notice of acceptance is necessary; but if it is contingent and indefinite in amount, notice must be given (4 Me. 521; 8 Conn. 438; 16 Johns 67); but the promisee has a reasonable time to give such notice (8 Gray 211).

A distinction is to be made between a guaranty and an offer to guaranty. No notice of acceptance is requisite when a guaranty is absolute (3 N.Y. 212; 2 Mich. 511); but an offer to guaranty must have notice of acceptance; and until accepted it is revocable (12 C.B. N. S. 784; 6 Dow. H.L.C. 239; 32 Pa. 10); and where acceptance is required, it may be implied by acts as well as by words, such as, by receiving the written guaranty from the promisor (8 Gray 211); or by actual knowledge of the amount of sales under a guaranty of the purchase money (28 Vt. 160).

The rule requiring notice is said to be based on "the nature and definition of a contract, which requires the assent of a party to whom a proposal is made, to be signified to the party making it, in order to constitute a binding promise. . . . The rule proceeds upon the ground that the case in which it applies is an offer or proposal on the part of the guarantor, which does not become binding as an obligation until accepted by the party to whom it is made; that, until then, it is just begun and incomplete and may be withdrawn by the proposer" (104 U.S. 159). When the guaranty is contemporaneous with the principal contract, notice is unnecessary (121 Ind. 465; 26 S.W. Rep. Tex. 941); so, where there has been a precedent request (27 N.E. Rep. Ind. 318; contra, 9 Pa. 320; see 34 Am. 1. Reg. & Rev. 257). Notice must be given of an offer to guarantee advances to be made by another to a third party, in order to bind the guarantor (1 M & S. 557). Knowledge that a guaranty is being acted upon is sufficient in the case of guaranties of existing debts or of contemporaneous debts (104 U.S. 159). But in the case of guaranties of repayment of future advances, the cases are in conflict as to whether notice is necessary. That notice is necessary, see 104 U.S. 159; that it is generally unnecessary, see 3 N.Y. 203 and 46 Mich. 70; that it is necessary where the amount of the proposed advance is uncertain, but unnecessary where it is certain, see 112 Ind. 293. One who as surety executes a bond with another, conditioned for payment of the moneys advanced the other, is not entitled to notice of acceptance of the bond by the obligee (34 Fed. Rep. 104).

Where a contract of guaranty is signed by the guarantor without any previous request of the other party, and in his absence and for no other consideration between them, except future advances to be made to the principal debtor, there must be acceptance of the guaranty by the other party in order to complete the contract (115 U.S. 527; 84 Fed. Rep. 605; 110 Pa. 285. 366).

CONSTRUCTION AND EXTENT OF OBLIGATION

The liability of a surety cannot in any event exceed that of the principal, though it may be less. The same rule does not apply to the remedies, which may be greater against the surety. But whatever may be the liability imposed on the surety, it is clear that it cannot be extended by implication beyond the terms of the contract. His obligation cannot be extended beyond the precise terms of the contract; 10 Johns 180; 2 Pa. 27; 9 Utah 260. Sureties are never held responsible beyond the clear and absolute terms and meaning of their undertakings, and presumptions and equities are never allowed to enlarge, or in any degree to change their legal obligations; 21 How. 66. And this rule has been repeatedly affirmed; 11 N. Y. 598; 29 Pa. 460; 2 Wall 235. "It is quite true, that in one sense, the contract of a surety is strictissimi juris, and it is not to be extended beyond the express terms in which it is expressed. The rule, however, is not a rule of construction of a contract, but a rule of application of the contract after the construction of it has been ascertained. Where the question is as to the meaning of the language of the contract, there is no difference between the contract of the surety and anybody else; 47 N. Y. Supp. 48.

The remedies against the surety may be more extensive than those against the principal, and there may be defences open to the principal, but not to the surety,—as, infancy or coverture of the principal,-which must be regarded as a part of the risks of the surety; 30 Vt. 122.

The liability of the surety extends to and includes all securities given to him by the principal debtor, the converse of the rule stated below in the case of collateral security given to the creditor; 26 Vt. 308. Thus a creditor is entitled to in equity to the benefit of all securities given by the principal debtor for the indemnity of his surety; 18 Mo. 136. If the surety receives money from the principal to discharge the debt, he holds it as trustee of the creditor; 6 Ohio 80.

A payment made by the principal before the claim is barred by the statute of limitations, keeps the debt alive as to the surety; otherwise if made after the statute has run; 114 U. S. 528.

In the common case of bonds given for the faithful discharge of the duties of an office, it is of course the rule that the bond covers only the particular term of office for which it is given, and it is not necessary that this should be expressly stated; nor will the time be extended by a condition to be bound "during all the time A (the principal) continues," if after the expiration of the time A holds over merely as an acting officer, without a valid appointment; 3 Sandf. 403. The circumstances of particular cases may extend the strict rule stated above, as in the case of officers annually appointed. Here, although the bond recites the appointment, if it is conditioned upon his faithful accounting for money received before his appointment, the surety may be held; 9 B. & C. 35; 9 Mass. 267. But the intention to extend the time, either by including past or future liabilities, must clearly appear; 4 B. & P. 175. See 101 Cal. 483; 76 Md. 136. Generally the recital cannot be enlarged and extended by the condition; Theob. Surety 66. And where the recital sets forth an employment for twelve months, this time is not controlled by a condition, "from time to time annually, and at all times thereafter during the continuance of this employment," although the employment is actually continued beyond the year; 2 B. & Ald. 431; 7 Gray 1.

So the obligation may cease by a change in the character of the office or employment; 3 Wils. 530; but an alteration of the obligees, by taking in new partners, does not necessarily terminate the obligation; 10 B. & C. 122. But where an essential change takes place, as the death of the obligee, the obligation, is terminated, although the business is carried on by the executors; 1 Term 18. Where one becomes surety for two or either of them, the obligation is terminated by the death of one of the principals; 1 Bingh. 452; but this where the obligation is essentially personal; and where a bond for costs was given by two as "defendants," the surety was not discharged by the death of one; 5 B. & Ald. 261. So a surety for a lessee is not liable for rent after the term, although the lessee holds over; 1 Pick. 332.

If the law provides that a public officer shall hold over until a successor is appointed, the sureties on the official bond are liable during such holdings over; 37 Miss. 518; 2 Metc. Mass. 522; contra, in the case of officers of corporations; 7 Gray 1; but the liability of such surety extends only for such reasonable time as would enable the successor to be appointed; 40 La. Ann. 241. And this provision is not controlled by an alteration of the law extending the term but leaving the provision intact; 15 Gratt. 1. But when the term of an office created by statute or charter is not limited, but merely directory for an annual election, it seems that the surety will be liable, though after the year, until his successor is qualified; 3 Del. Ch. 225.

In bonds, the penalty is the extreme amount of liability of the surety; but various circumstances may reduce the liability below this; 3 Cow. 151; 6 Term 303. If the engagement of the surety is general, the surety is understood to be obligated to the same extent as the principal, and his liability extends to all the accessories of the principal; 14 La. Ann. 183.

A surety on a cashier's bond is not liable for money collected by the cashier as an attorney-at-law, and not accounted for to the bank; 4 Pick. 314. So also where one was surety, and the bond was conditioned on the accounting by the principal for money received by him in virtue of his office as parish overseer, the surety was held not liable for money borrowed by the principal for parochial purposes; 7 B. & C. 491. But a surety on a collector's bond is liable for his principal's neglect to collect as well as failure to pay over; 6 C. & P. 106.

As the surety is only liable to the obligations fairly intended at the execution of the bond, he cannot be held for a breach of new duties attached to his principal's office; 4 Pick. 314; or if any material change is made in the duties; 2 Pick. 223. A surety on an official bond is said to be liable generally for the faithful performance of duties imposed upon the officer, whether by laws enacted before or after the execution of the bond, where such duties are properly within the scope of the office; Brandt. Sur. & Guar. @ 548.

If one guarantees payment for services, and the promisee partly performs the services, but fails of completing them from no fault of his own, the guarantor is liable to the amount of the part-performance; 12 Gray 445.

A bond for faithful performance of duties renders the sureties responsible for ordinary skill and diligence, as well as for integrity; 12 Pick. 303.

A continuing guaranty up to a certain amount covers a constant liability of that amount; but if the guaranty is not continuing, the liability ceases after the execution of the contract to the amount limited; 3 B. & Ald. 593.

A guaranty may be continuing or may be exhausted by one act. It is said that there is no general rule for determining the question; Brandt. Sur. & Guar. @ 156. The general principle may be thus stated: When by the terms of the undertaking, by the recitals in the instrument, or by a reference to the custom and course of dealing between the parties, it appears that the guaranty looked to a future course of dealing for an indefinite time, or a succession of credits to be given, it is to be deemed a continuing guaranty, and the amount expressed is to limit the amount for which the guarantor is to be responsible, and not the amount to which the dealing or whole credit given is to extend; 7 Pet. 113; 3 B. & Ald. 593. Thus a guaranty for any goods for one hundred pounds is continuous; 12 East. 227; or for "any debts not exceeding," etc., 2 Camp. 413; or, "I will undertake to be answerable for any tallow not exceeding," etc., "but without the word any it might perhaps have been confined to no dealing;" 3 Camp. 220. The words, "I do hereby agree to guaranty the payment of goods according to the custom of their trading with you, in the sum of 200 pounds," are held to constitute a continuing guaranty; 6 Bingh. 244; so of the words, "I agree to be responsible for the price of goods purchased at any time, to the amount of," etc.; 1 Metc. Mass. 24. The words "answerable for the amount of five sacks of flour" are clearly not continuous; 6 Bingh. 276. The court will look at the surrounding circumstances, in order to determine; L. R. 4C. P. 595.

The contracts of guaranty and suretyship are not negotiable or assignable, and in general can be taken advantage of only by those who were included as obligees at the formation of the contract; 3 McLean 279. Accordingly, the contract is terminated by the death of one of several obligees; 4 Taunt. 673; or by material change, as incorporation; 3 B. & P. 34. But where a bond is given to trustees in that capacity, their successors can take advantage of it; 12 East 399. The fact that a stranger has acted on a guaranty does not entitle him to the benefits of the contract; 20 Vt. 499; and this has been held in the case of one of two guarantees who acted on the guaranty; 3 Tex. 199. A guaranty is not negotiable, whether made by a payee or subsequent party to a bill or note; 8 Watts 361.

It is held that a guaranty addressed to no one in particular may be acted upon by anyone; 22 Vt. 160; but the true rule would seem to be that in such cases the party who had acted on the contract might show, as in other contracts, that he was a party to it within the intention at the making; the mere fact that no obligee is mentioned does not open it to everybody.

In an action against sureties for violation of a bond by the principals, it is not necessary to allege any violation on the part of the sureties; 31 Pac. Rep. (Cal.) 158.

The rule of construction applied to ordinary sureties is not applicable to the bonds of fidelity and casualty companies; any doubtful language should be construed most strongly against the surety and in favor of the indemnity which the insured had reasonable ground to expect; 2 U. S. App. 439.

Enforcement of the obligation. As the surety cannot be bound to any greater extent than the principal, it follows that the creditor cannot pursue the surety until he has acquired a full right of action against the principal debtor. A surety for the performance of any future or executory contract cannot be called upon until there is an actual breach by the principal. A surety on a promissory note cannot be sued until the note has matured, as there is no debt until that time. All conditions precedent to a right of action against the principal must be complied with. Where money is payable on demand, there must have been a demand and refusal. But it is not necessary that the creditor should have exhausted all the means of obtaining his debt. In some cases it may be requisite to notify the surety of the default of the debtor, or to see the debtor; but this depends upon the particular conditions and circumstances of each case, and cannot be considered a condition precedent in all cases. Even where the creditor has a fund or other security to resort to, he is not obliged to exhaust this before resorting to the surety; he may elect either remedy; and pursue the surety first. But if the surety pays the debt, he is entitled to claim that the creditor should proceed against such fund or other security for his benefit; 4 Jones, Eq. 212; 33 Ala. N. S. 261. And if the creditor having received such collateral security, avails himself of it, he is bound to preserve the original debt; for in equity the surety will be entitled to subrogation; 38 Pa. 98. A judgment against the principal may be assigned to the surety upon the payment of the debt; Metc. 489; 4 Jones Eq. 262; 77 Hun. 580. But an assignment of the debt must be for the whole; the surety cannot pay a part and claim an assignment pro tanto; 39 N. H. 150.

In general, it is not requisite that notice of the default of the principal should be given to the surety, especially when the engagement is absolute and for a definite amount; 14 East 514. The guarantor on a note is not entitled to notice as an endorser; 33 Ia. 293; 74 Pa. 351, 445; 56 Mo. 272. Laches in giving notice to the surety upon a draft of the default of the principal can only be set up as a defence in an action against the surety, in cases where he has suffered damage thereby, and then only to the extent of that damage; 3 N. Y. 203; it is no defence to an action against a surety on a bond that the plaintiff knew of the default of the principal and delayed for a long time to notify the surety or to prosecute the bond; 1 Zabr. 100. Mere passive delay in prosecuting a remedy against a principal does not release a surety; 37 Minn. 431; 30 S.C. 177; 99 N.C. 531; not even if prolonged until the statue of limitations has run; 69 Fed. Rep. 798.

Sureties on a supersedeas bond are not entitled to have a suit thereon stayed till attached lands of the principal are sold and the security exhausted; 57 Fed. Rep. 909.

A judgment against the principal is at least prima facie evidence against the surety, though he was not notified of the action; 66 Fed. Rep. 265.

Discharge of obligation. The obligation may be discharged by acts of the principal, or by acts of the creditor. Payment or tender of payment, by the one, and any act which would deprive the creditor of remedies in case of default would enure to the benefit of the surety, are instances of discharge. In the first place, a payment by the debtor would of course operate to discharge the liability. The only questions which can arise upon this point are, whether the payment is applicable to the payment in question, and as to the amount. Upon the first of these, this contract is governed by the general rule that the debtor can apply his payment to any debt he chooses. The surety has no power to modify or direct the application, but is bound by the election of the principal; 2 Bingh. N.C. 7. If no such election is made by the debtor, the creditor may apply the payment to whichever debt he sees fit; 7 Wheat. 20; 1 Pick. 336. This power, however, only applies to voluntary payments, and not to payments made by process of law; 10 Pick. 129. A surety on a promissory note is discharged by its payment, and the note cannot be again put into circulation; 12 Cush. 163; so also, extension of time by the holder of a note at the request of one maker without the knowledge of the other who signed as surety, releases the latter though the holder did not know of the relation between the two makers at the time the note was given; 23 U.S. App. 280.

When one of two sureties to a contract assented to a change which altered his liability to his prejudice, it was held that the other surety was released but the former was bound for the whole liability; 17 U.S. App. 442, 463. Whatever will discharge the surety in equity will be a defence at law; 7 Johns 337; 2 Pick, 223.

A release of the principal debtor operates as a discharge of the surety; A.C. 313; though the converse is not true 17 Tex. 128; (1893) App. Cas. 313; 63 Ill. 272; unless the obligation is such that the liability is joint only, and cannot be severed. But if the creditor, when releasing the principal, reserves his remedies against the surety, the latter is not discharged; L.R. 7 C.P. 9; 4

Ch. App. Cas. 204; and "a creditor who is fully indemnified is not released by the principal." Brandt. Sur. & Guar. @ 147. The release of one of several sureties is said to release the others only so far as the one released would have been liable for contribution to the co-sureties; 47 Ala. 390; but see 32 Ind. 438. Other cases hold that such a release to be a discharge of the co-sureties; 40 Ind. 225; 2 Ala. 694. When the discharge of one surety varies the contract; 2 Head 613; or increases the risk of the co-sureties, they are released also.

Fraud or alteration avoids a contract of suretyship. Fraud may be by the creditor's misrepresentation or concealment of facts. Unless, however, the contract between the debtor and creditor is unusual, the surety must ask for information; 12 Cl. & F. 109; 15 W.Va. 21. The creditor has been held bound to inform a surety of debtor's previous default; 33 Pa. 358; L.R. 7 Q.B. 666; contra, 21 W.R. 439; 91 Ill. 518; though not of his mere indebtedness; 17 C.B. N.S. 482. But to accept a surety relying on the belief that there are no unusual circumstances increasing his risk, knowing that there are such, and neglecting to communicate them, is fraud; 36 Me. 179; 81 N.Y. 518. The fraud must be practised on the surety; 9 Ala. 42. The forgery of the signature of a surety on a constable's bond will release another surety, signing the same upon the representation that such signature is genuine; 37 Ill. App. 490.

Any material alteration in the contract without the assent of the surety, or change in the circumstances, will discharge the surety; even though trivial, or to the advantage of the surety; 164 U.S. 238; 3 B. & C. 605. Such are the cases where the sureties on a bond for faithful performance are released by a change in the employment or office of the principal; 6 C. B. N.S. 550. But it seems that an alteration by the legislature in an official's duties will not discharge surety as long as they are appropriate to his office; 86 N.Y. 459. If the principal and obligee change the terms of the obligation without the consent of the surety, the latter is discharged; 4 Wash. C.C. 26. A change in the amounts of payments to be made under the principal contract releases the surety who had no knowledge of the change and did not consent; 61 Fed. Rep. 77.

If the creditor without the assent of the surety, gives time to the principal, the surety is discharged; 3 Y & C 187; 2 B. & P.

61; 8 Bingh. 156. So where he agrees with the principal to give
time to the surety; L.R.Ch. App. 142. But not if without consideration; 46 Ill. App. 418; 144 U.S. 97; nor does the reducing
the rate of interest on a debt and allowing it to run along after
maturity on payment of interest, without any binding contract
for an extension for a definite time; 148 Ill. 654. And not where
a creditor reserves his rights against the surety 16 M. & W. 128;
4 H.L.C. 997. The rule applies where a state is a creditor; 75
N.C. 515.

The contract must be effectual, binding the creditor as well
as the debtor; and it is not enough that the creditor merely forbears to press the debtor; 5 Gray 457; 15 Ind. 45. See also, 17
Johns 176; 9 Tex. 615; 9 Cl. & F. 45; 37 S.C. 463; 98 N.C. 111;
84 Va. 772; 71 Tex. 241; 140 U.S. 220. Mere forbearance or delay
of a creditor in enforcing his rights against the principal does
not release the surety, who may, if he chooses, pay the debt,
and, becoming subrogated to the creditor's rights, control the
claim to his own satisfaction; 45 La. Ann. 814.

The receipt of interest on a promissory note, after the note is
overdue, is not sufficient to discharge the surety; 6 Gray 319;
nor is taking another bond, as collateral security to the original,
having a longer time to run; 41 N.Y. 474.

As a requisite to the binding nature of the agreement, it is
necessary that there should be some consideration; 2 Dutch 191;
30 Miss. 424; a part payment by the principal is held not to be
such a consideration; 31 id. 664. Prepayment of interest is a good
consideration; 30 id 432; but not an agreement to pay usurious
interest, where the whole sum can be recovered back; 10 Md.
227; though it would seem to be otherwise if the contract is executed, and the statutes of usury only provide for a recovery of
the excess; 2 Patt. & H. 504.

It has been questioned how far the receipt of interest in
advance shows an agreement to extend the time: it may undoubt-
edly be a good consideration for such an agreement, but does
not of itself constitute it. At the most it may be said to be prima
facie evidence of the agreement; 30 Vt. 711; 1 Y. & C. 620.

The surety is not discharged if he has given his assent to the
extension of the time; 6 Boaw. 600; 16 Pa. 112. Such assent by
one surety does not bind his co-surety; 10 N.H. 318; and subse-

quent assent given by the surety without new consideration, after he has been discharged by a valid agreement for delay, will not bind him; 12 N.H. 320. He need not show notice to the creditor of his dissent; 12 Ga. 271.

Where one surety consents to a change in the original contract and the other does not, the former is bound and the latter is not; 61 Fed. Rep. 77.

The burden of showing a surety's consent to an alteration of the contract is on the plaintiff, when set up by him; 61 Fed. Rep. 77.

Where an execution against a principal is not levied, or a levy is postponed without the consent of the surety, he is discharged from his liability as surety, unless he has property of the principal in his hands at the time; if he has property in his hands liable for the principal's debts, the creditors of the principal may insist on an application of the property to the payment of their debts; 9 B. Monr. 235. A creditor must not only fail, but negligently fail, to enforce a lien, in order to exonerate sureties; 87 Ia. 56. Marriage of the principal and creditor, discharges the surety, destroying the right of action; 30 Ark. 667.

If the creditor releases any surety which he holds against the debtor, the surety will be discharged; 8 S. & R. 452; 23 Fed. Rep. 573; 80 Ill. 122; 84 Ind. 594; but if the security only covers a part of the debt, it would seem that the surety will be released only pro tanto; 9 W. & S. 36; 127 Mass. 386; so of an execution levied and afterwards relinquished; the surety is discharged to the extent to which he has been injured; 50 Ala. 340; 23 Cal. 94; but the surety is not discharged unless he is injured by the release of the levy; 2 G. & J. 243; 88 Pa. 157. Nor will it matter if the security is received after the contract is made; Brandt Sur. & Guar. @ 426; contra, 1 Drewry 333. A creditor who has the personal contract of his debtor, with a surety, and has also or takes afterward property from the principal as a pledge or security for his debt, is to hold the property fairly and impartially for the benefit of the surety as well as himself, and if he parts with it without the knowledge or against the will of the surety he shall lose his claim against the surety to the amount of the property so surrendered, in equity 43 Me. 381; 8 Pick. 121; 4 Johns. Ch. 129; 5 N.H. 353; or at law; 8 S&R 457. The fact that other security, as good as, or better than, that surrendered, was substituted for it, will not preclude the surety from availing himself of the discharge; 15 N.H. 119; 80 Ill. 122.

A creditor who has given up a lien on the debtor's property must prove that the surety was not injured thereby; 23 Fed. Rep. 573. If the relinquishment of the lien materially alters the contract, the surety is wholly discharged; 1 Q.B. Div. 669; when the creditor has, by way of compromise, given up a lien of doubtful validity, and applied the money received, as far as it would go, in payment of the principal debt, the creditor must show that an attempt to realize on the property against which the lien existed would have been successful; 67 Ia. 44. But a creditor is not under any obligation to take active steps to obtain a lien by execution. Generally, where a creditor has, by negligence, lost security held by him for the debt or undertaking, the surety is discharged. In some cases he has been held to diligence in realizing on such security; in other cases his inaction has been held not to discharge the security; Brandt. Sur. & Guar. @ 440.

But a surety is not discharged by the fact that the creditor has released or compounded with his co-surety; much less if his co-surety has been released by process of law. The only effect of such a release or composition is that the surety is not liable for the proportion which would properly fall on his co-surety; 6 Ves. 605. This at least is the doctrine in equity; although it may be questioned whether it would apply at law where the obligation is joint; 4 Ad. & E. 675.

But if the obligation is joint and several, a surety is not released from his proportion by such discharge of his co-surety; 31 Pa. 460.

The death of a surety on a bond conditioned for the repayment of advances to the principal does not terminate the liability, and his estate is liable for advances made after his death; 34 Fed. Rep. 111.

Rights of Surety Against Principal. Until default, the surety has in general, no rights against the principal, except the passive right to be discharged from the obligation on the conditions stated before. But after default on the part of the principal, and before the surety is called upon to pay, the latter has a remedy against the further continuance of the obligation, and he cannot in all cases compel the creditor to proceed against the debtor;

but the English courts of equity allow him to bring a bill against the debtor, requiring the latter to exonerate him; 2 Bro. C.C. 579. So a surety for a debt which the creditor neglects or refuses to enforce by proper proceedings for that purpose, may by bill in equity, bring both debtor and creditor before the court, and have a decree to compel the debtor to make payment and discharge the surety; 3 E. D. Smith 432; and in courts having full equity powers there can be no doubt of the right of a surety, after a debt has become due, to file a bill to compel the principal debtor to pay, whether the surety has himself been sued or not; 2 Md. Ch. Dec. 442; 4 Johns. Ch. 123; 107 Ill. 241; 41 N.J.Eq. 519. Where there is an accrued debt and the surety's liability is admitted, he has a right to compel the principal to relieve him, by paying off his debt. In sustaining such an action he need not prove that the creditor has refused to sue the principal debtor; 31 L.R. Ir. 181.

The surety, after payment of the debt, may recover the amount so paid of the principal, the process varying according to the practice of different courts; 2 Term 104; 4 Me. 200; 1 Pick. 121; 13 Ill. 68. A promise to pay the surety is implied, where there is no express promise; 70 Ala. 326; and assumpsit will lie; 6 M. & W. 153. But before a surety can recover of his principal because of his suretyship, he must first have paid the debt of his principal or some part of it; 41 Neb. 516. But he may pay the debt before it is due, without the request of the principal, and, after it is due, sue the principal; 47 Ind. 85; 125 id. 432.

And such payment refers back to the original undertaking, and overrides all intermediate equities, as of the assignee of a claim against the surety assigned by the principal before payment; 28 Vt. 391.

The payment must not be voluntary, or made in such a manner as to constitute a purchase; for the surety, by purchasing the claim, would take the title of the creditor, and must claim under that. By an involuntary payment is intended only a payment of a claim against which the surety cannot defend. It is not necessary that a suit should be brought. But a surety who pays money on a claim which is absolutely barred has no remedy against the principal; 3 Rand. 490.

A surety having in his hands funds or securities of the principal, may apply them to the discharge of the debt; 10 Rich. Eq.

557; but where the fund is held by one surety he must share the benefit of it with his co-surety; 3 Jones Eq. 170; 28 Vt. 65. But a surety who has security for his liability may sue the principal on his implied promise, unless it was agreed that he should look to the security only; 4 Pick. 444. A surety need not account to his co-surety for the simple indebtedness by himself to the principal; 77 N.Y. 280.

Payment of a note by a surety by giving a new note is sufficient payment, event if the new note has not been paid when the suit is commenced; 14 Pick. 286; 3 N.H. 366; contra, where judgment has been rendered against the surety; 3 Md. 47; or by conveyance of land; 9 Cush. 213.

If the surety pays too much by mistake, he can recover only the correct amount of the principal; 1 Dane. Abr. 197. If a surety discharges his obligation for a less sum than its full amount, he can only claim against the principal the actual sum paid; 4 Tex Civ. App. 526; with interest; 82 Mo. 660; and costs; 12 W.Va. 611.

Extraordinary expenses of the surety, which might have been avoided by payment of the money, or remote and unexpected consequences, are never considered as coming within the contract; 17 Mass. 169; 5 Rawle 106. Costs incurred and paid by the surety in litigating in good faith the claim of the creditor can be recovered of the principal; 30 Vt. 467; 5 Barb. 398; 12 W.Va. 611; but not so if the litigation is in bad faith; 24 Barb. 546; 26 W.Va. 412; or where the surety, being indemnified for his liability, incurred expenses in defending a suit contrary to the expressed wishes of the principal, and after being notified by him that there was no defence to such action; 22 Conn. 299. A surety cannot recover indirect or consequential damages from the principal; Brandt, Sur. & Guar. @ 213; or damages for the sacrifice of his property; 1 Hay 130; or for his failure in business due to his incurring the liability in question; 17 Mass. 169.

Joint sureties who pay the debt of the principal may sue jointly for reimbursement; 3 Metc. Mass. 169; 63 Vt. 609; and if each surety has paid a moiety of the debt, they have several rights of action against the principal; 20 N.H. 418.

Bail. "When bail is given, the principal is regarded as delivered to the custody of his sureties. Their dominion is a continuance of the original imprisonment. Whenever they choose to do so, they may seize him and deliver him up in their discharge, and if that cannot be done at once they may imprison him until it can be done. They may exercise their rights in person or by an agent. They may pursue him into another state, arrest him on the Sabbath, and, if necessary, may break and enter into his house for that purpose." 16 Wall 371; 85 Fed. Rep. 959.

Rights of Surety Against Creditor. It is not quite clear whether a surety can enforce any remedies on the part of the creditor before actual payment by the surety, and, of course, as connected with this, what is the effect of a request by the surety to the creditor to proceed against the debtor, and neglect or refusal to comply with the creditor. The objection to discharging the surety on account of such neglect is the fact that the surety may pay the debt and at once become subrogated to all the rights of the creditor; 6 Md. 210. But where there are courts in the exercise of full equity powers, the surety may insure a prompt prosecution either by discharging the obligation and becoming by substitution entitled to all the remedies possessed by the creditor, or he may coerce the creditor to proceed (by an application to a court of equity); 2 Johns. Ch. 554; 3 Sto. 393; though in the latter case he would probably be required to indemnify the creditor against the consequences of risk, delay, and expense; 2 Md. Ch. Dec. 442. The same indemnity would in general be required where a request is made; but it has been held that a simple request to sue the principal debtor, without a tender of expenses, or a stipulation to pay them, or an offer to take the obligation and bring suit, is sufficient to discharge the surety, unless the creditor at the time of the notice expressly puts his refusal to sue on the ground of the trouble and expense, and offers to proceed if that objection be removed; 18 Pa. 460. A creditor is not bound to make use of active diligence against a principal debtor on the mere request of a surety; 13 Ill. 376. There must be an express declaration by the surety that he would otherwise hold himself discharged; 29 Ohio St. 663; 90 Pa. 363.

There is a line of cases that hold that if the surety, after the principal debt is due, calls upon the creditor to bring suit against the principal who is then solvent, and the creditor fails to do so, and the principal becomes insolvent, the surety is discharged; Brandt. Sur. & Guar. @ 239; 17 Johns 386; 8 S. & R. 110; 2 Col. 614. So where the creditor has sufficient mortgage security, and, after request to sue and refusal, the property depreciates in value; 25 N.Y. 552. The request to sue must be clear and distinct; Brandt. Sur. & Guar. @ 240; and must be made after the debt matures; 44 Pa. 105. Such request must be in writing, see 76 Mo. 70. The great majority of cases hold that the surety cannot be discharged by a request to the creditor to sue, etc.; Brandt. Sur. & Guar. @ 242; 79 Ill. 62; 25 Neb. 448; 2 McLean 451.

In an able opinion in 4 Del. Ch. 258, Bates, Ch. reviews the cases and sustains this view. He points out that the contrary decision in 17 Johns. 386 was made by the casting vote of a lay senator, against the opinion of Kent, C.J. and that, while followed in New York, it has not been favorably regarded even there.

The surety who pays the debt of the principal in full is entitled to have every advantage which the creditor has in pursuing the debtor, and for this purpose may have assignment of the debt, or be subrogated either in law or equity; 39 N.H. 150. Whether the remedy will be by subrogation, or whether the suit must be in the name of the creditor, will depend upon the rules of practice in the different states; 38 Pa. 98. The right of subrogation does not depend upon any contract or request by the principal debtor, but rests upon principles of equity; 1 N.Y. 595; 4 Ga. 343; and, though originating in courts of equity, is now fully recognized as a legal right; 11 Barb. 159. In equity, payment of a debt by a surety does not extinguish it, but operates as an assignment to the surety, with all the creditor's rights; 100 Mo. 250. A surety may apply to the court by motion to compel the assignment of a judgment against him and his principal on his offer to pay the judgment; 77 Hun. 580.

A surety of a defaulting government contractor who completes the work may sue to recover a balance due his principal in his own name. 27 Ct. Cls. 185.

Rights of Surety Against Co-surety. The co-sureties are bound to contribute equally to the debt they became liable to pay when their undertaking is joint, or joint and several, not separate and successive; 3 Pet. 470; but the creditor may recover the whole amount of one surety; 1 Dana 355. To support the right of contribution, it is not necessary that the sureties should be bound by the same instrument; 30 Minn. 503; 14 Ves. 160. But where two sureties are bound by separate and distinct agreements for distinct amounts, although for equal portions of the same debt, there is no right of contribution between them; 3 Pet. 470. The right of contribution rests only on the principle of equity, which courts of law will enforce, that where two persons are subject to a common burden it shall be borne equally between them; 66 N.Y. 225; in such cases the law raises an implied promise from the mutual relation of the parties; 3 Allen 566. If contribution would, as between co-sureties, be inequitable, it will not be awarded; 24 Miss. 581. The right of a surety to seek contribution arises on making payment which discharges the sureties from action; 71 Miss. 426. Where a surety pays the debt of his principal, he cannot enforce contribution from one who signed simply as his surety; 62 Conn. 459.

It is not necessary that the co-sureties should know of the agreements of each other, as the principle of contribution rests only on the equality of the burden, and not on any privity; 2 B. & P. 270; 23 Pa. 294; 61 Ala. 440; but a volunteer is not entitled to contribution; there must be a contract of suretyship; 56 Pa. 80.

A surety may compel contribution for the costs and expenses of defending a suit, if the defence were made under such circumstances as to be regarded as prudent; 23 Vt. 581; 83 N.C. 183; 7 Ill. App. 192; this has been held to include attorney's fees; 87 Tenn. 226 (see 68 Tex. 423); whether the attorney employed was successful or not; 45 Mich. 584. And where the suit is defended at the instance or request of the co-surety, costs would be a subject of contribution, both on equitable grounds and on the implied promise; 1 Mood. & M. 406.

A claim for contribution extends to all securities given to one surety; 30 Barb. 403. If one of several sureties takes collaterals from the principal, they will enure to the benefit of all; 3 Dutch. 503. Where one of several sureties is secured by mortgage, he is not bound to enforce his mortgage before he pays the debt or has reason to apprehend that he must pay it, unless the mortgagor is wasting the estate; and if the mortgagor be squandering the mortgaged property, and the surety secured by the mortgage fails to enforce his rights, he is chargeable between himself and his co-sureties with the fair vendible value of the mortgaged property at a coercive sale; 11 B. Monr. 399. The surety in a suit for contribution can recover only the amount which he has actually paid. Any reduction which he has obtained must be regarded as for the benefit of all the co-sureties; 12 Gratt. 642.

And see 11 Monr. 297. But he is not obliged to account for a debt due by him to the principal; 10 W.N.C. (Pa.) 225.

The right of contribution may be controlled by particular circumstances; thus, where one becomes surety at the request of another, he cannot be called upon to contribute by the person at whose request he entered into the security; 37 N.H. 567.

One of several co-sureties cannot obtain contribution against the others until he has actually paid more than his own share, but he is entitled to a declaration of his right to contribution, and to a prospective order that on paying his own share he shall be indemnified against further liability; (1893) 2 Ch. 514.

The relation between co-sureties may be shown by parol evidence; 12 N.Y. 462; 43 Ind. 126; 62 Ga. 73.

A surety who if fully indemnified by his principal cannot recover contribution from his co-surety for money paid by him, but must idemnify himself out of the means placed in his hands; 21 Ala. N.S. 779, n. A co-surety has the same responsibility for keeping alive securities in favor of his co-surety, from whom he claims contribution, as a creditor has on behalf of sureties; 8 J. & Sp. 424. Ordinarily any indemnity, by way of a lien on property, obtained by one surety, after he became such, ensures to the benefit of all, and if he lose it by his neglect, it bars contribution. See Brandt, Sur. & Guar. @ 271.

The remedy for contribution may be either in equity or at law. The result reached either in law or in equity is the same, with one important exception; in the case of the insolvency of one of the sureties. In such cases the law takes no notice of the insolvency, but awards the paying surety his due proportion as if all were solvent. But equity does not regard the insolvent surety, but awards contribution as if he never had existed; 68 Tex. 423; 7 Dana 307; 6 B & C. 689. One surety cannot by injunction arrest the proceedings at law of his co-surety against him for contribution unless he tenders the principal and interest due such co-surety, who has paid the principal, or alleges he is ready and willing to bring the same into court to be paid to him as a condition of the court's interference; 4 Gill 225. Where surety has been compelled to pay co-sureties is out of the jurisdiction of the court, and others are within it, the surety who has paid is at liberty to proceed in a suit in equity for contribution against those co-securities only within the jurisdiction, by stating the fact in his bill, and the defendants will be required to make contribution without regard to the share of the absent co-surety 59 Vt. 365; 6 Ired. Eq. 115. See generally 1 Lead. Cas. Eq. 100. A bill in equity will lie, by one surety against a co-surety, before the principal debt is paid, to compel him to contribute. A surety who consents to the creditor's giving time to the principal loses the right of contribution as against one who does not consent; 8 Yerg. 158. In equity, in proceeding for contribution, it must be shown that the principal was insolvent; 2 Dana 296; but not at law; 34 Ala. 529; 50 Ind. 158; contra, 7 Dana 307; 99 N.C. 559.

The statue of limitations does not run as against a surety claiming contribution until his own liability is ascertained; (1893) 2 Ch. 514. It runs against partial payments on the debt, from the time he pays the creditor more than his proportion of the debt; 77 Wis. 435.

Conflict of Laws. The contract of suretyship like other contracts, is governed by the lex loci contractus; but the locus is not necessarily the same as that of the principal contract. Thus, the contract made by the endorser of a note is, not to pay the note where it is payable, but that if not paid where he will pay it at the place where the endorsement is made; 12 Johns. 142; 13 Mass. 20. The lex loci applies as well to the interest as to the principal amount. A question has been made in the case of bonds for faithful performance given by public officers; and in these it has been held that the place of performance is to be regarded as the place of making the contract, and sureties are bound as if they made the contract at the seat of the government to which the bonds are given. And under this rule the obligation of all on the bond is governed by the same law, although the principal and sureties may sign in different states; 6 Pet. 172. A letter of guaranty written in the United States and addressed to a person in England must be construed according to the laws of England; 1 How. 161.

GUARANTY

Guaranty is an undertaking to answer for another's liability, and collateral thereto. A collateral undertaking to pay the debt of another in case he does not pay it; Shaw, C.J., 24 Pick. 252.

A provision to answer for the payment of some debt, or the

performance of some duty in the case of the failure of some person who, in the first instance, is liable for such payment or performance; 60 N.Y. 438; Bayl. Sur. & Guar. 2.

A promise to answer for the debt, default, or miscarriage of another person; 94 Cal. 96 See 72 Ill. 13. It is distinguished from suretyship in being a secondary, while that is a primary obligation; or, as sometimes defined, guaranty is an undertaking that the debtor shall pay; suretyship that the debt shall be paid. Or again a contract of suretyship creates a liability for the performance of the act in question at the proper time, while the contract of guaranty creates a liability for the ability of the debtor to perform the act; Bayl. Sur. & Guar. 3. Guaranty is an engagement to pay on a debtor's insolvency, if due diligence be used to obtain payment; 52 Pa. 440.

The undertaking is essentially in the alternative. A guarantor cannot be sued as a promisor, as the surety may; his contract must be specially set forth. A guarantor warrants the solvency of the promisor, which an endorser does not; 8 Pick. 423.

The distinction between suretyship and guaranty has been expressed as follows: A surety is usually bound with his principal by the same instrument, executed at the same time, and on the same consideration. He is an original promisor and debtor from the beginning, and is held, ordinarily, to know every default of his principal. Usually, he will not be discharged, either by the mere indulgence of the creditor to the principal, or by want of notice of the default of the principal, no matter how much he may be injured thereby. On the other hand, the contract of the guarantor is his own separate undertaking, in which the principal does not join. It is usually entered into before or after that of the principal, and is often supported on a separate consideration from that supporting the contract of the principal. The original contract of his principal is not his contract, and he is not bound to take notice of its non-performance. He is often discharged by the mere indulgence of creditor to the principal and is usually not liable unless notified of the default of the principal; Brandt. Sur. & Guar. @ 1. See also, 52 Pa. 438, 525; 87 Ind. 560; 63 Ala. 419; 135 N.Y. 423. A written guaranty which fails to show on its face the person to whom the guaranty is made is void; 17 N.Y. Supp. 509; and where a contract contains no guaranty, parol evidence of one is inadmissible; 146 U.S. 42.

At common law, a guaranty could be made by parol; but by the Statute of Frauds, 29 Car. II c. 3, re-enacted almost in terms in the several states, it is provided that "No action shall be brought whereby to charge the defendant upon any special promise to answer for the debt, default, or miscarriage of another person . . . unless the agreement upon which such action shall be brought, or some memorandum or note thereof, shall be in writing, signed by the party to be charged therewith, or by some person thereunto by him lawfully authorized."

While, under this statute "no action shall be brought" on a contract not in writing, etc., yet such a contract may be enforced by a court against an attorney, by summary proceedings; 1 Cr. & J. 374.

"Any special promise" in the act does not apply to promises implied in law; Brandt. Sur. & Guar. @ 53.

The following classes of promises have been held not within the statute, and valid though made by parol.

First, where there is a liability pre-existent to the new promise.

1. Where the principal debtor is discharged by the new promise being made; 3 Bingh. N.C. 889; 28 Vt. 135; 8 Gray 233; 1 Q.B. 933; 8 Johns. 376; 13 Md. 131; Bro. Stat. Fr. @ 166, 193; and an entry of such discharge in the creditor's books is sufficient proof; 3 Hill. S.C. 41. This may be done by agreement to that effect; 1 Allen 405; by novation, by substitution, or by discharge under final process; 1 B. & Ald. 297; 18 S.W. Rep. (Tex.) 646; but mere forbearance, or an agreement to forbear pressing the claim, is not enough; I Sim. L. Cas. 387; 6 Vt. 666.

2. Where the principal obligation is void or not enforceable when the new promise is made, and this is contemplated by the parties. But if not so contemplated, then the new promise is void; Burge, Surety 10; 1 Burr. 373. But see, on this point 17 Md. 283; 13 Johns. 175; 6 Ga. 14.

3. So where the promise does not refer to the particular debt, or where this is unascertained; 1 Wils. 305.

In these three classes the principal obligation ceases to exist after the new promise is made.

4. Where the promisor undertakes for his own debt. But the mere fact that he is indebted will not suffice, unless his promise refers to that debt; nor is it sufficient if he subsequently becomes

indebted on his own account, if not indebted when he promises, or if it is then contingent; 4 Hill N.Y. 211; 82 Tex. 255. The provision of the statute does not apply whenever the main purpose of the promisor is not to answer for another, but to subserve some pecuniary or business purpose of his own, although it may be in form a promise to pay the debt of another; 141 U.S. 479. So if the vendee of land promises to pay the purchase-money on a debt due by the vendor; 82 Tex. 255.

5. Where the new promise is in consideration of property placed by the debtor in the promisor's hands; 1 Gray 391; 41 Me. 559; 23 Cal. 187; 72 Ill. 442. And where the new promise is made in a transaction which in substance is a sale to the promisor; Brandt. Sur. & Guar. @ 65.

6. Where the promise does not relate to the promisor's property, but to that of the debtor in the hands of the promisor.

7. Where the promise is made to the debtor, not the creditor; because this is not the debt of "another" than the promisee; 1 Gray 76; 11 Ad. & E. 438.

8. Where the creditor surrenders a lien against the debtor or on his property, which the promisor acquires or is benefited by; Fell. Guar. c. 2; Brandt. Sur. & Guar. @ 63, 64; 7 Johns. 463; 2 B. & Ald. 613; 21 N.Y. 412; but not so where the surrender of the lien does not benefit the promisor; 8 Metc. Mass. 396; 21 N.Y. 412; 3 Esp. 86.

In the five last classes, the principal debt may still subsist concurrently with the new promise, and the creditor will have a double remedy; but the fulfilment of the new promise will discharge the principal debt, because he can have but one satisfaction. The repeated dicta, that if the principal debt subsists, the promise is collateral and within the statute, are not sustainable; 30 Vt. 641. But the general doctrine now is that the transaction must amount to a purchase, the engagement for the debt being the consideration therefor, in whole or in part; 1 Gray 391; 5 Cush. 488.

Where one owes a debt to another, and promises to pay his debt to a creditor of such other party, the promise is not within the statute; 5 Greenl. 81; 3 B. & C. 842.

Second. If the new promise is for a liability then first incurred, it is original, if exclusive credit is given to the promisor; 5 Allen 370; 13 Gray 613; 28 Conn. 544; Browne, Stat. Fr. @

195. Whether exclusive credit is so given is a question of fact for the jury; 7 Gill 7. Merely changing the debtor on a bookaccount is not conclusive.

Whether promises merely to indemnify come within the statute is not wholly settled; Browne, Stat. Fr. @ 158; Brandt, Sur. & Guar. @ 59, 61. In many cases they are held to be original promises, and not within the statute; 15 Johns. 425; 4 Wend. 657. But few of the cases, however, have been decided solely on this ground, most of them falling within the classes of original promises before specified. On principle, such contracts seem within the statute if there is a liability on the part of any third person to the promisee. If not these promises would be original under class seven, above. Where the indemnity is against the promisor's own default, he is already liable without his promise to indemnify; and to make the promise collateral would make the statute a covert fraud; 10 Ad. & E. 453; 1 Gray 391; 10 Johns. 242; 1 Ga. 294; 5 B. Monr. 382; 20 Vt. 205; 10 N.H. 175; 1 Conn. 519; 5 Me. 504. The weight of American authority is said to be in favor of applying the statute to cases of indemnity; Brandt, Sur. & Guar. @ 59 n. When the promise to indemnify is in fact a promise to pay the debt of another it is within the statute. 21 N.Y. 412. A promise to indemnify another against loss in becoming surety on a replevin bond is within the statute; 12 Ohio St. 219. So on a bond for stay of execution; 111 Pa. 471. But a promise to indemnify one if he will become bail in a criminal case has been held not within the statute; B. & S. 414; 119 Ind. 85.

Third. Guaranties may be given for liabilities thereafter to be incurred, and will attach when the liability actually accrues. In this class the promise will be original, and not within the statute, if credit is given to the promisor exclusively; 2 Term 80; 1 Cowp. 227; 40 Ill. App. 275. But where the future obligation is contingent merely, the new promise is held not within the statute, on the ground there is no principal liability when the collateral one is incurred; Browne, Sta Fr. @ 196. But this doctrine is questionable if the agreement distinctly contemplates the contingency; 1 Cra. C.C. 77; 5 Hill, N.Y. 483. An offer to guarantee must be accepted within a reasonable time; but no notice of acceptance is required if property has been delivered under the guaranty; 8 Gray 211; 2 Mich. 511; 54 Fed. Rep. 846; 104 U.S. 159.

A contract of guaranty, like every other contract, can only be made by the mutual assent of the parties. If the guaranty is signed by the guarantor, at the request of the other party, or if the latter's agreement to accept is contemporaneous with the guaranty; or if the receipt from him of a valuable consideration, however small, is acknowledged in the guaranty, the mutual assent is proved, and the delivery of the guaranty to him or for his use completes the contract. But if the guaranty is signed by the guarantor, without any previous request of the other party and in his absence, for no consideration moving between them, except future advances to be made to the principal debtor the guaranty is in legal effect an offer or proposal on the part of the guarantor, needing an acceptance by the other party to complete the contract; 115 U.S. 524.

The agreement of a del credere agent to pay for goods sold by him is not within the statute; 23 Vt. 720; 14 N.Y. 267.

The form of the writing is not material: it may consist of one or more writings (provided they refer to each other on their face; 27 Mo. 388; 11 East 142. A minute of a vote of a corporation is sufficient; 14 Allen 407.

There is a conflict of authority as to whether the consideration need appear in the writing. It was finally settled in England that it must; 5 East 10; 4 B. & Ald. 595; but this is now changed by statute 19 & 20 Vict. The cases are reviewed in Brandt, Sur. & Guar. @ 82. A seal imports a consideration; id. As to the signature of the party to be charged, a seal alone is generally held sufficient; Stra. 764; so is a mark; 49 Barb. 62; 2 M. & S. 286; and a signature by the initials only 1 Den. 471; 9 Allen 474; and a signature on a telegram; 35 Barb. 463. The signature need not be at the foot of the writing; 2 M. & W. 653.

Guaranty may be made for the tort as well as the contract of another, and then comes under the term miscarriage in the statute; 2 B. & Ald. 613; 2 Day 457; 1 Wils. 305; 9 Cow. 154; 14 Pick. 174.

All guaranties need a consideration to support them, none being presumed as in case of promissory notes. A guaranty of the payment of a negotiable promissory note, written by a third person upon a note before its delivery, need express no consideration, even where the law requires the consideration of the guaranty to be expressed in writing; but the consideration which the note upon its face implies to have passed between the original parties is sufficient; 149 U.S. 298. Forbearance to sue is good consideration; Cro. Jac. 683; Browne, Stat. Fr. @ 190; 4 Johns. 257; 6 Conn. 81; 27 L. J. Exch. 120; 21 Fed. Rep. 836; 77 Ind. 1. Where the guaranty is contemporaneous with the principal obligation, it shares the consideration of the latter; 8 Johns. 29; 1 Paine 580; 2 Pet. 170; 3 Mich. 396; 36 N.H. 73.

A guaranty may be for a single act, or may be continuous. The cases are conflicting, as the question is purely one of intention of the particular contract; Brandt, Sur. & Guar. 156. The tendency in this country is against construing guarantees as continuing, unless the intention of the parties is so clear as not to admit of a reasonable doubt; Bayl. Sur. & Guar. 7, citing 32 Ohio St. 177; S. C. 30 Am. R. 572; Lent v. Padleford, 2 Am. Lead. Cas. 141; 24 Wend. 82; 145 Ill. 488. If the object be to give a standing credit to be used from time to time, either indefinitely or for a fixed period, the liability is continuing; 40 Ill. App. 383; 3 Ind. App. 1; but if no time is fixed and nothing indicates the continuance of the obligation, the presumption is in favor of a limited liability as to time; Bayl. Sur. & Guar. 7; 62 Barb. 351. A guaranty of any bills of account for goods sold another to a certain amount is a continuing guaranty; 40 Ill. App. 383. A sealed continuing guaranty is revoked by the death of the guarantor; 22 W.N.C. (Pa.) 457.

The authorities are not agreed as to the negotiability of a guaranty. It is held that a guaranty which is a separate and distinct instrument is not negotiable separately; 3 W. & S. 272; 4 Chandl. 151; 14 Vt. 233; 31 Me. 536; 31 Barb. 92; 21 Pick. 140. The right of an acceptor of a bill, to the benefit of a guaranty given to him, is not transferable to a holder of the bill, unless it was given for the purpose of being exhibited to other parties; 3 Ch. App. 756. But if a guaranty is on a negotiable note, it is negotiable with the note; and if the note is to the bearer, the guaranty has been held to be negotiable in itself; 24 Wend. 456; 6 Humphr. 261. But an equitable interest passes by transfer, and the assignee may sue in the name of the assignor; 12 S. & R. 100; 20 Vt. 506. It has been held that no suit can be maintained upon a guaranty except the person with whom it was made; Bayl. Sur. & Guar. 14; 8 Watts 361; but it has also been held that a guaranty of a note may be sued on by any person who advances

money on it, but that it is not negotiable unless made upon the
note the payment which it guarantees; Bayl. Sur. & Guar. 15; 26
Wend. 425.

It is held that a guaranty is not enforceable by others than
those to whom it is directed; 3 McLean 279; 1 Gray 317; 6 Watts
182; 10 Ala. N. S. 793; although they advance goods thereon;
4 Cra. 224.

In one case it was held that the guarantor was not bound
where the guaranty was addressed to two and acted upon by one
of them only; 3 Tex. 199. It was held, also, that the guaranty was
not enforceable by the survivor of two to whom it was addressed
for causes occurring since the decease of the other; 7 Term 254.

In the case of promissory notes, a distinction has sometimes
been made between a guaranty of payment and a guaranty of
collectibility; the latter requiring that the holder shall diligently
prosecute the principal debtor without avail; 4 Wis. 190; 25
Conn. 576; 6 Barb. 547; 26 Me. 358; 4 Conn. 527; 48 Minn. 207.

It has in some cases been held that an endorsement in blank
on a promissory note by a stranger to the note was prima facie
a guaranty; 37 Ill. App. 616. A second acceptance on a bill of
exchange may amount to a guaranty; 2 Camp. 447.

A guarantor is discharged by a material alteration in the
contract without his consent. Brandt, Sur. & Guar. @ 378; 137
N.Y. 307; 85 Ia. 617. Modification of a contract made by a contractor and the owner will not release the guarantor, if they are
such as are permitted by the terms of the contract; 155 Pa. 36.

The guarantor may also be discharged by the neglect of the
creditor in pursuing the principal debtor. The same strictness as
to demand and notice is not necessary to charge a guarantor as is
required to charge an endorser; but in the case of a guaranteed
note the demand on the maker must be made in a reasonable
time, and if he is solvent at the time of maturity of the note,
and remains so for such reasonable time afterwards, the guarantor does not become liable for his subsequent insolvency; 2
H. Bla. 612; 18 Pick. 534. Notice of non-payment must also be
given to the guarantor; 2 Ohio 430; but where the name of a
guarantor of a promissory note does not appear on the note,
such notice is not necessary unless damage is sustained thereby,
and in such a case the guarantor is discharged only to the extent
of such damage; 12 Pet. 497. One who guarantees that another

will pay promptly for goods to be purchased is not liable where the purchaser becomes insolvent after the guaranty is given, and the seller gives the guarantor no notice of the purchaser's failure to pay; 145 Ill. 488. A presentment for payment is now decided not to be necessary in order to charge one who guarantees the due payment of a bill or note; 5 M. & G. 559. It is not necessary that an action should be brought against the principal debtor; 7 Pet. 113; 2 Watts 128; 11 Wend. 629.

From the close connection of guaranty with suretyship, it is convenient to consider many of the principles common to both under the head of suretyship as was related.

Where an innocent person acts upon a guaranty, the execution of which was procured by misrepresentation, the burden devolves upon the guarantor to show that he was free from negligence; the rule in such cases being the same with respect to the execution of guaranties as to that of negotiable instruments; 17 N.Y. Supp. 764.

Whether a guarantee is absolute or special is a question of fact; 37 Ill. App. 616.

Where the guaranty of a written contract is executed on the same paper, notice of acceptance by the person for whose benefit it is made, is unnecessary; 130 Ind. 194.

It is not within the general scope of a partner's authority to give guaranties in the name of the firm; Wood's Byles, Bills 48; 35 Minn. 229. And an officer of a company cannot bind it as surety or guarantor; 91 Pa. 367.

A good advice to follow at all times is to never sign as a guaranty or surety unless you are perfectly willing to assume the payment of the obligation.

VI. AGENCY

IN GENERAL

Definition. An agent is a person employed by another to do some act or acts for the employer's benefit or on his account. The person for whom the agent acts is called the principal. Agency is the legal relation existing between the principal and the agent.

The principal must be a person competent to make contracts, for no one can make a contract through an agent which he has not the power to make for himself. The agent, since his acts are the acts of his principal, is not required to be competent to make a contract; therefore we find it to be the general rule that any person with sufficient understanding to transact the business committed to his charge may be an agent. Infants or married women may be so employed and may bind their principal with a contract which they could not make themselves.

As it is impossible for anyone to transact all his business without assistance, we can see how large a field agency covers and the great importance of the law of agency.

Classes of Agents. There are two classes of agents, general and special.

GENERAL AGENT. A general agent is one who is authorized to transact all his principal's business of a particular kind or in a certain place. If he has received from his principal a general authority to do certain acts, he is not limited to the performance of a specific act but is permitted a certain amount of discretion in carrying on the particular line of business for which he is employed. The acts of a general agent, while he is within the scope of his authority, will bind his principal, whether or not they are in accordance with his private instructions. If the agent is apparently clothed with authority, the principal is bound.

Munn v. Commission Co., 15 Johns (N.Y.) 44, is a case concerning a general agent; the court said: "The distinction is well settled between a general and a special agent. As to the former the principal is responsible for the acts of the agent, when acting within the general scope of his authority, and the public cannot be cognizant of any private instructions from the principal to the agent; but where the agency is a special or temporary one, there the principal is not bound, if the agent exceeds his employment."

SPECIAL AGENT. A special agent is one who is appointed for a special purpose or to transact a particular piece of business. He is given but limited authority. His acts do not bind the principal beyond the scope of the particular authority given him.

The distinction is a difference in degree rather than in kind. In the case of a general agent there has been general power delegated, the authority is necessarily broad, and a person dealing with such an agent may reasonably infer that he has the authority usually conferred on such agents under like circumstances; while in the appointment of a special agent the object is to accomplish a special purpose or to carry out a particular piece of business, and one would naturally infer that the authority is limited.

RELATION OF PRINCIPAL AND AGENT

Agreement. The relation of principal and agent may be created in several different ways. The ordinary way is by agreement, as where one man employs or appoints another to represent him in a certain transaction or in a general way. This is an agency by contract, except in the case of a gratuitous agent, and all the rules governing contracts govern also the relations of the principal and agent as between themselves.

The reason why a gratuitous agent is not an agent by contract is that there being no consideration, the agreement cannot be enforced as a contract.

An agent by agreement may be appointed orally, except in the following cases:

First. Where by the terms of the agency the service is not to be performed within one year; then, by the statute of frauds, the agreement must be in writing.

In Hinckley v. Southgate, 11 Vt. 428, defendant made a parol agreement in February with plaintiff that plaintiff would carry on defendant's grist mill for one year from April 1 next. Plaintiff offered to perform, but defendant would not allow him. It was held by the court that the case was clearly within the statute of frauds, since the work was not to be performed within one year. Consequently the parol agreement could not be enforced.

Tuttle v. Swett, 31 Me. 555, was an action on a parol agreement to employ plaintiff for three years to labor for defendant in making powder casks, for which he was to be paid a certain price per day. Defendant refused to permit him to work, and it was held that the agreement could not be enforced, since the labor was not to be performed within one year and the contract was not in writing.

Second. When the contract between the principal and the third party is required to be under seal, the authority of the agent to execute the instrument must itself be under seal.

In Hanford v. McNair, 9 Wend. (N.Y.) 54, A, by writing, not under seal, authorized an agent to enter into a contract for the purchase of a quantity of lumber. The agent entered into a sealed contract for such purpose. It was held that an agent cannot bind his principal by a sealed instrument unless he has authority under seal to do it.

In Johnson v. Dodge, 17 Ill. 433, the question was the proper authority of the agent to sell land. The court said that the power to convey land must be in writing and under seal, as the land can be conveyed only by deed, and the power to convey must be of equal dignity with the act to be executed.

Power of Attorney. The formal method of appointing an agent is by a written instrument under seal known as a power of attorney.

A form is used when the power conferred is the authority to sell and convey certain real estate. When the power conferred is to execute a deed, mortgage, or any other instrument that is to be recorded, the power must be so executed as to entitle it to be recorded in the same place. This requires that it shall be acknowledged before a notary public or some other officer empowered by law to take such acknowledgment.

This form may be used to confer other authority by inserting in place of the authority to sell real estate the exact authority intended.

Ratification. Ratification is the second way in which the relation of principal and agent may be created.

Assent of the principal to the act of the agent may be given before or after the act. If given before, then it is an agency by agreement, and has already been explained. If given after, the act has been performed by the agent, it is a ratification of the act and gives the same effect to it as though there had been a previous appointment. This may be true where the agent had no previous authority whatever or where the agent had some prior authority but exceeded it in the particular act. The ratification operates as an extension of the authority to the act.

In Merritt v. Bissell, 84 Hun. (N.Y.) 194, it was held that where a person was clothed with some authority as agent, ratification by his principal of his unauthorized acts relates back and makes such acts of the agent the acts of the principal from the beginning, the same as if he had been duly authorized at the start.

Power of Attorney
Know all Men by these Presents, That

I, Albert Anderson, of Chicago, Cook County, Illinois, have made, constituted and appointed, and by these presents do make, constitute and appoint Bert Boyd, of Galesburg, Illinois, my true and lawful attorney for me and in my name, place and stead to grant, bargain and sell real estate situated in the said Galesburg, Illinois, or any part thereof, for such price, and on such terms, as to him shall see in best, and to me and in my name, to make, execute, acknowledge, and deliver good and sufficient deeds and conveyance for the same, either with or without to covenants of warranty . . . . giving and granting unto my said attorney full power and authority to do and perform all and every act and thing whatsoever requisite and necessary to be done and in and about the premises, as fully to all intents and purposes, as I might or could do if personally present, with full power of substitution and revocation, hereby ratifying and confirming all that my said attorney or his substitute lawfully do or cause to be done by virtue hereof.

In witness whereof, I have hereunto set my hand and seal the 18th day of August 1966 in the year one thousand nineteen hundred and sixty-six sealed and delivered in the presence of

[Signed] A. B. Carlson   [Signed] Albert Anderson

[SEAL]

State of Illinois ⎫
City of Chicago ⎬ ss
County of Cook ⎭

On the eighteenth day of August 1966 in the year nineteen hundred sixty-six . . . . . . before me personally came Albert Anderson, to me known and known to me to be the individual, described in, and who executed the foregoing instrument and he duly acknowledged that he executed the same.

[SEAL]   [Signed] H. D. Chadwick
                                                        Notary Public

The ratification to bind the principal must be made with knowledge of all the material facts; if made under a misunderstanding or through a misrepresentation, the principal will not be bound. The principal must repudiate the agent's unauthorized act within a reasonable time after he learns of it, or he will be presumed to have ratified it. The ratification may be by express words or by accepting the benefits of the act.

In Pake v. Douglass, 28 Ark. 59, A without authority purchased a bill of goods for persons about to form a copartnership, in their name and on their credit as partners. They received the goods and sold them. One of the partners afterward repudiated the purchase, claiming that the other partner was to buy the goods and that the agent had no authority to buy for him, and he so advised the sellers. It was held that this was not sufficient. He should have restored the goods, but since they kept the goods, they were liable as partners; they had ratified the act by retaining the benefit.

But if the principal ratifies the act, it must be as a whole, for he cannot accept the benefits of a part and reject the remainder.

An axiom of the law is "A man cannot take the benefits of a contract without bearing its burdens."

In Eberts v. Selover, 44 Mich. 519, a subscription agent canvassing for a history to cost $10 had a book for signatures, and on this it was printed that no terms except those printed thereon should be binding. A justice of the peace consented to sign on condition that his office fees from time to time of delivery of the book be taken in payment. This was agreed to, and he was given a written memorandum by the agent to that effect. It was held that if the company ratified the contract, it must be on the terms agreed upon. As the agent went beyond his authority, they could repudiate the contract and refuse to deliver the book, but they could not repudiate part and still hold the subscriber.

Necessity. The third way in which the relation between principal and agent may be created is by necessity.

This is where the relations or positions of the parties are such that the authority of the principal is presumed. The leading illustration of this is the case of husband and wife. The wife can contract for the necessities of the household and bind the husband for their payment.

Benjamin v. Dockham, 134 Mass. 418, was an action for the price of milk delivered to defendant's wife, who because of his cruelty was living apart from him. It was held that as a wife is authorized by law to pledge her husband's credit; it is a case of compulsory agency, and her request is his request.

A shipmaster also has authority in case of necessity to purchase supplies for the ship and pledge the credit of the owner.

In McCready v. Thorn, 51 N.Y. 454, an action was brought against the owners to recover for services and advances rendered to the master of the ship. The master was running the vessel under an arrangement with the owners whereby he was to furnish everything and divide the profit, but plaintiff had no notice of this. The owners of the vessel were found liable for moneys and labor so advanced.

OBLIGATION OF PRINCIPAL TO AGENT

Compensation. The principal is under obligation to the agent to compensate him for his services.

When the agreement fixes the compensation the agent is to receive, this will control.

In Wallace v. Floyd, 29 Pa. St. 184, plaintiff agreed to work for a given time at a certain salary. He stayed beyond the time, and nothing was said about salary for the additional period. It was held that he could recover salary only at the rate agreed upon. It was said that the best valuation of services was that mutually agreed upon by the parties themselves.

In the absence of an express contract the law will imply an agreement to pay what the services are reasonably worth, unless it can be fairly inferred that the services were intended to be gratuitous.

Even if the service is unauthorized but is subsequently ratified and the benefit is accepted by the principal, the agent ordinarily can recover for the service to the same extent as if the service had been authorized originally.

In Gelatt v. Ridge, 117 Mo. 553, plaintiff was employed to sell real estate on the owner's terms. He sold on other terms, but the principal ratified the sale. It was held that the agent was entitled to his commissions as originally agreed.

The principal is also under obligation to reimburse the agent for any sums which he may have paid out or for which he may have become individually liable in the due course of his agency and for the principal's benefit.

Maitland v. Martin, 86 Pa. St. 120, is a case in which a broker purchased for B certain bonds which B left in his hands several years, when he directed that they be sold. It was learned that three of the bonds had been repudiated by the state where issued. It was held that the broker must be reimbursed; that the loss fell on B if the broker acted within the lines of his duty and in good faith.

The agent is further entitled to indemnity from his principal for the consequences of any act performed within his authority and the execution of his employment. But for him to be entitled to indemnity the act must be lawful, or the agent must have been ignorant of the fact that the act was illegal.

In Moore v. Appleton, 26 Ala. 633, plaintiff brought an action to be reimbursed for damages which he had been obliged to pay because of certain acts performed by him as agent for defendant in disposing of a third party of lands claimed by defendant and which plaintiff had reason to believe belonged to defendant. It was held that the act was not manifestly illegal, and that the law implies a promise of indemnity by the principal for losses which flow directly and immediately from execution of the agency.

OBLIGATION OF AGENT TO PRINCIPAL

Agent Must Obey Instructions. The agent is under obligation to his principal to obey the principal's instructions. So long as the agent carries out his instructions, he is protected, but if he goes contrary to them and loss ensues, he is liable for the damage, as where the agent is instructed by his principal to send a certain claim for collection to A and instead he sends it to B and loss ensues.

In Whitney v. Merchants Union Express Co., 104 Mass. 152, the express company received for collection a draft with instructions to return at once if not paid. It instead held the draft until the drawee wrote for some explanation. It then failed to present it for two days after the drawee had received a reply from the drawer, and at this time the drawee became insolvent. It was held that the express company was liable to the drawer.

Agent Must Use Judgment. The agent owes the duty to his principal to exercise the judgment and skill necessary to the prudent and careful discharge of his agency. This prudence and skill can generally be said to be the same as ordinarily observed by prudent and careful men under similar circumstances and engaged in similar business.

Whitney v. Martime, 88 N.Y. 535, is a case in which an attorney was employed as agent to loan money on bond and mortgage. He made loans when the parties giving the bonds were insolvent and took mortgages on realty already mortgaged. The principal lost, and it was held that the attorney was liable to his principal for the loss.

Thus an agent to purchase a carload of wheat must possess and exercise such knowledge and skill as is common to careful dealers in grain; an agent to purchase an expensive and intricate engine is bound to exercise the caution and skill of an engineer.

Fiduciary Relation. There exists between the principal and his agent what is said to be a fiduciary relation, which means that the utmost good faith is required in their dealings. An agent cannot therefore acquire any rights that are contrary to the interests of the principal. He must not act for both the principal and the third party in a transaction without their consent.

Walker v. Osgood, 98 Mass. 348, was an action by a real-estate agent for commissions. Defendant had employed him to sell or trade his farm, and the agent effected an exchange and made an agreement with the third party that he was to receive a commission from him. It was held by the court that the broker was the agent of the owner and could not act for the third party. And if he exacted from the third party a promise of compensation, he could not recover from the owner for his services, even though an exchange or sale was effected. The interests of the parties were adverse; the agent for one could not act for the other without the knowledge and consent of the first.

Neither must the agent use his position or authority for his own benefit.

In Bunker v. Miles, 30 Me. 431, defendant was employed by plaintiff to buy a certain horse for him for $80 or as much less as he could and was told to have $1 for his trouble. Defendant bought the horse for $72.50 but returned to plaintiff no part of the $80. The court allowed plaintiff to recover the balance of $7.50, holding that the agent could not make a profit for himself out of the transaction.

An agent authorized to sell or rent will not be permitted to buy or lease the property himself without the principal's consent.

In Kerfoot v. Hyman, 52 Ill. 512, plaintiff owned certain land and employed defendant to sell it for a certain amount. Defendant bought it himself and took title in the name of a third party, but for his own benefit without the owner's consent, and at the same time had a part of it sold for as much as he had obtained for the whole of it for plaintiff. It was held that the agent must account to plaintiff for the excess received, and the remainder not sold would revert to the principal.

Also, an agent commissioned to compromise a claim cannot purchase it at a discount and then enforce it in full against the principal. The agent is under obligation to his principal to render a true account of all the proceeds and profits of the agency.

In the absence of an express agreement to the contrary the agent must render an account to his principal on demand or within a reasonable time.

Subagents. Another obligation of the agent to his principal is to act in person, except when authorized either by his principal or by established custom to appoint subagents. The reason for this is obvious: the principal employs the agent because of his confidence and trust in the agent's ability and honesty to act in his stead, and the agent appointed cannot delegate to another the duty or trust which has been confided to him.

Still, an agent can in some cases appoint subagents to perform duties which do not involve exercise of discretion but are merely mechanical or ministerial acts.

In Renwick v. Bancroft, 56 Iowa 527, A was employed to sell a piece of realty and to fix the price, etc. After looking over the property, he employed B to find a purchaser, and B did find a purchaser and sold the property. It was held that the agent might properly appoint such a subagent, as there was no discretion placed in the subagent, and A could employ such party as he wished to help him in carrying out the agency.

Sometimes, from the nature of the case, it is implied that the agent is to appoint another agent for his principal. In that case the first agent is relieved from liability for the acts of the third party if he uses care and discretion in the appointment; whereas if he employs a subagent, he is personally liable to the principal for the acts of the subagent to the same extent precisely that he would be if they were his own acts.

An interesting illustration is the case of a man depositing in his home bank commercial paper payable at some other city. The question then is, Does the owner of the paper authorize the home bank to appoint subagents, or does he authorize it to employ additional agents in his behalf?

It is evident that whichever view is maintained, it is within the contemplation of the parties that the home bank cannot execute the agency alone but must have aid at the point where the note or paper becomes due. If the correspondent bank is a subagent, then the home bank is liable for its acts the same as for its own; but if the home bank has the authority to appoint the correspondent bank an agent for the principal, the correspondent bank is liable directly to the principal, and the home bank, if it used care in appointing the agent, is exonerated.

In New York, Michigan, and some other states the first theory is held.

Allen v. Merchants Bank, 22 Wend. (N.Y.) 215, is a case in which a draft was drawn by plaintiff in New York on a Philadelphia merchant and deposited by plaintiff in the Merchants Bank of New York. Defendant bank sent the draft to the Philadelphia bank. It was presented by the Philadelphia bank notary, but he did not properly protest it, and because of the lack of proper protest, plaintiff lost. It was held that the bank receiving a draft is liable for any neglect of duty in collection, whether arising from default of its officers, its correspondents abroad, or the agents of said correspondents.

The second theory is held in Iowa, Massachusetts, Pennsylvania, and other states.

In Guelich v. National State Bank, 56 Iowa 434, a bill of exchange was deposited with defendant bank of Burlington, Iowa, against a New York party. Defendant sent it to the Metropolitan Bank of New York for collection. This bank failed to present it for payment and protest in proper time. It was held that when the holder of a bill of exchange, payable at a distance, deposits it in a local bank for collection, he thereby assents to the course of business of banks to collect through correspondents, and the correspondent bank becomes his agent and is responsible to him directly for its negligence in failing to present the bill within the proper time.

Gratuitous Agent. In such a case the promise, being without consideration, is not enforceable, and the agent cannot be held liable for neglecting or refusing to perform.

In Thorne v. Deas, 4 Johns (N.Y.) 84, A and B were joint owners of a vessel. A voluntarily undertook to get the vessel insured but neglected to do so, and the vessel was lost. It was held that no action would lie against A for his non-performance, though damage resulted to B, as there was no consideration for A's promise.

But if the agent enters upon performance of the undertaking, he is bound to exercise skill and care in what he does.

In Williams v. Higgins, 30 Md. 404, a party undertook voluntarily and gratuitously to invest money for another. It was held that the gratuitous agent must use due diligence and exercise proper caution or he will be liable, and if he is given positive instructions, he will be liable if he disregards them.

The question of gratuitous agent comes up in the case of bank directors who fill their offices without compensation.

Delano v. Case, 121 Ill. 247, held that if bank directors are guilty of negligence in permitting their bank to be held out to the public as solvent when in fact it is insolvent and thereby induce parties to deposit their money there and it is lost, such depositors may recover from the directors, as they are bound to exercise care and diligence in their offices.

OBLIGATION OF PRINCIPAL
TO THIRD PARTY

Scope of Authority. The main purpose of agency is to effect
a contractual relation between the principal and the third party.
The identity of the principal may be disclosed or it may be withheld. In the case of either a disclosed or an undisclosed principal
is bound by such acts of the agent as are within the actual or
apparent scope of his authority.

A question difficult to answer is, What is the scope of authority of the agent? If the principal clothes the agent with apparent
authority to do an act, the principal is bound, although the agent
had private instruction to the contrary or had a limit put on his
authority.

A doctor might employ an agent to buy him a particular horse.
The agent has no apparent authority to buy a team or any other
horse. But when a stock dealer employs an agent to buy horses
for him, the agent has apparent authority to buy a team, although
he may have had private instructions to the contrary. The one is
clearly a special and the other a general agent.

It seems settled that when the agent has apparent authority,
the principal is bound. It is only required that the person dealing
with the agent, acting with average prudence and in good faith,
be justified in believing that the agent possesses the necessary
authority.

Notice to Agent. It is the rule that notice to the agent of anything within the scope of the agency is notice also to the principal. And the principal is chargeable with knowledge of all the
facts that have been brought to his agent's attention in the transaction in which the agent is acting for the principal.

Unless this were so, the principal would be in a position to
claim ignorance in whatever he might wish to do, and therefore
would be in a better position than if he dealt with the third party
directly.

LIABILITY OF PRINCIPAL FOR
TORTS OR WRONGS OF AGENT

General Rule. The principal is liable for the contractual
obligations of his agent in his behalf, and there are various ways

in which he can be rendered liable by the agent for the agent's torts or wrongful acts.

The rule is that the principal is liable for the wrongs committed by the agent in the course of his employment and for the principal's benefit.

This is true where the principal commands or ratifies the act, and we find that it is also true where the principal neither ratifies nor commands it. The law considers that when a person chooses to conduct his affairs through another, he must see that they are managed with due regard for the rights and safety of others.

Dempsey v. Chambers, 154 Mass. 330, was an action for damages in breaking a plate-glass window. It was proved that the party delivering coal for defendants and who in doing so broke the window was not authorized to deliver coal for them, and they did not know of his doing it. Later, after they knew of the broken window, they presented a bill for the coal. It was held that by ratifying the acts of this man they became liable for his negligent acts.

Fraud and Negligence. Fraud is a wrong of frequent occurrence in the relation of agency, the agent having made false and fraudulent representations in carrying out his principal's business. It is the general holding that the principal is liable for the agent's fraud in the course of the principal's business and for his benefit.

Negligence of the agent is among the wrongs for which the principal is liable, if such negligence was committed in the ordinary discharge of the agency.

In Brady v. Railroad Co., 34 Barb. (N.Y.) 249, an agent failed for four days to present a draft, and the party drawn on failed. It was held that the principal was liable for his agent's negligence in not presenting the draft in proper time.

When the wrong is committed by the agent in the course of his employment, and even to benefit himself personally and not his principal, some authorities hold that the principal is nevertheless liable.

In Cobb v. Railroad Co., 37 S.C. 194, an engineer willfully and unnecessarily blew the whistle and frightened a horse. It was held that the railroad company was liable for acts done by its engineer maliciously, wantonly, and willfully while in the exercise of his duties, whether in the course of his employment or not.

Others hold that the principal is not liable.

In Stephenson v. Southern Pacific Co., 93 Cal. 558, a railway engineer intentionally and wantonly backed his engine toward a streetcar that was crossing the track, with the simple intent of frightening the passengers, without colliding with the car. As a result plaintiff, a passenger, was frightened and jumped from the car and was injured. It was held that the act of the engineer was without any reference to the service for which he was employed, and not for the purpose of performing his employer's work, and that the principal was not responsible.

Malicious Wrongs. The principal is not liable for the malicious wrongs or crimes of the agent unless he expressly authorized the same. There is an old exception to this in the case of laws or statutes which are said to be in the nature of police regulations designed to promote the safety and health of the community. The principal is here liable, even though the agent directly acts contrary to instructions and without the principal's knowledge and consent. Laws regulating the speed of automobiles on public roads and laws prohibiting the selling of liquor on Sunday or to children are examples.

Commonwealth v. Kelley, 140 Mass. 441, relates to a statute which prohibited the closing on Sunday of curtains and blinds, so as to obscure the interior of premises where liquor was sold. The owner had given instructions that they be kept open, but the bartender, without his knowledge, closed them. It was held that the owner was liable. The statute forbade him to do the prohibited act or to permit it to be done, and it included the acts of his servants as well as his own.

OBLIGATION OF THIRD PARTY
TO PRINCIPAL

The third party is liable to the principal for contracts entered into with the agent within the agent's authority or subsequently ratified by the principal.

The third party is also liable to the principal for moneys or property obtained from the agent by duress or fraud; hence if an agent is compelled to pay illegal charges to protect his principal's interest, the principal may recover from the third party.

The third party may also be liable to the principal for fraud or wrong, or for collusion with the agent to injure the principal. Mayer v. Lever, I Q B 168, is an English case in which plaintiff was the proprietor of gas works. It was the duty of the company's manager to obtain and recommend bids for coal and supplies. Defendant bribed him to recommend his bid and added the price of the bribe to the bid. In an action against them it was held that plaintiff could recover the damages from the agent who had accepted the bribe, or from defendant, who had given it. They were joint wrongdoers and could be held jointly or severally.

The third party is also liable for unlawfully interfering with the agent in the performance of his duties as agent.

In Railroad Co. v. Hunt, 55 Vt. 570, it was held that maliciously to cause the arrest of plaintiff's engineer while running a train and then to delay the train and thereby damage the company was actionable, and the railroad company could recover for such damages from the person so causing the arrest.

OBLIGATION OF AGENT TO THIRD PARTY

When an agent makes a contract on behalf of his principal, he may in certain cases bind himself. If he holds himself out as having authority to act for a principal in a transaction in which he has no such authority, he is liable to the third party for damages suffered.

In Kroeger v. Pitcairn, 101 Pa. St. 311, A, agent for an insurance company, obtained and delivered to B a policy of insurance on B's store, containing a clause that no petroleum be kept on the premises. B told A it was necessary to keep a little, and A assured him that if he only kept a barrel, it need not be noted in the policy and was all right. The store burned, and B could not recover, because he had the barrel of petroleum. It was held that A, the agent, was liable, as he had given positive assurance in excess of his authority.

The agent is also presumed to represent not only that he has authority but that his principal is competent to give such authority.

Where there is no real principal, but the one so represented is fictitious, the agent himself becomes the principal and is liable as such.

Lewis v. Tilton, 64 Iowa 220, held that an unincorporated organization cannot be a party to a contract and that persons contracting in the name of such an organization are themselves personally liable either as being themselves in fact principals or as holding themselves out as agents for a principal which never in law existed.

In some instances the agent expressly pledges his credit, and he is then liable.

TERMINATION OF RELATION OF PRINCIPAL AND AGENT

The agency may be terminated by limitation, by acts of the parties, or by a change in the condition of the parties.

By Limitation. If the contract of agency is by its terms to continue for but a limited time, the agency terminates when the time expires; or if the particular business for which the agency was created has been completed, the agency is terminated.

In Moore v. Stone, 40 Iowa 259, an agent was employed to negotiate for the purchase of certain land. He obtained the contract for the conveyance, the first payment was made, and the agent was paid for his services. It was held that the agency was terminated when the object for which the agency was created had been accomplished. Here the agent, after he was paid for his services, bought in the property at a tax sale, and plaintiff sought to set it aside on the ground that he was still his agent, but the court refused to interfere.

By Act of Parties. Under certain conditions either party may terminate the relation. This may be done by mutual agreement, by the principal revoking the agent's authority, or by the agent renouncing the agency.

Since the principal appoints the agent and the relation is one of confidence for his own protection, he has the power to terminate it at will. It is therefore the general rule that the principal may terminate the agent's authority at any time and with or without good cause. This gives the agent a claim for damages if the agency is revoked contrary to agreement. We should note the distinction between the power to terminate the agency and the right to terminate it. The principal generally has the power, but if it violates an agreement with the agent, he does not have the right to terminate the agency, and he is therefore liable to the agent for damages.

In Standard Oil Co. v. Gilbert, 84 Ga. 714, there was a written contract for one year fixing the agent's compensation. This was renewed the next year, and from then on was lived up to, but nothing was said about the agreement. It was held that there was a tacit renewal from year to year and that the principal could not during the year deprive the agent of his salary, before expiration of the year. Though the power of revocation existed, the right to revoke did not exist.

Revocation of the agency by the principal need not be made in any formal way; it may be made by oral instructions or by written notice. It may be implied by the conditions; as when a principal gives an agent authority to sell his house and before the agency is executed it is destroyed by fire, in which case a revocation must be implied.

A revocation is binding only upon those who have notice of it. The principal must therefore give notice not only to the agent but to those who on the strength of the previous authority are likely to deal with him; otherwise he may be held for the acts of the agent after the revocation.

There is a class of cases in which the principal has no authority to revoke the agency. Here, it is said, the agency is coupled with an interest; as where the agent has an interest in the subject matter of the agency by way of security. For example, when a person has possession of personal property with power to sell and apply the proceeds to payment of a debt due the agent, such a case constitutes a power coupled with an interest.

In Knapp v. Alvord, 10 Paige Ch. (N.Y.) 205, a cabinetmaker, on going abroad, employed an agent to carry out his business and gave him full and entire control of his property, with written power to sell any or all of the furniture or stock and to apply the proceeds to the security or payment of a certain note, endorsed by said agent and a third party, or for any renewals upon which the agent might become liable. It was held that the agent had a power coupled with an interest which survived the principal's death and that the agent could sell after such death.

As to the right of the agent to renounce the agency, it seems that he has also the power but not the right to renounce at will. It may be either express or implied; as, if the agent abandons his work, the principal may consider the agency renounced.

By Change in Condition of Parties. The agency may also terminate by a change in the condition of the parties.

DEATH. The death of either the principal or the agent terminates the agency, and it no longer is binding on the estate of the deceased or of the survivor. In this case no notice of termination need be given to third parties. The agency terminates upon the principal's death, and any contract made thereafter by the agent is a nullity.

Farmers Loan and Trust Co. v. Wilson, 139 N.Y. 284, held that the power of an agent to collect rent due his principal ceased upon the principal's death unless the agency was coupled with an interest. And payments made thereafter did not bind the principal's estate, although made in ignorance of his death.

INSANITY. If either the principal or the agent becomes insane, the effect is to terminate the agency, as the principal is no longer competent to enter into a contract, or the agent is not competent to carry out the principal's intentions. But if the principal has not legally been declared insane, persons dealing with the agent in ignorance of his insanity are protected. Any other cause that may render the agent incompetent to carry out his duties, as his illness or imprisonment, terminates the agency.

BANKRUPTCY. Mere insolvency of either party does not affect the agency, but it will be terminated when either party becomes technically bankrupt, because when a party becomes a bankrupt his property passes out of his hands and he is unable to carry out any contract in reference to it. The above rule does not apply, however, when the agency is coupled with an interest. In the case of bankruptcy of the agent his authority ceases except to perform some formal act not involving the transfer of any property.

MARRIAGE. Under common law many restrictions were placed about a married woman, the control of her property passing to her husband. Consequently, upon her marriage, any contract of agency in which she was principal was dissolved, as she no longer had the power to deal with her own property. But every state has passed laws enlarging the rights of married women and in most instances giving them full power to own and manage their property and to carry on their own separate business. The result is that a married woman may appoint agents, and the act of marrying does not affect her status in a business way and therefore has no effect on the relation of principal and agent, nor does it dissolve an agency then existing.

WAR. It is the general law in the different states of this country that the existence of a state of war between the country of the principal and that of the agent terminates the agency. This is because of the rule prohibiting all trading or commercial intercourse between two countries at war.

VII. BAILMENT

IN GENERAL

Definition. Bailment is the delivery of some chattel by one party to another, to be held according to the special purpose of delivery, and to be returned or redelivered when that special purpose is accomplished. A bailment differs from a sale in that title to the property does not pass in a bailment. Practically every case in which one receives and holds or handles the property of another, without buying it or receiving it as a gift, is a case of bailment. When one borrows or lends a book, hires a car, or sends a package by express, he is within the rules of a bailment. Where possession and not title has passed to the vendee (as was learned in Sales), the vendee holds as bailee; for instance, when property is taken on trial.

Hunt v. Wyman, 100 Mass. 198, was an action for the price of a horse. Plaintiff had the horse for sale and agreed to let defendant take it and try it; if he did not like it, he was to return it, on the night of the day he took it, in as good condition as he got it. Almost as soon as the horse was delivered to defendant's servant, it escaped from him without the servant's fault and was injured so that defendant could not try it. The horse was not returned in the time stated. It was held to be a bailment and not a sale; therefore plaintiff could not recover.

In Nelson v. Brown, 44 Iowa 455, it was held that a contract acknowledging receipt of grain for storage, "loss by fire and the elements at the owner's risk," with the option to the party receipting for it to return grain of equal test and value, constitutes a bailment which is converted into a sale whenever the bailee disposes of the grain.

The parties to a bailment are the bailor, or the owner of the chattel who delivers it over, and the bailee, who is the party vested with temporary custody of the chattel.

Classification. Bailments are generally classified according to Roman law under five heads.

1. Deposit: a bailment of goods to be kept by the bailee gratuitously for the benefit of the bailor.

2. Mandate: a delivery of goods to the bailee who is to do something to them gratis.

3. Loan for use: a loan of personal property for the benefit of the bailee without recompense.

4. Pledge or pawn: a bailment as security for a debt.

5. Hiring: the loaning of a chattel for a consideration or reward.

Another and more practical division of the subject of bailment is made according to the benefit or recompense, as follows:

1. Bailment for the benefit of the bailor: deposit and mandate.

2. Bailment for the benefit of the bailee: loan for use.

3. Bailment for the benefit of both the bailor and bailee: pledge and hiring.

The last bailment, for the mutual benefit of both parties, is again classified as ordinary and exceptional. Exceptional bailments are those of postmaster, innkeeper, and common carrier; all other bailments for the mutual benefit of bailor and bailee are ordinary bailments.

Degrees of Diligence and Care. In all bailments a certain degree of diligence or care is requested of the bailee. Lack of it is termed negligence and renders the bailee liable.

By early authorities the diligence or care required of the bailee was classified into degrees, and to a certain extent this division is still adhered to. Absence of the required diligence renders one liable for negligence. Where the bailment is for the benefit of the bailor alone, no benefit or remuneration accruing to the bailee, it is not expected or required of the bailee that he exercise the degree of care or diligence necessary when he is paid for his services. So it is said he is bound to excercise slight diligence toward the property in his care and is liable for gross negligence.

In a bailment for the benefit of both parties, a benefit accrues to the bailee, and a greater degree of diligence is demanded of him than in the former case; therefore it is required that he exercise ordinary diligence, and he is liable for ordinary negligence.

The bailment for the sole benefit of the bailee being without any benefit to the bailor imposes on the bailee a greater degree of diligence than in either of the other cases, and it is said that great diligence is exacted of him, while he is answerable for even slight negligence.

Ordinary care is the care which persons of ordinary prudence under like circumstances are wont to bestow on their own property of like description. Slight degree of care is something less than ordinary care, yet not amounting to utter disregard of the property. It may be said to be the care that might be exercised by a very careless person. Great care or diligence, on the other hand, is that which would be exercised under similar circumstances by a more than ordinarily prudent and careful person.

In First National Bank v. Ocean National Bank, 60 N.Y. 278, plaintiff deposited bonds in defendant's vault for safekeeping, and defendant charged nothing. The vault was burglarized, and the bonds were stolen. The court held that a gratuitous bailee is liable only for gross negligence and is not bound to take any special or extraordinary measures for the security of the property intrusted to him.

In Mariner v. Smith, 5 Heisk (Tenn.) 203, Smith left $900 in gold at the counting house of Mariner & Curtis to be sold if 50 per cent premium could be had. The gold was placed in the presence of Smith in the safe of Mariner & Curtis where the firm kept their own money. The safe was afterwards broken open, and the gold, as well as the money belonging to Mariner & Curtis, was taken. The court held that the question whether the bailment was for reward or not depended on the intention and contract of the parties. The liability of a bailee without reward is to be determined by his bona fide performance of the fairly understood terms of the contract, which will be ascertained by the express contract explained by the surrounding circumstances, or by failure to perform the terms of the contract as it was understood by the parties at the time.

Besides the degree of care or diligence demanded of the bailee, the law requires that he act honestly and in good faith. He must not abuse his trust, nor sell, pledge, or otherwise deal with the property in his hands as if he were the owner.

Tortious Bailee. A tortious bailee is one who holds the possession of the property through an unlawful or wrongful act, as theft, trespass, or fraud, or having received it in a rightful way, misappropriates or applies it to a use other than that intended. He is liable to account absolutely for the property, and although it may be injured or lost while in his possession but without his fault, he must nevertheless account for it.

A thief who steals a horse, and while driving it is run into by a runaway team which kills the horse, is liable for the value of the horse, although he was guilty of no negligence. Or if a man hires a car to drive to Aurora, Illinois, and instead goes to Waukegan, Illinois, and on the way the car is damaged without the fault of the bailee, still he is absolutely liable.

In Fisher v. Kyle, 27 Mich. 454, defendant hired a horse of plaintiff to drive to a certain place. He drove beyond that place, and the horse fell dead while being driven. Defendant was held liable for the value of the horse. A person who hires a horse for a specific journey and drives him beyond that journey takes upon himself all the consequences of such additional drive and is liable if the horse dies while being so driven.

Liability Varied by Contract. As a general rule the parties to a bailment may by contract vary their rights or liabilities, making the liability of the bailee either greater or less than it would otherwise be, except that the law will not allow the bailee to be exempt, even by contract, for the consequences of his own willful misconduct.

In Archer v. Walker, 38 Ind. 472, A and B were partners in the banking business. To enable the firm to draw sight drafts on New York they borrowed from B a number of U.S. bonds and deposited them in New York as collateral security against overdrafts. The firm expressly agreed in writing that the bonds were "to be returned or accounted for to B." The bonds were stolen from the bailee in New York. It was held that the firm was liable to B for the loss.

BAILMENT FOR BAILOR'S SOLE BENEFIT

Deposit and Mandate. This is a common kind of bailment in everyday life. Every undertaking of a friend or neighbor to hold or convey an article of personal property gratuitously and as a favor comes under this class. A man may gratuitously take the chattel belonging to another to keep it in his custody. To illustrate, A stores B's car in his garage gratuitously; or he takes it to perform some work upon it, as to paint it, without charge; or it may be he carries it from one place to another, as to take B's car home with him. A bailment for the bailor's benefit may come under any one of these three classes, or it may combine two or all of them.

Two divisions of Roman law are included under this head. They are deposit, which is the placing of a chattel with the bailee to be kept by him without pay; and mandate, which is the bailment of a chattel on which the bailee is to do something gratuitously.

Liability of Bailee. An agreement by the bailee to carry out the gratuitous bailment cannot be enforced, because of lack of consideration, but when the bailee receives the property and carries out the bailment, he is bound to do it with care, and he will be liable for gross negligence or for wrongful acts in relation thereto. The act of the bailor in surrendering possession of the chattel on the faith of the bailee's undertaking furnishes sufficient consideration. A person who finds property and takes it into his possession is a gratuitous bailee and is bound to care for it as such.

It is often hard to determine whether a bailment is gratuitous or for the mutual benefit of the parties; that is, whether or not the bailee is entitled to compensation. The original intention of the parties is the test. If the bailee receives the chattel in the usual course of his business, and business usage and his ordinary method of dealing give him the right to demand compensation, the bailment is not considered gratuitous, even though nothing was said about compensation.

Pattison v. Syracuse National Bank, 4 T & C. (N.Y.) 96, was an action to recover the value of bonds stolen from defendant's bank, where they had been deposited by plaintiff for safekeeping. Nothing was said about compensation at the time of deposit. It was held that if defendant had the right to demand compensation by its course of dealings with depositors, the bailment was not gratuitous. The degree of diligence required of defendant depended on whether or not the bailment was gratuitous.

But if the bailee undertakes the service for a near relative or a personal friend, or out of mere charity or mere favor, and if the trust puts him to but little trouble and the bailment is out of his usual course of business, it is presumed to be without compensation.

In Dart v. Lowe, 5 Ind. 131, plaintiff, a merchant in Peru, Indiana, being about to go to Cincinnati, had placed in his hands by Thayer, another merchant, $81 with which to buy goods for Thayer. When Thayer handed plaintiff the money, he remarked that he would rather pay him for his trouble than go himself. To this plaintiff made no reply. This, with other money, was stolen from plaintiff on his way and through no negligence on his part. Plaintiff bought goods on credit for Thayer and charged him nothing for his services as buyer. The question arose whether it was a bailment for hire or a gratuitous bailment. The court held that to render the bailee liable for negligence as a bailee for reward when he is acting within the scope of his ordinary occupation, it must be expressly proved that he was to receive compensation; it further held that when a bailment is for the sole benefit of the bailor, the law requires only slight diligence and makes the bailee liable only for gross negligence.

Bailment Through Agent. Either party to a contract of bailment may act through an agent, and delivery to the agent of the bailee is delivery to the bailee.

Degree of Care Necessary. This class of bailment requires only the lowest degree of care and diligence of the bailee, which is slight care, and he is not held liable for loss or injury unless guilty of gross negligence, as was held in Dart v. Lowe.

Griffith v. Lipperwick, 28 Ohio St. 388, was an action to recover the value of certain government bonds deposited with plaintiff, with defendants as gratuitous bailees, and stolen from defendant's banking house. The bonds when deposited were in a tin box, the key of which was retained by plaintiff. Defendants had a small burglar-proof safe in which they kept similar bonds of their own and other depositors, but plaintiff's and similar bonds of another depositor were kept outside, the other depositor consenting that his should so be kept. It was held to be a question for the jury whether this was gross negligence. Good faith generally requires that such bailee should keep the goods entrusted to him with as much care as he ordinarily keeps his own of the same kind, and he should also keep them with such degree of care as would be reasonable considering the nature of the goods and the circumstances of the bailment.

McKay v. Hamblin, 40 Miss. 472, held that when there is no contract for the safekeeping of property and no compensation agreed to be paid for its custody, the party in possession is a mere depositary and in the event of loss is liable only for gross neglect.

Ordinary care may be defined as the care which a prudent man takes of his own property; less care might be expected when the bailor knows the bailee's habits and the place in which he is to keep, or the manner in which he is to handle, the goods, for when he knows these conditions the law presumes that he agrees that the goods be so treated.

Coggs v. Bernard, 2 Ld. Raymond 909, is an English case decided about the year 1700. Defendant, it seemed, undertook without compensation to move some casks of brandy from one place to another, but by his carelessness a quantity was spilled. It was held that when a man undertakes to carry goods safely and securely, he is responsible for any damage they may sustain in the carriage through his negligence, although he is not a common carrier and is to have nothing for his services.

In Spooner v. Mattoon, 40 Vt. 300, plaintiff and defendant were soldiers in camp, occupying tents ten rods apart. Plaintiff had considerable money, and fearing it might not be safe, left it with his friend, the defendant, without expectation of reward, for safekeeping. For two nights he so left it, and came for it each morning. On the third morning he did not call for it, and defendant started for plaintiff's tent with the money. He put it under his arm inside his vest, so that the pocketbook would not be seen. It slipped out and was lost. It was held that the defendant was not guilty of gross negligence and so was not liable.

A gratuitous bailee is under no absolute rule about just how he must care for the chattel under his charge. Circumstances control; different care is required of a person who receives a watch or a valuable vase from that of a person who receives a truck or a load of stone. It is said that a gratuitous bailment seldom demands skilled labor or care, and the gratuitous bailee is excused from the results of inevitable accident, accidental fire, etc.

Use of Property. A gratuitous bailee cannot make any use of the thing bailed except for the bailor's benefit. When the bailee accepts custody of an animal, he undertakes to feed and care for it. Proper care requires him to drive a horse, milk a cow, etc., but the profit derived from the use of the animal in this class of bailments go to the bailor. The bailee has the right to incur such expenses in caring for the thing bailed as are necessary.

In Devalcourt v. Dillon, 12 La. An. 672, A deposited in the hands of B merchandise to be sold, the proceeds to be applied on a debt which he owed to B. It was held that whatever useful and necessary expenses B incurred in fulfilling the bailment were chargeable to A.

Termination. This kind of bailment is terminated either by accomplishment of the purpose of the bailment or by express act of either party. The bailee may surrender the article bailed and so end the relation, or the bailor may demand and recover the chattel. When the bailment is for the purpose of accomplishing some act, as the delivery of a chattel from one place to another, the bailee after undertaking the bailment must accomplish it with at least slight care or be responsible for breach of contract. But by mutual assent the bailment may be ended at any time. Delivery of the identical chattel is necessary. If it is in better condition, the bailee derives no benefit, and if it is in worse, it is not his loss unless due to his gross negligence. If it is lost, he is liable so far as the loss is due to his lack of slight diligence and care.

BAILMENT FOR BAILEE'S SOLE BENEFIT

Definition. This kind of bailment consists in a gratuitous loan for use. The bailee is what we call the borrower. When a man lends his car or his bicycle to a friend to use, to be returned afterward, the loan is a bailment for the benefit solely of the bailee.

The bailor must voluntarily give possession of the article to the bailee without asking any recompense for its use. This bailment must be distinguished from the loan of something that is to be consumed and afterward paid back in kind, as flour or grain, which was under Roman law *mutuum*, "loan for consumption," but which is in fact no bailment at all but a barter; that is, the exchange of the particular property for another of like kind. The loan may be for a definite period or at the will of the bailor, who may end it whenever he pleases.

In Clapp v. Nelson, 12 Texas 370, plaintiff sued to recover possession of a wagon and two mules which he had loaned to defendant for "a day or two" but which defendant had neglected to return. It was held that when property is loaned for a definite period or for a day or two or a week or two, if it is not returned at the end of the longer period, the lender can bring an action for it without first making a demand for the property.

Responsibility of Bailee. The bailee being the only one benefited, the duty devolves upon him to exercise the highest degree of care or diligence in use of the chattel, and he is responsible for every loss occasioned by even slight negligence.

In Hagebush v. Ragland, 78 Ill. 40, defendant borrowed a horse of plaintiff to drive on a visit to his brother, and when the horse was returned it was so injured that it died. The court held defendant liable; it said that when an animal is borrowed without hire, the borrower is bound to take extraordinary care of it, and if failure of such duty results in injury to the lender, the borrower will be liable.

Bennett v. O'Brien, 37 Ill. 250, held that when the loan of domestic animals necessarily involves their keeping, the expense thus incurred by the borrower is not a compensation to the lender which changes the gratuitous character of the bailment. In a suit brought by the lender against the borrower of a horse which dies in the possession of the latter, it devolves upon the borrower to show that he exercised extraordinary care toward the property borrowed.

Wood v. McClure, 7 Ind. 155, held that the borrower is to use extraordinary diligence in regard to property loaned to him and is responsible for the slighest neglect; but if the property perishes or is lost or damaged without any blame or neglect on his part, the owner must sustain the loss.

Great diligence is such as one more than ordinarily careful would bestow on his property under like circumstances. Such high degree of care being required of the gratuitous bailee, he is held strictly to the terms of the bailment, and when he deviates from these terms he is liable for loss or damage ensuing.

In Martin v. Cuthbertson, 64 N.C. 328, plaintiff borrowed a

horse to ride to the residence of one Cline and return the next day, but instead he rode a mile and a half farther and in a different direction. The horse died during its absence on the third day after leaving home. It was admitted that there was no negligence. It was held that without regard to the question of negligence the bailee is liable for any injury which results from his departure from the contract.

But where the borrower, while the chattel is within the terms of the bailment, encounters some accident whereby the thing loaned is injured or lost without even slight negligence on his part, he is not liable.

Watkins v. Roberts, 28 Ind. 167, was an action for the value of a horse loaned by plaintiff to defendant. The defense was that while defendant who had borrowed the horse to go to a certain place and return was on his way, and without any fault or negligence on his part, he was met by some cavalry soldiers of the United States, who forcibly took the horse from him. It was held to be a good defense, rendering defendant free from liability.

If the chattel is injured or destroyed by inevitable accident or by fire, or if it is an animal and dies a natural death, the loss will not fall upon the bailee unless he is in fault.

In Beller v. Schultz, 44 Mich. 529, plaintiff loaned a flag to defendant. After it was hoisted, a hailstorm came up and damaged it. It was held that in the absence of proof that defendant had failed to take due care of the flag he was not liable. A borrower of property is not an insurer, even though it is gratuitously loaned.

Use of Property. This class of bailment carries with it the right to use the chattel subject to such conditions and limitations as the bailor may be reasonably supposed to have made. Such expense as may be necessary to preserve the chattel while in use is to be paid by the borrower, as for feeding and sheltering a horse or other domestic animal and for the gasoline, oil and garage rent of an automobile. But any extraordinary expense which wholly preserves the property for the owner may properly be chargeable to the bailor.

As soon as the bailment is ended, either by expiration of the term, act of the bailor, or mutual agreement of the parties, the borrower must immediately deliver the property to the bailor or his order.

BAILMENT FOR MUTUAL BENEFIT

Definition. This kind of bailment differs from those just considered in that the benefits derived are mutual instead of being confined to one side. It is a business transaction rather than an act of favor or friendship.

This kind of bailment may consist in (1) hired service about a chattel, (2) hired use of a chattel, or (3) pledge or pawn.

In mutual-benefit bailments it is essential that there be remuneration for use of the chattel or for work to be imparted upon it. The amount may be definitely fixed, or in the absence of an agreed price, it may be such as shall be determined to be just and reasonable.

In Chamberlin v. Cobb, 32 Iowa 161, plaintiff owned a horse for which he had no use, and to avoid the expense of keeping it, requested defendant to take it and to do his work with it in consideration of its feed and keep. It was held to be not a mere gratuitous loan, under which defendant would be required to exercise extraordinary care, but a contract for the mutual benefit of both parties, under which defendant was required to exercise ordinary care in the keeping and care of the animal.

As in all other bailments, possession of the chattel must be entrusted to the bailee, and as in other contracts, the parties must be competent to contract and the object of the bailment must be legal.

Hired Service About Chattel. In hired service about the chattel the bailment may be for the purpose of having the chattel stored or cared for or for the purpose of having work performed on it or for the purpose of having it carried from place to place. Among the hired custodians who store or care for property are safe depositaries, who for a consideration keep valuables in a safe place, and warehousemen, who for a certain charge keep goods and merchandise in storage. Hired work on a chattel includes that of the garage mechanic who takes a car to repair it, of the watchmaker who takes a watch to adjust it, and of other classes of mechanics who receive chattels to bestow labor of different kinds on them. Hired carriage of a chattel may be performed by a private carrier who for hire undertakes to transport a particular chattel or by a public or common carrier, who follows as a business the conveying of chattels or persons. Private carriers are within the usual rules of a mutual-benefit bailment, while public carriers, including railroads, airlines, and express companies, come within a special class, having exceptional liabilities imposed upon them by law.

Pennewill v. Cullen, 5 Harr. (Del.) 238, was an action against the owner of a boat for damage to a load of corn spoiled by water getting into it. Defendant's boat was generally employed to carry coal for a certain party from Philadelphia to New York and on returning to bring lime to defendant. Three or four times the boat had carried loads for other parties. The question was whether defendant was liable as a common carrier. The court held the test to be whether or not defendant held himself out to the public as engaged in the business of a common carrier. It was not necessary that his trips be regular between the same places. If engaged in the business of carrying grain for others generally to and from any point, he was a common carrier; but if he kept his vessel for his own use, he was not liable as a common carrier, even though he chartered or hired it to another by special agreement.

In bailment for hire the degree of care and diligence required of the bailee is said to be ordinary diligence, or such care as a prudent person exercises toward his own property under like circumstances. He is therefore liable for loss or injury to the chattel caused by ordinary negligence or failure to bestow ordinary care and diligence.

In Jones v. Morgan, 90 N.Y. 4, plaintiff stored certain household goods in a building owned by defendant and rented by him for that purpose. Plaintiff had a room allotted to her. Most of the goods were stolen by employees in charge of the buildings. It was held that defendant was a bailee for hire and bound to exercise ordinary care and prudence. Plaintiff was given judgment.

In Maynard v. Buck, 100 Mass. 40, defendant was a drover who received cattle to drive from Brighton to Worcester for hire. He received two head of cattle from plaintiff, and while he was driving them, the herd became frightened by a train and the two wandered away. It was held that defendant was bound to use the same care in regard to the cattle that men of ordinary prudence would exercise over their own property under the same circumstances. Plaintiff recovered.

When the chattel is in possession of a workman employed in working on it and it is destroyed by inevitable accident or through some natural cause and without any fault on his part, he will not be liable.

A greater degree of care is required of the safe depositary who stores jewelry or valuables than is required of a cattle keeper. So the exact care and precaution of the bailee depends much on the circumstance of the particular case.

Moorehead v. Brown, 51 N.C. 367, is a case in which a bailee, to store and keep cotton for hire, permitted it to remain with the roping of the bagging torn and the under portion in mud and water so that it became stained and much of it was destroyed. The court held that there was want of ordinary care and that defendant was liable.

A keeper of race horses who carelessly leaves doors or gates open so that the animals are lost or injured can be held liable.

In Swann v. Brown, 51 N.C. 150, defendant, keeper of a livery stable, permitted the owner of certain horses to go into the stable at a late hour of the night and take them out, in consequence of which a horse belonging to plaintiff made his escape and was lost either by passing out with the other horses or afterward, as the door was left partly open. It was held that defendant was guilty of lack of ordinary care and was liable. Ordinary care was said to be that degree of care which under the same circumstances a person of ordinary prudence would take of the particular thing were it his own.

When the bailee is to perform some work on the chattel, he must exercise such skill as a prudent workman of the same class would in a similar undertaking. And for failure to exercise ordinary skill he will be liable as for lack of ordinary diligence.

In Smith v. Meegan, 22 Mo. 150, defendant took plaintiff's boat to make certain repairs upon it. It was held that he was bound to use ordinary diligence in care of the boat and was liable for any damages to it occasioned by launching it into the river at a time and under circumstances of great danger, which ought to have been foreseen and which resulted in destruction of the boat.

Thus it is apparent that the skill required in different cases varies greatly according to the nature of the work required; but in all cases honesty and good faith are required of the bailee.

The bailee for hire has the right to undisturbed possession of the chattel while accomplishing the purposes of the bailment; and when the work is finished, he has the right to demand suitable compensation. The compensation may be fixed in advance or left to be computed later on the basis of what is just and reasonable.

Redelivery. When the service required by the bailment has been completed, it is the bailee's duty to deliver the chattel to the bailor, and it is the bailor's duty to pay the compensation. Delivery back must be to the bailor, to his agent, or to his order. It is customary for warehousemen who conduct places of storage, also wharfingers who keep wharves on which goods are received and shipped for hire, to give to the bailor, or owner of the goods, at the time the goods are delivered a receipt known as a warehouse or wharfinger's receipt. These receipts are generally considered as representing one person to another, and the warehouseman is held to be the bailee of the person to whom the receipt is transferred.

Dodge v. Meyer, 61 Cal. 405, held that a bill of lading represents the property for which it is given and that by its endorsement, or delivery without endorsement, the property in the goods may be transferred where such is the intent in making the endorsement or delivery.

Lien. Although it is the duty of the bailee to deliver back the chattel, still he may keep possession until he is paid for his services on the chattel or payment has been tendered to him. The bailee is therefore said to have a lien on the chattels for his services.

Harris v. Woodruff, 124 Mass. 205, held that a person has a lien for the expenses incurred and skill bestowed on a horse delivered to him to be trained to take part in running races.

Lowe v. Martin, 18 Ill. 286, held that a warehouseman has a lien for proper charges on grain in his warehouse and may retain possession of it to secure payment of such charges.

This lien holds only for service bestowed on the particular chattel and lasts only while the bailee retains possession.

In Tucker v. Taylor, 53 Ind. 93, defendant, a mechanic, received a wagon for repair. In payment for his labor he was to have use of the wagon and a horse to take a journey. After the work was done, defendant permitted the owner to take the wagon with the understanding that it was to be returned at a later day and the horse sent with it so that he could make the journey. The owner having failed to furnish the horse and wagon, defendant asserted his lien and sold the wagon. This action was brought by the original owner to recover the wagon. It was held that defendant lost his lien when he relinquished possession of the wagon to the owner. The court also held that there was no lien if the agreement was that the labor be paid for on a future day.

Hired Use of Chattel. The hiring of a chattel for use is often illustrated in daily transactions. The hiring of a car at a garage or the hiring of a rowboat on a lake is in this class. After the contract is made, it is the bailor's duty to deliver the chattel and to allow the bailee or hirer to have possession for the agreed purpose or during the stated time.

In Hickok v. Buck, 22 Vt. 149, defendant leased to plaintiff a farm for one year and agreed to provide a horse for plaintiff to use during the term. He furnished a horse at first, but took it away and sold it before expiration of the term. It was held that plaintiff had an interest in the horse for the period and could recover damages from defendant for having taken it away.

It is the bailee's or hirer's duty to use the chattel with care and for no other purpose than that for which it was hired. He has a further duty to return it at termination of the bailment and to pay the consideration for its use. The bailee must use ordinary care and diligence the same as in other mutual-benefit bailment. This is the rule when the chattel is used as agreed. But if the bailee uses the hired property in a way materially different from that mutually agreed upon, he is in most instances liable absolutely for any resulting loss or injury. This is illustrated in Fisher v. Kyle, 27 Mich. 454, as given under Tortious Bailee, *supra.*

Pledge or Pawn. This kind of mutual-benefit bailment consists in the loan or deposit of a chattel as security for some debt or agreement. This way of securing a debt differs from a chattel mortgage in that possession is transferred in the pledge, while in a chattel mortgage possession is generally retained by the owner.

In a mortgage title passes conditionally to the mortgagee, while in a pledge it remains in the bailor.

Collateral security is another name applied to this class of bailment, but the term has a broader meaning and includes chattel mortgage as well. The name "pawn" is the old expression, still in use as applied to a class of persons called pawnbrokers, who make a business of lending money on articles of personal property deposited with them. The same object is accomplished by the banker who lends money and accepts collateral security, stocks, warehouse receipts of grain, bills of lading, etc. Thus we see that the subject of a pledge may be any kind of personal property, including bills and notes, certificates of stock, bonds, and bank deposits. However, the thing pledged must be in existence, for if it has ceased to exist the pledge is void, as where a chattel has burned or an animal is dead.

Boynton v. Payrow, 67 Me. 587, held that the giving of a savings bank book to a third person for delivery to a creditor as security for a debt will create a valid pledge of the book and deposit.

The pledgee must exercise ordinary care and diligence toward the thing pledged, and when the property is delivered as security for a particular loan, it cannot be held as security for any other.

In Baldwin v. Bradley, 69 Ill. 32, a quantity of whiskey was pledged for money borrowed, and a few weeks later another lot was pledged for another loan. Each pledge and loan was separate from the other. It was held that each pledge was security for the loan made at the time, and not both for the first loan.

The bailee must keep the chattel in his possession, and if he voluntarily surrenders possession to the owner, the benefit of the bailment or pledge as security is lost. An exception is redelivery of the thing pledged to the bailor for some temporary purpose and with the understanding that the pledgee is again to have possession; in this case the security is not lost.

The pledgee has a right to use the chattel pledged if it is of such a nature that it requires use; for instance, a horse may be driven or ridden for its exercise. But if the article pledged would be the worse for use, the pledgee is prohibited from using it. All profits derived from the property pledged belong to the pledgor and must be accounted for to him, but all necessary expenses for keeping the property are chargeable to the owner.

In Androscoggin R.R. Co. v. Auburn Bank, 48 Me. 335, it was held that when a pledgee holds as collateral security bonds on which interest accrues at certain periods, the pledge necessarily implies authority in the pledgee to collect the interest and hold it on the same terms as the pledge itself.

The pledgee has the right to undisturbed possession of the chattel pledged. After the pledgor has made default in paying the debt secured, the pledgee may sell the chattel, after giving the pledgor reasonable notice of the time and place of sale, which notice must be preceded by demand of payment. The sale, unless the pledgee is a pawnbroker, must be by public auction, and the goods must be struck off to the highest bidder.

In Stearns v. Marsh, 4 Denis (N.Y.) 227, defendant sent plaintiff ten cases of boots and shoes as collateral security for a note of defendant's due November 5 which plaintiff held. From November 2 to 15 plaintiff advertised an auction sale of boots and shoes and sold the goods so pledged on the latter date without any notice to defendant. They sold for a very low price, and plaintiff sued for the balance of the note. The shoes were worth the face of the note. It was held he could not recover. The pledgee cannot sell the pledged property until he has called on the debtor to redeem the property, and he must also give him notice of the time and place of sale.

If the pledged property consists of notes, bills, or bonds which will soon become due, the proper procedure is to hold them until maturity and collect them if possible, applying the proceeds on the debt.

Union Trust Co. v. Rigdon, 93 Ill. 458, held that a pledge of commercial paper as collateral security for a debt does not, in the absence of a special power to that effect, authorize the pledgee to sell the security so pledged at either public or private sale upon default of payment of the original debt by the pledgor. The pledgee is bound to hold and collect the same as it becomes due and apply the net proceeds to payment of the debt so secured. The pledgee has no right, unless in extreme cases, to compromise with the parties to the security for a lesser sum than its face value.

The pledgor has the further remedy of bringing an action in equity court to foreclose his claim upon the article pledged; and when large amounts are involved, this is a frequent procedure.

When the original debt has been discharged without recourse to
the property pledged, the pledgor is entitled to return of his
chattels, the object of the bailment having been accomplished.
But before the pledgor is entitled to his return of the chattels
pledged, the principal debt and also the interest and all necessary expenses incidental to the pledge must be paid. A tender
made by the pledgor to terminate the pledge must include both
the interest, if any, and all such necessary expenses.

INNKEEPERS

Definition. Among the classes of mutual-benefit bailments
are exceptional bailments that require extraordinary diligence
and care of the bailee. Innkeepers and common carriers are the
main examples of this class.

An innkeeper is one who keeps a house, or inn, for the lodging and entertainment of travelers. Today he is a hotelkeeper,
an inn being the same as our hotel or tavern. The innkeeper, or
hotelkeeper, differs from a boardinghouse keeper in that his is
a public calling, and he is required by law to receive and give
accommodations to all persons of good behavior who apply and
offer to pay for their accommodations, unless his house is full.
Formerly boardinghouse keepers and restaurant keepers could
receive or refuse such persons as they pleased, but today under
civil-rights law, they have no right to discriminate or to refuse
any persons whom they are able to serve.

In Pinkerton v. Woodward, 33 Calif. 557, it was held that
an inn is a public place of entertainment for all travelers who
choose to visit it. It is distinguished from a private lodging or
boardinghouse in that the keeper of the latter is at liberty to
choose his guests, while the innkeeper is obliged to entertain and
furnish all travelers of good conduct and means of payment
everything they have occasion for as travelers on the way. A
traveler who enters an inn as a guest does not cease to be a guest
by proposing to remain a given number of days or by ascertaining
the price that will be charged or by paying in advance for his
entertainment. This question arose in a suit to recover gold dust

brought by plaintiff to defendant's hotel and at defendant's suggestion deposited in the hotel safe, from which it was afterward stolen. The court held the landlord liable and stated the rule to be that an innkeeper is liable as an insurer of the goods of the guest committed to his care unless the loss is occasioned by the act of God or by the public enemy or by the neglect or fraud of the guest.

Neither a company owning the sleeping cars attached to a train nor a steamship company can be held to be an innkeeper.

In Pullman Palace Car Co. v. Smith, 73 Ill. 360, Smith purchased a ticket on the Palace Car Company's car and while he was asleep on the trip his money was taken from his vest pocket, the vest being under his pillow. In an action for the money it was held that the car company was not liable as an innkeeper.

Clark v. Burns, 118 Mass. 275, held that a steamship company is not liable as an innkeeper for a watch worn by a passenger on his person during the day or kept out of reach at night, although the passenger pays a round sum for transportation, board, and lodging.

Guests. The relation of innkeeper arises only with reference to such parties as are guests of his, a guest being one who as a transient traveler partakes of the entertainment of the inn or hotel. He may be a guest although he does not stay overnight.

In Read v. Amidon, 41 Vt. 15, plaintiff and his father drove to defendant's hotel with their horse and wagon. They had their horse cared for, went in, laid off their coats, had dinner and stayed until evening, when they left. The court held that this created the relation of innkeeper and guest.

In Walling v. Potter, 35 Conn. 183, plaintiff resided about half a mile from defendant's hotel. Plaintiff went to the hotel one evening, stayed all night and had his breakfast, for which he paid. It was held that the relation of innkeeper and guest existed, and defendant was liable for money lost by plaintiff at the hotel.

A person receiving gratuitous accommodation is not a guest. To create the relation of guest, the innkeeper must receive pay for the accommodation.

Innkeeper's Liability. The innkeeper is bailee of the property and baggage of his guests, and this includes cars (as it included horses of old), wearing apparel, jewelry, and money. Under common law the responsibility of the innkeeper as bailee was exceptionally great. He was in most cases held to be an insurer of the goods and liable if they were lost, even without any fault on his part, unless the loss was occasioned by the guest's negligence or by an act of God—flood, lightning, etc.—as was illustrated in Pinkerton v. Woodward, 33 Cal. 557.

In Hulett v. Swift, 33 N.Y. 571, plaintiff's goods were destroyed by fire while he was a guest at defendant's hotel. The cause of the fire was unknown, but plaintiff was free from negligence. It was held that the innkeeper was liable. An innkeeper is an insurer of property committed to his custody by a guest unless the loss is due to the guest's negligence or fraud, or to the act of God or the public enemy.

Other cases go so far as to relieve the innkeeper from liability in case of loss if he can show positively that he was in no way negligent, but this is a modification of the common-law rule.

In Howth v. Franklin, 20 Tex. 798, it was held that when property committed to the custody of an innkeeper by his guest is lost, the presumption is that the innkeeper is liable for it but that he can relieve himself from that liability by showing that he used extreme diligence.

The innkeeper is responsible for the acts of his servants and employees the same as for his own acts.

Rockwell v. Proctor, 39 Ga. 105, was a suit against an innkeeper for a coat left by plaintiff, a guest. The coat had been given to a Negro in charge. It was held, that defendant was liable as innkeeper for the act of his servant.

Thereafter the innkeeper is liable for any theft of the guest's property, and he is not excused on the plea that he selected his servants carefully and performed his own duty well.

LIMITATION OF LIABILITY. The statutes in most states now allow the innkeeper to relieve himself from the extreme rigor of the common law, permitting him to limit his responsibility for money and valuables by requiring the guest to deliver them into his special custody. This is generally done by requiring that they be placed in the innkeeper's safe. But notice of this requirement must be given to the guest or the common-law liability will attach.

Bodwell v. Bragg, 29 Iowa 232, held that the mere posting of notices in the guest's room limiting liability of the landlord if certain directions are not observed does not operate as a notice to the guest unless he reads it or his attention is called to its contents.

Termination of Relation. Liability of the innkeeper for the guest's personal property exists as long as the owner of the property maintains his relation as guest of the hotel or inn.

MacDonald v. Edgerton, 5 Barb. (N.Y.) 560, held that after a person becoming a guest at an inn goes away for a brief period, leaving his property with the intention of returning, he is to be considered as still a guest, and if his property is lost during his absence, the innkeeper is liable.

Sasseen v. Clark, 37 Ga. 242, held that when a hotelkeeper sends his porters to the cars to receive the baggage of persons traveling, and there is delivered to the porter the baggage of a traveler who becomes the guest of the hotel, the liability of the innkeeper begins at delivery to the porter and continues until redelivery to actual custody of the guest. If the porter takes charge of baggage to deliver to the car, the liability of the innkeeper continues until the baggage is so delivered.

But after the relation of guest has ceased, the innkeeper is liable as only an ordinary bailee for property left with him.

Innkeeper's Lien. The innkeeper is compelled to receive any proper person who may apply for accommodations, but he need not receive those who cannot pay, and he may require payment in advance.

When he is not paid in advance, the law gives him a lien for all unpaid charges on the property which the guest has brought into the house and placed in custody of the innkeeper as bailee.

In Threfall v. Borwick, L.R. 10 Q.B. (Eng.) 210, A went to defendant's inn and stayed there with his family, taking with him to the inn as his own a piano which he hired of plaintiff. When A left the inn, he was in debt to defendant, and defendant detained the piano by virtue of his lien as innkeeper. It was held that defendant could hold the piano under such lien.

The innkeeper can detain the property until he is paid, but if he voluntarily surrenders it, the lien is lost. Statutes in most states now give boardinghouse keepers a like lien, but by common law it extended only to innkeepers.

COMMON CARRIERS

Definition. Common carriers also belong to the class of exceptional bailments. Like innkeepers they are as a general rule required to serve all alike and cannot choose their customers. They are also bound to use a greater degree of care and diligence toward property placed in their possession than any of the ordinary bailees.

A carrier is defined to be one who undertakes to transfer personal property from one place to another. He may be either a private carrier who comes under the class of ordinary bailees or a common carrier who is subject to special rules. A common carrier is one whose regular calling is to transport chattels for all who may choose to employ and remunerate him; a private carrier transports gratuitously or only in special cases.

Pierce v. Milwaukee Railway C., 23 Wls. 387, was an action to recover the value of eight bundles of bags which had been used in transporting grain and were then on their return empty. Defendants sought to evade liability as common carriers by showing that it was the usage of the railroads to carry empty bags free of charge and that they were responsible for gross negligence only. It was held that the consideration for such carriage was the patronage given the company in carrying the grain, that the carriage was not therefore gratuitous, and that defendant was liable as a common carrier.

Steele v. McTyer, 31 Ala. 667, was an action against defendant as a common carrier for loss of fifteen bales of cotton shipped by plaintiff on defendant's flatboat to Mobile. The boat was wrecked by running into a log. It was held that defendant was liable, as the damage was not due to an act of God or inevitable accident.

Allen v. Sackrider, 37 N.Y. 341, was an action to recover loss of a cargo of grain while being transported from Bay of Quinte to Ogdensburg by defendant for plaintiff. It was held that it was not enough, to charge as a common carrier, that he was the owner of a sloop and was specially employed by plaintiffs to make a trip for which he was to receive a stipulated compensation. Carrying for the public not being the business of defendant, he was held to be a special carrier and not liable for anything but his negligence.

Carriers may operate by land, water, or air, and the laws regulating their liabilities are much the same. Express, railroad, steamboat, and airplane companies are examples of common carriers. In order to constitute one a common carrier two things are necessary; first, a continuous offer to the public to carry, and second, the charge of a compensation for the service.

Haynie v. Waring, 29 Ala. 263, held that one who undertakes to carry goods for another gratuitously is liable only for gross negligence and not as a common carrier.

Goods and Payment for Carriage. Common carriers are said to be carriers of "goods," and this term includes animals, money, and in fact any article of personal property subject to transportation. Under common law a common carrier is bound to receive without respect of persons whatever may be offered him for transportation when the charges are paid or offered to be paid. Payment must be offered, as the carrier is under no obligation to carry free or upon credit. If he does not obtain his pay on receipt of the goods, he may hold them until the charges are paid, the law creating a lien on the goods for charges and expenses in favor of the common carrier. This compensation is sometimes called freight when applied to the charge for carrying goods. After goods have been delivered to the carrier, the shipper cannot retake them without paying the freight, and if they are intercepted before reaching their destination, the full freight can be recovered by the carrier. The consignor, or shipper, is the party primarily liable for the freight and not the consignee, or person to whom the goods are shipped, unless the consignee expressly agrees to pay for it.

In Wooster v. Tarr, 8 Allen (Mass.) 270, defendant shipped mackerel at Halifax upon plaintiff's vessel. In the bill of lading it was specified that the goods be delivered in Boston "unto Howe & Co. or their assigns, he or they paying the freight for said goods." They were delivered to parties to whom Howe & Co. had sold, and as plaintiff could not collect the freight from Howe & Co., who were insolvent, it was held he could recover of defendant, even though the goods were purchased for and account of Howe & Co. and shipped at their risk. The shipper is liable to the carrier for the freight, even though he does not own the goods and the carrier has waived his lien thereon.

Regulation of Charges. The charges that may be made are in some instances regulated by statute. In the absence of any statute regulating the subject, the carrier may agree to give one party a lower rate than others, but he cannot impose exorbitant or unreasonable conditions upon anyone.

In Johnson v. Pensacola R.R. Co., 16 Fla. 623, plaintiff sued defendant railroad company for excessive freight money claimed to have been charged and paid. He proved that he was charged more than another shipper of lumber. It was held that as common carrier defendant could not charge excessive or unreasonable rates of freight. Common law protects the individual from extortion and limits the carrier to a reasonable rate, but it does not require equal rates to all.

In 14 Blatchf. (U.S.) 453, the New Haven Ry. Co., owning a dock at New Haven, refused to receive coal on its cars on said dock from a canal boat thereat unless the master of the boat employed shovelers designated by the company, at a price fixed by the company, which was ordinarily the usual market price, to shovel the coal into tubs which were hoisted by derricks into the cars. The canal-boat carriers paid the company ten cents a ton for use of the tubs and machinery. It was held that the requirements of the company were unreasonable and could not be enforced.

The carrier can retain goods under his lien until all the freight and charges are paid.

Not only must he be a carrier for hire, but he must carry in the regular course of his business in order to be classed as a common carrier. That is, it is not sufficient that he carry goods in some particular business; he must undertake to carry for anyone who asks him. The test is whether he carries for particular persons only or for everyone who applies. If he holds himself out to carry for everyone who asks him, he is a common carrier; but if he does not do it for everyone, but carries for certain persons only, it is a matter of special contract. So a common carrier is one who follows the business as a public employment.

In Satterlee v. Groat, 1 Wend. (N.Y.) 272, defendant, who had been a common carrier between Schenectady and Albany, sold out all his teams but one which he used on his farm, and for a year or more entirely gave up the business. One Dows then engaged him to bring some loads for him from Albany to Schenectady. He sent his servant to bring these loads but expressly instructed him to carry for no one else. The man brought two loads, and when he went for the third, as it was not ready, he, contrary to his instructions from defendant, took a load from plaintiff to be delivered to Frankfort. On the way a box was broken into and stolen. The servant was afterward convicted of the theft. It was held that defendant could not be held unless he was at the time a common carrier, and if defendant was employed under a special contract for the goods, he was not liable. Defendant having abandoned his business as a common carrier, he stood on the same footing as if he had never been engaged in such business.

Right to Refuse Goods. A common carrier is bound by common law to receive whatever is offered to him to carry without respect to the persons offering. This rule is subject to three qualifications: first, the offer of the chattel must be for hire; second, the bailment must be within the carrier's means of safe conveyance; third, such carriage should be in the line of his vocation.

The first qualification has been discussed. In the second qualification it is but reasonable that the carrier may refuse to receive goods when he has not sufficient room or adequate facilities for carrying them safely. He is under no obligation to furnish extra equipment to satisfy an unusual demand. So if the article carried is larger or heavier than the carrier can handle, he may refuse it. He may also decline to receive particular property which may at the time be exposed to extraordinary danger or hazard on his route.

Phelps v. Illinois Central Ry. Co., 94 Ill. 548, held that it was a sufficient excuse for defendant to refuse to receive freight while the road was in military control of the U.S. Army during the Civil War, it not being safe for defendant to undertake the carriage of freight.

The article offered for transportation may not be in the line of the carrier's vocation. A freight carrier need not hold himself out to carry passengers. He need carry only the class of goods included in his public profession.

Johnson v. Midland Ry. Co., 4 Exch. (Eng.) 367, was an action for damages against the railway company for refusing to transport five tons of coal offered by plaintiff. Defendant never carried coal and did not hold itself out for any such business and could not unless it gave up its passenger traffic. It was held that a common carrier is not bound to carry every description of goods but only such goods and to and from such places as he has publicly professed to carry and for which he has conveyances.

Interstate Commerce Law. The carrier may prescribe reasonable rules as to the time and manner of receiving goods. He cannot be required to receive them at an unreasonable hour or place, and he may insist that the goods be packed in a reasonable way. But by statutes passed in most states the carrier is prohibited from discriminating in favor of one customer over another in rates or in privileges of any kind. The common carrier must not select his patrons arbitrarily but must furnish equal facilities to all.

In 1887 a statute was passed by Congress known as the Interstate Commerce Law. This law, designed to regulate commerce between the states, applies to all common carriers, either by water, land or air, who do business in two or more states. It provides that no discrimination shall be made between large or small, constant and occasional, shippers, and that no charges shall be unjust or unreasonable. It also provides that proportionate charges shall be made for long and short distances. The law further requires that the schedule of rates shall be published and filed with commissioners, known as the Interstate Commerce Commission, who are appointed to oversee enforcement of the law. The act also makes it unlawful for any common carrier who comes under the provisions to enter into any combination or agreement by which the continuous carriage of freight from one point to another shall be delayed or interrupted.

All the large railroad and express companies do business in more than one state and therefore come within the provisions of this act.

When Liability Begins. The common carrier becomes responsible for goods when they are delivered to him for carriage and accepted by him in the capacity of carrier. The delivery should be made to the agent or person whose business it is to receive freight, not to anyone who may be about the place of delivery. Trowbridge v. Chapin, 23 Conn. 595, was an action against the owner of a steamboat as a common carrier. It was the duty of the clerk of the boat to receive freight for transportation. Plaintiff's property was taken on board by a porter and left in a place pointed out by a person whose appearance and employment indicated that he was a common laborer. No inquiry was made by the porter as to whether the person had authority to receive the freight. It was held that it was not sufficient evidence of delivery to make defendant liable for loss of the property.

It is not necessary that the transportation actually begin before the common carrier's liability attaches, but rather the carrier is liable as soon as he accepts the goods. Thus expressmen and other carriers who go after goods and receive them at the shipper's residence or place of business begin their liability when they receive the goods.

Receipts. It is always prudent for the shipper or sender to demand of the carrier a receipt for the goods delivered. This is called a freight receipt, a way bill, or a bill of lading. Originally a bill of lading was given only by a carrier by water, but it is now given by all carriers. It consists of a writing showing receipt of the goods and the terms of the contract of carriage in brief form.

LIABILITY OF COMMON CARRIERS

Limits of Liability. Liability of the common carrier is exceptionally great. He is held as an insurer of goods against all risks of loss or injury, except when the loss arises from the following causes: (1) act of God or public enemy, (2) act of shipper, (3) act of public authority, (4) the nature of the goods. In early times this strict measure of responsibility was placed on the carrier for reasons of public policy. In an age of thieving and lawlessness the carrier had many chances to defraud his customers, and by collusion with thieves and robbers, to cause the shipper to be defrauded. To this absolute liability as an insurer there were only two exceptions under common law: losses occasioned either by act of God or by the king's enemies. But modern methods make the rule less urgent, and modern legislation has relieved the carrier's liability in the other cases just given.

Loss or Injury by Act of God. This includes those causes which man neither produced nor can contend against; as, accidents caused to the goods while the carrier is within the line of duty by lightning, tempest, earthquake, flood, sudden death, snow, rough winds, freezing, and thawing.

Denny v. New York Central R.R. Co., 79 Mass. 481, held that the rising of the Hudson River, caused by a flood, which ruined goods in defendant's warehouse was an act of God for which defendant was not liable.

Ballentine v. North Missouri R.R. Co., 40 Mo. 491, held that a snowstorm which blocks up a railroad to the extent that it delays and hinders the running of the cars is an act of God for which a carrier cannot be held liable.

But a prudent man will foresee the less violent of these causes, such as snow and freezing, and a carrier will not be excused for loss in such cases, unless he has exercised prudence and foresight in regard to them.

In Vail v. Pacific R.R., 63 Mo. 230, fruit trees shipped on defendant's road were frozen while en route, and the freezing was held to be an act of God for which the company was not liable, unless caused by unnecessary delay in transporting the trees or by their careless exposure to the cold.

In Parsons v. Hardy, 14 Wend. (N.Y.) 215, plaintiff received on November 19, at Albany, a quantity of merchandise to transfer by canal to Ithaca. When he arrived at Montezuma locks, winter set in, and he was prevented by ice from going farther, having had to stop on the way to repair an accident caused by being run into by a scow. Plaintiff took care of the goods at Montezuma, but defendant took them from there. It was held that plaintiff should have delivered them in the spring, but if the owner took them, it relieved plaintiff and he could recover pro rata for the part performed. As to the time of delivery, the carrier must exercise due diligence, and is excused by accident or misfortune. It is sufficient if he exercises due care and diligence to guard against delay.

Loss by Fire. Loss by fire, unless caused by lightning, is not an act of God, and a common carrier is not excused from loss by this cause unless it is expressly contracted for.

Parker v. Flagg, 26 Me. 181, held that unless a carrier limits his responsibility by the terms of a bill of lading or otherwise, he cannot escape the obligation to deliver the goods at their destination unless prevented by the public enemy or by an act of God. Loss by accidental fire is not a sufficient excuse unless the fire be caused by lightning.

Loss or Injury by Public Enemies. This is loss caused by those at war with one's country.

In McCranie v. Wood, 24 La. An. 406, defendant contracted with plaintiff, a carrier by boat, to remove certain cotton belonging to plaintiff to places deemed safe from hostilities during the Civil War. It was stored where it was deemed safe, but hostilities arose in that direction and the cotton was destroyed. It was held that defendant had performed, so far as was in his power, and the goods having been destroyed by the public enemy, he was not liable.

But the violence of mobs or rioters does not bring the participants within the term "public enemies."

Loss or Injury by Act or Fault of Consignor. This arises when the shipper packs the goods carelessly and they are injured or when he incorrectly addresses them so that they are delayed or lost. The carrier is not liable.

In Klauber v. American Express Co., 21 Wis. 21, plaintiff shipped some clothing which was not entirely covered and while being transported by defendent was damaged by rain. It was held that the owner was not required to cover goods shipped so that they would be safe from rain, mud and fire, and defendant here was liable. If there had been a hidden defect in the packing from which damage resulted in the ordinary course of handling, it would have been an act of the owner and the carrier would have been relieved.

In Congar v. Chicago Ry. Co., 24 Wis. 157, plaintiff shipped by defendant's road trees and other nursery stock from Whitewater, Wis., directed to "Iuka, Ia." The consignee was a resident of Iuka, Tama County, Iowa. Defendant took them to Iuka, Keokuk County, Iowa, in consequence of which delay the stock became worthless. Defendant proved that he examined the maps and found the place in Keokuk County. It was held that the company was not responsible. The negligence, if any, was on the part of plaintiff in not marking the goods with the name of the county or the road by which they were to go.

Any deception or bad faith on the part of the shipper as to the article shipped whereby it is made to appear less valuable or less liable to be injured will relieve the carrier from responsibility for any injury.

American Express Co. v. Perkins, 42 Ill. 458, was an action brought against the express company to recover the value of a package containing a wreath, made partly of glass, which was broken. The company was not informed of the fragile nature of the goods shipped. It was held that in order to charge a common carrier as insurer he must be treated in good faith, and concealment or suppression of the truth will relieve him from liability. When a package containing brittle articles is delivered to a carrier, he must be informed of the nature of its contents in order that he may use care proportionate to its character if he is to be held liable.

Loss or Injury Arising From Nature of Goods. When the loss arises not from any act of the carrier but from the inherent nature of the goods, the carrier is relieved. This applies to the natural decay of vegetables and fruit and other perishable commodities, also to the loss of livestock arising from their viciousness and habits, as when cattle gore and trample on each other. But the carrier must take such care of livestock as prudence and foresight demand, and must feed and water them unless the shipper undertakes this duty.

Clarke v. Rochester and Syracuse R.R. Co., 14 N.Y. 570, was an action for damages for loss of a horse shipped on defendant's railway from Rochester to Auburn, which upon arrival was found dead. It was held that the carrier was liable, unless the damage was caused by an occurrence incident to the carriage of animals in a railroad car and which defendant could not by the exercise of diligence and care have prevented.

Evans v. Fitchburg R.R. Co., 111 Mass. 142, was also an action for injury to a horse. The court held that a common carrier is liable for all accidents and mismanagements incident to transportation, but not for all injuries produced by or resulting from the inherent defects or essential qualities of the article which he undertakes to transport. If the injury is produced by fright, restiveness, or viciousness of an animal shipped, which defendant exercised all proper care and foresight to prevent, it would be unreasonable to hold him responsible for the loss.

Loss or Injury Caused by Public Authority. An example of such loss is seizure of goods by process of law or by the direct act of one's own government.

Ohio Ry. Co. v. Yohe, 51 Ind. 181, was an action against the railroad company for failure to deliver goods shipped by them. Their answer was that while the wheat was being shipped, one Johnson took out a writ of replevin, and by virtue of this writ the sheriff of the county seized the grain and took it out of the company's possession. It was held that a common carrier is excused from liability when the goods are seized by virtue of a legal process and taken out of his hands.

Limitation of Liability by Contract. In most states the carrier may limit his liability to a certain extent by contract with the shipper. That is, by special agreement a lighter degree of responsibility may be stipulated for. He may stipulate not to be liable for loss by fire, robbery, accidental delay, or dangers from navigation, provided he is not himself in fault; but he cannot contract away his liability for the fraud, misconduct, or negligence of himself, his agents, or his servants. He will be held to the responsibility of a mutual-benefit bailee, and he is required to exercise ordinary care and diligence, as well as honesty and good faith.

Camp v. Hartford Steamboat Co., 43 Conn. 333, was an action against the steamboat company as common carrier for the value of goods shipped by it and lost when the boat ran upon a rock and sprang a leak. The bill of lading given by the company when the goods were shipped provided that the company should not be responsible for damages to the goods from any perils or accidents not resulting from its own negligence or that of its servants. It was held that the exemption stipulated for was valid and lawful and that defendant was not liable.

Boorman v. American Express Co., 21 Wis. 152, held that an express company may exempt itself by special contract from its liabilities as an insurer; or for loss or damage of any package for over $50, unless the just and true value thereof is stated in the receipt; or on any property not properly packed and secured for transportation; or on any fragile fabric unless marked as such upon the package containing it, and when a receipt embodying such conditions is given to the shipper, his assent is presumed.

The carrier is also allowed to state a reasonable limit to the amount for which he shall be held liable in case of loss, unless the shipper states the valuation at the time of delivery of the goods to the carrier. Express companies generally contract that if no valuation is given, they will not be liable for a sum to exceed $50, and such provision is generally upheld.

In Belger v. Dinsmore, 51 N.Y. 166, plaintiff expressed a trunk by defendant company and received a receipt that contained a statement that as part of the consideration of the contract it was agreed that in case of loss the owner should not demand over $50, at which price the article was valued, unless otherwise expressed. It was held that by accepting the receipt and failing to give another valuation, plaintiff assented to the limitation and could claim no more.

In Hart v. Pennsylvania R.R. Co., 112 U.S. 331, plaintiff shipped five horses and other property in one car, under a bill of lading signed by him, which stated the horses were to be transported "upon the following terms and conditions which are admitted and accepted by me to be just and reasonable. First, to pay freight thereon at a specified rate on the condition that the carrier is liable on the stock to the extent of the following agreed valuation: if horses or mules not to exceed $200, etc." By the negligence of the railroad company one of the horses was killed and others were injured. It appeared that they were race horses worth $25,000. It was held that the liability of the company for the horses was limited to $200 each, the limitation in the bill of lading being just and reasonable and binding on plaintiff, even though the loss occurred through the company's negligence.

Delivery by Carrier. The carrier is bound to transport the goods with reasonable dispatch, and by the prescribed or customary route, and at termination of the journey to deliver them over to the consignee or his authorized agent within a reasonable time.

Berje v. Railroad Co., 37 La. An. 468, held that a stipulation in the bill of lading exempting the company from liability for loss arising from delay for any cause was unreasonable and did not relieve the carrier from liability for losses caused by negligence.

The carrier is liable absolutely to deliver to the right party. If he delivers to the wrong party, no matter how cautiously and innocently, he is liable. Delivery on a forged order or through the fraud of a stranger will not relieve him.

In Odell v. Boston R.R., 109 Mass. 50, plaintiff bought hay from one Swasey, to be delivered to plaintiff at the depot of defendants, who as common carriers were to carry the hay to plaintiff in Boston, where it was to be weighed. Swasey delivered the hay to defendants and directed them to market it in plaintiff's name and to carry it to him. After the hay reached Boston, Swasey directed defendants to deliver it to a third party. It was held that title passed to plaintiff on delivery of the hay to defendants and that they were liable to him therefor.

Powell v. Myers, 26 Wend. (N.Y.) 591, held that common carriers of passengers and their baggage are liable for the baggage until its safe delivery to the owner. Delivery of the baggage on a forged order will not discharge them.

When a bill of lading has been issued by the carrier, he must deliver the goods to the holder of it. He should therefore demand the bill of the consignee; otherwise, if it has been negotiated, he runs the risk of being required to make good the property to a purchaser holding the bill of lading.

Forbes v. Boston R.R., 133 Mass. 154, held that delivery of goods by a common carrier to a person unauthorized to receive them without requiring production of the bill of lading, but relying on such person's representation that he is the holder of it, renders the carrier liable to the person entitled to possession of the goods, without regard to the question of carrier's negligence or care.

When carriage is by water, a delivery on the usual wharf is sufficient, but while on the wharf, goods should be handled with reasonable care. A railroad company may deliver goods at the depot or freight house; and according to the laws of Alabama, New York, Wisconsin, Vermont, Michigan, Louisiana, and many other states, it must also notify the consignee, and it is liable as a common carrier until the consignee has had a reasonable opportunity to remove the goods.

In Moses v. Boston R.R., 32 N.H. 523, ten bags of wool were

delivered to defendant to be transported to Boston and then delivered to the consignee. The train arrived in Boston between one and three o'clock in the afternoon, and in the usual course of business two or three hours were required for unloading. The warehouse was closed at five o'clock, and during the night it burned. It was held that defendant was liable as a common carrier until the consignee had had reasonable opportunity during the hours in which such goods are usually delivered to examine them and take them away, after being informed that they were ready for delivery. He had no such opportunity to take the goods, and defendant was still liable as a common carrier.

Massachusetts, Iowa, California, Pennsylvania, and other states hold that delivery and safe storage of goods in the freight depot relieve the carrier from further liability, other than as a warehouseman.

In Francis v. Dubuque R.R. Co., 25 Iowa 60, plaintiff shipped goods by defendant's road to Ackley, where plaintiff resided. They arrived at 8:15 P.M. and were at once unloaded and safely placed in defendant's warehouse ready for delivery. That night the warehouse burned, and the goods were destroyed. It was held that the liability of a railroad company as a common carrier terminates and the company's responsibility as a warehouseman commences upon arrival of goods at the point of destination and their deposit in the company's warehouse to await the consignee's convenience.

If such carriers as express companies in cities, whose custom it is to deliver to the consignee at his residence or place of business, deliver at any other place or store the goods in the depot as is practiced by freight companies, such delivery will not be sufficient. This rule applies also to draymen and teamsters.

CARRIERS OF PASSENGERS

Definition. A common carrier of passengers is one who transports persons from one place to another for hire. A public carrier may be a carrier of both goods and passengers. Passengers may be carried by water, land, and air. The common carrier of pas-

sengers is bound to receive and carry alike all persons who apply
and are ready and willing to pay for their transportation.

In Bennett v. Dutton, 10 N.H. 481, it was held that the proprietors of a stagecoach who hold themselves out as common carriers of passengers are bound to receive all who desire passage
so long as they have room and there is no legal excuse for refusal.
It is not a legal excuse that they have agreed with a connecting
coach line that they will receive no passengers on certain days
from a given point unless they come on a coach on said line.

Rights and Duties. But the coach or bus driver may refuse to
carry when he has no more room or when the party applying is
not a suitable person. He need not receive a drunken person, a
notorious criminal, or a person infected with a contagious disease.
Neither is he obliged to take persons to a place which is not
on his route or at which he is not accustomed to stop.

Atchison R.R. Co. v. Weber, 33 Kan. 543, held that where
an unattended passenger becomes sick or unconscious or insane
after entering upon a journey, it is the duty of the company to
remove him from the train and leave him until he is in fit condition to resume his journey.

The fare required of the passenger must be reasonable, and
is regulated by statute as a rule or by the U.S. Commerce Commission. The carrier is bound to have means and appliances suitable to the transportation and to use all reasonable precautions
for the safety of passengers. He can prescribe reasonable rules
as to showing tickets, etc. The carrier is not an insurer of the
lives and safety of passengers, but he is held to a high degree of
care and will be liable for even slight negligence. While the
carrier does not warrant the safety of passengers, he is held to
the highest degree of care practicable under the circumstances.

In Ingalls v. Bitts, 9 Metc. (Mass.) 1, plaintiff was a passenger on defendant's coach. By reason of the breaking of the iron
axletrees, in which there was a small flaw that could not be seen,
he was injured. It was held that defendant was not answerable
for the injury thus received. Proprietors of coaches who carry
passengers for hire are answerable for injuries to passengers
which happen by reason of any defect in the coach that might
have been discovered by the most careful and thorough examination, but not for injuries which happen because of hidden defects
that could not upon such examination have been discovered.

In most states the carrier is not permitted to limit his liability for injury to passengers. It is considered contrary to public policy to exempt the carrier from liability for even slight negligence where the lives and safety of human beings are concerned.

Baggage. The passenger who pays his fare to the carrier is entitled to have certain baggage taken without charge, and for this baggage the carrier is liable, as for freight carried. Baggage in this sense includes such articles of personal necessity, convenience, and comfort as travelers under the circumstances are wont to take on their journeys. It does not include merchandise or a stock of goods used in the traveler's business.

In Purdue v. Drew, 25 Wend. (N.Y.) 459, plaintiff took passage at New York on defendant's boat and brought on board with him a trunk, which was put with the other baggage. It contained silks and other merchandise he had purchased in New York for his store. The trunk was lost, and this action was brought for its value. It was held that defendant was liable as a common carrier for baggage, but it must be for articles of necessity and personal convenience as are usually carried by travelers. In this case the carrier was not liable.

In Dexter v. Syracuse R.R. Co., 42 N.Y. 326, plaintiff sued for the value of the contents of his trunk which was lost by defendant. It contained, aside from his wearing apparel, material for two dresses purchased for his wife, and also material for a dress intended for his landlady. It was held that the common carrier is liable for the loss of such property received as baggage as is designed for the personal use of the passenger or his family, but it does not include articles purchased for persons not members of his family. In this case the company was held liable for all but the dress intended for the landlady.

The carrier is also liable for money which the passenger includes in his baggage for his traveling expenses and personal use, not exceeding a reasonable amount.

Duffy v. Thompson, 4 E. D. Smith (N.Y.) 178, held that a passenger on a voyage from a foreign country may keep money designed for small personal expenses in his trunk while on board the ship and hold the shipowner responsible for it.

If the baggage is not delivered into the actual custody and keeping of the carrier but is retained in possession of the passenger the carrier is under no such liability for its safety.

Carpenter v. New York R.R. Co., 124 N.Y. 53, held that the carrier was not liable for the effects of travelers not delivered into its custody, and that money retained at night and placed under a traveler's pillow was not in the custody of the carrier.

The carrier may by special contract make reasonable modifications of his liability for baggage. But the carrier cannot relieve himself wholly from liability, and the limitation must be brought to the passenger's notice and must be reasonable. Conditions limiting the carrier's liability to each passenger to a given amount have been upheld.

In Mauritz v. Railroad Co., 23 Fed. Rep. (U.S.) 765, it was held that a railroad company cannot limit its liability for the safe carriage of a passenger's baggage by a notice printed on the face of a ticket unless the passenger's attention is called to it when purchasing the ticket or unless the circumstances are such that it would be negligent of him not to read it. When the passenger cannot read and the agent makes no explanation when he sells the ticket, the passenger is not bound. The clause in the ticket was that the company would not be liable for lost baggage except wearing apparel, and then only for a sum not to exceed $50.

Liability of the carrier for baggage does not terminate until the passenger has had reasonable opportunity to take charge of it after it has reached its destination. If it is not claimed after a reasonable time, the carrier may store it, and his liability as a carrier ceases, he being liable thereafter only as a warehouseman.

Roth v. Buffalo R.R. Co., 34 N.Y. 548, held that when a passenger did not call for his trunk but left it in the hands of the company overnight without any arrangement with the company, and it was destroyed before morning by the burning of the depot, the company was not liable. The common carrier's liability for baggage terminates within a reasonable time after arrival of baggage at the place of destination if the carrier is ready to deliver it to the passengers.

VIII. PARTNERSHIP

IN GENERAL

Definition. Individuals may act alone in their business dealings. However, many important business and many smaller ones are undertaken by several persons joining themselves together, and thus by a union of their labor, ideas, and capital they are able to accomplish better results than if each had conducted his business alone. Two merchants in the same line of business in the same neighborhood may together run a store more economically than it could be run by either separately, and at the same time they will lessen competition. One may have business ability, an idea, or a patent, while the other may lack all these but have the capital. Together they can accomplish results which neither could accomplish alone.

When several persons join themselves together in business, they do so by forming either a partnership, a joint stock company, or a corporation. Partnership is a legal relation based on the express or implied contract of two or more competent persons to unite their property, labor, or skill in carrying on some lawful business as principals for their joint profit. The members of a partnership are called partners. The partners together are said to constitute a firm.

Executed Contract. The partnership is formed as the result of an agreement, and this agreement, or contract of partnership, must be executed. An agreement to form a partnership at some future time does not constitute the parties to such an agreement. A partnership differs from a corporation in that it is formed simply by the contract of the parties and requires no authority from the government.

Written Contract. It is a wise precaution to have the agreement in writing and all the terms and conditions of the partnership expressed. The written agreement setting forth the terms of the partnership and signed by the parties who are to compose the firm is called the articles of copartnership. A great many different clauses may be inserted, depending upon the actual agreement of the parties; the following is a brief form containing some of the more common provisions.

ARTICLES OF COPARTNERSHIP

This agreement made and entered into this twenty-eighth day of February, 1967, One thousand Nineteen Hundred and Sixty-seven, by and between Carl Swanson of Aurora, Illinois, of the first part and Elmer Carlson of Wheaton, Illinois, of the second part, witnesseth as follows:

1. The said parties, above named, hereby agree to become partners in the business of buying and selling dry goods under the firm name of Swanson & Company, said business to be carried on in the city of Aurora, or such other place or places as the parties may hereafter determine, and to continue for the term of five years from the date hereof.

2. The capital of the said partnership shall consist of the sum of Ten Thousand Dollars, to be contributed as follows: The party of the first part shall contribute his stock of dry goods and the good will of the business heretofore conducted by him, which are together valued by the parties hereto at the sum of five thousand dollars; and the party of the second part shall contribute the sum of five thousand dollars in cash. The capital stock so formed is to be used and employed in common between the parties hereto for the support and management of said business.

3. At all times during the continuance of their copartnership they and each of them shall give their time and attention to said business, and to the utmost of their skill and power exert themselves for their joint interest, profit, benefit, and advantage, and truly employ, buy and sell, and trade with their joint stock and the increase thereof in the business aforesaid; and they shall also at all times, during the said copartnership bear, pay, and discharge equally between them all rents and expenses that they may be required for the management and support of said business; and all gains, profits, and increase that shall grow or arise from or by means of their said business shall be equally divided, and all loses by bad debts or otherwise shall be borne and paid between them equally.

4. Each of said partners shall be at liberty to draw out of the funds of the firm each month for his private expenses the sum of one hundred dollars, and neither of them shall take any further sum for his separate use without the consent in writing of the other partner. The sums so drawn shall be charged against

the partners respectively, and if at the annual settlement, herein provided for, the profits of any partner do not amount to the amount so drawn out in that year, he shall at once repay such deficiency to the firm.

5. All the transactions of the said copartnership shall be entered in regular books of account, and on the first day of January in each year during the continuance of the copartnership account of stock shall be taken and an account of the expenses and profits adjusted and exhibited on said books; said profits shall then be divided, and one half carried to the separate account of each partner. Either party shall be at liberty to withdraw at any time the whole part or any part of his share of the accrued profits thus ascertained and carried to his separate account. Each partner shall have open and free access to the books and accounts of the copartnership at all times and no material or important changes shall at any time be made in the general business of the firm, either in the buying of stock or in any other respect, by either partner without the knowledge of the other.

6. And the said parties here mutually covenant and agree, to and with each other, that during the continuance of the said copartnership neither of them shall endorse any note, or otherwise become surety for any person or persons whomsoever, without the consent of the other of said copartners, each to the other, shall make a just and final accounting of all things relating to their said business, and in all things truly adjust the same; and all and every, the stock and stocks as well as the gains and increase thereof, which shall appear to be remaining, either in money, goods, wares, fixtures, debts, or otherwise, shall be divided equally between them.

IN WITNESS WHEREOF, the said parties have mutually covenanted and have hereunto set their hands and seals this twenty-eighth day of February, 1967.

                                                    [Signature]
                                                    CARL SWANSON
                                                    [Signature]
                                                    ELMER CARLSON

The agreement should be full and clear, and many other provisions may be inserted as the facts require.

Oral Contract. Articles of copartnership are desirable, but not necessary to form a partnership. Two neighbors, each being in need of a corn-picking machine on his farm, may purchase one, each paying half, and agreeing that each shall use it. The result is a partnership in the corn-picking machine; and if it should be disposed of, each would be entitled to his half of the proceeds unless the agreement between them provided otherwise. By the statute of frauds a contract of partnership for over one year must, in most states, be in writing.

In Morris v. Peckham, 51 Conn. 128, plaintiff agreed orally to assign to defendant one-half interest in an invention for making patent screwdrivers, defendant agreeing to furnish the capital to procure the patents and to purchase the machinery and stock, and they were then to engage in manufacturing the screwdrivers. After conducting the business for one year, defendant refused to continue and to furnish more funds. Plaintiff brought an action to compel specific performance of the partnership agreement, claiming that the partnership was to continue for seventeen years, the life of the patent; but the court held that such a contract, by its terms not to be performed within one year, is void under the statute of frauds unless it is in writing.

Virginia and some other jurisdictions hold to the contrary, and expressly declare that a contract of partnership for over one year, when made orally, is not within the statute of frauds.

Implied Partnership. A partnership may be implied from transactions and relations in which the word partnership has never been used but in which the law will imply a partnership whether it was so intended by the parties or not. This implied partnership may be an actual partnership by implication or a partnership by implication as to third parties.

Partners. When does partnership exist, and who are the partners? The number of persons who may unite to form a partnership is not limited, but to become a partner, a person must be competent to contract. An infant's contract of partnership, like most of his contracts, is voidable, and may be affirmed after he becomes of age, in which case he has all the rights and is subject to all the duties, of a partner.

In Bush v. Linthicum, 59 Md. 344, plaintiff and defendant entered into a written agreement of copartnership in the grocery business. After the business had been conducted for a time, plaintiff brought an action to dissolve the partnership and to have the assets applied on the debts of the firm. Defendant pleaded that he was an infant, but the court held that this did not prevent dissolution of the partnership and sale of its assets, and applying the same to payment of the debts. Although an infant may become a partner, he cannot be held for the contracts or deals of the firm individually unless he affirms them after becoming of age.

Kinds of Partners. Partners are (1) ostensible, or public, (2) secret, or unknown, (3) nominal, (4) silent, (5) dormant, or (6) special, or limited.

PUBLIC PARTNER. A public or ostensible partner is one of the active and known parties. He usually participates in the business and is held out to the world as a partner.

SECRET PARTNER. A secret, or unknown, partner is one who is in reality a partner active in the management of the business, but conceals that fact both from the public and from the customers of the partnership. This course is often taken when a person risks money or credit in a business but does not wish to assume the risks and liabilities of a partner. So long as his concealment is perfect, he is protected; but if he is at any time discovered to be an actual partner, he may be held the same, as an ostensible partner.

In Milmo National Bank v. Bergstrom, 1 Tex. Civ. App. 151, defendant and one Carter were engaged as partners for one year in dealing in hides, wool, and produce, under the name of A. N. Carter. At the time that Carter opened the credit account with plaintiff he informed plaintiff that defendant was his partner. The money sued for had been loaned after defendant withdrew from the firm, but this was not known to plaintiff. Defendant contended that as he was a secret or dormant partner, he was not bound to give notice of the dissolution. It was held that he was liable to plaintiff for debts contracted after dissolution of the partnership if plaintiff was not given notice, as the credit was extended on the strength of defendant's membership in the firm.

NOMINAL PARTNER. A nominal partner is one who is held forth as a partner with his own consent, and is liable as a partner because he has given his credit to the firm and authorized engagements and contracts on the strength of this relation. He has no interest whatever in the business, and as between himself and the true owner there is no actual partnership; but there exists what was spoken of as an implied partnership as to third parties, and the nominal partner will therefore be held to the same liability as to third parties to whom he has suffered himself to be held out as a real partner.

In Hicks v. Cram, 17 Vt. 449, defendants were sued as partners doing business under the name of Cram & Hutchinson. Defendant Hutchinson claimed that he was not a partner and had no interest in the business but that his son was the partner. It was shown that defendant had held himself out as a partner, and that when Cram had stated that Hutchinson was a partner, he made no denial. It was held that defendant Hutchinson was liable and that a person who suffers himself to be held out to the world as a partner in a firm will be liable for all debts which the firm contracts on the credit of his being a member.

SILENT PARTNER. A silent partner is one who as between the members of the firm is an actual partner but who takes no active part in the business of the firm except to recover his share of the profits. He may be known to the outside people as a partner, but in the business itself he takes no active part.

DORMANT PARTNER. There is very little difference from a silent partner except that a dormant partner is not known to the outside world. He is both a secret and a silent partner, being both unknown as a partner and inactive in the business.

SPECIAL PARTNER. A special, or limited, partner exists only in those states where the statutes provide for limited partnerships. By complying with the statute, such a partner may contribute a certain amount of capital and not become liable for the debts of the firm beyond the amount so contributed.

REALITY OF PARTNERSHIP. In the case of a partnership by implication, the question often arises whether a partnership really exists. The agreement or understanding between the parties to a transaction may be such that the law will say they are partners, that although they did not contemplate becoming partners, the effect of their agreement created this relation. The early test in English and American courts was the sharing of profits. A person who was to share in profits was a partner, but later holdings of the courts have departed from this rule, and now the test in England and in most states seems to be the intention of the parties.

If the parties either expressly or impliedly enter into an associ-

ation the law regards as a partnership, they will be held to stand
in that relation. Whether such an association is intended to be
formed depends on the facts in each case.

There may be a partnership as to third parties though the
parties are not partners as between themselves, as when one
holds himself out as a partner and by his conduct induces others
to trust the firm on the strength of his being a partner. As to
such outside parties, he will be so held though the intent and
agreement of the parties between themselves does not create such
a relation.

Powell v. Moore, 79 Ga. 524, was an action brought against
Marbut and Powell, doing business under the firm name of S. P.
Marbut. Powell denied being a partner. He contributed the use
of a dwelling, storehouse, and $200, which he called a loan, and
Marbut contributed his time and $200. No agreement was made
as to the rent of the house or the interest on the money, but
Powell was to receive half the profits of the business as profits
and not as compensation for use of the house and money. It was
held that this constituted a partnership as to third parties.

In Hackett v. Stanley, 115 N.Y. 625, defendant entered into
an agreement whereby in consideration of his loaning one Gorham $750 for use in the heating and ventilating business, which
sum was secured by notes of Gorham's and by a chattel mortgage,
etc., and in further consideration of defendant's services in securing sales, and also in consideration of any other sums he might
in his option advance, Gorham was to divide the net profits of
the business equally with him. Any money advanced was to draw
interest. Gorham was to have $1,000 for his services in managing
the business, which was to be carried on in his name. It was held
that as to creditors of the business defendant was chargeable as
a partner, and that this was so although the creditors were ignorant of the agreement at the time of giving the credit.

Caldwell v. Miller, 127 Pa. St. 442, held that an agreement
between persons engaged in business that each is to share directly
in the profits as such constitutes them partners as to third persons, whatever their arrangements may be between themselves.

In determining whether the parties are partners, the fact that
they are to divide the profits and share the losses is evidence of
an intent to become partners, though this does not absolutely
create such a relation. That each such party is to have a voice

and control in the business and that each is to invest his capital and labor in the undertaking and is not to occupy the position of clerk or manager are generally considered facts sufficient to determine the relation as one of partnership.

Meehan v. Valentine, 145 U.S. 611, held that one who lends a sum of money to a partnership under agreement that he be paid interest thereon and also be paid one tenth of the yearly profits of the partnership business if those profits exceed the sum lent does not thereby become liable as a partner for the debts of the firm.

Manhattan Brass Co. v. Sears, 45 N.Y. 797, held that an agreement to share in the profits of a business is sufficient to constitute a partnership as to third parties. It is not necessary that the agreement be to share in the losses.

Authorities differ very widely as to the rules that will control in determining who are and who are not partners; and the only safe guide seems to be to discover whether the parties intended to enter into a relation which the law will consider a partnership. If so, even though they themselves did not intend to become partners and expressly stated that they were not, still they will be considered partners.

In Bush v. Beecher, 45 Mich. 188, Beecher owned a hotel, and Williams agreed in writing to hire the use of it from day to day, to keep it open as a hotel, and to pay Beecher daily a sum equal to one third of the gross receipts. Plaintiff sold Williams a bill of goods and then sought to hold Beecher as a partner. The goods were sold to Williams, and Beecher was never held out as being in partnership with him. It was held that their agreement did not constitute a partnership. The court said that there can be no such a thing as a partnership as to third persons when there is none as between the parties themselves, unless the third persons have been misled by deceptive appearances or concealment of facts.

In Farnum v. Patch, 60 N.H. 294, certain persons took a number of shares, at $25 each, in an enterprise which, according to their written agreement, was for the purpose of starting a grocery store. They thought they would not be liable for any debts except in the amounts which they subscribed and did not consider that they were partners. It was held that their arrangement constituted their relation that of partners.

RIGHTS OF PARTNERS
BETWEEN THEMSELVES

Right to Choose Associates. The first right of a partner is to choose whom he is to be associated with in this relation, for as a person cannot be compelled to go into a partnership against his will, so he cannot be compelled to allow anyone to come into the partnership without his consent. If a partner draws out or dies, no one can purchase his interest and can come in without the consent of the other partners; and if they give their consent, and he comes in, the result is that a new partnership is created.

Noonan v. Nunan, 76 Cal. 44, held that the mere purchase of interest in the partnership property of the estate of a deceased partner does not create a new partnership between the purchaser and the surviving partner of the old firm.

Right of Purchaser or Inheritor. The person who buys or inherits the interest of a partner in a firm merely has the right to demand settlement of the affairs of the company and payment to him of his share, after the debts of the firm have been paid.

Partner May Sell. Each partner has the absolute right to sell the whole or any part of the partnership property included in the regular course of business, but a sale of any property of the partnership not ordinarily kept for sale and not within the course of business is not within the power of one partner. For example, one partner in a grocery business can sell the stock the regular way, but not the fixtures and store, as such sale would not be in the regular course of the business.

In Drake v. Thyng, 37 Ark. 228, Drake and Thyng were partners in the brickmaking business. While Drake was away, Thyng sold the stock and plant to a third party for an insignificant and inadequate sum. Drake brought this action to set aside the sale. It was held that while a partner may sell a part or the whole of any of the effects of a firm which are intended for sale, if the sale is within the scope of the partnership business, yet he cannot, without consent of the other partners, dispose of the partnership business itself or of all the effects, including the means of carrying it on, as this is beyond the range of a partner's implied powers.

Capital. The capital of the partnership consists of such properties or amounts as are contributed to the common fund by the different partners at the beginning or as may be put in thereafter. The claim of each partner to this partnership capital extends not to any particular article but to an interest in the whole, consisting of a right to share in the proceeds after the firm debts are paid. Aside from this, individual property of the partners may be used in the business. The store in which the business is conducted may belong to one of the partners, and he can deal with this as his own and not as a partner.

In Nichol v. Stewart, 36 Ark. 612, one partner mortgaged a certain number of bales of cotton out of the partnership crop for payment of an individual debt. The mortgagee had notice of the partnership. It was held that the mortgagee had no right to the specific property but only a right to the ultimate interest of the mortgagor in the partnership effects, after all the firm debts were paid, to an amount equal to the value of the cotton.

Good Will. The good will of the firm is partnership property. Good will is defined to be the benefit arising from the connection and reputation of the firm, the fact that the business is established and going, that it has customers and is advertised throughout the section to which it looks for trade. The sale of the business as a whole, including stock, fixtures, etc., is understood to include the good will. So the trade-marks and trade name of a business are property belonging to a firm and pass with the sale of the business in the same manner as the good will, although either may be sold separately.

In Merry v. Hoopes, 114 N.Y. 415, Hoopes and Merry were copartners engaged in manufacturing galvanized iron under two trade-marks, the Lion brand and the Phoenix brand. Upon dissolution of the firm defendant bought the business. Thereafter plaintiff brought action to restrain him from use of these trade-marks, nothing having been said about them in the bill of sale. It was held that the exclusive right to use the trade-marks belonging to the firm passed to defendant.

In Williams v. Farrand, 88 Mich. 473, it was held that an assignment of all the stock, property, and effects of a business, or the exclusive right to manufacture a given article, carries with it the exclusive right to use a fictitious name under which such business has been carried on and such trade-marks and trade names as have been used in such business.

Good Faith. The first duty of each of the partners to the others is to exercise the utmost good faith toward them, because each partner is at the mercy of the others. Each partner really acts as agent in the transaction of business for the firm and for the other partners.

Kimberly v. Arms, 129 U.S. 512, held that if one partner is the active agent of the firm and as such receives a salary beyond what comes to him from his interest as a partner, he is clothed with a double trust in his relations with the other partners, which imposes on him the duty of exercising the utmost good faith in his dealings; and if he obtains anything for his own benefit in disregard of that trust, a court of equity will compel him to account for it to the other partners.

Individual Liability. Each partner is chargeable with any loss to the firm which arises from his own breach of duty, whether through fraud, negligence, or ignorance, but he is not liable to the company for loss arising from an honest mistake of judgment.

Charlton v. Sloan, 76 Iowa 288, held that although a partner may act unwisely in incurring liabilities for the firm, the resulting loss cannot properly be charged to him personally upon dissolution, when it is not shown that his acts were wanton or fraudulent.

If one partner takes a secret advantage of the partnership whereby he makes a profit for himself at the firm's expense, he can be required to restore it, the courts holding that he acted for the partnership and it will be entitled to the benefits. If the lease of a building occupied by a firm expires, one member cannot secretly take out a new lease in his own name and seek to sublet to the firm at an increased rate. The new lease taken in the name of one member of the firm will be declared by the courts as held by him for the benefit and use of the firm.

In Hodge v. Twitchell, 33 Minn. 389, Hodge, Twitchell, and Ruby agreed to purchase real property together, to pay one third of the cost each and to divide the property equally. Twitchell called their attention to a lot and advised its purchase. While they were considering it, he secretly made an agreement with the owner that if he, Twitchell, found a purchaser for the remainder of the lot at $2,500, the original price, the seller would give him a certain part of the lot for his services. Twitchell then told his partners that a part was sold but that the balance could be obtained for $2,500, and urged its purchase. It was taken on his recommendation, and the portion promised Twitchell was conveyed to his wife in pursuance of the owner's agreement. The court decided that the wife held the lot in trust for Hodge and Ruby to the extent of their agreed interest in the venture.

Records of Transactions. The firm must keep books of account in which each member is bound to enter, or have entered, all transactions for the firm, as each partner has a right to know of all transactions in the business.

Van Ness v. Van Ness, 32 N.J. Eq. 669, held that a member of a firm whose duty it is to keep the accounts and who claims he has omitted to enter credits to which he is entitled will be required to furnish satisfactory proof of the mistake he asks to have corrected.

Compensation. One partner is not entitled to any special compensation for his services in the partnership unless it is expressly provided for. Each partner is supposed to do all he can for the good of the partnership, and whatever he does gives him no claim for extra compensation beyond his share of the profits of the business unless he has consent of the other partners.

Burgess v. Badger, 124 Ill. 288, held that in the absence of an agreement to that effect, one partner is not entitled to charge his copartners for his services because he has done more than his just proportion of the work.

In Gregory v. Menefee, 83 Mo. 413, the claim of the surviving partner of a firm for compensation for his services in closing up the partnership business was not allowed. The court held that a surviving partner is not entitled to any compensation for such services.

Heath v. Waters, 40 Mich. 457, held that the sickness of a partner is one of the risks incident to a partnership and does not give another partner any claim for personal services in conducting the entire business unless the articles of copartnership provide for such compensation.

Partners May Sign Negotiable Paper. It is the general rule that one member can bind the firm by signing the firm name as maker, endorser, or acceptor of negotiable paper if it is done in the connection with the firm business and not for a private debt or account.

In Wagner v. Simmons, 61 Ala. 143, defendants were partners in the business of buying and selling cattle and produce. The court held that each member had the right to draw, accept, or endorse bills of exchange in the firm name, and bind the partnership as to third persons, dealing fairly and in good faith, regarding matters usually incident to the business. It was immaterial, as to persons thus dealing with one of the partners, that the other partner was not informed of the transaction and repudiated it as soon as it came to his knowledge.

The power of any partner to use the firm name on negotiable paper is presumed, and a stipulation between the parties that certain members of the firm shall not so use it will not affect third persons having no knowledge of such agreement. But this rule will not apply if it is obvious that the instrument is signed not for the firm but for the individual benefit of a partner.

Power of Majority. A majority of the partners may control the ordinary conduct of the firm's business and have power to act in all matters within the scope of partnership affairs, but they have no power to change the nature or location of the business.

In Clarke v. Slate, 136 Pa. State 408, it was held that as a majority of the partners, while acting fairly and in good faith and keeping within the scope and purposes of the partnership, have power to direct the course of the partnership affairs, they may give a valid warranty of attorney in the name of the firm, authorizing suit on a contract made by it, and this notwithstanding the dissent of a minority.

In Staples v. Sprague, 75 Me. 458, five persons had agreed to cut and pack a quantity of ice for sale, and after deducting all expenses, to divide the proceeds equally. One of the members, with the consent and approval of two others, sold a large quantity of ice. The remaining two brought suit to charge the others for damages in selling the ice at what they claimed was too low a price. It was held that the agreement constituted a partnership, and if there was no fraud, the majority of a firm could make a valid sale of property belonging to the firm without consent of the minority.

LIABILITY OF PARTNERS
TO THIRD PARTIES

A partner is liable for all the debts of the partnership, whether he is a secret, a nominal, or an ostensible partner.

In Richardson v. Farmer, 36 Mo. 35, defendants had been doing business under the name of W. H. Jopes. It was shown that Farmer was a secret or dormant partner. It was held that while credit was given to an ostensible partner, because no other was known to the creditor, yet the creditor might also sue the secret partner when discovered, and the credit would not be presumed to have been given on the sole responsibility of the ostensible partner.

Effect of Notice. However, if fair notice is given that the company will not be liable for any particular acts of a partner, and if the notice that such acts are forbidden is given to the person with whom the partner deals, he can no longer bind the firm.

In Yeager v. Wallace, 57 Pa. St. 365, it was held that the partnership relation makes each partner the agent of the other when acting within the scope of his power, but when the agency is denied and the act forbidden by the copartner, with notice to the party assuming to deal with him as agent of the firm, the act is then his individual act and not that of the firm.

Limit of Authority. The authority of a partner to bind a contract is limited to transactions within the scope of the partnership business, and if he seeks to charge the firm with matters outside that scope, he must show special authority from the other partners to do so. A partnership to work a farm would not therefore give one partner any implied authority to draw bills of exchange or borrow money, while a partner in a mercantile or manufacturing company would have such authority.

In Randall v. Merideth, 76 Tex. 669, Tiernan, Randall, Sawyer, and Dwyer, residing in Galveston, made a joint investment in mining property in Mexico. Tiernan was the manager in charge of the work of developing the mine. Assessments were made for the work each year for three years, and when the money for each year gave out, the work was to be suspended. In 1885, although the home partners gave express orders that the work

should stop when the money gave out, Tiernan kept up the work
and raised money by loan from Merideth and Ailmon, local bankers, who dealt alone with Tiernan, not having knowledge of his
partners. Upon suit brought by the bankers against all the partners, it was held that they could not recover of Randall, Sawyer,
and Dwyer without showing affirmatively that Tiernan had express authority from them to borrow money on their credit for
the mining enterprise. The partners to a mining enterprise, have
no implied power to borrow money on the credit of the partnership.

While the presumption is that a partner has no authority to
use the goods or credit of the firm to pay his personal debts or
to buy goods for his personal use with the partnership funds,
still he may have express authority to do so, and the transaction
is then valid.

In Dobb v. Halsey, 16 Johns. (N.Y.) 34, one Moore and plaintiff were partners in the lumber business. Moore gave defendant
some lumber belonging to the firm in payment of a personal debt.
In this action by plaintiff to recover the value of the lumber the
court held that when one partner delivers partnership property
to a third person in payment of a private debt, and the third person knows it is partnership property, he cannot hold it against the
other partners but is liable to pay the price of the goods.

In Hartness v. Wallace, 106 N.C. 427, Connelly and Deitz
were copartners in the business of selling wagons until they made
an assignment to Hartness. Before the assignment one Hobbs
purchased a wagon from them and gave his note. Connelly assigned the note to Wallace in part payment of his individual
indebtedness to him. Assignment of the note was made without
the knowledge or consent of Deitz. The note was afterward paid
to Wallace. In this action by the receiver to recover this amount
from Wallace it was held that plaintiff could recover.

In Guice v. Thornton, 76 Ala. 466, it was held that when
money is borrowed by one partner on his own individual credit,
subsequent execution of a note for it in the partnership name
without consent of the other partners is a fraud on the partnership
and does not give the creditor a right to recover from the firm on
such a note.

Name. A partnership should adopt some particular name
under which to do business. This may be simply the name or

names of one or more of the partners, either with or without the words "and Company" added or any other designation that the parties may adopt; but by statute in New York State the term "and Company" must not be used unless it actually represents a partner.

Fraud. The partners are held liable for the fraud and the false representations of one partner when they are made in the course of the firm business.

In Taylor v. Jones, 42 N.H. 25, it was held that one partner is not liable for the wrongful acts of another partner unless they are done within the proper scope of the business of the partnership or are authorized or adopted by him.

Notice to One Partner Is Notice to All. That notice to one partner is notice to all is an established principle. An example is the case of negotiable paper that has been dishonored; notice of the dishonor to one partner is notice to the firm.

In Tucker v. Cole, 54 Wis. 539, it was held that where timber is purchased by a firm, prior notice to one member of the firm that it was cut from land not belonging to the vendor is notice to all the partners. In Frank v. Blake, 58 Iowa 750, it was held that where a partnership seeks to recover as a bona fide purchaser of a promissory note fraudulently procured, the burden is on it to show that all the members of the partnership were ignorant of the fraud at the time of the purchase.

REMEDIES AGAINST PARTNERSHIP

A partnership does not have an individuality of its own like a corporation but is looked upon as a collection of persons, and it must be sued not in the firm name but in the names of the persons composing it. In some states this rule has been changed, and partnerships may sue and be sued in the firm name. The members of a partnership are proceeded against for a debt of the firm in the same way as is an individual. When creditors of the partnership and individual creditors of the partners come in conflict, a distinction is made: the law says they must proceed in a particular way, the object being to give the individual creditor his due out of the individual property of the partner, and the firm creditor his due out of the partnership property. If after the partnership debts have been paid, there remains a surplus, the creditor of a partner may proceed against this partner's share; but if, on the other hand, there are not sufficient partnership assets to satisfy the firm creditors but there remain individual assets after the individual creditors are satisfied, such surplus is liable for the firm debts.

Wilder v. Keeler, 3 Page (N.Y.) 164, held that upon the death of one of the partners of a firm, a joint creditor of the partnership has no claim for payment of his debt out of the estate of the deceased partner until all the separate creditors of such partner have been paid out of the estate, and the creditors of the individual partners have no claim on the partnership property until all the partnership creditors have been satisfied.

If there are no partnership assets, the firm's creditors are entitled to share in the individual assets of any partner equally with his individual creditors.

In Brock v. Bateman, 25 Ohio St. 609, it was held that when a partnership and several members of the firm are insolvent and there are no partnership funds for distribution among the creditors, the creditors of the firm are entitled to share equally with the creditors of each partner in the distribution of his individual assets.

DISSOLUTION OF PARTNERSHIP

Duration. When the partnership is formed, the articles of copartnership usually state how long it shall continue. Other circumstances, however, may operate to change the time. When the relation terminates, the partnership is said to be dissolved.

Forms of Dissolution. Dissolution may take place in any one of the following ways: (1) by provision in the articles of copartnership; (2) by mutual consent of all the partners; (3) by act of one or more of the partners; (4) by change in the partnership; (5) by death of a partner; (6) by decree of a court of equity; (7) by bankruptcy.

BY CONTRACT. When the period for which the partnership was formed has elapsed, it is thereupon dissolved unless continued by the parties. The partnership may be formed for a temporary purpose; when the purpose has been accomplished, the partnership ceases.

BY MUTUAL CONSENT. The partnership may be dissolved at any time by mutual consent of all partners, though the period for which it was formed has not elapsed.

BY ACT OF PARTNER. The firm may be dissolved by the act of one or more of the partners. This is accomplished when one of the parties makes an assignment for the benefit of his creditors or becomes bankrupt, or when, he being insolvent, his interest is sold upon execution to pay his creditors. In these cases his property passes beyond his control, and he can no longer perform his part as a partner. Also, where the partnership was formed for no definite period but at the will of the parties, any partner can terminate the relation by notice to the other partners.

In Blake v. Sweeting, 121 Ill. 67, Blake, Huston, and Sweeting were engaged as partners in manufacturing brick. After continuing the business for about three years, Huston went away, abandoned the business, and wrote to Blake, authorizing him and Sweeting to settle the business as they pleased. Thereafter Blake and Sweeting formed a new partnership and conducted the business themselves. It was held that the acts of Huston operated as a dissolution of the old firm. A partnership not formed for any definite time may be dissolved by any member of the firm at his pleasure. Withdrawal of one member is a dissolution of the firm.

BY CHANGE IN PARTNERSHIP. Dissolution of a partnership may be made by a change in the membership of the firm. A partner may withdraw from the firm, or he may transfer his interest to a stranger. In whatever way the membership of a partnership is changed, the act at once terminates and dissolves the partnership. One party may sell his interest to another party who is satisfactory to the remaining members of the firm, and they may agree to take him in as a partner; the old partnership is dissolved and a new one formed. After the partner has retired or sold out, he is still liable on all the contracts of the firm made before dissolution, and he is entitled to his share of the firm's assets after debts have been paid.

In Goodspeed v. Wiard Plow Co., 45 Mich. 322, it was held that a retiring partner is bound by all previous contracts made within the lines of the business, but after dissolution of the partnership he is not bound by any new contracts made by his former partner.

Notice. The retiring partner, if the business is to be continued by a new firm, which may have the same or a somewhat similar name, will be liable for the debts and contracts of the firm even after he is out if they were entered into with parties who had dealt with the firm while he was a member and had no notice of his retirement. Therefore, to render himself free from liability for debts and contracts of the new firm, he must give notice of the dissolution of the old firm. This notice must be given either orally or in writing to those who have had previous dealings with the old firm, for the retiring partner is bound unless those who have dealt with the old firm can be shown to have had actual notice.

National Shoe & Leather Bank v. Herz, 89 N.Y. 629, was an action brought against defendant as an alleged partner in the firm of Martin Herz & Co. to recover on four promissory notes endorsed in the name of the firm. Prior to the endorsing of the note, Herz had sold out to his partner, Rosenberg, who carried on the business in the same name. Notice of dissolution was given in the papers and sent by mail to persons who had dealt with the firm. Such a notice was sent to the bank, which never received it. It was held that defendant was liable. To release himself he must show that the bank had actual notice of the dissolution.

But direct notice from the firm or the retiring partner is not required if the customer has actual knowledge of withdrawal of the partner.

Aside from notice of former customers, notice to the world is necessary to enable the retiring partner to escape liability for future debts of the continuing firm or partner. The ordinary method of giving such notice by publication in a newspaper is usually held sufficient, but the paper must be one that circulates in the vicinity.

In Meyer v. Krohn 114 Ill. 574, it was held that as to persons who have never had any business transactions with a partnership, notice of its dissolution by withdrawal of a member by publication in a newspaper published at the place of business of a firm is sufficient; but as to those who have had previous dealings with the firm actual notice or its equivalent must be shown in order to protect the retiring member from liability for debts subsequently incurred in the firm name.

A change in the firm name under which the name of the retiring partner is dropped and general attention is called to the fact that the firm has dissolved is sometimes held to be sufficient notice to the general public to protect the retiring partner against future dealings of the new firm.

In Coggswell v. Davis, 65 Wis. 191, it was held that a change in a partnership name which in itself indicates who the individual partners are may be sufficient evidence of dissolution of the partnership; but when the name under which the business is transacted gives no indication of the names of the persons composing the firm, a change in name is not notice of the retirement of a person who is known to have previously been a partner in the business.

A new or incoming partner who purchases the interest of a retiring partner and becomes a member of the new partnership is liable for all debts incurred after he becomes a member of the firm, but not for any old debts, unless he has expressly agreed for a consideration to assume them.

In Kountz v. Holthouse, 85 Pa. St. 235, it was held that an incoming partner may by agreement become liable for debts contracted by the firm previous to his entering it; but the presumption is against any such liability.

BY DEATH OF PARTNER. The death of a partner will work a dissolution of the partnership. (This also comes under change in the partnership.) Dissolution of the partnership necessarily follows immediately upon a partner's death. The surviving partners have the exclusive right to possession and management of the partnership business for the purpose of closing it out. Often the articles of copartnership provide how the surviving partners shall close out the business; and when such provision is made, it must be followed. The surviving partners hold the partnership assets in trust for the purpose of closing up its affairs, paying the firm debts, and distributing the remaining assets among the partners or their representatives.

In Sellers v. Shore, 89 Ga. 416, it was held that upon the death of a partner, title to the personal assets of the firm is in the survivor, who is charged with their administration, first for payment of partnership debts and second for paying over the deceased partner's share in the surplus to his legal representatives. Unless there is a surplus, none of the assets constitutes any part of the estate of the deceased.

BY DECREE OF COURT. A court of equity may decree a dissolution of the firm for good cause upon application of one or more of the partners. This relief will be granted when the partnership was entered into through fraud or for a wrongful and illegal purpose. After the partnership has been formed, dissolution may be decreed because of misconduct of one or more of the partners; but this relief will not be granted for any slight cause. Wild speculations, gross extravagance, quarrelsome and oppressive conduct, habitual intemperance, indolence, inattention to business, or any conduct which brings disgrace and discredit on the firm, if sufficiently serious, will constitute grounds justifying such action by the court.

In Cottle v. Leitch, 35 Cal. 434, it was held that when one partner having charge of management affairs makes false entries in the books and defrauds his copartners of a portion of the partnership receipts, the partners thus defrauded are entitled to dissolution of the partnership and an accounting.

In Loomis v. McKenzie, 31 Iowa 425, it was held that ill feeling and differences between partners will not justify appointing a receiver to wind up the affairs of the firm when the term for which the partnership was created has not expired and it does not clearly appear that the parties will suffer loss by continuing in possession of the property.

In Groth v. Payment, 79 Mich. 290, it was held that denial by one partner of all rights of his copartners in the partnership property and his claim of the right of exclusive possession and use of it entitled his copartners to dissolution of the partnership.

When the parties cannot longer be associated together with harmony and profit, the court will decree dissolution rather than cause the partnership to be injurious to innocent parties. So also the financial inability of one partner to fulfill his part of the transactions of the firm, whether from his fault or from his misfortune, will be sufficient cause for dissolution. Insanity or permanent failure of health because of incurable disease are sufficient grounds for dissolution.

In Raymond v. Vaughn, 128 Ill. 256, it was held that insanity does not in itself work dissolution of the partnership but may constitute sufficient grounds to justify a court of equity in decreeing its dissolution.

Bankruptcy. Bankruptcy of either a partner or the firm operates as a dissolution of the partnership. This is also true when the firm or any partner makes an assignment for the benefit of creditors.

JOINT STOCK COMPANIES

Definition. A joint stock company is a form of association in appearance resembling a corporation while in reality it is nothing more than a partnership.

Incorporation is expensive in England, and there the joint stock company is common; but in the United States, where the corporate form is so often adopted, the joint stock company is in many states but seldom found.

Joint stock companies resemble corporations in form. They have officers and bylaws. Their capital is divided into shares which under their bylaws are transferable. Their bylaws generally regulate the mode of conducting their business and electing their officers. A member of a joint stock company, although he may style himself but a stockholder, is a partner and as such is liable to the same extent and in the same manner as any ordinary partner.

In Davison v. Holden, 55 Conn. 103, defendants and others associated themselves together without incorporation under the name of Bridgeport Cooperative Association for the purpose of procuring meat and provisions at a lower rate for the members of the organization. Sales were made to persons not members at a higher rate, but no profit was expected beyond the expense of management. The members held meetings and elected officers. It was held that the individuals composing the association were liable personally as partners for goods purchased by the managers of the association for its benefit. It made no difference that they did not intend to become individually responsible or that they did not know or believe that they would.

Sale of Shares. Usually it is held by the bylaws of the company that a member may sell or transfer his shares without working dissolution of the company, as would be the result in a partnership, and the death of a member does not work its dissolution. In some states joint stock companies are given certain privileges by statute; for instance, to sue or to be sued in the name of their president or treasurer. The business of a joint stock company cannot be changed or extended without consent of all the members, although in its ordinary business arrangements a majority will govern.

IX. CORPORATIONS

IN GENERAL

Origin. Modern railroads, steamship lines, airlines, large manufacturing plants, etc., which are controlled by private parties, have made it desirable and necessary for a great number of persons to join in a single enterprise that can be more successfully promoted by means of their joint capital and endeavor. There has also arisen the need for some method of organization that shall be free from certain features of the copartnership law. A necessary feature of the organization is that it shall survive the life of any one member; another is that the interest of any member may be sold or transferred without affecting the organization. To interest people freely in an organization of this kind, it has also been found desirable that a member shall not be personally liable in the enterprise beyond the amount which he invests.

Under common law there was no provision for any association of persons to meet these demands unless by special permit or authority from the government, known as a charter, which was much too slow and costly for commercial use. Now the statutes of all states provide for the formation of corporations, the purpose of which is to enable a number of persons to associate themselves together under a corporate name with the protection and privileges before stated.

Definition. A corporation is defined as a collection of individuals united by authority of law into one body, under a special name and with the capacity of perpetual succession and of acting in many respects as an individual.

In Sebastian Fietsam v. James Hay, 122 Ill. 293, a corporation was held to be an artificial being created by law and composed of individuals who subsist as a body politic under a special denomination with the capacity of perpetual succession and of acting within the scope of its charter as a natural person.

In the eyes of the law corporations are separate from the members who compose them. The property of the corporation is owned by it and not by the members, and a conveyance or sale of the property must be made by the corporation, and cannot be made by the members as individuals.

In Wheelock v. Moulton, 15 Vt. 519, it was held that the stockholders, as such, cannot convey the real property of the corporation, though they all join in the deed. The name and seal of the corporation must be affixed by an officer or agent having authority.

Suits to which a corporation is to be party must be brought by or against the corporation and not the individuals who compose it personally. The corporation may convey to or take from its individual members and may sue them and be sued by them.

In Waring v. Catawba Co., 2 Bay (S.C.) 109, it was held that a member of a corporation may maintain an action against the corporation on any just demand.

The authority of the government is always necessary for the creation of a corporation. No agreement among the members can accomplish such a result. The mere act of the members alone would result in a partnership. The corporation, therefore, being created by the government, has only such powers as are conferred on it by its charter or act of incorporation.

Public Corporations. There are several classes of corporations, but the only division of sufficient importance to consider here is that into public and private corporations. Public corporations are created for the purposes of government and the management of public affairs. Cities, towns, and villages, are examples of such corporations. The legislatures give them certain powers to pass laws or ordinances, build bridges, improve streets, etc. They may take and hold property and may sue and be sued in their corporate names.

Private Corporations. Private corporations are such as are created for private purposes and for the management of affairs in which the members are interested as private parties. When private individuals are interested in a personal way in a corporation which is of even a public nature, as a railroad, airline, bank, or insurance company, it is a private corporation. Private corporations are also either stock or non-stock corporations. Those formed for the pecuniary benefit of their members generally have a capital stock divided into a certain number of parts called shares of stock. A member's interest is determined by the number of shares he holds in the company. This stock is represented by a written or printed certificate, which can be transferred from one person to another without consent of the other members of the company. This transfer of stock may usually be effected through a stock broker at the various stock exchanges, such as the New York and American Stock Exchanges, if the stock is listed there.

Certificates. The form of the certificate of stock is like the following:

INCORPORATED UNDER THE LAWS OF THE STATE OF ILLINOIS

No. 270   10 Shares

THE COOK COUNTY CANDY COMPANY

Capital $700,000   Shares $100 each

This certifies that Bert B. Broome is the owner of ten shares of $100 each, of the Capital Stock of the Cook County Candy Company of Chicago, Illinois, transferable only on the books of the Company, in accordance with the By-laws thereof, in person or by attorney, upon the surrender of this certificate.

In witness whereof, the said corporation has caused this certificate to be signed by its duly authorized officers, and to be sealed with the seal of the corporation, this twenty-seventh day of March 1967.

[SEAL]   [Signed] John Auds, President
                                          [Signed] Fred Fern, Secretary

Non-Stock Corporation. A non-stock corporation is one in which there is no stock to be transferred, and the membership of any individual depends on the consent of the other members. Incorporated societies and mutual-benefit societies are examples.

Private Stock Corporation. The most common corporation in the United States is the private stock corporation.

The powers and attributes of practically all private stock corporations are (1) to have continuous succession under a special name; (2) to receive and grant property, to enter into contracts, and to sue and be sued in the corporate name; (3) to purchase and hold real and personal property; (4) to have a common seal; (5) to make bylaws; and (6) to limit the personal liability of its members for corporate debts to the amount invested.

Name and Perpetual Succession. The attribute of perpetual succession under a special name is essential to all corporations. The corporation is not subject to dissolution by the death or withdrawal of a member. A member may transfer his shares without consent of his associates, and the transferee comes into the corporation as a member without in any way changing or affecting its existence. A necessary attribute of every corporation is a corporate name. This is essential because the corporation being distinct from the members, it could not otherwise be known.

In Elgin Butter Co. v. Elgin Creamery Co., 155 Ill. 127, it was held that issuance of a charter to "Elgin Creamery Company," notwithstanding the previous licensing of "Elgin Butter Company," did not violate the corporation act, which forbade issuing licenses to corporations having the same name.

In State v. McGrath, 92 Mo. 355, it was held that a company was not entitled to a charter under the name of Kansas City Real Estate Exchange when there was a duly incorporated company doing business under the name of Kansas City Real Estate and Stock Exchange, as the names were substantially the same.

Real Estate. The power to hold real estate is common to most corporations, but it is not essential to a corporation's existence. So also, the power to use a seal is ordinarily included in the privileges of a corporation, but it is not essential, as a corporation can contract without a seal.

Bylaws. The right to make bylaws is a common incident of a corporation's powers. It is unnecessary to make them when the charter is sufficiently full to provide for all contingences, but usually matters of detail are not included in the charter, provision for them being made in the bylaws, and every private corporation has the implied power to make them. But the bylaws, to be valid, must be reasonable, consistent with the charter, and within the purposes of the corporation. They are generally adopted by majority vote of the stockholders, and having once been adopted, bind all the stockholders, whether they have assented to them or not.

Limited Liability. A most important attribute of a corporation is exemption of the stockholders from liability for debts of the corporation. In a partnership a partner is personally liable for debts of the firm, but this is not so in a corporation, except when by statute the personal liability of a stockholder is increased. The stockholder of a bank is liable not only for his investment in stock but also for a further sum of the same amount. This is called double liability of the stockholder.

Incorporation. As has been said, a corporation can be created only by act of the government. This act may be by the enactment of a special law which creates and gives power to a particular company. The constitutions of most states prohibit the legislature from creating a corporation by a special law except in some particular cases. The great majority of corporations are formed under the general law, which does not of itself create the corporation but authorizes persons to form a corporation by taking certain prescribed steps. It generally requires that articles of incorporation be executed by the incorporators and filed in some public office. These articles must usually set forth the names and residences of the incorporators, the name by which the proposed corporation shall be known, its principal place of business, the objects and legal purposes of the association, the period of time for which it is to exist, the amount of capital stock and the number of shares into which it is divided, the number of directors, and the names of those who are to act as directors until an election is held.

Any person who has the capacity to enter into a contract may be an incorporator. The statutes generally prescribe the number of incorporators necessary to organize.

In the matter of Globe Mutual Benefit Association, 63 Hun (N.Y.) 263, it was held that a cooperative insurance company incorporated and having bylaws under which losses are payable from weekly dues collected from policyholders cannot insure infants. The relation existing between the company and its members is one of contract and the legal disability of an infant is inconsistent with such relation.

In Slater v. Critchett, 37 Minn. 13, a statute provided that the articles of incorporation should be signed by any number not less than nine. So articles of incorporation signed by but two were invalid.

Most states require that a certain number of incorporators be residents of the state in which the company is incorporated.

POWERS AND LIABILITIES
OF CORPORATION

Powers Limited. A corporation has only such powers as are conferred on it by its charter or articles of incorporation. These powers may be expressly conferred, or they may be implied, either because they are incidental to a corporate existence, as the right of successor and the right to have a corporate name, or because they are necessary in order to exercise the powers expressly conferred.

In Downing v. Mt. Washington Road Co., 40 N.H. 230, a charter which gave defendant authority to make and keep in repair a road to the top of Mt. Washington, to take toll of passengers and carriages, to build and own toll houses, and to take land for a road, was held not to authorize the corporation to establish a stage and transportation line, nor to buy carriages and horses for that purpose. Corporation have no powers except such as are given them by their charter, or such as are incidental and necessary to carry into effect the purposes for which they were established.

Implied Powers. The powers that are incidental to corporate existence and that will always be implied are these: to have perpetual succession during the life of the corporation, to have a corporate name under which to contract and to sue and be sued, to purchase and hold real and personal property, to have a common seal, and to make bylaws.

A corporation has also the implied power that is reasonably necessary to execute the powers expressly granted and not expressly or impliedly excluded. A corporation generally has the implied power to borrow money whenever the nature of its business renders it necessary or expedient to do so.

In Nelson v. Eaton, 26 N.Y. 410, it was held that an insurance corporation, in the absence of any statutory restriction, has the power to borrow money, and incident thereto, the power to transfer its assets in trust as security for the loan.

In Bradbury v. Boston Canoe Club, 153 Mass. 77, it was held that a corporation formed for the purpose of encouraging athletic exercises has the power to borrow money for building a clubhouse on lands leased by it, under the provision of the statute that such corporation may hold real and personal estate and may purchase or erect suitable buildings for its accommodation. It also has the power to make, endorse, or accept bills of exchange and promissory notes if such is the usual and proper means of accomplishing the results for which it was created.

In Moss v. Averell 10 N.Y. 449, a corporation organized for the purpose of raising and smelting lead ore was held to be a corporation having power to purchase property necessary for carrying on the business, and unless expressly prohibited by statute, to give promissory notes in payment for such purposes.

To sell or mortgage real property owned by it is another important power of a corporation, unless it is a railroad or other company of a public nature.

In Dupee v. Boston Water Power Co., 114 Mass. 37, it was held that a corporation chartered with power to purchase and hold water power created by the erection of dams and to hold real estate may, when its water privileges can no longer be profitably used, sell its land.

But a corporation has no implied power to enter into a contract of partnership.

In Mallory v. Hanaur Oil Works, 86 Tenn. 598, an agreement between corporations engaged in manufacturing cottonseed oil to select a committee composed of representatives of each corporation and to turn over to this committee the properties and the machinery of each company, so that the business of each might be operated and managed for a specified time by this committee for the common benefit, the losses or profits to be shared in certain proportions, was held to be a contract of partnership. A partnership contract is not within the express or implied power of a corporation and is void even though authorized by both stockholders and directors.

In Central R.R. Co. v. Smith, 76 Ala. 572, it was held that the Central R.R. and Banking Co. of Gregory, which was authorized by its charter to construct and operate a railroad between the cities of Savannah and Macon and to organize and carry on a banking business, had no power, express, implied, or incidental, to purchase and run a steamboat on the Chattahoochee River, which was no part of its route, nor to form a partnership with a natural person for carrying on that business.

As a general rule, when a corporation is given general authority to engage in business, it takes the powers of a natural person to make all the necessary and proper contracts to enable it to attain its legitimate objects.

In Wright v. Hughes, 119 Ind. 324, it was held that a corporation organized as a life-insurance company has power to borrow money and secure its payment by mortgaging its real estate. When general authority is given a corporation to engage in business, it takes the power, in the absence of charter restraint, just as a natural person enjoys it with all its incidents, and may borrow money to attain its legitimate objects the same as an individual.

Acts Ultra Vires. When a corporation performs acts not within its power to perform, the acts are said to be *ultra vires.* An ultra vires contract, if executory, cannot be enforced; but most courts hold that if the defense of ultra vires will work an injustice, it will not be allowed, and this is also true if the party seeking to enforce the contract has performed his part.

In Nassau Bank v. Jones 95 N.Y. 115, plaintiff, the bank, subscribed to stock in a railroad corporation and in this action sued for its share of the profits. It was held that plaintiff was not authorized to make such a contract, and the court would not enforce it.

Liability for Acts of Agents. A corporation is liable to the same extent as a natural person for the frauds and wrongs of its agents and servants committed in the course of their employment.

In Goodspeed v. Bank, 22 Conn. 530, plaintiff brought an action against defendant, a banking corporation, for damages for maliciously bringing vexatious and unjust lawsuits against plaintiff. The defense was that a corporation is not liable for such a wrong, but the court held that a suit of this nature may be maintained against a corporation.

DISSOLUTION OF CORPORATION

A private corporation may be dissolved in any one of four ways: (1) by expiration of its charter; (2) by surrender of its charter with consent of the state; (3) by act of legislature repealing its charter, under the power reserved by the state when granting the charter; (4) by its forfeiture of its franchise or charter, upon judgment of a proper court, for misuse or non-use of its powers.

By Expiration of Charter. The charter usually stipulates that the corporation shall be formed for a certain time, as for twenty of fifty years. When this period expires, the association no longer has an existence and is therefore dissolved.

Sturges v. Vanderbilt, 73 N.Y. 384, held that upon expiration of the term of existence of a corporation as limited by its charter it becomes extinct, and no formal decree of dissolution is necessary.

A charter when granted to the corporation and accepted by it constitutes a contract between the state and the corporation. This contract exists under the clause in our Constitution prohibiting any state legislature from passing a law impairing the obligation of a contract. The state cannot, therefore, repeal the charter of a company unless it has expressly reserved that right or unless the corporation assents.

In Ruggles v. People, 91 Ill. 256, a railroad company was in its charter expressly granted the right to fix rates of toll to be charged. This was held to confer not unlimited power but only the right to charge reasonable rates, and a statute fixing what are reasonable maximum rates does not impair the contract contained in the charter. The charter of a railway corporation is a contract between it and the state by which it may exercise the rights and privileges conferred until expiration of its charter, unless by some act it forfeits its privileges and franchise, and under the federal Constitution, the obligation of such contract cannot be impaired by subsequent legislation.

By Surrender of Charter. Dissolution may be effected by the association's surrendering its charter, but the charter being a contract between the state and the association, this can be done only with consent of the state. The statutes generally provide certain formalities which must be complied with before dissolution will be granted.

By Repeal of Charter. The state may institute a suit in the proper court to cause a corporate charter to be forfeited. Ground for such a suit is abuse or misuse, or neglect, of corporate powers. But mere abuse or misuse alone does not work forfeiture of the charter. This results only from the judgment of the court after a hearing in which the corporation has a chance to appear and

present its side of the case. Forfeiture will be decreed by the
courts when the corporation is guilty of acts or has omitted to do
certain things which by statute are expressly made causes of
forfeiture of its franchise.

People v. North River Sugar Refining Co., 121 N.Y. 582, is a
famous trust case. Defendant had entered an agreement with
other sugar refineries which constituted a partnership between
them, whereby control of their several businesses was to be under
one board of managers and the profits were to be divided according to a certain proportion. The court held that such action was
in excess of its corporate powers, illegal and contrary to public
policy, and so authorized dissolution of the corporation; it said:
"To justify the forfeiture of corporate existence the transgression
on the part of the corporation must be not merely formal or
incidental, but material and serious, and such as to harm or
menace the public welfare; for the state does not concern itself
with the quarrels of private litigants. It furnishes for them sufficient courts and remedies but intervenes as a party only where
some public interest requires its action."

By Forfeiture. Continued neglect to exercise rights under
corporate franchises and failure to perform the implied conditions
on which the charter was granted amount to non-use, for which
the charter may be forfeited.

State v. Atchison R.R. Co., 24 Neb. 143, held that when a
railway company without authority of law leases its road to another railway company with all of its rights, property, and
franchises for a long period of time, it thereby abandons operation
of the road and is subject to forfeiture.

Combinations with other corporations to form an unlawful
trust or monopoly is sufficient ground for dissolution. This is illustrated in People v. North River Sugar Refining Co., *supra.*

Distilling Co. v. People, 156 Ill. 448, was an action brought
to dissolve the Distilling and Cattle Feeding Co., which had been
formed for the purpose of taking over the plants of five or six
other distillers and running them under one head, the profits
to be divided among the several stockholders. It was held that
a charter authorizing a corporation to engage in a general distilling business and to own the property necessary for that purpose
gives it no power to enter into a scheme of getting into its hands

all the distilleries of the country and establishing a virtual monopoly of the business.

Method of Dissolution. The effect of dissolution is that thereafter the corporation no longer exists for any purpose; but the statutes in nearly all the states now make provisions under which the business of dissolved corporations may be liquidated and settled and the rights of stockholders and creditors adjusted. The usual method of doing this is to appoint a receiver to wind up the corporate affairs, collect bills due the corporation, and pay its creditors, and after that divide the remainder among the stockholders, according to the amounts of stock they hold.

Mason v. Pewabic Mining Co., 133 U.S. 50, held that on dissolution of a corporation at expiration of the term of its corporate existence, each stockholder has the right, as a general rule, to have the corporate property converted into money, whether it is necessary for the payment of debts or not.

MEMBERSHIP IN CORPORATION

Stockholders. Membership in a private stock corporation is acquired by the ownership of one or more shares of the captial stock. This may be acquired by subscription to the capital stock either before or after incorporation by purchase from the corporation or by transfer from the owner. The certificate of stock is a written acknowledgment of the holder's interest in the corporation. When the stock is subscribed for after incorporation of the company, it is simply a contract between the corporation and the subscriber.

In Greer v. Railway Co. 96 Pa. St. 391, Greer, soliciting subscriptions for the building of a railway, took a subscription book, signed therein himself and persuaded others to subscribe. He kept the book about six months, and then, because of a disagreement with the company, cut out his own name from the book and returned it to the company. It was held that by placing his name in the book he had perfected a contract with the company and was just as much bound as if he had left his name in the book.

Stock Subscriptions. The subscriptions of several persons to an agreement to take stock in a corporation thereafter to be formed is a continuing offer to the corporation to be formed, which may be accepted by the corporation, and is binding. Delivery of the certificate is merely evidence of the ownership of the shares, and is not necessary to make a subscriber a stockholder. A stockholder has a right to inspect the books and papers of the corporation if he has a reason to do so.

In Phoenix Iron Co. v. Commonwealth, 113 Pa. St. 563, a stockholder wishing to prepare a bill setting forth certain grievances against the corporation asked to see the papers and books of the company. It was held that the books and papers of a corporation are the common property of the stockholders and that unless the charter provides otherwise, a stockholder has the right, at proper times, to inspect them personally and with the aid of a disinterested expert to make extracts from them for a definite and proper purpose.

Dividends. Out of the surplus or net profits of the corporate business the directors may vote a dividend. This is a certain per cent on the capital stock, and when the dividend is declared the stockholders are entitled to their respective shares. Until such dividend is declared, a stockholder has no legal right to a share of the profits, although upon its being wrongfully withheld a suit in equity may be brought to compel the corporation to declare it.

In Hyatt v. Allen, 56 N.Y. 553, plaintiff transferred to defendant twenty shares of stock of a corporation under an agreement by which all profits and dividends on said stock up to January 1, 1872, were to be paid to plaintiff. No dividends were to be declared until April 9, 1872. In an action to recover part of this dividend as having been earned before January 1, it was held that plaintiff was not entitled to any part of it. A stockholder has no legal title to profits until a dividend is declared.

Preferred Stock. The dividend declared must be equal on all the stock except where part of the stock is "preferred." This means that a certain part of the capital stock is declared on the certificate to be preferred and the balance common stock. The rights of preferred stock usually include a prior claim on dividends. Six per cent preferred stock entitles the holder to an annual dividend of 6 per cent before any dividend can be declared on the common stock.

Transfer of Stock. Shares of stock are transferred from one holder to another by an assignment, which is usually on the back of the stock certificate and in a form somewhat like the following:

For value received I hereby sell, assign, and transfer unto John J. Jones twenty shares of the capital stock represented by the within certificate, and do hereby irrevocably constitute and appoint Bert B. Boyd my attorney to transfer the said stock on the books of the within named corporation, with full power of substitution in the premises.

Dated January 27, 1967
In the presence of
Elmer Ekblad   [Signed] Howard E. Holt

The attorney named to transfer the stock is generally the secretary of the company.

Stock in a corporation is subject to sale and transfer like any other kind of personal property. The transferee of stock acquires all the rights and assumes all the liabilities arising after the date of transfer. He is entitled to dividends declared after the transfer and has the right to vote at stockholders' meetings (if his is voting stock) and all other rights arising from his ownership.

In March v. Eastern R.R. Co., 43 N.H. 515, it was held that the purchaser of a share of stock in a corporation takes with it all its incidents, one of which is the receiving of all future dividends declared on such shares, and it does not make any difference at what time or from what sources the profits thus divided may have accrued.

When the statute imposes a personal liability on stockholders, the transferee is liable under such statute if the liability arises after the transfer. The transfer of stock must be recorded on the books of the company and a new certificate issued before the transferee appears as a stockholder on the books and has the right to vote.

MANAGEMENT OF CORPORATION

Vote of Stockholders. As a general rule each stockholder in a corporation is bound by all acts adopted by majority vote of the stockholders, provided such acts are within the scope of powers and authority conferred by the charter.

In Dudley v. Kentucky High School, 72 Ky. 576, a corporation was authorized to receive and hold for the benefit of a high school any land by gift, devise, or purchase. A stockholder brought action to restrain the corporation from purchasing certain real estate, claiming that the corporation could not afford it and the result would be brankruptcy. It was held that the action could not be maintained, as the majority of the stockholders had voted for the purchase. Every stockholder contracts that the will of the majority shall govern in all matters coming within the limits of the act of incorporation. But the majority cannot bind the minority by any acts outside the powers conferred by the charter.

In Barton v. Enterprise Loan Association, 114 Ind. 226, it was provided in the articles of association of the company that it should continue in operation eight years, unless it should earlier have sufficient funds to pay its debts and redeem its stock. A resolution was passed by a majority of the stockholders dissolving the association before the time limit, and it was held that without consent of all the stockholders, and with unredeemed stock outstanding, such a resolution was of no effect.

In some cases management of the corporation is vested in the directors, and then the authority vested in the stockholders is the election of the directors. The directors alone are authorized to act in managing the business. The right to make bylaws is generally in the majority of stockholders, although in some cases that power is by charter vested in the directors.

Notice of Meeting. Notice of the time and place of a stockholders' meeting must be given to each stockholder unless it is definitely designated by the charter or the bylaws. Each stockholder is usually entitled to one vote for each share of stock owned by him, although at common law each stockholder had but one vote without regard to the number of shares of stock he owned. At common law the right to vote could be exercised only in person, but now the right to vote by proxy (power of attorney) is generally conferred by statute. The proxy or authority to vote is in the form of a written power of attorney and is revocable at the pleasure of the person executing it.

Directors. Active management of the corporate business is usually vested in a board of directors selected by a majority of the stockholders. The directors act by majority vote. The powers and duties of the directors and other officers are generally fully defined in the bylaws.

RIGHTS OF CREDITORS OF CORPORATION

In General. The creditors of a corporation generally have the same rights and remedies against the corporation and its property as they would have against a natural person. They may obtain a judgment against it and issue an execution against its property, and adopt the other remedies that they would have against an individual. Aside from the rights of creditors to proceed against the property belonging to the corporation, there are cases in which the creditor may also look to the stockholder, notwithstanding the general rule that a stockholder is not individually liable for debts of the corporation.

Liability of Stockholders. In the first of these cases the stockholder is indebted to the corporation on his stock, and the payment of the amount is necessary to pay the creditors. It is held that a stockholder must contribute the full amount of his subscription for stock if it is needed by creditors. This amount is part of the capital stock of the company, and the capital is held by the courts to be in the nature of a trust fund for payment of corporate debts.

In Payne v. Bullard, 23 Miss. 88, it was held that where a person subscribes for a certain number of shares of bank stock and does everything in order to secure his right to the stock but does not fully pay for it, he cannot afterward by an agreement with the bank diminish the number of his shares so as to affect the creditors of the bank. Stock subscribed to a bank is in the nature of a trust fund for payment of its liabilities.

Hatch v. Dana, 101 U.S. 205, held that creditors of a corporation who have exhausted their remedy against the corporation can, in order to satisfy their judgment, proceed against a stockholder to enforce his liability to the company for the amount remaining due on his subscription for stock.

The stockholder is also liable to creditors of the corporation if any part of the capital stock has been unlawfully distributed or paid out to him, directly or indirectly, leaving creditors unpaid. This may be accomplished by distributing funds as dividends when there are no surplus profits, or in other ways, but however accomplished, the stockholder may be compelled to refund for the benefit of creditors the amount so received.

In Bartlett v. Drew, 57 N.Y. 587, defendant was a stockholder in the New Jersey Steam Navigation Co. Three boats of the company were sold for a gross sum of $15,000, which was divided among the stockholders. This action was brought by a creditor of the company to reach the amount so received by defendant. It was held that plaintiff could maintain an action to reach whatever defendant had so received. It was immaterial whether he got it by fair agreement or by a wrongful act, the creditors had the right to be paid first out of the assets of the company.

The statutes which in some states have imposed additional liabilities on stockholders vary greatly. Some make the stockholder liable for all debts until the whole capital stock is paid in. Others make him liable for a sum equal to the amount of stock held by him in addition to the amount yet due on his stock, and so on, many different provisions being found in the different states.

McDonnell v. Alabama Gold Life Insurance Co., 85 Ala. 401, held that by statute in that state a stockholder in a life-insurance company was liable for debts of the company, not only for his unpaid subscription for stock but also for an additional sum equal to the amount of his stock.

X. INSURANCE

IN GENERAL

Insurance Companies. Certain catastrophic events may happen which, although by no means frequent in the experience of the average man, are so important and may entail upon him such severe loss that he seeks a mode of protection. The impending loss may be destruction of his property by fire, flood, or cyclone; or it may be loss of his earning capacity by accident to his person; or loss to his family by reason of his death.

To afford protection against these calamities there exist many large corporations, known as insurance companies, which engage in the business of assuming such risks for a certain compensation known as a premium. These premiums, although comparatively small, being contributed by the many, form a large fund out of which the losses to the few are indemnified.

Definition. Insurance is defined as a contract whereby for a stipulated consideration one party undertakes to compensate the other for loss on a particular subject for a specified peril. The party agreeing to make the compensation is called the insurer or underwriter; the other party to the contract is the insured. The written contract is called the policy, and the event insured against, the risk.

Every state has an insurance official whose duty it is to regulate and inspect the insurance companies doing business in his state to see that they are solvent and that their affairs are properly conducted.

FIRE INSURANCE

Insurable Interest. The insured must have an insurable interest in the risk or property insured. This means that he must have an interest of such nature that the fire insured against would directly injure him. If the person had no interest in the property on which he obtained insurance, the only object would be mere speculation, and the contract would not be upheld in law.

Riggs v. Insurance Co., 125 N.Y. 7, is a case in which a stockholder in a steamship company had one of the company's boats insured in his favor, and the question was whether or not he had an insurable interest in the property. It was held by the court that he had such an interest. The stockholder in a corporation has no legal title to its assets, but he has an equitable right of a pecuniary nature which may be prejudiced by destruction of property belonging to the corporation, as a loss of the property would affect the dividends distributed by the company and would also lessen the assets distributed among the stockholder upon dissolution.

This interest may be an existing interest; for example, the absolute ownership, or a life interest, or a right by mortgage or lien. Or it may be only an interest in expected profits or goods, as a shipowner's right to insure goods on which he has a claim for freight.

In National Oil Filtering Co. v. Citizens Insurance Co., 106 N.Y. 535, plaintiff had an agreement with Ellis & Co. by virtue of which Ellis & Co. was to pay plaintiff royalties for the use of plaintiff's patents, which royalties were guaranteed to amount to $250 per month. Plaintiff insured the plant of Ellis & Co., the agreement of the insurance company in the policy being that in case the buildings occupied by Ellis & Co. should be damaged by fire, so as to cause a diminution in said royalties, defendant would pay the amount of the diminution during repairs of said premises. It was held that plaintiff had an insurable interest in the property.

The owner of property does not lose his insurable interest by mortgaging, leasing, or giving an executory contract of sale, as more than one person may have an insurable interest in property. For example, A owns a house and lot; he leases it to B, mortgages it to C, and gives an executory contract of sale to D. Each one of these four parties has an insurable interest in the house.

Davis v. Insurance Co., 10 Allen (Mass.) 113, held that omitting to state in an application for insurance on a building that a written agreement had been given by the applicant to convey the building to a third party in consideration of a certain sum of money being paid within a fixed time did not affect the right to recover the full amount of insurance.

Divided Interest. Each person having an insurable interest in a house cannot recover the full value of the house in case of fire but merely the value of his interest. The owner can recover the market value at the time of loss, and the mortgagee can recover the value of the house up to the amount of his mortgage.

In Kernochan v. Insurance Co., 5 Duer (N.Y.) 1, it was held that the mortgagee's insurable interest in the mortgaged property corresponded in amount to the debt secured and that in the event of total loss he could recover the full sum insured, provided it did not exceed the amount due on the mortgage. This recovery could not be defeated by showing that the property, notwithstanding the loss, was still ample security for the mortgaged debt.

Form of Contract. The contract of insurance is usually in writing, although it may be oral, unless expressly required by statute to be written. The forms adopted by the various companies are much alike and generally set forth in detail all the agreements between the parties.

The contract requires a meeting of the minds of the parties, and certain terms must be definitely settled upon, viz., the property insured, the risk insured against, the rate of premium, and the term of duration of the insurance.

In Goddard v. Insurance Co., 108 Mass. 56, defendant insured a building as a machine shop against fire. The representation that it was such was made by an insurance broker without the knowledge or consent of plaintiff. It was in fact used as an organ factory. The risk on an organ factory was greater than on a machine shop, and it was held that the policy was void, as the minds of the parties had never met on the subject matter of the contract.

Description of Property. The policy must contain a description of the property insured. This is generally set forth briefly and gives the nature of the building or article. It also gives the title or interest of the insured in the same, that is, whether he is the owner, mortgagee bailee, etc. The risk insured against must also be agreed upon. The property may be insured against fire, flood, tornado, or other unforeseeable casualty.

Oral Contract. The contract is binding and in force as soon as the agreement is completed, although the written policy may not have been actually delivered nor in fact ever issued.

Fish v. Cottenet, 44 N.Y. 538, held that if an agreement for insurance is made with an agent authorized to bind the company but through the negligence of the agent the application is not received in time to be acted on by the company before the loss occurs, the company is liable.

In Ellis v. Insurance Co., 50 N.Y. 402, plaintiff applied to an insurance agent for insurance on a quantity of cotton. The amount and the premium were settled upon, and the agent agreed to insure as requested. It was left with the agent to select the companies with which to insure, and he decided to place $6,100 with defendant, entering it on his books, and crediting defendant with the premium, which was forwarded to defendant before the loss. It was held that this constituted a contract to issue the policy and was binding on defendant.

Effect of Fraud. A contract of insurance requires good faith between the parties, and the party seeking insurance is bound to disclose any circumstance that will affect the risk. Any fraudulent dealing is fatal to the rights of the party responsible for it. Any concealment of a material fact inquired into by the insurer will, if made intentionally by the insured, avoid the policy. Still, neither party is bound to volunteer information regarding matters of which the other has knowledge or of which in the exercise of ordinary care he ought to have knowledge. But the insured must not withhold information which would affect the insurer's judgment.

In Armenia Insurance Co. v. Paul, 91 Pa. St. 520, one of the questions in the application for insurance was "What is the distance, occupation, and material of all buildings within 150 feet?" No answer was made to this question, and the company sought to avoid the policy on that ground. It was held that it might have refused to issue the policy or sought further information but that by issuing the policy it waived the answer to the question.

Representation. A representation is said to be a statement of fact made at the time of or before the contract relating to the proposed adventure and on the good faith of which the contract is made. A material misrepresentation of fact, whether innocent or fraudulent, avoids the contract.

In Armour v. Insurance Co., 90 N.Y. 450, defendant issued a policy of insurance on plaintiff's warehouse, by the terms of which losses should be apportioned between the different policies on the building, and also any misrepresentation whatever would avoid the policy. Plaintiff's agent, who applied for the policy, stated through mistake that there was already $200,000 insurance on the building, when in fact there was but $30,000. It was held that the misrepresentation was material and that plaintiff could not recover on the policy.

Warranty. A warranty is a statement of fact or promise of performance relating to the subject of insurance or to the risk, inserted in the policy itself or expressly made part of it, which, if not literally true or strictly complied with, will avoid the contract. It differs from a representation, which, as we have seen, is a collateral inducement outside the contract and need be only substantially complied with; the warranty must be contained in the policy and must be strictly performed.

In Wood v. Insurance Co., 13 Conn. 533, it was held that any statement or description on the part of the insured on the face of the policy which relates to the risk is an express warranty, and such a warranty must be strictly complied with or the insurance is void.

If questions in the application are not answered or if the answers are incomplete but not false, there is no breach of warranty, provided the insurer accepts the invitation without objection.

Although breach of warranty or misrepresentation of a material fact may not contribute to or cause the loss, nevertheless the policy is avoided, for the risk is different from that which the insurer undertook to assume.

In Ripley v. Aetna Insurance Co., 30 N.Y. 136, at the time the insurance was obtained the question was asked whether there was a watchman in the buildings during the night. The insured answered, "There is a watchman nights." It appeared that by the custom of the mill no watchman was kept from 12 o'clock Saturday night until 12 o'clock Sunday night. The above answer was referred to and made part of the policy. It was held that the answer was understood to mean that there was a watchman at the mill every night and that failure to keep a watchman every night constituted a breach of warranty and avoided the policy without regard to whether it had anything to do with producing the loss.

FIRE INSURANCE POLICY

Uniformity. Statutes have been passed in New York and in several other states adopting a standard form of fire-insurance policy, the object being to establish uniformity of contract and to avoid conflict between different companies insuring the same property.

Loss by Fire. Insurance in the policy against loss by fire includes loss which is caused by the burning of the property insured or which is the result of fire in close proximity, the heat from which damages the property insured. It also includes loss or damage by water from fire engines or from exposure or theft of goods during their removal to a place of safety at the time of the fire.

White v. Insurance Company, 57 Me. 91, is a case in which it was held that the damage and expense caused by removing, with a reasonable degree of care suited to the occasion, insured goods from apparent immediate destruction by fire, are covered by a policy insuring the goods against "loss and damage by fire," although the building in which they were insured and from which they were removed was not in fact burned.

It includes loss caused by lightning but only if a lightning clause is inserted; therefore it is customary to include such a clause.

In Babcock v. Montgomery Insurance Co., 6 Barb. (N.Y.) 637, it was held that under a policy of insurance against loss or damage by fire, one of the conditions being that the insurer will be liable for "fire by lightning," the company is not liable for destruction of the building by its being shattered and torn by lightning without its being burned. Unless the loss is the effect of actual ignition, the insurers are not liable.

If the fire is caused by the act of an incendiary or by the acts of the insured while insane or by the careless acts of a third person, the insurance company is liable.

Location. The standard policy contains a statement of the location of the property insured, and if the property is removed to another or different place without consent of the insurer, the policy is no longer in effect. So if a party insures his household

furniture while living on a certain street and then moves to
another street, the insurance ceases to be in force. The reason
for this rule is plain; the risk is likely to vary in different locations,
and whether it does or not, the insurer has the right to know what
risk he is assuming, as he may wish to decline placing any more
insurance on property in the same building.

In Lyons v. Insurance Co., 14 R.I. 109, a policy of insurance
against fire was issued on furniture described as contained in a
house on McMillen Street, Providence, R.I. The insured, without
knowledge of the insurer, moved the articles to a house on another street, in which they burned. It was held that the insured
could not recover. Statement of the location of the goods is a
continuing warranty.

Bradbury v. Insurance Co., 80 Mo. 396, is a case in which
plaintiff had a fire-insurance policy on a "frame stable building,"
specifically described, and on his "carriages, sleighs, hacks, horses,
harnesses, blankets, robes and whips contained therein." It was
held that the insurance did not cover damage by fire to plaintiff's
hack while in a repair shop one eighth of a mile away and on
another street, without the knowledge and consent of the insurer,
for the temporary purpose of being repaired.

Amount Recoverable. The market or cash value of the property
at the time of the fire is the amount that can be recovered of the
insurance company if this sum does not exceed the amount of
the policy. If the property is only partly destroyed, the amount
that may be recovered is the difference in the value of the
property before and after the fire. The insurer generally reserves
the right to rebuild or repair, and if he elects so to do, this takes
the place of money damages.

Additional Insurance. The standard policy of insurance contains a clause which provides that the policy shall be void in
case the insured now has, or shall hereafter make or procure, any
other contract of insurance, whether valid or not, on property
covered in whole or in part by the policy, without an agreement
endorsed or added thereon allowing such additional insurance.
The reason for this provision is that the companies do not wish
to have the property insured for more than its value, and also
they desire to know whether any other insurance is carried on the
property, as in case of loss, if insured in several companies, each
need contribute only its proportionate share.

Sanders v. Cooper, 115 N.Y. 279, held that where one of the conditions of a policy declares it void in case of other insurance on the property insured, not endorsed on the policy or consented to in writing by the insurer, the fact that there was such other insurance outstanding whose existence was not communicated or known to the company is a breach of the condition of the policy that renders it void.

Alienation Clause. The standard policy also contains a clause known as the alienation clause, which renders the policy void if any change other than the death of the insured takes place in the interest, title, or possession of the subject insured (except change of occupants without increase of hazard), whether by legal process or by judgment or by voluntary act of the insured. This section means any parting of or sale of the premises, and does not include the giving of a mortgage upon the premises.

Judge v. Insurance Co., 132 Mass. 521, is a case in which the insurance policy contained practically the above clause. After the policy was issued, the insured gave a mortgage on the property covered by the policy, but the mortgagee had made no move to foreclose; in fact, the mortgage was not yet due. It was held that the policy was not avoided.

Assignment. A fire-insurance policy is not assignable, and if assigned without consent of the insurer, it is void.

In Lett v. Insurance Co., 125 N.Y. 82, defendant issued a policy of insurance on property owned by B, the loss being payable to A as mortgagee. B afterward conveyed the property to C, who in turn conveyed it to plaintiff. At the time of the last conveyance, B executed to plaintiff an assignment of his interest in the policy, but consent of defendant was not endorsed on the policy, although such endorsement was a condition of its remaining in force. It was held that the policy was invalid because of failure to obtain defendant's consent to the assignment.

If with consent of the company the property insured as well as the policy is assigned, a new contract is formed which will not be affected by any act of the assignor.

Unoccupied Dwelling. The standard form of policy also provides that if the property is a dwelling and remains vacant or unoccupied without consent of the company for a period of ten days, the insurance is of no effect. This clause is held to be a reasonable restriction, as the insurer is entitled to know that the premises are receiving ordinary supervision. It means that the dwelling must have a tenant living in it.

In Corrigan v. Insurance Co., 122 Mass. 298, the insurance policy provided that it should be void if the house insured should remain vacant or unoccupied for ten days without written notice to, and consent of, the company. It was held that if the house had not been used by someone as a dwelling place within ten days of the date of loss, the policy would be void, consent of the company not having been obtained. If the former tenant had moved his family into another house in which they slept and took their meals, the fact that he retained the key and that some of the furniture was still in the house did not constitute occupancy of the premises.

Factory Buildings. There is a further provision rendering the policy void if the subject insured is a factory building and is operated after ten o'clock at night or some other given hour, or is not operated for ten consecutive days or some other specific length of time.

In Day v. Insurance Co., 70 Iowa 710, a policy of insurance on a flour mill contained the provision that if the mill were shut down or remained idle from any cause whatever for more than twenty days without notice to the company, the policy would be suspended from expiration of that time until the mill resumed work. It was held that stoppage of the mill for more than twenty days without the required notice suspended the policy, though the stoppage was for necessary repairs to the mill or race.

Renewals. The policy is often renewed by a short form of receipt which obviates the necessity of a new policy. This renewal, which may be either in writing or by parol, in substance creates a new contract on the same terms and conditions as those agreed on in the old policy.

Hay v. Insurance Co., 77 N.Y. 235, held that an agreement to renew a policy of fire insurance in the absence of evidence that any change was intended implies that the terms of the existing policy are to be continued.

Cancellation. The standard form of policy contains a stipulation that the policy may be canceled at any time by the company, or at the request of the insured upon giving five days' notice of such cancellation. In case of such cancellation the unearned premiums paid shall be returned to the insured.

Mortgaged Property. When the property insured is mortgaged and it is desired that in case of fire the insurance shall be paid to the mortgagee to satisfy his claim, it is the custom to attach a mortgagee clause which provides that the insurance shall be paid to the mortgagee named as his interest may appear.

Notice of Loss. After loss it is the duty of the insured to give the company immediate notice. Under the standard form of policy this notice must be in writing. The damaged goods must be inventoried, and proof of loss duly sworn to must be filed within sixty days.

Knickerbocker Insurance Co. v. McGinnis, 87 Ill. 70, is a case in which a policy of fire insurance required immediate notice to be given by the insured in case of loss. In the great Chicago fire, October 9, 1871, plaintiff's property was burned and notice of loss was given November 13. It was held to have been given in sufficient time in view of the great derangement of all kinds of business caused by the fire.

Unless notice is given as stated and proof of loss is filed within the specified time, no recovery can be held on the policy.

Pro Rata Clause. The standard policy contains a pro rata clause under which the insured cannot recover more than the amount of his loss in the property where there is more than one policy on the property. Thus a man might have his house insured in three companies, as follows: in number one for $4,000, in number two for $6,000, and in number three for $2,000. The house is damaged by fire to the amount of $6,000. The insured can recover only this amount, and the companies will be required to pay their pro rata portions—that is, number one, $2,000; number two, $3,000; number three, $1,000. This rule does not apply to the case of several persons with different interests in the same property; it applies to any one insurer who, if he recovered the full amount of all policies, would be getting double insurance on the loss.

LIFE INSURANCE

Definitions. Another form of insurance becoming more general every year is life insurance. This kind of contract appears in an almost endless number of forms. It is in its simplest form an agreement on the part of the insurer to pay a specific sum of money upon the death of a certain person, called the insured, to a specific person, called the beneficiary. The consideration paid by the insured is called the premium, and it is generally a certain amount payable annually or monthly. The agreement may take the form of what is termed endowment insurance, whereby the insured, after paying the premium for a given number of years, will receive a certain sum of money, or if he dies before expiration of the period, the amount of the policy will go to the beneficiary. The beneficiary, instead of being a specific person, may be the estate of the insured.

Insured Interest. In life insurance, as in other classes of insurance, the applicant for the policy must have an insurable interest in the life of the insured; otherwise the insurance would be a mere speculation on the life or death of the person insured, placing a premium on the death in favor of one who had no other interest in him. Every person has an insurable interest in his own life, and also in the life of any person on whom he depends either wholly or in part for education and support, and in the life of any person who is under a legal obligation to him for payment of money. So a person may be said to have an insurable interest in the life of anyone whose death would naturally cause him a pecuniary loss or disadvantage.

In Bevan v. Insurance Co., 23 Conn. 244, plaintiff advanced to one Barstow $300 and some articles of personal property under an agreement that Barstow should go to California and labor there for at least a year and then account to plaintiff for half the profits. Plaintiff then insured Barstow's life for $1,000. It was held that plaintiff had an insurable interest in Barstow's life and could recover the amount of the policy.

A partner has an insurable interest in the life of his copartner, and a creditor of the partnership in the life of each partner.

In Connecticut Mutual Life Insurance Co. v. Luchs, 108 U.S. 498, A and B formed a partnership with a capital of $10,000 to which each was to contribute half. A temporarily contributed B's half, and after B's failure to comply with the agreement he had B's life insured for $5,000. It was held that A had an insurable interest in B's life to the amount which B should have contributed to the firm.

Morrell v. Life Insurance Co., 10 Cush. (Mass.) 282, held that a creditor of a firm has an insurable interest in the life of one of the partners, although the other partner may be entirely able to pay the debt and although the estate of the insured is perfectly solvent.

A woman has an insurable interest in the life of her prospective husband as well as in the life of her actual husband, and a man has the same interest in the life of his wife. Mere relationship is not enough to give an insurable interest: there must be an element of dependency coupled with the relationship. A nephew has no insurable interest in the life of his uncle nor has one brother in the life of another.

Lewis v. Insurance Co., 39 Conn. 100, held that one brother did not, from the mere relationship, have an insurable interest in the life of another brother.

If the person taking out the policy has an insurable interest at the time, the fact that the interest ceases does not affect the policy. Therefore, if a man insures the life of his debtor and the debtor subsequently pays the debt, the policy may be continued and enforced at the death of the party insured.

Where the insured designates another person as beneficiary, the right of such beneficiary as a general rule becomes vested at once, and it cannot be disturbed by assignment or in any other way without consent of such beneficiary, unless the right to make a new appointment is reserved in the policy itself.

In Glanz v. Gloeckler, 104 Ill. 573, it was held that when a father takes out a policy of insurance on his own life in favor of an infant daughter, paying all the premiums himself and retaining the policy, the contract is between the insurance company and the daughter, and upon the father's death legal title to the policy vests in her and she is entitled to possession of it.

Premiums. Premiums of life insurance are graded according to the age of the risk. The person insured must undergo a physical examination, as only healthy persons are insured. The amounts of the premiums are determined by average results computed on the length of life of a large number of persons and carefully arranged and tabulated. These results so arranged are called mortuary tables.

Effect of Concealment. The contract of life insurance, like that of fire insurance, requires the exercise of good faith between the parties, but to avoid the policy the concealment of a material fact not made the subject of an express inquiry must be intentional.

In Mallory v. Travelers Insurance Co., 47 N.Y. 52, defendant company issued an accident policy of insurance on the life of A. Prior to issuance of the policy, A had been a canvasser for defendant company and while so acting had been directed to be careful not to insure insane persons. Before the policy was issued, A had been insane but had been discharged from a hospital cured. He did not disclose this fact, but said that there were no circumstances rendering him peculiarly liable to accident. It was held that no fraudulent concealment was shown and the policy was not void if the insured did not conceal any facts which in his own mind were material in making the application.

Misrepresentation. A material misrepresentation will avoid the policy. The same rules apply to misrepresentations in life insurance as in fire insurance, but warranties are statements of facts which are a part of the policy and must be strictly performed or the policy is avoided.

Cushman v. Life Insurance Co., 63 N.Y. 404, is a case in which, by the terms of a life-insurance company, the statements made by the insured in his application were made part of the contract, and it provided that if they were untrue the policy was avoided. The applicant stated that he had never been afflicted with a certain disease. It was shown he had twice been ill with this disease before the policy was issued. It was held that the statement was a warranty and that its breach avoided the policy.

Life-insurance companies generally ask many questions in their applications, and unless the application is expressly incorporated in and made part of the policy, the answers to these questions are considered representations and not warranties. If they are included as warranties, they must be strictly true.

Dwight v. Germania Life Insurance Co., 103 N.Y. 341, is a case in which, in an application for insurance on his life, the applicant, asked whether he was then or had been engaged in or connected with the manufacture or sale of intoxicating liquors, answered, "No." By the terms of the policy the assured warranted the truth of his answers, and it was stipulated that any substantial deviation from the truth in an answer would avoid the policy. It was shown that the insured had kept a hotel for three and one-half years prior to issuance of the policy, and while he had no bar he kept wine and liquors which he sold to his guests. It was held that the answer was false and the policy avoided.

If the questions are not answered or are only partly answered, there is no misrepresentation or breach of warranty.

Phoenix Life Insurance Co. v. Raddin, 120 U.S. 183, is a case in which in the application the question was asked "Has any application been made to this or any other company for insurance on the life of the party? If so, with what result?" To this inquiry there was no answer. It was held that failure to disclose unsuccessful applications for additional insurance did not avoid the policy. Issuance of the policy without further inquiry was a waiver by the company of the right to inquire further.

Forms of Policies. There is no standard form of life-insurance policy, and the forms of different companies vary materially. It is customary to have the policy provide that the application be made part of the contract, thereby making the statements in the application express warranties. So a denial that one is affected with a disease avoids the policy if untrue. The application often inquires as to what other insurance is carried, and a deceptive statement on this point is fatal to the policy. So also a statement as to age is material, and the answer must be correct.

In Aetna Life Insurance Co. v. France, 91 U.S. 510, the insured in his application agreed that if the answers made by him were untrue, the policy should be null and void. It was held that the insurance company was not liable if the statements were untrue. In this case the applicant's age was asked, and he answered thirty, but it was shown that he was from thirty-five to thirty-seven.

Payment. If the policy contains a provision that the insurance ceases unless the premium is paid when due and that the policy is not to take effect until the first premium is actually paid, the condition must be strictly complied with or the policy fails. Prompt payment is essential.

In Holly v. Life Insurance Co., 105 N.Y. 437, the policy on plaintiff's life contained a provision that in case of non-payment of premium when due by the terms, the policy should be forfeited. It was held that punctuality in payment of premiums for life insurance is of the very essence of the contract, and if payment is not made when due, the company has the right to forfeit the policy if such is the contract.

Sickness or other inability to comply with the terms of payment offers no excuse. If the insurer accepts payment of the premium after it is due, the breach will be waived.

Suicide. If the policy contains no express stipulation to the contrary, the insurance company is liable on a policy if the party insured commits suicide, if a third party is the beneficiary. If the insured is the beneficiary, the rule will be otherwise. The policy frequently contains a clause exempting the company from liability if the insured commits suicide within a certain date.

Fitch v. Life Insurance Co., 59 N.Y. 557, was an action on a policy of life insurance taken out for the benefit of the wife and children of the insured. It contained no clause forfeiting it in case of death by suicide. The court held that the insured's suicide did not defeat the policy. The parties interested were not bound by the acts of the deceased after the policy was issued unless in violation of some condition thereof.

When the exemption does not expressly state that the company shall not be liable whether the insured is sane or insane, the suicide clause does not vitiate the policy if suicide is committed while the person is insane. If the clause contains these words, it is vitiated in any event.

Bigelow v. Life Insurance Co., 93 U.S. 284, was an action on a life-insurance policy which provided that it should be null and void if the insured died by suicide, "sane or insane." The company pleaded that he died from a pistol wound inflicted by his own hand and that he intended inflicting such a wound to destroy his own life. It was held that the policy was avoided, even though the deceased was of unsound mind and unconscious of his acts when he inflicted the wound.

Notice of Death. In life insurance the company generally requires immediate notice of death and due proof that the person insured is dead.

MARINE INSURANCE

Definition. Marine insurance is a contract by which the insurer agrees to indemnify the insured against certain perils or risks to which his ships, cargo, and profits may be exposed during a certain trip or during a specified time.

Insurable Interest. The rules governing this class of insurance closely follow the laws of life insurance. The person procuring the policy must have an insurable interest in the property insured. The owner always has an insurable interest, even though the property has been chartered to a person who agrees to pay its value in case of loss. The charterer also has an insurable interest in the ship. Practically the same rules apply to the insurable interest here as in fire insurance.

Oliver v. Greene, 3 Mass. 133, held that a part owner of a vessel who has chartered the remainder with a covenant to pay the value in case of loss may insure the whole vessel as his property.

Effect of Fraud. The requirement of good faith between the parties is greater in marine insurance than in any other branch of insurance. The reason is that the insured has every opportunity to know all the facts and the insurer has only limited opportunity to determine them. Concealment of a material fact, either innocently or fraudulently, avoids the contract.

In Proudfoot v. Montefiore, L.R. Q. B. (Eng.) 511, plaintiff in Liverpool had an agent in Smyrna to buy madder for him and ship it. The agent shipped a cargo and advised plaintiff on January 12, sending the shipping documents on the 19th. On the 23rd the ship sailed, but it was stranded and the cargo destroyed on the same day. The agent got word of the loss on the 24th, and on the 26th, the day that the next mail went to Liverpool, he wrote to plaintiff informing him of the loss, but purposely abstained from telegraphing him in order that plaintiff might not be prevented from obtaining insurance. On the 31st plaintiff, after receiving the letters of the 12th and 19th, but before receiving the letter of the 26th and without knowledge of the loss, obtained insurance. It was held that plaintiff could not recover, as the agent should have telegraphed.

A material fact was concealed in this case which rendered the policy void by reason of concealment and misrepresentation.

Misrepresentation. So a material misrepresentation of a fact, whether innocently or fraudulently made, avoids the contract. The rule is even more strict here than in fire insurance.

Hodgson v. Richardson, 1 W. Black. (Eng.) 463, was an

action on a policy of marine insurance at and from Genoa. The load was put on at Leghorn, bound for Dublin, but the vessel put in at Genoa and was there about five months before sailing. Defendants contended that the policy was vitiated because of non-disclosure to the insurer that the vessel was not loaded at Genoa. It was held that plaintiff could not recover. Concealment of the port of loading vitiated the policy.

Warranty. A warranty, as in fire insurance, must be strictly performed. In marine insurance there are three implied warranties which are understood in every contract. They are in respect to seaworthiness, deviation, and legality.

Seaworthiness. There is implied the warranty that the ship is seaworthy at the time of commencement of the risk. A ship is seaworthy when reasonably fit to perform the services and encounter the ordinary perils incident to the voyage. This means that the ship shall be stanch, properly rigged, and provided with a competent master and a sufficient number of seamen.

In Thebaud v. Insurance Co., 52 Hun. (N.Y.) 495, under a policy of marine insurance plaintiff insured with defendant the steamboat Dos Hermanos on a voyage from Philadelphia to Frontera, Mexico. The defense set up was that the boat was unseaworthy. It appeared that the boat was built simply for river navigation, and sank during the ocean voyage. It was held it was not sufficient to show that the vessel was stanch and strong for river and smooth-water navigation; in order to comply with the implied warranty the plaintiff was obliged to show that everything that could be done to render the vessel fit for the voyage had been done. When the evidence was not disputed that the voyage was one for which the vessel was not fitted, and to the effect that no precautions were taken to provide for the perils to be encountered, plaintiff could not recover.

Deviation. The second implied warranty is that there shall be no voluntary deviation or departure from the course fixed by mercantile usage for the voyage contemplated by the policy; also that there shall be no unreasonable delay in commencing or making the voyage.

In Burgess v. Marine Insurance Co., 126 Mass. 70, a vessel was insured against perils of the seas, "at and from Plymouth to Banks, cod-fishing, and at and thence back to Plymouth." The premium was a certain rate per month, and the policy was to

end with the voyage. The vessel sailed with the usual quantity
of bait, expecting, as usual, to catch more at the Banks. In previous years bait at that place had been plentiful, but this year it
was scarce; so, being unable to get a supply, the master went to
the nearest port for bait, and then returned to the fishing grounds.
The vessel was afterward lost by the perils of the sea. It was
held that in the absence of evidence of usage to put into port for
bait under such circumstances, doing so was a deviation which
discharged the insurer.

If no course has been fixed by mercantile usage, such course
must be pursued as would appear reasonably direct and advantageous to a master of ordinary skill. Deviation is justified when
caused by circumstances over which neither the owner nor the
master had any control, as when forced from the course by stress
of weather, a mutinous crew, etc.

Turner v. Insurance Co., 25 Me. 515, held that if the master
of a vessel which has been insured, in departing from the usual
course of the voyage from necessity, because of leaking of the
vessel, acts in good faith and according to his best judgment,
and has no other object than to conduct the vessel by the safest
and shortest course to the port of destination, the insurance will
not be forfeited.

LEGALITY. The third implied warranty is that the voyage shall
be legal, both in its nature and in the manner in which it is
prosecuted. Smuggling voyages and trading trips to an enemy's
port are cases of illegal voyage.

Losses. Loss may be total, in which case the whole insurance
is ordinarily recoverable; or it may be partial, and then only a
pro rata part can be recovered. When loss is total, it may be
actual total loss or constructive total loss.

Actual total loss occurs when the subject insured wholly
perishes, as when a vessel is so completely wrecked that it
cannot be repaired.

Carr v. Insurance Co., 109 N.Y. 504, held that when a policy
of insurance on a vessel is against "actual total loss only," if the
vessel is afloat or it is practicable to put her afloat, or if she
is capable of being repaired, at any expense, she is not such a total
loss.

A constructive total loss occurs when the article insured is so
far damaged or lost that it cannot be reclaimed or repaired,

except at greater cost than its value. For example, a vessel may be sunk in shallow water, but the cost of raising her may be greater than what she is worth.

Insurance Co. v. Fogarty, 19 Wall. (U.S.) 640, is a case in which a sugar-packing machine was insured and no part was delivered capable of use. It was held to be a total loss, though more than half the pieces, in number and value, may have been delivered and though they would have some value as old iron. To constitute a total loss, it is not necessary that there be absolute extinction or destruction of the thing insured so that nothing of it can be delivered at the point of destination.

The rule adopted in some jurisdictions is that if the property insured by a marine insurance policy is damaged to such an extent that its value is reduced one half or more—that is, if there is a one-half loss or more—the person insured may abandon the property as a constructive total loss and claim the full amount of insurance. Notice of the abandonment must be given the insurers so that they may take measures to claim the property and avail themselves of whatever may be salvaged.

CASUALTY INSURANCE

Definition. Casualty insurance is indemnity against loss resulting from bodily injury or the destruction of certain kinds of property. It may be accident insurance, which is indemnity against personal injury by accident, or it may be one of the numerous classes of insurance that have sprung up within the past few years and grant indemnity against almost every conceivable form of catastrophe. Among these special forms of casualty insurance are plate-glass, boiler, tornado, employer's liability, fidelity, credit, and title insurance.

Accident Insurance. Accident insurance is a branch of life insurance. This class of insurance usually provides a certain payment in case of accidental death, a weekly indemnity for either permanent or total disability by reason of accident, and a fixed sum for such permanent injury as loss of one or both hands, feet, or eyes. An accident in this sense is an unforeseen event which results in injury to one's person. Being thrown from a wagon in a runaway and being struck by falling timber are accidental injuries.

In North American Insurance Co. v. Burroughs, 69 Pa. St. 43, injuries were caused while the insured was pitching hay. The handle of the fork slipped through his hands and struck him in the body, inflicting an injury which caused inflammation resulting in his death. It was held that death was the result of an accident.

Fidelity & Casualty Co. v. Johnson, 72 Miss. 333, held that death at the hands of a mob by hanging is within the terms of a policy insuring against "bodily injuries sustained through external, violent, and accidental means."

Unless it expressly excludes poisoning, the accident policy is held to cover death due to the accidental taking of poison.

Healey v. Mutual Accident Association, 133 Ill. 556, held that death caused by accidentally taking and drinking poison is death produced by bodily injuries received through "external, violent, and accidental means," within the meaning of a policy of insurance providing indemnity in case of death resulting from such causes.

Employer's Liability Insurance. Employer's liability insurance is a class of protection afforded to employers of men engaged in manufacturing or other business, against liability for damages for personal injuries caused by negligence of the employer or his servants. This class of insurance has arisen because as soon as an employee in a factory is killed by reason of some faulty machinery, his survivors sue the company for damages. The insurance company in which the employer has insured the risk defends the case, and if the proprietor is defeated, the insurance company pays the loss.

In People's Ice Co. v. Employers' Liability Assurance Co., 161 Mass. 122, plaintiff in his application for insurance represented that he was an ice dealer and that the work carried on by his employees was cutting and handling ice. The insurance was to cover an expenditure in wages of $5,000 a year. Plaintiff warranted his statements in the application to be true. It was held that injuries caused to employees by the fall of an ice house while in the process of construction by him, not in the season for cutting ice, were not within the policy.

Fidelity Insurance. Fidelity or guaranty insurance is a contract by which an employer is insured against loss by fraud or dishonesty of his employees. It is in fact a guarantee of the honesty of an employee. These insurance companies issue bonds guaranteeing faithful performance of contracts as well, and in all cases in which bonds are required it is now the common practice to purchase them of a fidelity-insurance company.

In People v. Rose, 174 Ill. 310, the court said that the business of guaranteeing the fidelity of persons holding public or private places of trust, and the performance by persons, firms, and corporations of contracts, bonds, and other undertakings, is guaranty insurance.

Credit Insurance. Credit insurance protects merchants and tradesmen from loss through insolvency or dishonesty of their customers. For a certain premium the insurance company guarantees the merchant against bad debts. The merchants must usually bear a certain small percentage, and all losses over that amount are paid by the insurance company.

In Tebbets v. Mercantile Credit Guarantee Co., 73 Fed. Rep. (U.S.) 95, defendant, in consideration of a premium paid, insured plaintiffs against losses in their business during the year 1893. The application, which was part of the policy, stated the amount of their gross sales for the preceding 14 months and their total losses for that period. Defendant agreed to purchase of plaintiffs an amount, not to exceed $15,000, of uncollectible debts arising during 1893 in excess of one half of one per cent of their total gross sales and deliveries, subject to certain conditions. The policy contained this provison: "The contract is issued on the basis that the yearly sales of the insured are between $1,800,000 and $2,500,000." It was held that this was not a stipulation that they would equal that amount, requiring that the one half of one per cent be computed on at least $1,800,000, but that plaintiffs were entitled to receive their losses, not in excess of one half of one per cent on their actual total sales.

Title Insurance. Title insurance is a guaranty to the owner of real property that his title is clear. It is insurance against defect in title to the property insured, and in case of loss by reason of liens or encumbrances prior to the interest of the insured, the company indemnifies him.

Plate-glass Insurance. Plate-glass insurance is another branch of casualty insurance often employed. Many stores and offices have plate-glass fronts representing a large investment, and to avoid danger of loss the owners employ insurance companies to take the risk of breaking of these windows. The premium charged is based on the cost price of the windows.

Elevator Insurance. Elevator insurance consists of a contract which covers the risk incidental to the use of elevators, including damage both to the elevators themselves and to persons or property that may be injured by use of, or by accident occurring to, such elevators.

Steam-boiler Insurance. Because of the frequent explosions occurring from the use of steam boilers, not only the boilers themselves but surrounding property is insured under this head. The insurance does not cover loss by fire, even though it is caused by the explosion, but does cover injury to persons or property from such cause.

XI. REAL PROPERTY

IN GENERAL

Definition. Real property, or real estate, is defined as including such things as are fixed, permanent, and immovable, composing land and whatever is affixed to and issues out of the land. It will therefore be seen that it includes not only the land itself but buildings erected thereon, as well as trees growing therefrom, and oils and minerals in the land extending downward to the center of the earth and upward indefinitely.

Aiken v. Benedict, 39 Barb. (N.Y.) 400, is a case in which it was held that an action for damage would lie against one who erected a building on the line of his own premises so that the eaves or gutters projected over the land of his neighbor.

Standing water belongs to the owner of the soil, but the owner of the land has only the right to use and enjoy running waters, having the exclusive right to fish, sail, etc., in the waters over his land.

Ocean Grove v. Asbury Park, 40 N.J. Eq. 447, is a case in which plaintiffs bored in their own land for water over 400 feet, and secured a flow of 50 gallons per minute. Defendants then sank a shaft 8 feet less in depth than plaintiffs' on land of a third party where they had permission to bore. This shaft was 500 feet from plaintiffs' well, and a flow of 30 gallons per minute was obtained. As soon as this well started, plaintiffs' flow decreased to 30 gallons per minute. Defendants proposed to sink other shafts still nearer to plaintiffs'. It was held that they had the right to do so, and the court would not enjoin defendants from either sinking other wells or continuing to use this well.

In the case of navigable waters there is no such right, as title to the soil under them is held by most authorities to belong to the state. In waters that are not navigable the owners of the land

on each side, as a general rule, own to the center of the stream
or lake.

Cooley v. Golden, 117 Mo. 33, held that a grantee from the
United States of land in Missouri on the banks of a navigable
river, such as the Missouri River, takes only to the water's edge
and not to the middle of the stream. The owner of the bank
is not the owner of an island which springs up in the river, no
matter whether it is on one side or the other of the center of
the stream.

Ice belongs to the owner of the land over which it forms,
except when it is on navigable waters, in which case it belongs
to the one first appropriating it.

State v. Pottmeyer, 33 Ind. 402, held that when the water of
a flowing stream, not navigable, freezes while in its natural
channel, the ice attached to the soil constitutes part of the land
and belongs to the owner of the bed of the stream, who has the
right to remove it. A person who owns the land on one side and
cuts the ice beyond the center of the stream is liable to the
owner of the land lying under the ice taken.

In Wood v. Fowler, 26 Kan. 682, it was held that the owner of
a bank along the Kansas River, a navigable river, did not own
to the center of the stream, nor did he own the ice formed on
the stream adjacent to his land without first taking possession
of it.

Cases in which trees, crops, and grass are part of the realty,
also the question as to when fixtures become realty and when
they retain their character as personalty, have heretofore been
considered and should be reviewed.

Corporeal and Incorporeal Real Property. Corporeal real
property includes the land itself and the buildings, trees, minerals, and other tangible appurtenances thereto. The examples
of real property just discussed belong to this class. Incorporeal
property is an intangible right in the land which does not amount
to ownership of it. The principal illustration is an easement,
which is defined as a right that the owner of one tract of land
may exercise over the land of another. A right of way which a
man has over the land of his neighbor for the purpose of reaching his own land is an easement. Lots in the city are sometimes
sold with the covenant that the purchaser will not build within
a given number of feet from the street. This creates an easement

in favor of the seller. The easement may be granted perpetually or for a limited time.

In Wolfe v. Frost, 4 Sandf. Ch. (N.Y.) 72, it was held that an agreement between the owners of adjacent city lots that if one will build a building on his lot three feet back from the line of the street the other will set his buildings back the same distance when he builds, creates an easement in the party so building in the land of the other.

Peck v. Conway, 119 Mass. 546, is a case in which A, owner of a large tract of land, conveyed a portion to B with the reservation in the deed that "no building is to be erected by the said B, his heirs, or assigns, upon the land herein conveyed." A retained the balance of the land as his homestead and later sold to C. B afterward sold to D without making any mention of the reservation. It was held that the reservation created an easement in B's land and for the benefit of A's adjoining property and that it could be enforced by C against B's grantee.

ESTATE IN LAND

Definition. Estate is the interest which one has in land. This interest may amount to absolute ownership, or it may be only temporary or conditional ownership. Under early English law, what is called the feudal system was in force, and absolute title to all real property was in the king, all others holding under him as tenants. The king generally granted large tracts of land to his nobles or followers, who in return for the grants rendered him certain military services. Each follower of the king had his followers or servants to whom he rented the land and who gave him a certain amount of their time as soldiers for the king. The estate of the tenant in the land was called "fee." This feudal system does not exist in the United States, but many terms and rules still used in real property law are derived from it.

Estate in Fee Simple—Eminent Domain. Estate in fee simple is the nearest approach to complete and absolute ownership of real property. Excepting the right the state has to take his land for taxes or under the power of eminent domain, it cannot be taken from him without his consent, except by creditors to pay his debts. It is an estate which exists for a man during his life and which if not displaced by him descends to his heirs. When an estate of this nature exists in land, the owner can use the land as he chooses, provided he does not cause injury to others, and he may dispose of it or grant privileges in reference to it as he may desire. The land may be taken by the state, under the right of domain, for public use only, as for a road or railway, and in every case just and adequate compensation must be given the owner. The right is often delegated to corporations or private persons who perform some public function, as railroad companies and telegraph companies.

Beckman v. Saratoga R.R. Co., 3 Paige (N.Y.) 45, held that eminent domain remains in the government, which can resume possession of private property not only when the safety but also when the interest or even the convenience of the state is concerned, as when the land is wanted for a road, canal, or other public improvement; but it cannot be taken without just compensation to the owner.

Were it not for this right in the state, construction of a highway or a railroad might be prevented by the arbitrary acts of a single individual.

Life Estate. The fee in all real property must rest in someone, but there may be carved out of it various lesser estates. The absolute owner has a right to do what he will with his land; therefore he may grant use of it for life or for a term of years to another person. Estates ranking next to estates in fee are life estates. There are estates in land which are limited by the life of some human being. It is not necessary that the estate shall last during the life, but that an estate be created which may continue for that period. An estate to a widow is during her widowhood a life estate, although she may remarry and thus defeat it before her death.

In Warner v. Tanner, 38 Ohio St. 118, Tanner and one Bartlett executed an instrument under seal by which Tanner leased to Bartlett two acres of land with use of water and the privilege of conducting it to a cheese house to be erected by Bartlett. Bartlett agreed to pay $30 per year for the premises while he should use them for the manufacture of cheese, and when the premises were no longer to be used for that purpose, they were to revert to Tanner, Bartlett having the privilege of removing all buildings and fixtures erected by him. It was held that the agreement created a life estate in Bartlett provided he continued to use the premises for the manufacture of cheese and paid the rent.

Tenant for Life. The owner of the life estate, or tenant for life, as he is called, unless restrained in the grant to him, may dispose of his interest in the land, or out of it may grant a lesser estate, as for a certain number of years, but he can grant to another no rights in the land that will extend beyond his life. The life tenant can recover nothing for any improvement which he makes on the property, and he is bound to make ordinary repairs at his own expense.

In Hagan v. Varney, 147 Ill. 281, it was held that a life tenant, by placing permanent improvements on the land, however much they may enhance the value of the estate, cannot create a charge for the moneys thus expended against the party who takes the next estate or the remainder. Such improvements are deemed to have been made by the life tenant for his own benefit and enjoyment during the pendency of his own estate.

In re Mary E. Steele, 19 N.J. Eq. 120, it was held that a life tenant is bound to keep the premises in repair. If a new roof is needed, he must put it on, and if paint wears off, he must repaint.

The life tenant has the right to cut timber on the land for use as fuel and for the purpose of repairing the building and building fences.

Elliot v. Smith, 2 N.H. 430, was an action against a life tenant of certain premises for cutting down and carrying away two oak trees. They were cut and sold for the purpose of paying for labor and material in building fences on the land. It was held that a tenant for life may cut trees for fuel, wood, and fencing but cannot sell wood to pay for fencing the land. To justify the cutting, the trees themselves must be used for these purposes.

A tenant for life must not commit waste, that is, cause or allow any permanent and material injury to the property that would affect the interest of the owner of the fee. The one who is entitled to the property after the estate for life has terminated has the right to have it come to him without being impaired by injury to any part of the premises.

In Proffitt v. Henderson, 29 Mo. 325, Proffitt at his death was seized of a certain tract of land, in which he devised to his wife a life use, and at her death the remainder went to his children. The widow conveyed her interest to defendant. This action was brought by the children against defendant for waste in cutting and carrying away timber worth $600. It was shown that the property was timberland and not valuable for anything else. It was held that the cutting of timber may be waste, although necessary for the profitable enjoyment of the land and although the land is valuable for timber only. Waste is lasting damage to the reversion, caused by the destruction by the tenant for life of such things on the land as are not included in its temporary profits.

The tenant may continue to work mines or take gravel from pits that have been previously worked, but if he opens new mines or quarries, he is guilty of waste.

Sagers v. Hoskinson, 110 Pa. St. 473, was an action for waste brought against life tenants for mining coal and quarrying limestone. It was shown that the quarries and mines were opened and had been worked before life estate of defendants began. It was held that mines and quarries opened at the beginning of a life estate may be worked by the life tenant even until they are exhausted, without rendering him liable in damages for waste.

Emblements. Emblements are annual products of the land which are the result of the tenant's labor and which he is entitled to take away after his tenancy has ended. All grains and other products which are planted and cultivated by one having an interest of uncertain duration may be removed by him, if that interest terminates without his fault before they are harvested.

In Harris v. Fink, 49 N.Y. 24, it was held that when, under a parol contract for the sale of land, the vendee, with consent of the vendor and in pursuance of the terms of the contract, enters into possession and puts in crops, the fact that the contract to sell is invalid does not affect title of the vendee to the crops, and if the vendor refuses to perform the contract and ejects the vendee, the latter does not lose title to the crops.

Therefore the representative of a tenant for life is entitled to emblements, since the tenant's estate is of uncertain duration.

In Bradley v. Bailey, 56 Conn. 374, it was held that the executor of a tenant for life is entitled to crops sown during the tenant's lifetime but maturing after his death. It does not affect this right that the life tenant was rapidly failing in health and had reason to expect his early death when the land was sown.

If the life tenant terminates the estate by his own act, he cannot claim emblements.

Debow v. Colfax, 10 N.J.L. 128, is a case in which a minister of a certain church was entitled to possession of the parsonage land, and while in possession, sowed the land with grain. He sold the crop to B before it was harvested and voluntarily ceased to be minister of that church, removing to another charge. It was held that B could not claim the grain. If a person has an estate in land, the duration of which is uncertain and may continue until the grain is ripe, he will, if he sowed the land, be permitted to reap the grain, although the estate is previously ended, unless the estate is terminated by act of the tenant himself before the crop is harvested.

ESTATES BY MARRIAGE

Classification. Estates by marriage may now be included, under the three heads of Curtesy, Dower, and Homestead. Under common law there existed an estate during coverture, or during marriage, but this has been practically abolished by statute in all the states. The estate during coverture arose from the common-law disability of a married woman to hold property; therefore the husband acquired an interest in all the wife's real property, which gave him the right to the use and profits of it until the marriage was terminated by death or divorce. If the wife died first, her real property at once descended to her heirs, unless a child was born of the marriage, in which case the husband was entitled to curtesy.

Curtesy. Curtesy is the estate for life of the husband in the real estate of his wife. Under common law such an estate was created, when there existed a valid marriage, if the wife died before the husband and a child had been born which might have inherited the property. These conditions existing, the husband had a life estate for the remainder of his life in the real property of which the wife died possessed. It was not necessary that the child live until the mother's death; if it lived but a moment after birth, that was sufficient to vest this estate in the husband. This estate by curtesy has been abolished by statute in some states, while in others it exists only in case the wife dies without disposing of her real property by will. In other states still the husband takes the same interest in the wife's estate as the wife takes in the husband's.

Breeding v. Davis, 77 Va. 639, held that by common law husband and wife were jointly seized of her real property, and after a child was born the husband had an interest as tenant by curtesy, by reason of which after the wife's death he had a life interest in said land. By the Virginia married women's act no interest in the wife's property vests in the husband during coverture. But if a child is born and the husband survives the wife, he has an estate by curtesy of the land which she held in fee when she died and which she had not alienated during the coverture.

Dower. Dower is the provision which the law makes for the support of a widow out of the lands of the husband. Under common law it was a life interest in one third of the husband's realty. By statute in a few states this has been changed to a life interest in half his realty. To give rise to this estate, it is necessary that there be a legal marriage, that the husband own the land during some time after their marriage, and that the husband die before the wife. The husband may own the real property but an instant; still that will be sufficient to cause the wife's right of dower to attach. Therefore, if A buys a piece of land of B today and sells it to C tomorrow, the right of A's wife attaches. But this is not so if it is the same transaction; as, if A buys a farm and gives back a purchase-money mortgage, the wife of A gets a dower interest in the farm subject to the mortgage .

In King v. Stetson, 11 Allen (Mass.) 407, it was held that if at the same time that a deed of land is received, and as part of the same transaction, the grantee mortgages the land to a third party for the purpose of procuring money to enable himself to obtain his deed, his seizing is only instantaneous, and the mortgage will bar his wife's dower, although she did not sign it.

Under her right of dower the wife has no vested interest until the husband dies. He may sell the land without her consent, and she will have no right in it until his death; but after that event, into whatever hands it comes the wife can claim her interest. Therefore, if one takes land from a married man, the wife must join in the conveyance in order to cut off her right of dower. But the wife cannot release her dower interest to her husband nor to anyone else except the person to whom the land is conveyed.

In re Rausch, 35 Minn. 291, we have a case in which Maria Rausch, by an instrument in writing which recited that in consideration of the sum of $100 paid to her by her husband, Henry Rausch, and the further sum of $300 agreed to be paid to her by him in two years, she did "remise, release, convey, and set over to the said Henry Rausch" all her estate or claim to all real and personal property now owned or hereafter acquired by said Henry Rausch. She further agreed to make no claim on him or his heirs for any further interest in his property. At his death she applied for her dower interest. It was held that she could recover. A married woman cannot so release to her husband her contingent interest in his real property as to exclude her, as his widow, from dower.

Statutes in many states have changed the law as to dower. In a few states the wife is not required to join in a conveyance with her husband, as she takes dower only in the property of which he dies possessed.

Homestead. Homestead right is an exemption of certain property from sale for debts, generally the home and a certain number of acres of ground or land of a given value. Under common law there was no such provision, but statutes have been passed in many states creating a homestead law. These statutes vary in the different states, and grant the exemption only to the head of a family or one on whom there rests the duty to support dependent persons living with him. A husband and wife constitute such a family.

Powers v. Sample, 72 Miss. 187, held that an aged widower living with a married son in a house built and controlled by the son, though on the land of the father who receives no rent for it, but who contributes nothing to the support of the family beyond what is necessary for his own maintenance, and who is under no moral or legal duty to contribute to the support of the family, is neither a householder nor the head of a family, and so is not entitled to homestead exemptions.

Marsh v. Lazenby, 41 Ga. 153, held that an unmarried man whose indigent mother and sisters live with him and are supported by him is the head of a family in the sense in which the term is used by the state constitution and is entitled to a homestead. This homestead exemption is acquired by occupancy of the premises as a homestead.

Estate for years is an estate in real property less than a life estate. The tenant for years is called the lessee or tenant, and the owner, the lessor or landlord. This will be treated under the subject of Landlord and Tenant.

Equitable Estates. The estates which we have been discussing are termed legal estates. There also exist equitable estates; that is, legal title may be in one party, while equitable title is in another. Property may be conveyed to A to hold in trust, or as trustee, for the benefit and use of B. A is the legal owner but holds the property only for the purpose of turning over the profits to B, who is the equitable owner. In this case A is the trustee and B is the beneficiary.

Estates in Severalty and Joint Estates. Estates are divided, according to the number of owners, into estates in severalty and joint estates. Estates in severalty are those in which ownership is in one person. Joint estates are those owned by two or more persons. The common classes of joint estates are joint tenancies and tenancies in common. The chief distinction between the two is that in joint tenancy, upon the death of one of the joint tenants his interest vests in the survivor or survivors, while upon the death of a tenant in common his interest passes to his representatives. In the United States all joint estates are presumed to be tenancies in common, unless it appears that there was a contrary intention.

SALE AND CONVEYANCE
OF REAL ESTATE

Title. Title to real property is the means by which ownership is acquired and held. It is, in other words, the evidence which a person has of the right to possession of property. It may be either by descent or by purchase. Title by descent is acquired either by will or by the law of descent which controls disposition of the real property of a person dying without a will. Purchase includes all other means of acquiring title to real property, whether by gift or for a valuable consideration.

Land Contract. When title is acquired by purchase, the transaction is the result of a contract or an agreement of one party to purchase or take the property on the prescribed terms, and of the owner to sell and convey the property for the stated consideration. This agreement is often called a land contract, and it is required by the fourth section of the statute of frauds to be in writing. It must be remembered that this contract does not convey land but agrees to convey at some future time. If the conveyance immediately follows the making of the agreement, the contract to convey is unnecessary, but in the passing of title to real property much care is necessary to ascertain that title to the person about to sell, or the grantor, is clear; that is, that no third party or parties have any claim on it. To ascertain that title is clear, a search of the records in the public office where all deeds, mortgages, and other important documents are kept is made, usually by a lawyer or some officer or company accustomed to perform such duties. When the results of this search are put in writing, the document shows all the transactions affecting the particular piece of land; it is called an abstract of title. It requires some time to obtain this abstract of title and to perfect other arrangements for the conveyance of property, and the land contract binds the parties to their agreement during this interval. Sometimes the purchaser has not the ready money to pay for the property, and this contract is given until he has paid a certain amount by installments, at which time a deed will be given him.

DEEDS

Definition. Conveyance of title to property may be absolute, in which event it is made by deed, or conditional, in which event it is made by mortgage.

A deed in real-property law is defined as a written contract, signed, sealed, and delivered, by means of which one party conveys real property to another. The two principal kinds of deeds are warranty and quitclaim. A warranty deed is a conveyance which, aside from granting the land, contains certain warrants or covenants concerning title. A quitclaim deed merely grants what interest the grantor has, and nothing more.

Conditions. All deeds must be in writing (or printing) and must have parties to contract. To constitute a valid deed, or conveyance of property, it is also requisite that there be (1) property to be conveyed, (2) words of conveyance, (3) description of the property, (4) writing signed, and in some states sealed, by the grantor, (5) delivery and acceptance, (6) acknowledgment in some states, witnesses in others, and in still others registry of the instrument.

PROPERTY TO BE CONVEYED. The first condition is self-evident, as a valid deed cannot be given unless there is real property to convey.

WORDS OF CONVEYANCE. The deed must contain words of conveyance, called the granting clause; it consists of words sufficient to transfer the estate to the grantee. The words, "give, grant, bargain, and sell" are sometimes used in the granting clause, or again the phrase, "grant, bargain, sell, remise, release, convey, alien, and confirm."

Hummelman v. Mounts, 87 Ind. 178, held that a writing as follows, "This indenture witnesseth, that I, Jacob Smith, warrant and defend unto Christena Smith, her heirs and assigns forever," certain real estate that was then described, the instrument being then signed, sealed, and acknowledged like a deed, was not effective as a conveyance, as it contained no granting clause, nor words signifying a grant.

The granting clause should contain the names of the parties, also words defining the estate, as the words, "unto the second party of the second part, his heirs and assigns forever." By this clause an estate in fee is granted. Under common law, if the word "heir" was omitted and the grant was to the grantee alone, only a life interest would be conveyed.

In Adams v. Ross, 30 N.J.L. 505, it was held that a grant to A for her natural life and at her death to her children conveyed life estate to A and then an estate to her children during their lives, but that they did not take it in fee, as the grant contained no words of inheritance.

Sedgwick v. Laflin, 10 Allen (Mass.) 430, held that a grant to A and "his successors and assigns forever" conveyed only a life estate. The court said it is a well-settled rule of common law that the word "heirs" is necessary to create an estate of inheritance.

But this rule has been changed by statute in some states, and a conveyance showing an intent to grant a fee will be so construed.

The conveyance clause may contain exceptions; that is, there may be reserved something that would otherwise pass with the property conveyed. The exception, for instance, might be of a right of way over the land, or the right to mine coal or minerals and oil. The exception must be stated and particularly described.

The habendum is that part of the conveying clause which begins with the words "To have and to hold." It designates the estate that is to pass. If it is repugnant to the granting or conveying clause, it is void, and if the conveying clause defines the estate granted, the habendum clause is not necessary, although it is usually employed.

Ratliffe v. Marrs, 87 Ky. 26, held that where the granting clause grants an absolute estate to A, and the habendum recites that a life estate was given to A, remainder to B, A takes an absolute estate. When the granting clause and the habendum do not agree, the latter gives way to the granting clause.

DESCRIPTION. The deed must contain a description of the property sufficient to identify it. The description may include references to maps, monuments, distances, or boundaries.

Travelers Insurance Co. v. Yount, 98 Ind. 454, held that a creek is a monument which may be referred to as a boundary in a deed or mortgage.

The description often closes with the words "with privileges and appurtenances thereto belonging." But it is not considered that this clause adds anything to the deed. The appurtenances are such rights as water courses, rights of way, and rights to light and air, and these are all included in the general grant, unless they are expressly reserved.

SIGNATURE AND SEAL. At common law a seal was necessary to the legality of a deed, but in many states this requirement has been abolished. Between the parties themselves to a deed a consideration is not necessary to its validity, although it may in some cases be attacked by creditors of the grantor. A date is not strictly necessary to the validity of a deed, and when used may be placed in any part of the instrument. It is generally at the commencement or just before the signature at the end. A deed takes effect from the time of delivery, and the presumption is that the date of delivery is the date of the instrument.

It is usual for the deed to close with the testimonium clause, which recites, "In witness whereof the party of the first part has hereunto set his hand and seal the day and year first above written," and immediately thereafter the grantor signs his name. By the statute of frauds the deed has to be signed. In some states the statutes require that the deed be "subscribed," and in that case it must be signed at the end; otherwise it may be signed at any other place.

In Devereux v. McMahon, 108 N.C. 134, it was held that while the laws of North Carolina require all deeds conveying land to be signed by the maker, the signing is not required to be at the end of the deed; if the signature is in the body of the instrument, it is sufficient. Nor is it essential that the maker actually sign his name. He may authorize it done in his presence, or he may affix his mark, which will have the same effect as his own writing.

DELIVERY AND ACCEPTANCE. A deed does not become operative until it is delivered and accepted, that is, the instrument must pass out of control of the grantor; but it must be his voluntary act, and if taken without his consent, as by theft, it is not a delivery.

In Fisher v. Hall, 41 N.Y. 416, a conveyance of real property had been subscribed and sealed by the grantor and attested by witnesses under a clause stating that it had been sealed and delivered in their presence, but the grantee was not then present, and remained ignorant of the deed until long after the death of the grantor, who continually retained the deed in his possession until his death. It was held that such a conveyance did not pass title to the grantee, as there was no delivery to him. The court further held that it is not necessary that the grantee be present at signing of the deed or that he have actual possession of it, but if he does not receive the deed, it should be placed within the power of some third person for the grantee's use.

The instrument may be entrusted to a third person to be delivered to the grantee on the performance of some condition. This is a delivery in escrow. To constitute a valid delivery in escrow there must be no power in the grantor to recall it.

James v. Vanderheyden, 1 Paige Ch. (N.Y.) 385, is a case in which a mortgage and a deed were delivered to a third person, to be kept by him during the pleasure of the parties and subject to their further order. It was held that the papers were not delivered in escrow, such delivery as in this case amounting to a mere depositary. To constitute a delivery in escrow the papers must be placed in the hands of a third person, who is to deliver to the grantee upon the happening of some event or the performance of some condition.

Not only must there be a delivery, but there must be an acceptance by the grantee, though acceptance will sometimes be presumed from the grantee's having possession of the deed or from the beneficial character of the instrument.

Jackson v. Phipps, 12 Johns (N.Y.) 418, held that delivery of a deed is not complete until it has been accepted by the grantee. The grantor agreed to give the grantee a deed of his farm as security for a debt, and upon returning home executed and acknowledged a deed as agreed, and left it in the clerk's office to be recorded. Neither the grantee nor any person in his behalf was present to receive it. It was held that this did not constitute delivery and acceptance.

ACKNOWLEDGMENT. In some states acknowledgment is necessary to entitle the instrument to be recorded, and in other states it is necessary to give it validity. Acknowledgment consists in the grantor's going before an officer designated by law and declaring the deed to be genuine, and that it is his voluntary act, the officer making a certificate to this effect.

Blood v. Blood, 23 Pick. (Mass.) 80, held that if a deed of land is recorded without having been acknowledged before a magistrate, it is of no effect. In some states one or more witnesses to a deed are required by statute in case there is no acknowledgment in order to entitle it to be recorded, while in other states they are necessary to give it validity.

Acknowledgment

KNOW ALL MEN BY THESE PRESENTS,   THAT

I, Paul J. Schlundt, of Chicago, Cook County, Illinois, party of the first part, for and in consideration of the sum of Three Thousand Dollars ($3000.00) . . . . . lawful money of the United States, to me in hand paid, at or before the ensealing and delivery of these presents by Raymond Heim of the same place, party . . . . of the second part, the receipt whereof is hereby acknowledged, have bargained and sold, and by these presents do grant and convey unto the said party of the second part, his executors, administrators and assigns, one Chevrolet Automobile named the "Camaro" and four new extra white wall tires.

To have and to hold the same unto the said party of the second part, his executors, administrators and assigns for ever. And I do for myself, my heirs, my executors and administrators, covenant and agree, to and with the said party . . . . of the second part, to warrant and defend the sale of the said property, ... hereby sold unto the said party of the second part, his executors, administrators and assigns against all and every person and person whomsoever.

In Witness Whereof, I have hereunto set my hand and seal the nineteenth day of December, in the year one thousand nine hundred sixty-seven.
Sealed and delivered in the presence of
[Signed] Howard R. Hanson   [Signed] Paul J. Schlundt
                                                       [SEAL]

State of Illinois ⎫
City of Chicago ⎬ S.S
County of Cook ⎭

On the Nineteenth day of December in the year one thousand nine hundred . sixty . seven . . before me personally came . . . . Paul J. Schlundt . . . . . to me known, and known to me to be the individual described in, and who executed the foregoing instrument, and . . . he . . . acknowledged that he executed the same.

[Signed] A. B. Carlson
Com. of Deeds

Record. The statutes of all the states provide for the registration or recording in some public office of all deeds and other instruments affecting real property. Instruments so recorded are notice to the whole world that they exist, as everyone can examine the records. Therefore the first instrument recorded has priority over another like instrument on the same property. But as between the parties themselves and all parties having actual notice, the instrument is in most states equally valid without recording. It is only against subsequent purchasers who buy in good faith that unrecorded instruments are of no effect.

Warranties. A deed may be a full warranty deed which contains the five covenants of title, or it may be a simple warranty deed containing only the covenant of quiet enjoyment and the covenant warranting title of the grantor. Upon breach of the covenant the grantor is liable for damages. They are contracts by which the grantor warrants certain facts to the grantee.

Seizin. In the full warranty deed above mentioned the first covenant is that of seizin and right to convey. This is a covenant that the grantor has possession of the property granted and has the right to convey it. He must have the very estate in quantity and quality which the deed purports to convey. This covenant is broken when the grantor is not the sole owner, or when the property is in adverse possession of another, or when the land described does not exist or there is a deficiency in the amount of land conveyed.

Bacon v. Lincoln, 4 Cush. (Mass.) 210, was an action for breach of covenant of seizin. The land conveyed was described as a tract of land in the county of Hamilton and state of New York, and known on a map of Township No. 38, filed in the office of the clerk of Montgomery County as No. 5. At the trial it was shown that there was no such map on file in the Montgomery County Clerk's office, that Township No. 38 had never been surveyed or subdivided, and that no such lot as the one described in the deed existed. It was held that this constituted a breach of the covenant of seizin. Defendant covenanted that he was seized of the lot described in the deed, and if no such lot existed, the covenant was broken.

This covenant is often set forth in the deed in more elaborate form after the following manner: "The party of the first part does hereby covenant and agree that at the time of the ensealing and delivery of these presents he was the lawful owner and was well seized, in fee simple, of the premises above described, free and clear of all lien, right of dower, or other incumbrances of every name and nature, legal or equitable, and that he has good right and full power to convey the same."

Quiet Enjoyment. The second covenant is that of quiet enjoyment, and is to the effect that the grantee and his heirs and assigns shall not be legally disturbed in their quiet and peaceable possession of the premises, but that they shall possess it without suit, trouble, or eviction by the grantor or his heirs or assigns.

In Underwood v. Birchard, 47 Vt. 305, it was held that a covenant of quiet enjoyment relates to the grantor's right to convey the premises. It is a covenant that the grantee shall not rightly be disturbed in his possession, and not that he shall not be disturbed at all. So where it appears that the grantee was kept out of possession by a party who had no right or claim, it is not a breach of covenant.

Encumbrances. Number three is a covenant against encumbrances and warrants that there are no outstanding rights in third parties to the land conveyed. It is a covenant against both mortgages and easements in favor of third parties. It is broken by an outstanding mortgage, an unexpired lease, an easement, unpaid taxes, or judgments that are unsatisfied.

Clark v. Fisher, 54 Kan. 403, is an action brought for breach of covenant against encumbrances in a deed given by defendant. It seemed that one Dent was a tenant under a lease under which he was to give up possession to the grantor on thirty days' notice in case of sale, but Dent was to have the right to harvest sixty acres of wheat which he had sown. It was held that this right to gather a growing crop was an encumbrance, and the amount of damages which plaintiff could recover was the value of the crop less the cost of harvesting and marketing. This case also held that an outstanding lease was an encumbrance. An encumbrance is defined as any right to or interest in the land which may exist in a third person to the diminution of the value of the land but which does not prevent the passing of fee by conveyance.

Hall v. Dean, 13 Johns (N.Y.) 105, held that a judgment against the grantor outstanding at the time of execution of a deed is a breach of the covenant against encumbrance.

In Hill v. Bacon, 110 Mass. 387, it was held that taxes assessed to the grantor on the land conveyed, before execution of the deed and which are not paid by the grantor, constitute breach of the covenant against encumbrances.

Further Assurance. The fourth covenant is one of further assurance, and is an agreement by the grantor to perform any acts that may be necessary to perfect the grantee's title, including execution of such further instruments as may be required for the purpose.

In Colby v. Osgood, 29 Barb. (N.Y.) 339, it was held that

release of a mortgage is a further assurance, and an action may be brought for breach of this covenant if the grantor refuses to clear title to the premises by obtaining such release, unless the property was expressly conveyed subject to the mortgage.

Warranty of Title. The fifth and last covenant is warranty of title, which is assurance by the grantor that the grantee shall not be evicted from part or all of the premises by reason of superior title in anyone else. This covenant is broken by eviction from any or all of the premises, removal of fixtures by one having the right, or taking of the premises by one having paramount title.

Norton v. Jackson, 5 Cal. 262, held that eviction by process of law is required to enable one to maintain an action for breach of covenant of warranty.

Quitclaim Deed. The quitclaim deed contains none of the covenants of a warranty deed and purports to grant only what interest the grantor has, if any. The quitclaim deed does not even aver that he has any title. If he has defective title, the grantee has no claim on him. The words of conveyance differ from those in the warranty deed. This form of deed is used when the grantor has an interest in land, as one of several heirs or as a joint owner, and wishes to convey his share to another heir or to the other joint owner. It is also employed when a person having an easement or other minor estate in land wishes to transfer his estate to the owner in fee for the purpose of clearing title.

Covenant against Grantor. The covenant against grantor is the only covenant used in a quitclaim deed. It is also sometimes used in a warranty deed, when the grantor is not willing to warrant title absolutely, but is willing to covenant that he has not himself done or permitted to be done anything that would injuriously affect title to the premises. Such a deed is called a special warranty deed.

WARRANTY DEED

This Indenture Witnesseth, That the Grantors, MABEL PALMER NELSON (formerly Mabel E. Palmer) and C. WILBUR NELSON, her husband, of Rock Island, County of Rock Island and State of Illinois, for and in consideration of Four Thousand and no/100 DOLLARS in hand paid, CONVEY and WARRANT to ELMER C. JOHNSON of Oxnard, in the County of Ventura and State of California, the following described real estate, to-wit:

All of Lot 3 of the South Half of the South West Quarter of
Section 19 except the East 177 feet thereof; a part of Lot 4
of the South Half of the South West Quarter of Section 19 described as beginning at a point 346 feet North and 344 feet
West of the Southeast corner of Lot 1 of Crawford's First Addi-
tion to Woodhull, thence running North 161 feet, thence West
751 feet to the Cemetery, thence South 161 feet, thence East
751 feet to the point of beginning; and a tract in the South
Half of the South West Quarter of Section 19 described as be-
ginning at a point located South 88° 15' West 312 feet and
North 346 feet from the Southeast corner of Lot 1 of Crawford's
First Addition to Woodhull, thence running South 556 feet to
Russell's Addition to Woodhull, thence West 1061 feet, thence
North 461 feet to the Cemetery, thence East 250 feet to the
Southeast corner of the Cemetery, thence North 93 feet, thence
East 799 feet to the point of beginning, excepting therefrom a
tract in the Southwest corner thereof 20 feet North and South
by 180 feet East and West and also excepting therefrom a tract
described as beginning 312 feet West of the Southeast corner of
Lot 1 of Crawford's First Addition to Woodhull, thence running
South 211½ feet, thence West 466 feet, thence North 208½ feet
and thence East 466 feet to the point of beginning—all of said
real estate being in the South Half of the South West Quarter
of Section 19, Township 14 North, Range 2 East of the 4th P.M.,

situated in the County of Henry in the State of Illinois, hereby
releasing and waiving all rights under and by virtue of the Homestead Exemption Laws of the State of Illinois.

The grantors intend to and do hereby convey to the grantee
all of the real estate of the grantor Mabel Palmer Nelson in the
South West Quarter of Section 19, Township 14 North, Range 2
East of the 4th P.M. Said real estate is described on the tax
records of Henry County, Illinois as the West 180 feet Lot 3, 2.75
acres West of Lot 3 to the Cemetery, and the balance of Lot
1 of Lot 4 of the South West Quarter of Section 19, Township
14 North, Range 2 East of the 4th P.M., containing 11.35 acres.

This conveyance is subject to the 1965 general taxes, assumed
by the grantee.

Dated this 30th day of July, A.D. 1965.

[Signature]
Mabel Palmer Nelson   [SEAL]
[Signature]
C. Wilbur Nelson   [SEAL]

State of Illinois } ss
Rock Island County }

I, ... , the undersigned, a Notary Public, do hereby certify that MABEL PALMER NELSON (formerly Mabel E. Palmer) and C. WILBUR NELSON, her husband, personally known to me to be the persons whose names are subscribed to the foregoing instrument, appeared before me this day in person and acknowledged that they signed, sealed and delivered the said instrument as their free and voluntary act, for the uses and purposes therein set forth including the release, and waiver of the right of Homestead.

Given under my hand and official seal, this 30th day of July, A.D. 1965.

[SEAL]   [Signed] Elmer C. Johnson
                          Notary Public of
                          Cook County, Illinois

My Commission expires
October, 1969

QUIT CLAIM DEED—Statutory
(ILLINOIS)
(INDIVIDUAL TO INDIVIDUAL)

Approved By { Chicago Title and Trust Co.   (The Above Space
            { Chicago Real Estate Board   For Recorder's Use Only)

The Grantors MABEL PALMER NELSON and C. WILBUR NELSON of the City of Rock Island, County of Rock Island, State of Illinois for the consideration of Ten Dollars, CONVEY and QUIT CLAIM to Elmer C. Johnson of the Village of Maywood, County of Cook, State of Illinois, all interest in the following described Real Estate, to wit: This land is outside of Village of Woodhull in Clover Township: .466/1515 Acre Lot 1 SW Section 19, Township 14, Range 2 as is indicated by the boundary description and diagram drawing hereby attached that forms part of this quit claim deed, situated in the County of Henry in the State of Illinois, hereby releasing and waiving all rights under and by virtue of the Homestead Exemption Laws of the State of Illinois.

DATED this Tenth day of April 1962

[Signed] Mabel Palmer Nelson   [SEAL]

PLEASE
PRINT OR
TYPE NAME(s)   Mabel Palmer Nelson
BELOW   [Signed] C. Wilbur Nelson   [SEAL]
SIGNATURE(s)   C. Wilbur Nelson

State of Illinois, County of . . . . ss., I, the undersigned, a Notary Public in and for said County, in
the State aforesaid, DO HEREBY CERTIFY that

. . . .

IMPRESS   personally known to me to be the same persons
SEAL   whose names subscribed to the foregoing in-
HERE   strument appeared before me this day in per-
               son, and acknowledged that they signed, sealed
               and delivered the said instrument as their free and
               voluntary act, for the uses and purposes therein set
               forth, including the release and waiver of the right
               of homestead.

Given under my hand and official seal, this 10th day of April,
1962. Commission expires October 1, 1969

                                        [Signed] E. C. Johnson
                                                   NOTARY PUBLIC

                          ADDRESS OF PROPERTY:

MAIL { NAME Elmer C. Johnson	THE ABOVE ADDRESS IS FOR STATISTICAL PURPOSES ONLY AND IS NOT A PART OF THIS DEED.
TO: { ADDRESS Box 9119	SEND SUBSEQUENT TAX BILLS TO:
{ CITY AND STATE Chicago 90 Illinois	(NAME)

DOCUMENT NUMBER 16677890

                          AFFIX "RIDERS"
                          OR REVENUE
                          STAMPS HERE

    In New York State the form of this covenant used is: "The
said party of the first part covenants with said party of the second
part that the party of the first part has not done or suffered any-

thing whereby the said premises have been encumbered in any way whatever."

In Buckner v. Street, Fed. Rep. (U.S.) 365, it was held that a deed with a special warranty against all persons claiming by, through, or under the grantor cannot be extended to a general covenant of warranty against all persons.

MORTGAGES

Definition. A mortgage is a conveyance of land as security for a debt or some other obligation, subject to the condition that upon payment of the debt or performance of the obligation the conveyance becomes void. The debtor, or person who gives the mortgage, is called the mortgagor; and the creditor, or person to whom it is given, is the mortgagee. In Chapter XII, Chattel Mortgages are described in detail; in Chapter XIII, Real Estate Mortgages.

Equity of Redemption. Under common law the mortgage was strictly a conveyance, and the mortgagee held legal title to the property. His title was subject to be defeated upon payment of the debt secured; in default of payment his estate became absolute. This often led to hardship and injustice, for the value of the property might be greatly in excess of the mortgage debt. The courts of equity recognized this injustice and extended relief by giving the mortgagor the right to redeem the land by paying the debt with interest. This right was termed equity of redemption, and to cut off such right an action was brought in court giving the mortgagor a certain time in which to pay or else lose the right entirely.

Lien. In many states the mortgage is now looked upon as a lien which the mortgagee has in the mortgaged premises, the mortgagor still being the legal owner subject to the lien which the mortgagee holds upon the land as security for his debt.

In Dutton v. Warschauer, 21 Cal. 609, it was held that the doctrine respecting mortgages which prevails in the state of California is that a mortgage is a mere security operating on the property as a lien or encumbrance only, and is not a conveyance vesting in the mortgagee any estate in the land.

Any Realty Interest Subject to Sale May be Mortgaged. A widow may mortgage her right of dower; a mortgagee may mortgage his mortgage; an heir may mortgage his undivided interest.

In Neligh v. Michenor, 11 N.J. Eq. 539, A and B entered into a written contract by which B bound himself to convey certain lands to A. It was held that A might mortgage his interest in the land under this contract. Everything that is subject of a contract or that may be assigned is capable of being mortgaged.

Form. A mortgage is in substantially the same form as a deed, with the addition of the defeasance clause. This is a clause containing a statement that the conveyance is made conditional on payment of a specified amount, which, being paid, renders the instrument void. A mortgage is executed with all the formality of, and in practically the same manner as, a deed. As a rule, when the mortgage is given to secure a debt, it is accompanied by a note or bond or other evidence of indebtedness, making the mortgagor personally liable, so that the mortgagee may look to him personally in case the mortgaged property is not sufficient to pay the debt. This is not necessary to the validity of the mortgage, as there may be a valid mortgage without any personal liability on the part of the mortgagor, for example when the creditor's only right to payment is out of the mortgaged property.

Hodgdon v. Shannon, 44 N.H. 572, held that the validity of a mortgage depends on the genuineness of the debt described in the condition thereof. This debt need not exist in the form of a promissory note.

An ordinary form of mortgage will be given later.

Defeasance Clause. Often the words "Provided Always" open the paragraph of the defeasance clause. No particular form is necessary for this clause; so long as it shows the conveyance is made to secure payment of a debt, it will constitute the conveyance a mortgage. And although on its face the instrument may be a deed, a court of equity will permit it to be shown that the agreement really is that the conveyance shall be made security for a debt and not absolutely; therefore when this is shown, although the instrument is a deed in form, it will be declared a mortgage, the defeasance clause in this case being made orally.

In Morrow v. Jones, 41 Neb. 867, Jones gave Morrow a real-estate mortgage to secure a loan of money, and after it matured

Morrow brought an action to foreclose the mortgage and sold the property, for a sum considerably less than the debt and costs. Before the sale was confirmed, Morrow wrote a letter to Jones enclosing a deed of the property, in which Morrow was named as grantee, and made a proposition that if Jones would execute and return the deed, she could redeem the property at any time by paying the amount of the mortgage, costs, and interest. Jones accepted the proposition, executed the deed, and returned the same to Morrow, who immediately placed it on record. It was held that the relation of mortgagor and mortgagee was not changed by delivery of the deed on the terms on which it was obtained, and that the deed was taken as further security for, and not as payment of, the mortgage debt. A deed of real estate, absolute in form, may be shown by parol to have been intended by the parties as security for a debt, and as between such parties it will be construed to be merely a mortgage.

Covenants. The mortgage may or may not include one or more of the three covenants designated as first, second, and third in a mortgage. They are often inserted for the security of the mortgagee. The first clause usually gives the mortgagee the right to sell the property, that is, to foreclose the mortgage on default of payment of any part of the principal as agreed, although the time for which the balance is to run has not yet expired.

The second clause is known as the insurance clause, and is inserted when the mortgagee does not deem the land, aside from the buildings, ample security for the loan.

The third clause, usually called the interest, tax, and assessment clause, compels the mortgagor to pay the interest, taxes, and all assessments levied against the property; and in case of default for a given number of days, the mortgagee may, if he chooses, consider the whole amount of the debt due and proceed with the same remedies as if the time within which the debt was to have been paid had expired.

Bond. As has been said, the debt is usually represented by a note or bond by which the mortgagor personally obligates himself to pay the debt which the mortgage is given to secure. If a note is given, it is drawn in the usual form; if a bond is given, it is drawn in such form as to contain the same covenants as the mortgage.

Assignment. The mortgagee may desire to sell the mortgage

or transfer it to another party. This he may do, as the interest of the mortgagee in the property mortgaged is subject to sale as well as the interest in the property remaining in the mortgagor. The assignee takes the mortgage with all the rights of the assignor, but no others. The mortgage can be assigned only by an instrument in writing and under seal.

In Warden v. Adams, 15 Mass. 233, Adams delivered a mortgage to a third party for the purpose of having him draw an assignment thereof to Warden. Before this assignment was prepared, Adams assigned the mortgage by written instrument to Hamilton, another creditor. Hamilton knew that the mortgage was in the third party's hands for the purpose of drawing an assignment to Warden. It was held that Hamilton was entitled to the mortgage. Delivery to the third party did not constitute an assignment. Assignment of a mortgage can be made only by written instrument.

Foreclosure. The remedy of the mortgagee when the debt secured by the mortgage is not paid as agreed is to foreclose his lien. This is called foreclosure of the mortgage, and means the proceedings by which the mortgaged premises are applied to payment of the mortgage debt and by which the equity of redemption is barred or cut off. The remedy usually consists in an action in the courts from which a judgment is obtained, decreeing that the property be sold and the proceeds applied to payment of the mortgage debt. If anything remains after the costs of the proceedings and the mortgage debt have been paid, it is turned over to the mortgagor. This action bars all rights of the mortgagor to the property and cuts off his equity of redemption. All parties interested in the property must be made parties to the action, so that they will have notice of the proceedings and can present their claims to the court if they desire. The statutes generally require that the property be advertised for sale in the papers for a certain length of time before the sale takes place. If the property does not sell for enough to satisfy the debt, a personal judgment on the note or bond is taken for the balance, this being called a deficiency judgment.

Record. Mortgages are required to be recorded in the same manner as deeds, in order to give notice to subsequent purchasers of the property. If not so recorded, they are in most states valid as between the original parties but not against persons who have purchased in ignorance of existence of the mortgage. But in some states the statutes require the mortgage to be recorded in order to render it valid.

Discharge. If the mortgage is paid according to its terms when it becomes due, it is discharged; or payment after it is due, but before an action is brought to foreclose, discharges the mortgage. In order to cancel the mortgage on the records, a formal discharge is executed and filed; otherwise the mortgage, although paid, will still appear by the records to stand against the property.

Second Mortgage. The mortgagor may place a second or subsequent mortgage on the property. Unless otherwise stipulated, the mortgages take priority according to their date; that is, the second mortgage gets nothing until the first is paid in full. But if the first mortgage is not recorded and the second mortgagee has no notice of it, the second mortgage will, if recorded, have priority.

Any mortgagee may foreclose his mortgage when it is past due or the mortgagor is in default, but he cannot affect the interest of a prior mortgagee by such proceeding, although he may cut off any subsequent mortgagee. By foreclosing his mortgage, therefore, the holder of a first mortgage will bar the second mortgage, and if the property sells for only enough to pay the first mortgage, the second mortgagee will lose. Of course, if the property sells for more than enough to pay the first mortgage, the balance will be applied on the second mortgage. If the second mortgagee forecloses, he must sell the property subject to the lien of the first mortgage. (More detailed illustrations are given in Chapter XIII.)

LANDLORD AND TENANT

Estates for Years. Freehold estates and estates for life have been discussed. But estates in real property may be created for a shorter definite period. These are called estates for years. The grantor is known as the lessor, or landlord, and the grantee as the lessee or tenant.

Leases. By the statute of frauds in most states the lease must be in writing if for a longer time than one year. Generally, if for one year or less it may be made orally, and this is true even though the term is to commence at a date in the future. In a few states leases can be made for only a limited number of years, while in others a lease for more than a certain number of years must be recorded.

Toupin v. Peabody, 162 Mass. 473, is a case in which a lease for a term of five years contained a provision that the lessee was to have the privilege of renewing the lease on the same terms for a further period of five years. It was held that it was a lease for more than seven years under the meaning of the statute, which provided that all leases for over seven years are invalid as against all but the parties to them and persons having actual notice of their existence. Therefore, so far as it purported to give the grantee the privilege of renewing, it was invalid as against a purchaser of the premises without actual notice of the lease, it never having been recorded.

Covenants. Aside from the provisions, any further agreement between the parties may be incorporated in the writing. A lease is but a contract, and the full agreement of the parties should be set forth. Frequently the following covenant is inserted: "The party of the second part hereby covenants not to sublet said premises, or any portion thereof, without the written consent of said party of the first part;" or the following: "It is further mutually covenanted and agreed that, in case the buildings or tenements on said premises shall be destroyed or so injured by fire as to become untenantable, then this lease shall become thereby terminated, if second party shall so elect; and in such case, he shall vacate said premises and give immediate written notice thereof to said landlord, in which case rent shall be due and payable up to and at the time of such destruction or injury."

Term. The term of the lease is the time for which it is to run. If the tenant has been in possession under a lease for one or more years and he retains possession without executing a new lease, he is presumed, in the absence of some agreement, to be a tenant from year to year, which means that his term after expiration of the lease is one year and if he remains in possession after the next year, he is a tenant for another year.

In Haynes v. Aldrich, 133 N.Y. 287, defendant leased certain premises for a year, the term expiring May 1. Before expiration of the time, defendant informed plaintiff that she did not wish to renew the lease for another year. May 1 was a holiday, and possession was retained until May 4, the excuse given being the difficulty of getting trucks to move defendant, also that on May 3 one of the boarders was ill. On the afternoon of May 4 the keys were tendered plaintiff and refused. It was held that plaintiff was entitled to consider the lease renewed for another year. It was in the landlord's option so to regard it or to accept surrender of the premises.

Express and Implied Covenants. The covenants contained in a lease are either expressed or implied. Implied covenants exist whether they are mentioned or not; express covenants must be included in the express conditions of the lease, and may be many or few.

Implied covenants on the part of the lessor are those regarding quiet enjoyment and payment of taxes. The usual words of grant in a lease are "demise and lease," or "grant and demise," these words being said to import a covenant of quiet enjoyment. This covenant is broken when the tenant is evicted by someone who has paramount title.

Duncklee v. Webber, 151 Mass. 408, was an action for breach of an implied covenant of quiet enjoyment of a written lease for one year. Within the time the property was sold under a mortgage; and plaintiff, on receiving notice to quit, followed by threats of ejectment, moved away. It was held that plaintiff could recover.

The landlord also impliedly covenants that he will pay all taxes assessed against the premises during the term. There is no implied covenant on the part of the lessor, or landlord, that the premises are in tenantable condition.

Reeves v. McComeskey, 168 St. 571, held that no implied covenant that the landlord warrants the leased premises to be tenantable, or that he undertakes to keep them so, arises out of the relation of landlord and tenant; and in the absence of a provision in a lease that the lessor shall make repairs, it is no defense to an action for rent that the premises are not in a tenantable condition.

Lucas v. Coulter, 104 Ind. 81, was an action for rent of a store leased to defendant. The defense was that the store was rented for the manufacturing and selling of musical instruments, and that it was so imperfectly and defectively constructed that rain and sand came through the roof and ceiling, causing damage to the instruments. It was held that in the letting of a store, room, or house, there is no implied warranty that it is, or shall continue to be, fit for the purpose for which it is let. The tenant must determine for himself the safety and fitness of the premises.

On the part of the lessee, or tenant, there is an implied covenant that he shall pay the rent stipulated for; and although no sum is specified in the lease, the tenant must pay a reasonable rent, unless it appears that it was the intention of the parties that none be paid.

The lessee also impliedly covenants to repair, and if the leased premises consist of a farm, it is implied that he is to cultivate it in a husbandlike manner. The covenant to repair is not to rebuild when the property is burned down, but, it is said, to keep it "wind and water tight," that is, to keep the roof from leaking and the siding tight. The premises must be kept in repair, except for ordinary wear and tear.

Turner v. Townsend, 42 Neb. 376, is a case in which the tenant sued the landlord for the value of a front window in the leased store. The window had been broken by a storm during the tenancy and replaced by the tenant, the landlord having refused to put in a new one. It was held that he could not recover. The landlord is not bound either to repair leased premises himself or to pay for repairs made by his tenant unless he has expressly contracted to do so.

Auworth v. Johnson, 5 C. & P. (Eng.) 239, held that the tenant of a house from year to year is bound only to keep it wind- and water-tight.

Rights and Liabilities Under Lease. Aside from the covenants in a lease there are certain rights and liabilities which arise from the relation of landlord and tenant. In the absence of an agreement to the contrary the tenant is entitled to exclusive possession of the premises. He is liable for waste and is estopped from denying his landlord's title, that is, the tenant cannot for any purpose claim that the premises do not belong to his landlord.

Gray v. Johnson, 14 N.H. 414, held that if a tenant recognizes title of his landlord by accepting a lease or by paying rent, he will be estopped during the term of his tenancy from disputing it, although want of title may appear from the landlord's own testimony.

Hamilton v. Pittock, 158 Pa. St. 457, held that the lessee of an oil lease who takes a second lease on the same premises from a person claiming adversely to the original lessor cannot refuse to pay rent under the second lease on the ground that the lessor in the first lease has the better title to the land.

A life tenant is entitled to emblements when the estate is cut off by some contingency without his fault.

In Gray v. Worst, 129 Mo. 122, Shoemaker owned some land, of which he gave a deed to Toms to secure a loan. Shoemaker afterward leased the land to defendant for a year, and defendant paid the rent in full. Before defendant had harvested his crops, Toms foreclosed his claim and sold the property to plaintiff. Plaintiff at once claimed the crops as owner of the land, but defendant as lessee gathered them before leaving. In this action for the value of the crops it was held that the lessee was entitled to them and that plaintiff could not recover.

The landlord is under no obligation to repair unless the lease expressly binds him to such duty. And he is entitled to the fixtures annexed to and made part of the realty. The question when the fixtures may be removed by the tenant and when they may be claimed by the landlord has been discussed under Sales.

Assigning or Subletting of Lease. Unless the tenant is restrained by an express covenant against subletting or assigning, he may sublet or assign his lease without consent of the landlord. If the interest granted by the lessee is for a shorter time or for rights inferior to those granted in his own lease, it is a sublease.

In Collins v. Hasbrouck, 56 N.Y. 157, it was held where a lessee executes an instrument conveying the whole of his unexpired term, but reserving rent at a rate and time of payment different from those in the original lease, and the right of reentry on non-payment of rent and breach of other conditions, and also providing for surrender of the premises to him at expiration of the time, the instrument is a sublease and not an assignment.

In a sublease the subtenant is not liable for rent to the original lessor, but only to the original lessee.

Trustees v. Clough, 8 N.H. 22, held that he to whom the lessee sublets for but part of the term is only a subtenant and not an assignee of the term. Such subtenant is not liable for rent to the original lessor.

If the interest conveyed by the tenant is his whole interest in the lease, it is an assignment of the lease, and the assignee is liable to the original lessor for rent. In an assignment the landlord may look to either the original lessee or the assignee of the lease for rent. The assignee takes all the interest of the original tenant and is bound to pay rent and to repair and to use the property in any special way provided for in the lease. But these obligations of the assignee of the lease do not in any way release the original lessee from his obligations to his lessor.

In Sanders v. Pertridge, 108 Mass. 556, the lessees of real estate granted to them for ten years by a written lease delivered the lease to defendant with an endorsement by which they assigned him all their "right, title and interest in, and to the within lease." Neither the lessee nor defendant personally occupied the premises, but after the assignment the rents were turned over to defendant. It was held that the landlord could maintain an action against defendant for rent.

Eviction. At expiration of the lease the landlord is entitled to possession of the premises, and if the tenant does not surrender it, the landlord may institute proceedings to evict him. The statutes in the different states provide the procedure by which the tenant holding over after his lease has expired may be evicted on short notice. This is termed summary proceedings. This form of procedure is also provided by statute for eviction of a tenant when he does not pay his rent. The landlord who wishes to evict a tenant by summary proceedings obtains a process from some court which is served on the tenant, and if it is found by the court when the case comes up for hearing that the landlord is entitled to possession of the premises, the court empowers one of its officers to evict the tenant.

When the tenancy is not for any fixed period but from year to year, or month to month, it cannot be terminated by either party except by notice. Under common law a tenancy from year to year could be terminated by notice six months before expiration of the period, and a tenancy for a shorter period, as from month to month, by a notice equal to the length of the period.

In Steffens v. Earl, 40 N.J.L. 128, it was held that in monthly tenancies a month's notice to quit is sufficient, but the notice must be given at the end of one of the monthly periods.

Until this notice has been given, the landlord cannot evict the tenant, and until the tenant has given like notice to the landlord, he is liable to be held for rent, unless the landlord accepts his surrender of the premises. The statutes in many states have changed the common-law rule so that a shorter notice is sufficient.

XII. CHATTEL MORTGAGES

A chattel mortgage is a written instrument, in the form of a lien, against any particular personal property, or chattel. If John gives James a mortgage against twenty head of cattle, the court will hold, under modern law, that when the mortgage matures, or comes due, if John, the mortgagor, cannot pay the amount of the mortgage, he will have the right of redemption for a reasonable period of time after the due date before James can foreclose in an equitable proceeding. The same process is followed in equitable foreclosure proceeding where the subject matter is personal property as where it is real property. The court will hold, in case John gives a chattel mortgage to James, that legal title to the personal property or chattel, would vest in the mortgagee, James. It will hold that the chattel is subject to the privilege of redemption on the part of John, its mortgagor and original owner. When John pays the mortgage, title to the chattel will be revested in him.

The court will also hold that a chattel mortgage must be in writing, just the same as a real-estate mortgage must be, in order to comply with the statute of frauds, which provides: "All contracts for the sale of goods, wares, and merchandise which amount to a certain amount of money must be written." According to the modern method of handling chattel mortgages, the party who buys the mortgage will insist that it be written in order that he may record it and thus protect himself from other parties who might innocently buy the property against which the mortgage is given. Under modern conditions the mortgagor, or owner, of the chattel usually keeps it in his own possession, and an affidavit is ordinarily attached to the mortgage which says that the mortgagor executed the mortgage in good faith. The court will hold that any personal property subject to present sale may be mortgaged. However, the court will not permit a fixture which has become part of the real estate because of the manner of attachment to it to be made the subject matter of a chattel mortgage.

ILLUSTRATIONS

Suppose John gives a chattel mortgage on five hundred head of cattle. The court will hold that this mortgage must be written, describing the cattle in detail; it must be signed by the mortgagor; it need not be sealed; the mortgage itself must be delivered by the mortgagor to the mortgagee and be accepted in order to be valid.

Suppose John gives James a chattel mortgage on ten head of horses. John, the mortgagor, delivers the horses into the possession of James, the mortgagee. James, while he has the horses in his possession, hires them out to haul brick. When the mortgage matures, John pays it. The court will hold that when John has tendered the money in payment of the mortgage, James has to release the mortgage, deliver back to John possession of the horses, and pay John whatever the horses have earned, less the reasonable cost of feeding and caring for them. The court will also hold, if John did not, on giving the mortgage, deliver the horses into James's possession but instead kept them and used them and hired them out, that John will not have to pay James any money the horses may have earned while in John's possession.

Suppose John, the original mortgagor of the ten horses, sells his title or interest in them to Henry. The court will hold that Henry has the right to redeem the horses in case the chattel mortgage has matured and provided John has not paid it. Henry's interest in the horses, however, will of course be subject to the chattel mortgage held by James, the mortgagee. The court will also hold that James may assign the mortgage. This may be done by written assignment or else by James's delivering the chattel covered in the mortgage to the assignee. The debt must be assigned to the assignee at the same time as the chattel mortgage itself.

Where the original mortgagor fails to pay the mortgage at maturity, he has a reasonable length of time, according to the nature of the property, within which to exercise his right of redemption. Under the modern method of drawing up mortgages for chattels the mortgagee usually has the power of sale, inserted in the mortgage itself; it provides that if the mortgage is not paid when due, the mortgagee may act as agent of the original mortgagor and without judicial proceeding sell the chattel which is the subject matter of the mortgage to the highest bidder and retain the face value of his mortgage, plus interest. The balance of the money, he must turn back to the original mortgagor or owner of chattel. This sale of the chattel by the mortgagee, as agent of the mortgagor must be public, and published notice made according to the statutes of the state. The publication must give the time and place of sale of the property. If the chattel mortgage itself does not contain this power of sale, then regular foreclosure proceedings must be instituted in the proper court, just the same as in a foreclosure sale of real property, and the same procedure is followed.

XIII. REAL ESTATE MORTGAGES

ILLUSTRATIONS

Suppose James lends John $5,000 on John's farm. In consideration of the loan John gives James a mortgage on the farm. John is now the mortgagor and James the mortgagee. The mortgage is actually a lien on the farm itself; it states that if John fails to pay James the $5,000 when the real-estate note matures, James will have the privilege of foreclosing the mortgage, or lien. If at the foreclosure sale James himself buys in the farm, the court will order that he be given title to the farm in fee simple.

A mortgage on real estate is an interest in the land itself; and here the mortgage is a lien against the farm itself, and not against John, the party who owns it. A real-estate mortgage is personal property, and a real-estate mortgage is also a right in rem. Here the court will hold that after John has given James a mortgage on his farm, title to the farm remains in John, and does not pass to James, because James, when he receives the mortgage, simply has a lien against John's farm and title cannot vest in him. But if John is unable to pay the mortgage when it falls due, or even after a reasonable time has elapsed, after the mortgage has fallen due, which period of time is called the period of redemption, then John's right of redemption has expired, and James may institute a bill to foreclose the mortgage and thus forever kill John's right of redemption. If John neglects to pay the mortgage on the day of foreclosure, then James will secure title to the farm if he is the only bidder at the foreclosure sale. But if an outside party bids at the sale and bids more than $5,000 for the farm, the court will order James's $5,000 mortgage to be paid out of the money which the court receives from the outside party. After court costs have been paid, the balance of the sale price of the farm will be turned over to John, the original mortgagor, and new title to the farm will be issued to the outside party who bought the farm at the foreclosure sale. The right of redemption which John has, to pay the mortgage after the mortgage itself has matured, is called the equity of redemption; and the court will hold that if John entered into any contract with James to transfer this equity of redemption to James, the mortgagee, the contract is absolutely null and void unless James bought the equity of redemption outright when the mortgage was given, and for its reasonable value. Only in this case could the equity of redemption pass to James.

The courts hold that John's ownership of a farm in fee simple; John's ownership of a life estate; John's ownership of an estate for years; John's ownership of a lease on the farm; John's dower right or interest in the farm—all may be mortgaged. The courts hold that John can mortgage any legal or equitable right or interest which he may possess or own in the farm, or in any real estate he owns, except that he cannot mortgage real estate which he expects to get possession of in the future. John cannot mortgage this kind of estate because he cannot sell it at the present time. The courts have also said and held that if John owns a farm and gives James a mortgage against it, the mortgage will cover the farm lands and all the farm buildings.

If John gives James a mortgage against his farm in the form of a deed, which may be done, title to the farm passes to James, the mortgagee, and John no longer has title; but John, the mortgagor, has the right of redemption in the farm. This right of redemption may be written up in the form of a separate contract, on a separate piece of paper from the deed. The right of redemption may be inserted in the deed as a condition, as a redemption or defeasance feature. The right-of-redemption clause, if it is drawn up on a separate sheet of paper from the deed, must be made and executed at the same time the deed is executed, as part of the same transaction. James should record his mortgage in the form of a deed. John, the mortgagor, should record his right of redemption, in case it is a separate instrument, on a separate piece of paper. The court will hold that John can introduce oral evidence, where the mortgage is in the form of a deed, to show that the deed which James receives is not a sale but only a mortgage.

Suppose John receives a loan of money from James and wishes to secure James by means of a mortgage in the form of a trust deed. John may execute a mortgage and deliver it to a third party, who will act as a trustee of it. When John pays James the money for the mortgage, the trustee reconveys title to the farm to John, the original mortgagor. Suppose John does not pay the money which he owes James and for which he has given the mortgage as security, in the form of a trust deed, to a third party called the trustee. The trustee will have power to sell John's farm and pay the money due James and secured by the trust deed. After the trustee has sold the farm, he will pay James the amount of the mortgage; the balance of the money received from the sale will be returned to John, after paying court costs incident to the foreclosure sale.

Suppose John gives James a mortgage against his farm. James records this mortgage; John retains possession of the farm. John may give other mortgages on the same farm, subject, of course, to the first mortgage, which James holds. John may rent his farm or sell it. If he dies intestate, that is, without leaving a will, his heirs will receive whatever title he had in the farm, after mortgages, liens, and judgments against the farm have all been paid. This is the law of mortgages in all states where the lien theory prevails, that is, where title remains in the mortgagor.

In states where the title theory prevails, that is, where title to the farm, passes to the mortgagee, when the original mortgagor gives a mortgage on his property. In states where the title theory prevails in regard to mortgages, the mortgagee is entitled to immediate possession of the farm the moment he buys the mortgage, unless an agreement is entered into in the mortgage which permits the mortgagor to remain in possession of the farm after the original mortgagor gives the mortgage. If the mortgagor commits waste in regard to the houses on the farm or in regard to the trees, water rights, etc., the mortgagee may bring suit against him for any such waste. In states where the title theory prevails the mortgagee may retain possession of the farm until the mortgagor pays the mortgage and thus redeems title.

Thus we see that in lien-theory states the original mortgagor retains title to the land which he mortgages, and that in title-theory states the mortgagee gets title to the land and is entitled to possession of it until the mortgage is paid.

The courts hold that where John, the mortgagor, redeems the

mortgage when James, the mortgagee, is in possession of the farm, James has to pay John at that time all rents and incomes that James has received from the farm while in possession of it as mortgagee. If James has been grossly negligent in managing the farm or in collecting rents, John will be entitled to receive damages for the reasonable amount the farm should have brought in under proper management and what the rents should have been. All this money will be turned over to John when he redeems the farm.

Suppose John, mortgagor of a farm and in possession of it, gives Harry a lease on the farm for five years. If the mortgage matures before the lease expires, Harry, the lessee, will be permitted to retain the farm under the lease, whether the mortgage is foreclosed or not. The courts will hold that Harry received good title to the farm for five years, which John, the original mortgagor and owner of the farm, had the right to give, in states where the title remains in the mortgagor. In states where title passes to the mortgagee, the mortgagor cannot give a lease on the property after a mortgage is put on the property.

Suppose John gives a second mortgage on his farm to James. Suppose James, the mortgagee, pays off the first mortgage when it matures. Suppose James pays taxes on the property. The courts will hold that where James, the second mortgagee, pays off the first mortgage on the same farm when it matures, in order to protect his own title, he is entitled to recover from John, the original mortgagor and owner of the farm, the amount, with accrued interest, of the first mortgage. The courts will also hold that James can recover from John any money which James paid out for taxes on the farm to protect his title and which John should have paid. The courts will hold that where John still owns title to the farm, no matter how much mortgage he gives against it, he will have an insurable interest in the farm to its total value. The courts will also hold that where James has an insurable interest in the farm to the value of the mortgage, that interest will continue until the mortgage is paid. The original mortgagor's insurable interest in the farm will continue to exist until his right of redemption has expired.

Suppose John gives James a mortgage on a farm which John does not own. The court will hold that James does not have title to the farm, nor interest in it, by virtue of the mortgage, because John cannot convey to James, by means of mortgage, deed, or any other instrument, any more interest in the farm than John himself possesses.

Suppose John owns a farm and gives James a first mortgage on it. Shortly afterward John sells and transfers his title to the farm to Harry, the transferee. While Harry has title, the mortgage matures, and James brings suit against Harry personally to hold him for the amount of the mortgage which James bought from John. The court will hold that James, the mortgagee, cannot hold Harry, the transferee, personally liable for the amount of the mortgage even though Harry owns title to the farm, because a mortgage against a farm is a lien against that specific farm itself, and no one can be held personally liable for the mortgage. James will have to foreclose against the farm itself.

Suppose Harry, transferee of the farm, agrees at the time that John, the original mortgagor, transfers it to pay the mortgage personally. The court will hold that Harry thereby becomes the principal and John a surety. Suppose Harry goes to James, the mortgagee, and asks him to extend the time of payment of the mortgage and James does so. The court will hold that John, the original mortgagor, who afterward became a surety for the payment of the mortgage, with Harry as principal, is released from any liability for payment of the mortgage after James without John's consent extended the time of payment for Harry.

Suppose John gives a mortgage on his farm to James. When the mortgage matures, John pays it. James has the mortgage recorded. A mortgage recorded in the county where land is situated becomes a cloud on title to the land. When John pays the mortgage, he should get a release, and have the release recorded in the same county in order to remove the cloud from the title.

Suppose in the same case, when John goes to pay James the money on the mortgage, James refuses to give the mortgage up, and refuses to sign a release. John may file a bill in equity, and the court will compel James to execute a release of the mortgage when John tenders the money in payment of it. Thus John gets a release by paying the money to the court, and he may file this release in the county where the land is situated and thus remove the cloud on his title.

In the same case, if John does not pay the mortgage to James when the mortgage matures, the court will hold that John has the right of redemption before foreclosure proceedings can be instituted. The statute of limitations will run against the original mortgagor's right of redemption, and when the period specified in the statutes has expired, the property may be foreclosed. Some courts have held that the right of redemption of the original mortgagor runs for twenty years. In these states if the mortgagor fails to redeem within twenty years, the mortgagee, or the assignees of the mortgage, will be said to have title in fee simple by right of adverse possession.

Most courts hold that a mortgagee has twenty years in which to foreclose the mortgage. If he neglects to foreclose within twenty years, his right to foreclose is barred by the statute of limitations. In most states, after a mortgage has matured, and if there is nothing in the mortgage itself to the contrary, the mortgagee can start foreclosure proceedings within a reasonable time after the mortgage has become due. This reasonable time is called the original mortgagor's redemption period and right.

Under the law of mortgages, we have two kinds of foreclosure: strict foreclosure and equitable foreclosure. Suppose John gives James a mortgage on his farm, and when James buys the mortgage, he also buys the right of redemption which John has as original mortgagor, or owner, of the farm. When the mortgage falls due, James immediately starts foreclosure proceedings to secure his money, or to take title to the farm in his own name. This is called strict foreclosure. Suppose John simply sells James a mortgage on the farm. In this case, when the mortgage falls due, John will be given a reasonable time thereafter to redeem his title to the farm. After the redemption time has expired, James files a bill to foreclose. The court receives the evidence; and if the mortgage is valid, it will order that the farm be sold at public sale, after due notice has been published in the county where the land is located and foreclosure proceedings are instituted. On the day of the sale the party who bids highest will be granted title to the farm by order of the court through valid foreclosure proceedings. If the original mortgagor, John, has the money and bids highest, he gets back title to the farm. If James bids highest, the court will issue new title to the farm in James. The money received by the court from sale of the farm will be

redistributed as follows: The court will pay James, the mortgagee, the face value of his mortgage, plus interest; all costs will
be deducted from the balance of the money, and any residue
will be turned over to John, the original mortgagor, as his equity
in the farm. This is called an equitable foreclosure.

Suppose John executes a mortgage to James. The mortgage
contains a clause which provides for power of sale, that is, the
mortgage reads that when the mortgage falls due, the mortgagee
will have the privilege of putting the farm up for public sale
in order to pay himself as mortgagee. The court will hold that
when the mortgage matures, James may sell the land, not as
owner of the farm but as agent for John. This is called selling
the farm without judicial proceedings.

Suppose James, the second mortgagee, brings a foreclosure
sale against the farm belonging to John. In starting this foreclosure suit, James will have to make defendants in the suit all
parties interested in the farm who have lesser title than James;
they must be made parties so that they will have the right to
defend their own titles. Suppose Frank holds a third mortgage
against the property when James brings his foreclosure proceeding against John, the original mortgagor. If Frank wishes to keep
his mortgage alive, he must pay the second mortgagee, or see
to it that John pays it; otherwise, when the court in charge of
foreclosure gives new title to the party who buys James's title,
that party will secure clear title as against all others who have
title inferior to the second mortgage; but the party who gets
new title to the farm as a result of the foreclosure sale takes
that title subject to all higher titles which others may have in the
farm. For example: A first mortgage will not be interfered with
by foreclosure proceedings on a second mortgage, and the holder
of the first mortgage need not be made party to the suit, or even
given notice of the foreclosure sale. In other words, the party
who buys title of James to the second mortgage in foreclosure
proceedings takes that new title from the court, subject to all
superior rights and liens but free from all inferior rights or
liens.

XIV. TRUSTS

DEFINITION AND CLASSIFICATION

In a popular sense the term trust is often used to designate combinations of capital or combinations among businessmen for the purpose of destroying competition or of regulating prices. The term trust as used here, however, means an estate of some kind held for the benefit of another. A trust has been defined as "an obligation upon a person, arising out of a confidence reposed in him, to apply property faithfully according to such confidence." A, by will, appoints B trustee of his farm for the benefit of C. Upon A's death—if B accepts the duty imposed on him by will—a trust is thereby created in which B holds legal title to the farm for C's benefit.

Trusts are sometimes classified as general and special. If property is conveyed by deed or will to another to be held in trust for a third person without specifying any of the duties of the second person, it is said to be a general trust. If the duties of the second person or trustee are defined, the trust is called a special trust. A trust for the benefit of an individual or individuals is a private trust, while one for the benefit of a public institution or of the public is a public trust. If A gives his property to B to care for the poor of Chicago, the trust is public. As to their method of creation, trusts are usually divided into express trusts, implied trusts, resulting trusts, and constructive trusts.

PARTIES TO TRUSTS

The party creating a trust is called the grantor or settlor. The party to whom title to the property is given to hold for the benefit of another is called the trustee. The party for whose benefit the trust is created is called the cestui que trust; if there are two or more such parties, they are termed cestui qui trust. If X deeds his land to Y for the benefit of Z, X is the settlor, Y is the trustee, and Z is the cestui que trust.

WHO MAY BE PARTIES TO TRUST

Persons of legal age and competent to make contracts, including corporations, may create trusts. Any person competent to make contracts, including corporations, may act as trustee. Even a legal infant may act as trustee if the duties require no exercise of discretion. An infant may hold the legal title of trustee, and if the duties require the exercise of discretion, the court will remove him or appoint a guardian to perform his duties. Anyone capable of holding legal title to property may be a cestui que trust. This includes corporations, aliens, and in case of charitable trusts, infants. Any kind of property, real or personal, may be given in trust. This includes lands, chattel property, promissory notes, accounts, and kindred property rights, regardless of where the property is located.

EXPRESS TRUSTS

An express trust is one created by the express written or oral declaration of the grantor. If X gives a deed on his farm to Y by the terms of which Y is to hold the farm in trust for Z, X, the grantor, has created an express trust in favor of Z, Y as trustee holds legal title to the farm, and Z, as cestui que trust or beneficiary, holds the beneficial or equitable interest. X, before giving the deed of trust, was absolute owner of the farm; that is, X held the legal title and the equitable interest in the farm. By creating the trust, he placed the legal title in one person and the equitable or beneficial interest in another.

Originally, in England, at common law, trusts could be created by oral declaration as well as by written instrument. At that time land could be transferred without written instrument. The seller took the buyer onto the land to be conveyed and in the presence of witnesses delivered to him a symbol of the land, such as a piece of turf or a twig. About 1676, the Statute of Frauds was passed by Parliament requiring that conveyances of lands, including the creation of trusts therein, be by written instrument. This provision of the Statute of Frauds has been reenacted by most of our states. At the present time trusts in real estate must generally be created by written instrument. A trust may be created by will to take effect at the grantor's death. A trust may be created in personal property. Except when created by will, a trust in personal property may be created by oral declaration of the grantor. A grantor may create a trust voluntarily. If actually carried out or if the grantor's intention to create the trust is expressed as final, it requires no consideration to support it. If the declaration of trust amounts to a mere agreement to create a trust and is not carried out, it requires a consideration to enable the beneficiary to compel its execution. After an express trust is completed, it cannot be revoked by mutual agreement between the grantor and the trustee without consent of the cestui que trust.

The most common forms of express trust are created by deed, by will, or by contract. Any declaration of the grantor, no matter how informal, if expressing his intention to create a trust, is sufficient to create a trust. A trust cannot be created for an immoral or illegal purpose.

IMPLIED TRUSTS

When a person by deed or will does not use language expressly creating a trust but uses language showing his intention to create a trust, one will be implied. Such a trust is known in law as an implied trust, as distinguished from an express trust. If X devises all his property to his son Y, the will containing the following language, "I request my son Y to pay his cousin Z $25 per month during his life," this language is held to create a trust in favor of Z, wherein Y is trustee.

RESULTING TRUSTS

One party may so conduct himself or so deal with another that a court will declare the transaction to be a trust even in the absence of any express declaration or intention of the parties to create a trust. Such a trust is known in law as a resulting trust. X, to avoid paying his creditors, purchases property in the name of his wife Y. Y is trustee for X, and creditors can by suit in equity subject X's interest in the property.

If X buys property and takes the deed in the name of Y, Y is trustee for X. Y is the legal owner, and X is the beneficial or equitable owner. If a third person buys the property from Y without notice of X's rights and for value, the third person takes good title to the property free from X's claim.

Each state generally requires by statute that deeds and mortgages of real estate be recorded. If an equitable owner does not have a properly recorded written instrument showing his interest in the real estate in question, thereby giving future buyers notice of his interest, he cannot complain unless the third person has actual notice of his rights, or purchases without giving a valuable consideration. A resulting trust is created not by agreement or contract to that effect but by the trustee's using money or funds of the cestui que trust to purchase property in his own name.

CONSTRUCTIVE TRUSTS

If one person is in a confidential relation to another and misappropriates his money, this act is said to create a constructive trust in which the defrauding party is trustee and the defrauded party is beneficiary, or cestui que trust. A constructive trust differs from a resulting trust in that the former involves fraud on the part of the trustee, exercised on the cestui que trust, while the latter never involves fraud between the trustee and the cestui que trust, although created for the purpose of defrauding third persons.

If X, an attorney, is employed by Y to collect a note of $1,000 and fraudulently reports a collection of $600, keeping $400, a constructive trust results, in which X is trustee for Y for $400. If X, for the purpose of defrauding his creditors, deposits his money in a bank in Y's name, a resulting trust arises in which Y is trustee for X, and X's creditors can take the property.

Anyone defrauding another by duress, by taking advantage of old age or mental weakness, or by fraud becomes trustee for the wronged party in the amount lost.

RIGHTS AND LIABILITIES OF TRUSTEE

The designated trustee of an express trust need not accept the trust against his will. If X, by deed, will, or written declaration, names Y as trustee of certain property for Z, Y need not accept. If Y refuses, the trust does not fail by reason thereof. A court may appoint another trustee or may itself administer the trust. After accepting a trust, a trustee cannot resign without consent of the cestui. He may be removed by the court for misconduct, or he may transfer his duties, if so stipulated in the instrument creating the trust.

During the reign of Henry VIII a statute was passed in England, called the Statute of Uses, declaring that real property given to one person and his heirs in trust for another and his heirs should vest legal title in the trustee. Thus, if X gives real estate to Y and his heirs in trust for Z and his heirs, Y takes legal title. The Statute of Uses is in force in most of our states. It does not apply to personal property, and if the trustee is given some duties, such as to collect rents, or to do anything except to hold legal title as trustee, the case is not within the Statute of Uses, and the trust will be carried out.

A trustee holds legal title to the trust estate. Suits against the estate must be brought against him as trustee, and suits for protection of the estate must be brought by him as trustee. A trustee has the right to possession af all personal property covered by the trust and to possession of the real property if necessary to execute the terms of the trust. A trustee must protect the estate and perform his duties with care or be liable to the beneficiary for any damages resulting. He is not permitted to keep any profit made out of his office; any profit so made belongs to the beneficiary.

RIGHTS AND LIABILITIES OF BENEFICIARY

A cestui que trust has the right to receive the benefits of the trust estate as outlined in the instrument creating the trust. If the trustee fails to perform his duties properly, the cestui que trust may bring legal action to have him removed. A trustee has legal title to the trust property and may convey good title to one who purchases for valid and without notice of the trust. The cestui que trust can follow and regain trust funds or property if these are conveyed to persons not bona fide purchers.

LIVING TRUST

A living trust is essentially an arrangement whereby you transfer certain assets to the chosen trust company of a bank as your trustee. They retain in the trust those assets in the investment program which you have approved, and dispose of other, possibly less desirable assets, reinvesting the proceeds to fit your program. From then on they supervise the investments and pay the income to you or to those you name to receive it. The trust may last for your life and the lives of certain persons you name. Such persons need not be, but usually are, the income beneficiaries. When the last beneficiary dies, the trust ends, and the assets remaining are paid over to those you have selected. Such a trust may be revocable—that is, you may change it or revoke it completely at any time; or it may be irrevocable—that is, it may be permanent, unchangeable transfer of property. Several of the many living-trust advantages are avoidance of estate settlement delays, experienced investment management, simplified preparation of income-tax returns, and minimized taxes, and may include a pour-over will.

MODERN, TAX-SAVING PLAN— "MARITAL DEDUCTION"

Mr. and Mrs. Jones owned total property worth about $300,000. Of this amount $100,000 was in real estate and $200,000 in securities. All the property was in their joint names, although Mr. Jones had paid for practically everything with his money.

Mr. Jones discovered that the full value of the property, $300,000, would be subject to federal estate tax at his death. However, there would be a "marital deduction" allowed on account of the property passing to his wife, and the tax would come to about $17,500. A tax of this amount did not seem too disturbing.

But Mr. and Mrs. Jones were disturbed when they discovered

that the tax on their property when Mrs. Jones died would probably come to about $54,000. Her estate would not receive the benefit of any marital deduction, assuming she did not remarry. In other words, there would likely be a tax bite of over $71,000 taken out of the property before it passed to the children.

To avoid this severe taxation, here is the new plan that Mr. and Mrs. Jones adopted: First they divided up the $200,000 in securities. They had $100,000 registered in Mr. Jones's name and $100,000 in Mrs. Jones's name. Title to the real estate was not changed but remained in the joint names of Mr. and Mrs. Jones.

Then Mr. Jones made a will leaving his securities in trust for Mrs. Jones. When Mr. Jones dies, she will receive the income from the trust for the rest of her life, and at her death the trust principal will be turned over to the children. If any child is under twenty-one at that time, all shares will stay in trust until the youngest child attains his majority.

Mrs. Jones provided in her will for a similar trust of her securities, with income payable to her husband for life and principal to go to the children.

There were clauses in both wills providing that the real estate should go to the children at the death of the surviving parent but that it was to be held in trust until all children attained their majority. (These practical provisions are designed to avoid many of the problems of disagreeable and expensive guardianship arrangements that often come when minors inherit property.)

The new arrangements adopted by Mr. and Mrs. Jones indicate a substantial saving in estate taxes in the distribution of their property. Here is the specific comparison:

	Old Plan		New Plan	
Total property	$300,000		$300,000	
Tax at Mr. Jones's death	$17,500		$ 4,800	
Tax at Mrs. Jones's death	$54,270		$31,500	
Total Tax	$71,770	$ 71,770	$36,300	$ 36,300
Left for children	$228,230			$263,700
Tax Saving	$35,470			

Like many people, Mr. Jones had placed too much reliance on joint ownership. Before he changed his plan, his estate was in effect all set to pay an unnecessary tax bill of $35,000. He is very happy about the time he spent in reviewing and revising his arrangements.

What happened to Mr. Jones is not unique. Many persons, particularly married couples, have found that a little time spent in reviewing the merits of jointly owned property has led to great savings for their families.

Where property is held by two persons in joint ownership, a will is still necessary to provide for effective disposition of the property when the surviving joint tenant dies. Both parties should have wills to cover all possibilities. With a will one can give the children the benefit of competent trust management of the property.

XV. TORTS

The study of law is divided into two parts: rights and wrongs. A tort is a wrong committed against an individual or against his property rights. For example: John hits James; John is said to have committed a tort against James. John breaks a window in James's house by throwing a stone, either intentionally or accidentally; this is a tort against James's property. John calls James a thief in the presence of James's creditors; this is a tort, because John has wrongfully injured James's credit or reputation if he cannot prove that James is indeed a thief.

ILLUSTRATIONS

Suppose John hits James. This is a tort. Suppose John shoots James with a revolver and kills him. This is a crime. Let us study these two illustrations closely. When John hit James with his fist, the blow affected only James himself, personally. When John shot James and killed him, the act affected not only James but the entire society or community, or the public at large, because John might shoot somebody else. People would be afraid to live near John; if he took James's life, he might take someone else's. Therefore, when a crime is committed, the criminal act and its implications affect everybody, but in a tort the act affects only individuals.

When John commits a tort against James by hitting him with his fist, James may bring a tort action for damages against John. Thus, we see, money is the basis for adjusting damages in tort action. But when John commits a crime by killing James, the public at large, or the state, prosecutes John, and he will either go to the penitentiary or, in states where capital punishment is in vogue, be executed. We see that money is not the basis for damages where one party commits a crime against another. In the category of crimes are murder, larceny, arson, and burglary. All these offenses affect the public at large and not merely the individuals against whom they are committed.

In the law of torts we have what is known as trespass. Instead of giving a definition of trespass, I shall illustrate. Suppose John actually hits James with his fist, so that John's person comes into contact with James's person. We then have what is known as trespass in the form of a battery. Suppose John holds his fist in the air in preparation to strike James; John is close enough to strike James and also has the physical ability to do so, but he holds his fist in the attitude of striking and does not actually strike. This is what we call trespass in the form of an assault. Suppose John puts dynamite all around James's house and warns James that if he comes out of the house the dynamite will be discharged. Here we have a trespass in the form of what is called imprisonment; it takes away James's personal liberty. All these different forms of trespass are classified under the term tort. A tort action for damages may be brought against any party who commits any of the above trespasses against another party—with this exception, that if a man commits one of these acts in self-defense, an action for tort will not lie against him. (There are a few other exceptions, not worthy of mention here.)

Under the subject matter of trespass: If John walks on James's cornfield, he is said to have committed a trespass against James's real property. To have a trespass against real property, the act of touching the property must be intentional, or by virtue of negligence, or by some act of the party who goes upon the land.

Suppose John takes James's overcoat. This is a trespass against personal property. Suppose John cuts the overcoat into pieces or burns it up or indefinitely keeps it in his possession. In all these cases John will have committed a trespass against James's personal property. Thus, we see, a trespass, may be committed against a person, against real property, or against personal property.

Suppose John, in an airplane, happens to be flying along a public highway and suddenly there comes up a very strong wind, and against John's best endeavors to avoid flying over another's property, the wind blows his plane over into James's pasture. The machine strikes the ground and tears up a bunch of sod before John can get it under control again and back over the highway. Clearly John has committed a trespass against James's property. The court will hold, however, that this trespass, being purely accidental and unintentional, is to be excused, especially since John made extraordinary efforts to avoid committing it.

In the above case John was performing a lawful act; he had the right to fly his plane. But suppose John hits James in the face unintentionally. This is a trespass, because John has committed an unlawful act: hitting a person in the face is in itself unlawful. John has committed the tort known as trespass, and James can bring an action for assault and battery. The court will find for James on the ground that striking anyone in the face is an unlawful act, as a breach of the peace.

Suppose John, in digging a cellar, by mistake digs away some of James's lot, thinking he is on his own lot. James brings an action for trespass against real property. The court will hold John liable for damages, because when he removed soil from James's lot, it was a voluntary, intentional act, even though performed as the result of a mistake. Suppose John, cutting down trees on his own lot, by mistake cuts down trees on James's lot. The court will hold that James can bring suit for damages in an action for trespass against personal property, because John intentionally cut down James's trees, even though he was mistaken as to how far his own land extended. Suppose John is cutting hay in his meadow. James comes up to him in the field and starts an argument. During the argument James picks up a rock, intending to strike John. John in self-defense strikes James in the face and knocks him down. James afterward brings an action against John for assault and battery. The court will hold that where John was defending his person, or his real property or chattels, he will not be liable in trespass. The court will further hold that John did not have to wait until James had committed a battery against him to begin defending himself; rather, John had the right to act in self-defense at the very moment the battery was attempted. Suppose James and other persons take John by surprise and the weapons they carry and their menacing actions cause John to believe that his life is in peril. It is impossible for John to get away safely, and in self-defense he kills James and one of the others. The court will hold that John is to be excused for killing while acting in self-defense, that is, in the preservation of his own life. But a court will hold that John may not kill anyone while in defense of his property, real or personal, except when his home is being attacked and it is vitally necessary that he protect it.

Suppose John, a minor, while playing, commits a trespass against James's property. James brings suit against John's father for damages. The court will hold that James cannot hold the parent liable for any tort which John committed, unless the minor committed it while acting as agent for his father and within the scope of that authority. The courts also hold that if a person is insane or drunk, and while in this condition commits a tort, he will be held liable for his tort despite his condition. The minor, John, can be held liable for his own tort committed against James, but the father cannot be held liable.

Suppose John is arrested by an officer, and the process, or written instrument, calling for the arrest seems to be regular on its face and the court that issued the process is a court of proper jurisdiction, but the process is not perfectly valid. John brings an action for damages in trespass against the officer who served the process and thus caused his unlawful arrest. The court will hold that so long as the instrument was apparently valid on its face, the officer cannot be held for trespass and damages. But a court will hold, if John is arrested by an officer serving a process or instrument which on its face is not valid, that John can bring suit for damages against the officer for unlawful arrest, and secure damages. A court will hold that an officer who is serving a valid criminal process can break into a man's house for that purpose and be free from arrest for trespass. But if an officer who is serving process or instrument in a civil suit breaks into the house of the party, he will be liable for damages for trespass.

A private nuisance is "anything done to the hurt, or to the annoyance, of the lands of another, and not amounting to a trespass." Suppose John has an apartment house filled with tenants, and James, who lives next door, converts his private dwelling house into a factory. In the manufacturing process James keeps noisy machinery going night and day, so that it became a private nuisance to John and his tenants. John can enter James's factory; and if he can remove the nuisance peaceably, James cannot bring an action against him for trespass in having entered the house converted into a factory. If, however, John cannot remove the nuisance peaceably, he can then request a court of equity to issue an injunction against James restraining him from continuing the nuisance.

Suppose John takes James's boat, and while using it, breaks the oars. James can bring suit in trespass for damages against John for the injury which John caused by breaking the oars, and judgment will be rendered in James's behalf. The court will hold that in every action for trespass in which judgment is entered against defendant, plaintiff can recover damages only for the injury actually committed against the thing itself; and the thing itself may be either an individual, real property, or personal property.

Suppose, in this same case, James, instead of bringing an action for trespass, brings an action in trover for conversion of the boat. The court will hold that where an action is brought by James in trover for conversion and judgment is given him, the amount of damages to be awarded will be not for the injury suffered but instead for the entire value of both the boat and the oars which John converted to his own use; and when judgment has been rendered, the personal property, the boat, will be considered to belong to John, and no longer to James. So when an action is brought in trover for conversion, the plaintiff will not retain the personal property converted.

An action in trover for conversion can be brought only where the article converted is personal property. Thus the distinction between an action in trespass and an action in trover for conversion: An action in trespass may be instituted where the subject matter is either real property, personal property, or the person of an individual; and plaintiff, or the injured party, always retains the property, real or personal, injured. In an action brought in trover for conversion, the subject matter must always be personal property, and the property becomes the property of defendant, or the party who did the converting. One more distinction: In an action in trover for conversion, the damages awarded plaintiff are always for the entire value of the personal property, and not for just the injury done the property by its conversion. The party who converts personal property must obviously have it under his control or in his actual possession in order to perform the conversion. Again, the party who converts personal property must do so intentionally, either to withhold it from the rightful owner or for the purpose of keeping it in his control or possession; otherwise there can be no conversion and no action in trover. Under common law an action in trover lies only for the act of conversion; it will not lie where the subject matter is real property.

Suppose John goes into the woods and takes a rabbit out of a trap which belongs to James and converts the rabbit to his own use. When he arrives home, he decides to return the rabbit to James, and he actually does return the rabbit, so converted. James can still bring action in trover for conversion against John, even though James willfully and intentionally accepted the rabbit which John returned to him. The court will take into consideration, however, the fact that John returned the rabbit, and damages against him will be mitigated.

Suppose John takes some wheat belonging to James and converts it to his own use, making flour out of it and in turn bread. Clearly John has converted the wheat, and by additional labors, has changed the nature of the property converted. James can bring an action in trover for conversion against John and receive damages for the value of the wheat, but as wheat only and not as wheat in its more valuable transformed condition of bread.

Suppose John calls on a merchant who sells pianos. He picks out a piano and asks to have it charged to his account. The merchant inquires of John whether he owns any property, and John, with intent to deceive, falsely tells him that he owns a house and lot. On the basis of this statement of John's, the merchant grants the charge and delivers the piano. John afterward sells the piano, and the merchant is unable to collect the sale price. He brings suit against John on the ground of deceit. The court will hold that the merchant can recover.

Suppose John injects deadly poison into an orange and gives it to James with intent to kill him. That evening Henry visits James, and James gives him the orange to eat. Shortly afterward Henry dies from the effects of the poison. John will be held guilty of killing Henry, though he intended to kill James, because a person is responsible for any intentional tort he commits: John started in motion the machinery by which Henry got killed, and must therefore be considered directly responsible for Henry's death.

When an action is brought for damages on the ground of negligence, plaintiff must allege in his petition that defendant has violated, or neglected to use care and diligence in carrying out, a duty or responsibility which defendant owes plaintiff. In order that plaintiff's petition be good, it should state or allege that defendant owes plaintiff a certain duty or obligation, and that defendant has violated it. Defendant must use ordinary care in carrying out the duty or obligation owed plaintiff, in accordance with the peculiarities of the case. In his petition plaintiff must also allege that the injuries he sustained were a direct result of defendant's negligence. This is according to the law of torts.

Suppose John takes his family for a ride. After they have driven into the country ten miles, they stop on a river bank. The road runs alongside, and nearby a wooden railroad bridge crosses the road over a trestle. John builds a fire to fry some chickens. After they have eaten their lunch, they return home; meanwhile a wind comes up and fans into flames the embers of the fire which John had made and neglected to put out completely. Some dry grass immediately contingent catches fire and burns up to the bridge, and the bridge burns. That evening a freight train comes along, the bridge gives way, and several boxcars are hurled into the river and their contents destroyed. The railroad company brings an action in damages for tort against John, basing it on the natural-and-proximate consequence rule. The court will hold that John is liable; even though he never intended to burn the bridge, his negligence nevertheless contributed directly and naturally to the burning. The court will further rule that John is to be held responsible, in a tort action for damages, for all natural and probable consequences of his negligence in not having put out the fire which he started.

A court would hold that John was not to be held liable if the burning of the bridge was not the natural and proximate result of John's negligent act. John would also not be liable if the bridge was caused to burn as an unnatural and remote consequence of his having built the fire. For instance, suppose John carried all the wood to the spot, piled it up ready to build a fire, put kerosene on the wood to make it burn more rapidly, and then left the pile in this condition. Later some tramps came wandering by and lighted the pile for their own convenience, and the bridge burned because of this fire. The court would hold that the railroad company could not bring a damage suit in tort against John for having burned the bridge, because John's piling on the wood and putting on the kerosene was an unnatural and remote cause of the bridge's having burned. The tramps would be held responsible in damages, and not John. But if John acted concurrently with the tramps and his negligent act helped to burn the bridge, the railroad could then hold him for damages. For example, suppose John, after he had piled the wood up and put the kerosene on it, gave a tramp a match and told him to light the wood and build a fire, and the bridge burned as a direct result of the fire. The court would hold that even though John himself did not light the fire, he nevertheless acted concurrently with the tramp in having assisted in setting the machinery in motion which resulted in destruction of the bridge; so, as a natural and probable consequence of John's concurrent action with the tramp, the railroad company was injured, and it could bring an action for damages in tort against John and recover.

Suppose in this same case, where John starts the fire which burns the bridge, that the foreman of the railroad section gang discovers the bridge burning but neglects to notify the dispatch office and several hours later the freight train comes by, and as a result of the bridge's having burned, several cars are damaged. The court will hold that in the case of the cars the railroad cannot hold John for damages in tort, because it did not use ordinary care in protecting itself against the wreck, in that its agent was negligent in not having notified it of the condition of the bridge in time to avoid the wreck. The court will hold that the railroad's contributory negligence relieves John of liability for the wrecked train. But the court will of course hold that the railroad can sue John in tort action, and recover against him, for damage done to the bridge.

Suppose John is James's chauffeur, and while driving James's automobile, he skids into one owned and driven by Henry. Henry was using due care in driving his own car. As a result of the chauffeur's negligence Henry's car is damaged. Henry brings an action in tort against James for damages. The court will hold that Henry can recover against James, John's principal, for damages sustained while John was acting within the scope of his authority as James's chauffeur, explaining that John's negligent act is to be imputed to James.

Suppose, in the same case, Henry, in driving his car, is himself negligent. The court will not then permit Henry to recover damages in an action of tort against James, because Henry's contributory negligence directly caused the damage to his own car. James will thus be relieved.

Suppose John goes to James's garage and hires an automobile and chauffeur to drive to Urbana, to a football game, and return to Chicago. But John, instead of stopping at Urbana, directs the chauffeur to drive him to Peoria, and between Urbana and Peoria an accident occurs and the car is damaged. James, owner of the car, brings suit against John in tort for damages done to it. The court will hold that John, while driving between Urbana and Peoria, was in unlawful possession of the car, and James will be permitted to recover against him, even though he did not cause the accident. The court will hold that while John was in unlawful possession of the car, driving between Urbana and Peoria, from the moment he left Urbana he became an insurer of the car belonging to James.

Suppose John builds a fire in his store building, and the fire spreads and burns the entire block, containing a number of stores which belong to other people. Common law would hold John responsible for damages in tort for all the property damaged. But under modern law, unless John was negligent in having caused the fire, he will not be held responsible in a tort action for damages to the property of other parties directly resulting from the fire which he started in his own building.

Suppose John has a number of fine horses. One of the horses gets loose, strays to James's field and eats considerable oats there. James brings an action in tort for damages against John. The court will hold that James may recover, even though John was not at all negligent in permitting the horse to get away from his own property.

Suppose John has a fine bunch of fatted calves, and while driving them to market, one of them strays from the highway without any negligence on John's part and walks into a country grocery store along the highway, doing considerable damage there. The storekeeper brings an action in tort for damages against John. The court will hold that the storekeeper cannot recover, because John had a perfect right to drive his calves along the public highway, and while doing so, was not committing a trespass.

Suppose John is organizing a bank in Illinois and has secured subscriptions to all the shares of stock. After the cashier has signed his subscription and just before he pays the money in on it, he talks with the secretary of the state banking board. The secretary tells him that he would not grant a charter to any bank that John had anything to do with. Now, the laws of the state provide that the banking board must grant a charter to any group of citizens in the state who can qualify as to residence and who bring to the board the required amount of capital to start a bank in any particular town in the state, according to the state banking laws. After the secretary of the board has told the cashier that he would not grant a charter to any bank that John had anything to do with, the cashier refuses to pay on the subscription, and John is unable to proceed further with organization of the bank, after having expended considerable money for sundry expenses. John brings suit for damages against the secretary of the state banking board, and the court will hold that John can recover.

Suppose John makes a defamatory remark about James, intending to injure or disgrace him. James can bring an action against John for defamation of character. Defamation may be in the form of libel or of slander. If the defamation is written or printed, it is called libel; if it is published or circulated orally, it is called slander. If the libel or slander is caused by negligence or by a willful, intentional act, the party it is directed against can bring an action in tort for damages or injuries sustained. A party libeled does not need to prove that he has been injured; a party slandered must prove the damages which he has actually suffered or sustained. In an action for damages for libel or slander, defendant must prove that the defamatory remarks attributed to him are actually true or he will be held liable.

Suppose John is engaged to be married to a young woman, and James tells him that his fiancée had a child by a third party named Henry. As a result of this remark John breaks off the engagement. The girl brings an action against James. In such a case a court held: "The action lies here, for a woman not married cannot by intendment, have so great advancement, as by her marriage, whereby she is sure of maintenance for life, or during her marriage, and dower or other benefits, which the temporal law gives, by reason of her marriage; and therefore, by this slander, she is greatly prejudiced, in that which is to be her temporal advancement, for which, it is reason, to give her remedy, by way of action at common law, and the man who thus slandered her will be held liable in damages." The action will lie, and damages will be awarded the girl if James cannot prove the statement he made to John.

Suppose John has a daughter or a servant employed in his home and James injures the daughter or servant. John brings an action against James. The court will hold that John has a perfect right to recover damages for loss of the daughter's or servant's services, and besides, for any mental suffering caused him.

Suppose James entices John's wife away from John's home. John brings an action against James. The court will permit John to recover damages for the value of the wife's affection, and will also take into consideration any anguish which John has suffered.

Suppose James has a criminal conversation with John's wife and has improper relation with her. John may then bring an action for damages against James, and will not have to prove any loss of services which he has sustained.

Suppose that John's wife alienates the affections of Mary's husband. Mary will be permitted to bring an action for damages against John's wife for having alienated her husband's affections.

XVI. DOMESTIC RELATIONS

DEFINITION

The subject of domestic relations deals with the various phases of domestic life and with legal marriage as the basic unit of community civilization where Christianity prevails.

PRENUPTIAL CONTRACT

Suppose John enters into an agreement with Cora to transfer title to a house and lot to her in consideration of her promise to marry him. Such an agreement is called a prenuptial contract; it is a contract entered into by the parties to a contemplated marriage. The contract is binding, and each may hold the other to it. When the marriage is completed, and John becomes the husband and Cora the wife, by virtue of either a religious ceremony or a civil process, the prenuptial contract must be complied with.

A prenuptial contract may be written or unwritten. If the marriage is to take place more than one year from the date the prenuptial contract is entered into, the contract must be written to be binding; if the marriage is to take place within one year, the contract may be unwritten and perfectly valid. If either party violates the agreement to marry, the other may bring suit for damages for breach of promise. Either party may prove that there was a contract to marry by the parties' words, actions and conduct.

ILLEGAL OR UNLAWFUL CONSIDERATION FOR PROMISE TO MARRY

Suppose John enters into a contract with Cora to marry. If the consideration for marriage, or for the promise of one party to marry another, is illegal or unlawful, to arrangement to marry will be null and void. For example: Suppose John is married and

Cora is unmarried. John enters into a contract with Cora to marry her, though she knows that he is already married. He then refuses to marry her. Cora brings suit for damages against John for breach of promise. The court will hold that she cannot collect, because the consideration for the contract to marry is illegal and unlawful, it being unlawful for a man to marry again while he is still married to another woman.

Suppose John is married, and Cora does not know it. The parties enter into a contract to marry as a result of John's promise to marry Cora. Cora permits John to injure her. Afterward John refuses to marry her. Cora brings an action for damages against John for breach of contract to wed. The court will hold that Cora can collect.

MARRIAGE LICENSE–STATUTORY MARRIAGE— COMMON-LAW MARRIAGE

According to certain statutes regulating marriage, the parties who intend to marry must secure a marriage license. Marriages are usually performed by a minister or a justice of the peace. After the ceremony a record of the marriage is made, containing the data of the marriage, and this is preserved in the form of a public record. This type of marriage is a statutory marriage.

Suppose John and Lucy agree to get married, and instead of having a statutory marriage, they agree to live together as husband and wife and do actually so live together. This is a common-law marriage. It is perfectly valid. Any children resulting from it will be legitimate, and entitled to inherit property from their parents just the same as children resulting from a statutory marriage. For a common-law marriage to be valid, it is absolutely essential that the time when the marriage is to take place be definitely agreed upon.

AGE OF CONSENT FOR MARRIAGE— MINOR'S MARRIAGE— HABEAS CORPUS

In days of old, when common law prevailed and there were no statutes to the contrary, if John was fourteen years old and Gladys was twelve, the two children could consent to and enter into a valid marriage contract. If John, however, was less than fourteen and Gladys less than twelve, and the children married, the marriage contract would be voidable; that is, when either John or Gladys attained the age of fourteen or twelve, respectively, he or she could annul the marriage and thus invalidate the marriage contract.

Under the law as it exists today, if John and Gladys marry before they have attained their majority or age of consent, the contract of marriage will be considered valid, until it is avoided; and they must avoid it at a reasonable length of time after they have attained their majority or age of consent, otherwise it becomes binding on both parties and can no longer be avoided.

Suppose John, who is twenty-two, marries Karen, who has not reached the age of consent. If Karen is content and wishes to remain with her husband, her parents will not be permitted to sue out a writ of habeas corpus and thus secure custody of her from John.

Suppose John is not yet seven years of age, and likewise Karen is not yet seven. If these children get married, the agreement to marry, and the subsequent marriage, will be absolutely null and void.

MARRIAGE BY FORCE

Suppose John marries a girl who is insane. The agreement of marriage will be null and void, because an insane person cannot enter into a valid contract, except a contract for the necessaries of life.

Suppose John gets Karen to marry him against her will, either by using physical force or by threatening to take her life. This marriage will be null and void.

Suppose John marries a girl, and they cannot have any children. John sues his wife for divorce on the ground of impotence. The court will hold that the marriage cannot be annulled.

Suppose John marries Karen in Nebraska, and the marriage contract is valid under the laws of that state. The wedded couple then go to New York to make their residence. The state of New York will recognize the marriage valid in Nebraska. Every state recognizes a valid marriage performed in any other state.

DIVORCE—GROUNDS—
ALIMONY—CHILDREN

Divorce is a legal procedure by which the marriage contract is dissolved. Grounds for divorce are enumerated by state statutes, and vary from state to state. The commonest grounds for divorce among the states as a whole are desertion, non-support, insanity, cruel and inhuman treatment, adultery, and habitual drunkenness. There are many other grounds.

Suppose Jane sues John for divorce on the ground of cruel and inhuman treatment. Attorney for Jane may secure an order from the court requiring John to pay temporary alimony, so that Jane can pay her attorney for legal services and pay the living expenses of herself and the children and thus enable her to carry on the divorce proceedings. If it happens that Jane was living apart from John for some time after he gave her cause to sue for divorce, and before she started suit, most courts will grant her alimony before she actually receives her divorce decree. If Jane prevails in her suit and the court grants her a divorce, and she is absolutely blameless for the acts whch John committed, the court may grant her permanent alimony for support and maintenance, so long as she remains unmarried; the court may do this because the husband is obligated by law to supply the wife with the necessaries of life, according to their situation in life; and if they have children and custody of them is granted the wife, the husband will also have to pay for their support. These expenses are usually figured up by the court and allowed the wife as monthly alimony when she secures her divorce. If the husband neglects to pay this alimony, the wife can sue him for contempt of court. He must then pay, or the court may send him to jail.

When there are children involved, the court granting the divorce will have absolute discretion in giving custody of them to either the wife or the husband, as it sees fit.

Suppose in the same case, where Jane has secured a divorce from John, that the court has granted alimony to Jane and also divided up the estate between them. If John now dies, Jane will have no further interest in what he accumulated or was possessed of after the divorce was granted. If, following the divorce,

Jane dies, John likewise will have absolutely no right to any part of her estate.

PROPERTY RIGHTS AFTER MARRIAGE

Suppose John and Jane were married in days when the old common law had not been amended by modern statutes. Under common law, at the moment John married Jane, all the property that Jane owned on the day they were married and all property that might come to her afterward, whether real estate, chattels, negotiable instruments, bank accounts, diamonds, or what not, became John's property. But modern statutes are more lenient toward married women. If John and Jane are married today, any personal or real property that she owns, or may come to own, in her own name, as her own separate property, for her own separate use, will remain so, just as if she were not married, and John will have nothing to say about her separate estate. And if John's business fails, and has piled up a great many debts, John's creditors will not be permitted to attach any of Jane's own, separate property for payment of those debts.

Under the old common law, if John married Jane and Jane had property, John had the right to administer Jane's estate and thus receive the rents and issues and keep them for his own use. Under common law, if Jane worked and drew a salary, that salary became John's property. The statutes of today are not so one-sided; and when Jane, a married woman, works and earns a salary, the money she earns belongs to her personally, and John will have no interest in it whatsoever. But it must be understood that today, after Jane marries John, she cannot charge him for services which she renders as a wife, as in taking care of the home and the children, for the wife is as much interested in home and children as the husband is. If John and Jane have property which they together hold in fee, John cannot deed away this property unless Jane signs the deed with him, for under modern law husband and wife hold their property as tenants in common.

The right of a married woman to enter into a valid contract was denied her under common law, but modern statutes have gradually enlarged the powers of a married woman to contract, so that today if, for example, a married woman makes a contract with a plumber to do some work on her personal estate, held in her own name as her separate property, the plumber can bring suit against her on the contract and collect a debt against her own property just as if she were unmarried.

Suppose John marries Jane, and Jane has separate real estate in her own name. Jane wishes to transfer this estate to Henry in trade for some Portland Cement stock. She will be permitted to give a valid deed to her own property without having John sign; but according to general business custom, John will be required to sign the deed with Jane in order to protect the third party against John's dower, or homestead right, in Jane's property.

Modern law has gone so far in granting the married woman the power to contract as to permit her to make valid and lawful contracts with the husband; and likewise the husband may contract with the wife. Under common law, a woman could not make a valid contract with her husband. Suppose John marries Jane. John has property in his own name; Jane has property in her name. Suppose, as the husband, John is managing Jane's property, and he mismanages it. Jane brings suit against John for the mismanagement. The court will hold that Jane has a perfect right to bring suit against John in all cases where the subject matter of the suit involves property belonging to Jane in her own name. But neither Jane nor John may bring suit against the other for services rendered.

Suppose John marries Jane, and before they were married, John gave Jane his personal note. Under common law, after John married Jane, this note would be null and void, because the marriage would have invalidated it, and Jane could not bring suit against John to recover on the note for money loaned him previous to their marriage. But under modern law Jane can bring suit against John on the note and secure judgment, for the reason that today the note is considered Jane's own individual property.

We have learned that under common law, when a man married, he took all his wife's personal and real property as his own estate. Under the same theory the husband became responsible and liable for all prenuptial torts and contracts of the wife. But under present law the husband is not liable for torts and contracts which his wife committed and entered into before their marriage. Under old common-law theory, if the wife committed a tort after she was married, the husband was liable; but under today's law the husband is not responsible or liable for the wife's postnuptial torts.

Today, if the husband refuses to buy the necessaries of life for the wife, she can contract for them and charge them to his account. If he refuses to pay for them, the third party who furnished them can bring suit against him and recover.

Suppose John marries Gladys. Harry negligently injures Gladys, and John brings an action against him for damages. The court will hold that John is entitled to recover damages against Harry for loss of the wife's services, and the damages will be the damages which John actually sustains as a result of the injury to his wife. The courts will further hold that Gladys can bring suit against Harry in damages, for any pain or suffering caused her, or for loss of actual earnings if she was earning money, outside of her household duties; and the court will grant her appropriate damages.

The above is the law as it exists today. Under common law John would be privileged to bring both actions against Harry, and Gladys would have no action, because when a woman married, her husband took all her rights, whatever they pertained to—real property, chattels, commercial paper, choses in action, etc.

Suppose John is married to Gladys and Harry has a criminal conversation with Gladys or commits adultery with her. John brings an action against Harry in tort. The court will hold that John has the right to sue Harry, and to receive damages for the act of adultery, whether loss of the wife's services was actually suffered by John, or not. Under common-law theory, if John committed adultery, Gladys had no right of action against the other woman. But under present law the wife has the same privilege of suing for adultery of the spouse as the husband does.

ALIENATION OF AFFECTIONS

Suppose John marries Gladys, and Harry alienates Gladys's affections and causes her to leave John and live abroad, away from him. John brings an action against Harry. The court will hold that John can recover damages for loss of his wife's services and her society.

CUSTODY OF CHILDREN

Suppose John is married to Gladys and they have three children. Under common law the husband and father had absolute right to custody of his children, and the wife and mother had no right. But under modern law both parents have the right to custody of their children, and if one parent wishes to secure sole custody, that parent may request the court to issue a writ of habeas corpus. The court has absolute discretion in awarding custody. It usually grants the mother custody of very young children, because she is in the better position to care for them.

Parents, of course, have the right to custody of their children in preference to any outside party.

NECESSARIES OF LIFE FURNISHED MINOR CHILD

Suppose John marries Gladys and they have two minor children. Suppose the children leave home. While away from home and yet minors, they buy clothing, groceries, and other necessaries of life and charge them to John's account. The grocer, clothier, etc., bring suit against John. Under common law the court would hold that the father was not liable for any necessaries of life furnished his minor children. But under modern law the court will hold that the grocer, clothier, etc., can collect against the parent for necessaries of life furnished his minor children provided the children had not been away from the parent's home or provided they had not left home against the father's will.

MINOR CHILD'S WAGES

Suppose John and Gladys are married and they have a minor son. The son works for a banker; the banker pays the son his wages. John brings suit against the banker for his son's wages.

The court will hold that John has the right to all the earnings of this minor son and that the banker was negligent in paying the son instead of making the check payable to the father. The court will therefore permit John to recover against the banker for the wages of the minor child. The court will also hold that John can assign the wages, by either written or unwritten assignment, revocable by John if it is not under seal. If John dies, then Gladys is entitled to receive the wages which the minor son earns, until he reaches his majority. She may assign the child's wages in the same way that John could have done.

LOSS OF MINOR CHILD'S SERVICES

Suppose John is married to Gladys and they have a son fifteen years of age. Harry commits some tort against the child and injures him. John brings suit for damages in tort against Harry. The court will hold that John can secure damages for actual loss of services of his minor son and for any money which the child may have earned, if he were not injured, between the ages of fifteen and twenty-one. The court will further hold that the minor child can bring an action against Harry and recover for his pain and suffering and for his probable future earnings, after the age of twenty-one.

Suppose John is married to Gladys and they have a daughter fourteen years of age. Harry injures the daughter. John brings an action against Harry in tort for damages. The court will hold that John can secure damages against Harry for his injured feelings and for loss of the daughter's services.

The court will hold, if the daughter has reached her majority and Harry commits the same act toward her, that unless the daughter is staying at home and working for the father as a servant, the father cannot collect damages against Harry for loss of wages. If the daughter is of age and Harry commits the act against her while she is away from home and employed for wages by a third party, the father cannot secure damages against Harry for loss of the daughter's wages, even though she had to leave her employment and return home, because the father will not be considered to stand in the de facto relation to her of master and servant. But if Harry commits the act against the daughter when she is staying at home with her father in the de facto relationship of master and servant, then the father may bring an action for damages against Harry for loss of wages due to injury done the daughter, even though she is of age.

Suppose John is married to Gladys and they have a daughter. John injures the daughter, and she brings an action in tort against him. The court will hold that the father is liable to a penitentiary offense but that the daughter cannot sustain her tort action against him. Further, the court will hold, if a third party commits a tort against the daughter, that the father is not liable for the tort, nor for any tort which the daughter commits, unless she commits it as the father's agent.

ILLEGITIMATE CHILD

Suppose John is married to Gladys. Suppose before their marriage they had an illegitimate child. Under common law an illegitimate child belonged to nobody, and had no right to inherit anything from either of his parents. If this illegitimate child, after becoming of age, married, accumulated property, had children, and died, the children could inherit the property left by their parent, who was himself an illegitimate child. If the parents of the illegitimate child afterward married each other, the child would become legitimized.

The court will hold, according to modern law, that the illegitimate child can inherit property from his mother. And the mother can inherit from the illegitimate child, in case the child accumulated property and then died intestate and childless.

ADOPTED CHILD

Suppose John marries Gladys, and they have no children as a result of the marriage. Suppose they adopt a child. According to modern procedure, if John and Gladys accumulate property and die intestate, the child is privileged to inherit the estate just the same as a natural child.

Suppose an adopted child grows up and by his industry and

ability accumulates property, and then dies intestate and without leaving any children. The court will hold that the adoptive parents are entitled to inherit the property.

POWER OF MINOR CHILD TO MAKE WILL

Suppose John marries Gladys and they have two children. While still minors, these children draw up a will, giving away some real property and some personal property. The father brings an action to set aside the will on the ground of the children's minority. The court will probably hold that minor children have no power to make a will to dispose of real property, but can make a will disposing of personal property after a son is fourteen and a daughter is twelve. Most states have statutes which provide that an infant cannot will away real property; if there is no such statute in the state, the child can do so. Very few states have statutes which prohibit a minor from willing away personal property.

CONTRACTS OF MINOR CHILD

Suppose John and Gertrude marry and have a minor son. The son makes a contract with Harry to build a woodshed and then refuses to carry out his side of the contract. The court will hold, if the son pleads his minority, that it is a valid defense and Harry cannot enforce the contract.

In this same case, suppose the son is an infant, and he fraudulently induces Harry to believe that he is of age, and as a result Harry makes the contract with him. To the injury of Harry, the minor saws up a large quantity of lumber and then refuses to complete the contract. Harry brings an action at law against the minor for damages. The court will hold that according to legal procedure, minority is a valid defense and therefore Harry cannot collect against the minor in a court of law. But let us say the court of law sends the case to be tried in an equity court. The equity court will hold that because the minor used fraud in making Harry believe that he was of age, and as a result Harry made a contract with the minor and was damaged, Harry is entitled to damages.

The courts hold that a contract made with an infant is voidable on the part of the infant and cannot be enforced against the infant, except a contract to furnish him with the necessaries of life. But the courts also hold that one cannot collect the contract price of the necessaries of life furnished the infant unless it is the reasonable value of those necessaries.

Suppose John is married to Gladys and they have an infant son fifteen years of age. Suppose the son sells a horse to Harry for $200 and then spends $100 of it. When he becomes twenty-one, the son disaffirms the contract of sale and sues Harry to recover the horse sold him while he was yet a minor. The court will hold that the minor can recover the horse, and all that he has to return to Harry is whatever he has left of the money which he received for the horse.

Suppose, again, the minor buys a horse of Harry, and pays $200 for it. When the minor attains his majority, he rescinds the contract of purchase and brings suit against Harry for the $200 he paid for the horse. The court will hold that the minor can rescind the contract and receive back the $200, less reasonable value for the minor's use and services of the horse. The court will also order the infant to tender the horse back to Harry.

MINOR AS PARTNER

Suppose a minor enters into a partnership to buy and sell horses. When he reaches his majority, he can rescind all the contracts entered into in behalf of the partnership. Creditors will not be permitted to secure judgment against the minor personally for partnership debts, but may secure judgment against the other partner, Harry, who is of age. The creditors may collect their claims out of all the partnership assets, including the minor's share in the partnership, prior to the right of the infant to set up his claim of minority.

Suppose the infant secures the services of Harry as an agent. In the course of his agency Harry makes several contracts with third parties, at the infant's direction. When the infant reaches his majority, he cannot disaffirm these agency contracts, and thus obligate Harry. Should the infant desire to bring suit, the suit must be prosecuted in his guardian's name or in the name of his next friend.

In the same case, the infant will be held to account for his own torts or crimes if he is more than fourteen years of age; and an infant who is under seven will not be held for crime, because at this tender age a person cannot have the intent to commit a crime. A minor will not be permitted to hold public office, because he has not reached the age at which he can perform duties and assume obligations which call for the exercise of discretion.

XVII. COMMUNITY PROPERTY

COMMUNITY SYSTEM IN GENERAL

The common law, recognizing that one spouse is entitled to some economic activity in the property of the other, evolved the interests known as dower and curtesy. These interests applied only with respect to land. The husband enjoyed the additional economic advantage that would come from management and control of the wife's property. This advantage has disappeared with the coming of married women's acts, which confer on married women the right to manage their own separate estates. Statutes have enlarged the idea of dower and curtesy to include chattels by providing for a statutory share that one spouse may claim upon the death of the other spouse. However, these changes fail to take into consideration that both spouses contribute to the acquisitions made during marriage and both should have an interest in such increases. That is the concept of community property. The idea came from Germany, was adopted in France and Spain and was taken to the colonies in the New World.

Community Property States: The community-property system in Louisiana shows the influence of the law of both France and Spain. California owes the origin of its community-property law to an 1848 treaty between the United States and Mexico. The Spanish-Mexican civil law was the law of California at the time of its cession by Mexico to the United States as a result of this treaty. The treaty expressly provides that the property rights of the inhabitants of the ceded territory are to be protected. This forced the community-property system to be continued in California. In some states constitutional or legislative enactments gave origin to the community system. To some measure the system may be adopted by judicial decree. The community system is not followed in Florida; yet in a recent decision from that state the court said: "In the southwest where community property is recognized, the husband and wife share equally in all property accumulated during coverture. There is a perfectly sound basis for this rule and it will be applied in this state when the circumstances warrant." Since the community system is one of the oldest forms of concurrent ownership known, it is expected to survive even legislative and judicial attempts to tax it out of existence.

NATURE OF INTERESTS

A. It is now recognized in all community-property states that the wife's interest in community property is a present and existing interest and not only an expectancy. So it is a vested interest.

THEORIES OF OWNERSHIP

There are three theories underlying community ownership of property. One view is that the community is regarded as a sort of legal entity much like, although to be distinguished from, a commercial partnership. This could be called the quasi-legal-entity theory. Washington and some other states follow this theory. In the state of Washington community property is not liable for the separate debts of either husband or wife (Katz v. Judd, 108 Wash. 557), and also in Arizona (Forsythe v. Paschal, 34 Ariz. 380). In Texas the view is followed that legal title to land or chattels is vested in the spouse to whom the conveyance or transfer is made. The other spouse has an equitable interest in the property. (Edwards v. Brown, 68 Tex. 329.) The view followed in most community-property states is that regardless of the fact that title may be conveyed to one spouse, the other spouse has legal title to the extent of his or her interest in community property.

EXISTENCE OF COMMUNITY

Putative Marriage. At common law, dower and curtesy depend on the existence of a marriage legally recognized under the civil law; even though a marriage is absolutely void, a party who entered into the relationship in good faith may assert rights thereunder. The relationship is known as a putative or good-faith marriage, and it produces the same civil effects as a valid marriage. Not only is the issue of such a marriage considered to be legitimate, but property acquisitions during continuance of the relationship constitute community property. In U.S. v. Robinson, 40 Fed (2d) 14, the wife was not entitled to war-risk insurance, because a putative spouse is not entitled to benefits under federal legislation. Where there are both a legally recognized spouse and a putative spouse, the putative spouse is entitled to half the acquisitons made during continuance of the putative relationship (Hubbell v. Inkstein, 7 La. Ann 252; Morgan v. Morgan, 1 Tex. Civ. App. 315). In determining whether one entered into a marriage relationship in good faith, a subject test is applied (Figoni v. Figoni, 211 Cal. 354; Knoll v. Knoll, 104 Wash. 110). Under this view a putative marriage may result even though a marriage ceremony was not performed as required by local law.

Contracts. The general rule is that husband and wife may agree that their property acquistions, whether joint or several, are not to be considered community property. There is a minority rule that such an agreement may be made only prior to marriage. In Arizona and Louisiana there is an exception in cases where parties move to the state after marriage; a valid marriage contract may be made within one year thereafter. In all states the contract must be in writing, and it is usually provided that it must be executed with the formalities required for the conveyance of land. Such an agreement is prospective in its operation and is to be distinguished from an agreement that merely fixes the status of presently existing property. In Texas the rule is followed that husband and wife cannot contract away their rights under the community-property laws. It is considered that the constitution of the state defines community property. Since the legislature of the state is without power to define what is or what is not community property, the parties to the marriage are likewise without such power (Arnold v. Leonard, 114 Tex. 535; Myles v. Arnold [Tex. Civ. App.], 162 SW[2d] 442).

SEPARATE AND COMMUNITY PROPERTY DEFINED

In General. The prevailing rule is that husband and wife may own land or chattels as community property, joint tenants, tenants in common, or tenants in partnership. In Squires v. Belden, 2 La. 268, capacity was denied on the ground that a married woman cannot bind herself for the debts of her husband. In Miller v. Marx & Kempner, 65 Tex. 131, it was held that a married woman cannot become a partner in business with her husband. But the modern rule is to the contrary (156 Cal. 195).

Presumptions. There is a general presumption that all property acquired after marriage is community property. In some states there are special presumption rules where title is acquired by a married woman by an instrument in writing (196 Cal. 547; 119 Wash. 631).

Community Property Defined. Community property is usually defined as including all property acquired after marriage other than by gift, devise, bequest, and descent; and the rents, issues, and profits from separate property form a part of the community. In California it is provided by statute that the earnings and accumulations of a married woman and of her minor children living with her or in her custody while she is living separate from her husband constitute her separate property (Makeig v. United Security Bank & Trust Co., 112 Cal. App. 138).

TIME OF ACQUISITION

In General. Since land or chattels acquired before marriage, or after termination of marriage, constitute separate property, the time of acquisition plays an important part in determining the status of property as being separate or community.

Inception of Contract Theory. According to this theory, the status of land or chattels as community property is determined according to conditions as they exist at the time of inception of the right that resulted in acquisition of title. In Commissioner of Internal Revenue v. King, 69 Fed. (2d) 639, during continuance of his marriage King, a lawyer practicing in Texas, agreed to represent a railway company on a contingent-fee basis. Almost five years later he received his fee of $52,000. His wife had died less than two years prior to payment of this fee. The court held that this money was community property because the marriage relationship existed at the time the contract was made (Bishop v. Williams [Tex. Civ. App.] 223 SW 512). Similarly it is held that if one takes possession of property adversely prior to marriage, without any legal or equitable right, it will be community property if the marriage relationship exists at the time of expiration of the statutory period (Bishop v. Lusk, 8 Tex. City App. 30). In re White's Estate, 43 N.M. 202, the deceased, White, while in the U.S. Navy, took out a $10,000 policy of government insurance. Four months later he had it canceled, and while yet in service he married Mildred White. He received his discharge in 1918, and in 1919 he applied for reinstatement of his insurance quired. Three months after reinstatement White died. Following the view that a reinstatement of insurance continues the original policy in force, the court held that the policy constituted the separate estate of the deceased. A policy of insurance payable to the estate of the insured is separate estate if the policy was acquired prior to his marriage. The same conclusion was reached in Succession of Lewis, 192 La. 734.

Acquisition of Title Theory. According to this theory, the status of land or chattels as community property is determined according to conditions existing at the time of acquisition of title. In re Monaghan's Estate, 60 Ariz. 342, during continuance of her marriage plaintiff, an attorney practicing in Arizona, entered into a contract of employment on a contingent-fee basis. Thereafter she separated from her husband, and he died at the time she received payment for her services. The court held that the money constituted part of her separate estate because the marriage relationship did not exist when title to the money was acquired. A Washington court reached the same conclusion in a case where as provided by law. No additional physical examination was re-a contract to purchase land was entered into during continuance of the marriage but legal title to the land was not acquired until after dissolution of the marriage. The court held that the property constituted the separate estate of the husband, who was the purchaser under the agreement (Kuhn's Estate, 132 Wash. 678). In Wooley v. Louisiana Central Lumber Co., 204 La. 801, Wooley applied for a homestead entry. Three months after his death his widow made final proof to the land and the government issued a patent conveying the land to her. The court held that the land constituted part of her separate estate because the marriage relationship did not exist at the time title was acquired.

Apportionment Theory. According to this theory, the status of land or chattels as community property is determined by the extent to which community property was used in its acquisition. In the early California case of Estate of Webb Myr. Prob. (Cal.) 93, Webb paid the first year's premium of an endowment policy prior to his marriage. He paid the second year's premium after his marriage and died shortly after making a payment on the third year's premium. The court held that the proceeds derived from the policy should be considered community property to the extent that community funds were used in paying the premiums. Accordingly, two-thirds of the proceeds derived from the policy was held to be community property. In Vieux v. Vieux, 80 Cal. App. 222, the same rule was applied where a contract to purchase land was involved. While an application of this theory accomplishes exact justice in many cases, there are some situations where its application is not practical. In Gelfand v. Gelfand, 136 Cal. App. 448, the husband secured policies of life insurance at a time when he was domiciled in a non-community-property state. Thereafter he established a domicile in California and paid premiums amounting to $24,000, using community funds for the purpose. In divorce proceedings it became necessary for the court to determine the status of the policies. Unlike other insurance-policy cases, apportionment of the proceeds derived from the policies was not involved. The court held that since such apportionment was not possible, the policies should be awarded to the husband as part of his separate estate and the community should be reimbursed to the extent that community funds had been used to pay premiums.

SOURCE OF ACQUISITION

General Rule. A change in the form of property does not change its status. In Estate of Clark, 94 Cal. App. 453, about two weeks after the death of his son by his first marriage, Clark married Eliza Simpson. He then instituted proceedings to contest his son's will, and the case was compromised by payment to Clark of an amount in excess of $150,000. After Clark's death his widow claimed that this money was community property. Her argument was that all property acquired after marriage other than by gift, devise, bequest, and descent, and the rents, issues, and profits therefrom, constituted community property. The court held that the money formed part of the separate estate of the deceased Clark. Prior to his marriage he had a valuable property right, that is, the right to contest his son's will, and this right was a part of his separate estate. Consequently the money received in settlement of this right was separate property.

Credit Acquisition. Property acquired on the separate credit of the wife constitutes her separate property, but property acquired on the basis of community credit is community property (Dyment v. Nelson, 166 Cal. 38; Gleich v. Bonzio, 128 Tex. 606). Property acquired on the separate credit of the husband constitutes part of his separate estate (Estate of Ellis, 203 Cal. 414); however, a contrary view was held in Morris v. Waring, 22 N.M. 175, which is a minority rule. Some courts take the position that the intention of the creditor is the controlling factor. If the evidence shows that he intended to extend credit to the husband or to the wife, then the acquisition is separate property. The intention can usually be gathered only from circumstances. In Fortier v. Barry, 111 La. 776, a creditor of the husband sought to seek his alleged interest in two lots. The wife claimed that she owned the lots as part of her separate estate. She bought one of the lots, paying $350 from her separate estate, and gave a mortgage on the lot to secure the balance of the purchase price in the amount of $2,050. She gave a $3,000 note in payment for the second lot. Other than these lots, the wife's separate estate consisted only of a $2,000 lot rented at $20 a month. The court held that the lots in question were community property because acquired on the strength of community credit. The wife did not have sufficient separate property to justify the conclusion that the acquisitions were on the strength of her separate credit (Lotz v. Citizens Bank & Trust Co., [La. App.] 17 So. [2d] 463). This does not seem to be sound, because the issue should be resolved on the basis of legal liability rather than of the creditor's intention (Morris v. Waring, 22 N.M. 175). A similar view is expressed in Gorman v. Gorman (Tex. Civ. App.), 180 SW (2d) 470.

Damages for Injuries to Personalty. In the absence of statute, damages recovered for injuries to personalty suffered by either husband or wife are community property. This is true because of the rule that all property acquired after marriage other than by gift, devise, bequest, or descent falls into the community. Some states have a statute which declares a contrary view (McFadden v. Santa Ana, Orange & Tustin Street Ry. Co., 87 Cal. 464). If one spouse seeks to recover damages for personal injuries where it appears that the other spouse was guilty of contributory negligence, recovery will be denied. This theory is carried over into wrongful-death cases. In Dallas Ry. & Terminal Co. v. High, 129 Tex. 219, the surviving mother and son of Mrs. Godwin claimed damages under a wrongful-death statute alleging that her death resulted from defendant's negligence. At the time of the accident Mrs. Godwin was riding in the sidecar of a motorcycle. Her husband, who was operating the motorcycle, was guilty of negligence. He was fatally injured in the accident, living only a few hours. Recovery was denied. It was reasoned that if Mrs. Godwin had lived, she could not have successfully maintained an action to recover damages for her personal injuries, because her husband's negligence would bar such recovery. Assuming that damages recovered for personal injuries constitute community property, another question may arise as to time of acquisition. In Franklin v. Franklin, 67 Cal. App. (2d) 717, the wife secured an interlocutory decree of divorce. Before a year had passed by, during which time the parties were still husband and wife, the husband suffered injuries in an automobile accident. The wife petitioned for a final decree and an order that would entitle her to a half interest in the cause of action vested in her husband. It was her contention that the cause of action constituted community property. The court held that the cause of action did not constitute community property, because such a right is personal to the injured party. In this case the husband did not recover such damages during continuance of the community. In Ostheller v. Spokane & Inland Empire R.R. Co., 107 Wash. 678, the same conclusion was arrived at as in Dallas Ry. & Terminal Co. v. High, 129 Tex. 219, on the ground that since the husband and wife were engaged in a community activity at the time of the accident, the negligence of the husband was the negligence of the community, the community being considered a quasi-legal entity. An action could not be maintained in wrongful death.

Earnings of Wife. Usually the earnings of the wife are community property unless the community interest is released by the husband. In some states the statute provides that the wife may apply to do business as a sole trader. Where such application receive judicial approval, the earnings of the wife constitute part of her separate estate. This helps the wife to get her necessaries where the husband is unwilling or unable to provide them.

Improvements Erected on Separate or Community Property. An improvement erected on land may become part of the land under the rules concerning fixtures. If the husband uses community funds to erect an improvement on his own separate estate, the improvement thereby becomes a part of his separate estate, but the community must be reimbursed to the extent of the expenditures (Estate of Chandler, 112 Cal. App. 601). If the husband uses community funds to erect an improvement on the wife's separate estate, the presumption is that it is a gift to the wife (Shaw v. Bernal, 163 Cal. 262).

Commingling Cases. Sometimes property is acquired by the use of both community and separate assets. Where the proportion contributed by each can be ascertained, the acquistition will be considered separate property to the extent that the separate property contributed to its acquisition. Trouble arises where it is impossible to find the extent of contribution. In re Torrey's Estate, 54 Ariz. 369, the husband at the time of his marriage owned two restaurants appraised at $3,035. His widow claimed that the income from these restaurants after marriage was community property. It was shown that both separate and community assets contributed to the acquisition. Since the restaurants were owned by the deceased as part of his separate estate, the rents, issues, and profits from them would be his separate estate. The community contributed the management. It was considered im-

possible to segregate and evaluate these contributing factors. It
was held that the chief contributing factor was the effort and
skill of the husband in managing the business. So the income
was community property (Estate of Gold, 170 Cal. 621). The
separate estate of the husband should be entitled to reimbursement to the extent that the separate estate was used. This could
be determined on the basis of a reasonable rate of return on the
value of the investment at the time of marriage (Pereira v.
Pereira, 156 Cal. 1 103 P. 488). The weight of authority is that
rents, issues, and profits from land follow the status of the land,
regardless of such contributing factors as effort and skill (Estate
of Pepper, 158 Cal. 619). In Van Camp v. Van Camp, 53 Cal.
App. 17 199 P 885, at the time of his marriage the husband
owned stock in the Van Camp Sea Food Company. After his
marriage he devoted his entire time and skill to management
of the business, and through his efforts the stock increased greatly
in value. The wife claimed that this increase should be considered
community property. The court followed the general rule that
the increase in value of property follows the status of the property itself. It was indicated that the community received the
value of the community contribution in view of the fact that
the husband received good salary for his services. (Katson v.
Katson 43 N.M. 214).

STATUS FIXED BY AGREEMENT

General Rule. The husband and wife may fix the status of
existing land or chattels by agreement. Such agreement does
not result in a conventional community but only operates regarding existing chattels.

Consideration. According to the prevailing rule, husband and
wife may agree as to the status of land or chattels and the agreement will be operative, even though not supported by a consideration (Schwartz v. Schwartz, 52 Ariz. 105).

Conveyance. In Estate of Watkins, 16 Cal. (2d) 793, during
continuance of their marriage husband and wife accumulated
an estate of some $300,000. It was all community property at
the time of acquisition, but its status was changed to separate
estates of husband and wife because it was held by them as

joint tenants. Where husband and wife acquire title as joint tenants, the undivided interests are separate property (Siberell v. Siberell, 214 Cal. 767). In the Estate of Watkins case, before the death of the husband, the parties executed joint and mutual wills in which it was declared that all property owned by the parties was community property. The court held that this declaration was sufficient to change the status of both land and chattels from separate estates to community property.

Statute of Frauds. While it would seem that the statute of frauds is applicable where the husband and wife purport to change the status of property from separate to community or vice versa, there is authority that such a change, at least in the case of chattels, may be brought about by oral agreement. In Estate of Harris, 169 Cal. 725, it was held that chattels may be converted into a joint tenancy; but a different rule is applicable in the case of land (Estate of Harris, 6 Cal. [2d] 649).

CONFLICT OF LAWS

Domicile Case. In Shilkret v. Helvering, 138 Fed. (2d) 925, husband and wife were domiciled in New York. In 1935 the husband entered into an exclusive personal service contract with RKO Studios, Inc., located in Hollywood, California. The contract was for two years, with employer's option to renew for two additional years. The husband left New York for California about November 14, 1935. The wife followed in February, 1936. While in California she signed a new lease on their New York apartment, running into 1937. Later there was a renewal for another year. The husband returned to New York in 1938. He contended that he was domiciled in California in 1936 and 1937, and that husband and wife were entitled to file separate income-tax returns for those years. The court held that the evidence justified the conclusion that husband and wife did not have the fixed purpose to remain in California permanently or indefinitely; consequently the old domicile continued. The rule is then declared to be that the status of chattels as separate or community property is determined according to the law of the domicile at the time of acquisition (Snyder v. Stringer, 116 Wash. 131). Under this view the income for the years in question did not constitute community property. In Brookman v. Durkee, 46 Wash. 578, husband and wife were domiciled in New York. While so domiciled the husband purchased land in Washington, a community-property state, the consideration being paid with his earnings accumulated after his marriage. Under New York law the earnings involved constituted the separate estate of the husband. The court held that the land was part of the husband's separate estate. It was not community property, because the money used in its acquisition was separate property. In Depas v. Mayo, 11 Mo. 314, the husband used community funds to purchase land in Missouri, a non-community-property state. The court held that the wife's interest in the land could be protected by declaration of a constructive trust.

Change of Domicile. In Estate of Thornton, 1 Cal. (2d) 1, husband and wife were domiciled in Montana during the time when the property in question was acquired. Under Montana law these acquisitions constituted part of the separate estate of Mr. Thornton. Thereafter husband and wife established a domicile in California and changed the status of the property in question to California. After Thornton's death his widow claimed that the property constituted community property. A California statute supported this claim. The court held, however, that this statute was unconstitutional to the extent that it purported to give extra territorial application to the definition of community property. The federal Constitution provides that no state shall make or enforce any law which shall abridge the privileges and immunities of citizens of the United States (14th Amendment). A citizen has the right to establish a domicile in any state without thereby forfeiting substantial property rights. Shortly after this decision a statute was enacted in California providing that property such as that involved in the case would be distributed as community property upon the death of the owner. In other words, the state of domicile may enact such a statute where it is a statute of inheritance (Estate of Schnell, 67 Cal. App. [2d] 268).

Agreement Case. In Black v. Commissioner of Internal Revenue, 114 Fed. (2d) 355, husband and wife were domiciled in Oregon. The husband acquired land in Washington, a community-property state, that constituted part of his separate estate. Husband and wife entered into an agreement by whose terms they purported to provide that all property owned by them, or either of them, and property thereafter acquired was to be community property. Thereafter husband and wife claimed the right to file separate income-tax returns with respect to income subsequently derived from the property. The court sustained the right. It was held, however, that the portion of the income due to the personal services of the husband, as manager of a partnership formed to look after the land, was separate property. As to that part of the income, therefore, separate returns were not proper. It was pointed out that the agreement was valid according to the law of the situs of the land. The mere fact that the parties were domiciled in another state was not controlling. The case is unlike Lucas v. Earl, 281 U.S. 111, where the agreement pertained to future acquisitions. In the instant case the agreement fixed the status of existing property as community property. The subsequent income from that property would also be community property. If the owner of land desires to create a joint tenancy with another, there certainly can be no constitutional objection to a holding that as to subsequent income from the property, each concurrent owner will be entitled to file a separate income tax with respect to his share of the income. There would be constitutional objections to any other conclusion.

Rent Case. In Commissioner of Internal Revenue v. Skaggs, 122 Fed. (2d) 721, Skaggs, a husband domiciled in Texas, owned land in California as part of his separate estate. The issue pertained to the income from this land. Under California law the income from separate property was separate property. It was held that California law was controlling as to the status of the income from land located in that state. The court pointed out that income from land could not be disassociated from the land itself. To hold that the wife was entitled to half the income from this land would be to hold that she had a half interest in the land during the period of the marriage. The rent on the land belonged to the husband the moment it became due. The Texas law, being a statute real, did not operate to change ownership. It was a statute real because it applied only to things within its jurisdiction.

Personal Injury Case. In Matney v. Blue Ribbon, Inc., 202 La. 505, plaintiff, Mrs. C. W. Matney, a married woman domiciled in Texas, suffered personal injuries while in Louisiana, in an accident resulting from her husband's negligence in driving a

car in which she was riding as a guest. This action was brought
in Louisiana to recover damages from the husband's employer,
it appearing that at the time of the accident the husband was
acting within the scope and course of his employment. It was
stipulated that under Texas law, the items of damages claimed
by plaintiff would belong to the community and that an action
to recover such damages could not be maintained by plaintiff
in the courts of Texas. Such an action could be maintained only
by the husband in his own name. Under Louisiana law the right
of a married woman to recover damages for personal injuries
sustained by her through the fault of another is her separate
property, for which she alone can bring suit. The court held
that plaintiff could maintain the action. It is pointed out that all
matters relating to the right of action in tort are governed by the
lex loci delicti, that is, by the law of the place where the wrong
was committed (W. W. Clyde & Co. v. Dyess, 126 Fed. [2d] 719;
Traglio v. Harris, 104 Fed. [2d] 493).

MANAGEMENT AND CONTROL
OF COMMUNITY PROPERTY

BY HUSBAND

General Rule. With exceptions to be noted, the management
and control of community property is entrusted to the husband.
His management is somewhat restricted, however, by statutory
enactments. These statutes have been enacted from time to time
in the various states for the purpose of protecting the wife from
his mismanagement of the community property. In Arnett v.
Reade, 220 U.S. 311, husband and wife were domiciled in New
Mexico. Land was acquired in 1889 and 1893, and it formed
part of the community estate. A statute was passed in 1901 providing that the husband could not convey real property unless
the wife joined in the conveyance. It was contended that this
statute could not be applied with respect to land acquired prior
to its enactment because such retroactive application would
divest the husband of a vested right, that is, the right to convey
without such joint action. The court held that the statute could
be applied retroactively without violating any constitutional

provisions. It is stated that where the interest of the husband and wife in community property is a present, existing, and equal interest, the husband does not have a vested right in its management. The legislature may change the rules respecting management at any time.

Gifts. In Nimey v. Nimey, 182 Wash. 194, the husband deposited community funds in the name of his mother. The court held that the attempted gift could be set aside by the surviving wife. According to the California rule, the wife can set the gift aside in its entirety if proceedings are instituted during continuance of the marriage relationship (Britton v. Hammell, 4 Cal. [2d] 690).

Courts follow the view that while the husband does have management and control of the community property, he does not have the right to make a substantial gift of such property without consent of the wife (In re McCoy's Estate, 189 Wash. 103; Occidental Life Insurance Co. v. Powers, 192 Wash. 475).

Conveyance or Transfer for Value. It is usually provided by statute that husband and wife must join in any conveyance of community real property or in any instrument creating an interest therein. In Fargo v. Bennett, 35 Idaho 359, the statute provides that the husband cannot sell, convey, or encumber the community real estate unless the wife joins with him in executing and acknowledging the deed or other instrument of conveyance. It has been held that a lease is an encumbrance within the meaning of the statute. Short-term leases may sometimes be excepted. Even if the wife does not join in execution of a lease or conveyance, she may be estopped from questioning its validity where she has subsequently sanctioned the transfer (Rice v. McCarthy, 73 Cal. App. 655; Bowman v. Hardgrove, 200 Wash. 78).

Bona Fide Purchasers. According to the rule followed in Texas, legal title vests in the spouse named as grantee and title of the other spouse is equitable. Thus it follows that if the husband is the owner of record and conveys to a bona fide purchaser for value and without notice, such purchaser acquires an indefeasible title on the ground that where the equities are equal the legal title will prevail (Edwards v. Brown, 68 Tex. 329). In other states, unless changed by statute, a bona fide purchaser or mortgagee will take subject to the rights of the spouse not joining in the conveyance (Ewald v. Hufton, 31 Idaho 373; Mark v. Title Guarantee & Trust Co., 122 Cal. App. 301).

BY WIFE

General Rule. Since the right to manage and control community property is entrusted to the husband, that right is denied to the wife. In some states she may maintain an action to recover damages for any personal injuries which she may suffer without joining the husband in such action. To this extent, therefore, management and control of this type of community property is entrusted to the wife.

Absence or Disability of Husband. In Wampler v. Beinert, 125 Wash. 494, while living with her husband the wife sustained personal injuries through the negligence of defendant. In this action to recover damages defendant sought to avoid liability on the ground that the husband executed a release to defendant from all liability growing out of the accident, and in consideration therefor defendant paid him $350. At the time of the alleged release the husband had deserted plaintiff. The court held that while the damages involved constituted community property, and the husband had management and control of the community, he ceased to be a necessary party to the litigation and had no authority to release or discharge the claim after he had deserted the wife. It is stated that after repudiating his duties, the husband releases his authority to manage the community (2 Idaho Law Jr. 120).

LIABILITY FOR DEBTS

SEPARATE PROPERTY OF WIFE

Liability for Her Own Debts. The general rule is that a married woman is liable for her own debts incurred either before or after marriage. This liability is measured by any limitations that may exist on the contractual capacity of a married woman. Under the law in Texas, a married woman can bind her separate estate by contract only if the contract has as an objective the preservation of her separate estate (Borders v. Moran [Tex. Civ. App.], 51 SW [2d] 434). A married woman may be bound by a representation that a contract is made for the benefit of her separate estate (Willson v. Manasco [Tex. Civ. App.], 63 SW. 910).

Family Expense. It is often provided by statute that the separate estate of the wife may be charged for the care and support of her husband if he has not deserted her and because of infirmity he is unable to support himself (DeNison v. National Bank of Commerce of Seattle, 197 Wash. 265).

Agency. The wife may be held liable for debts incurred by the husband where it appears that he acted as her agent (Powell v. First National Bank of Harlingen [Tex. Civ. App.], 75 SW. [2d] 471).

SEPARATE PROPERTY OF HUSBAND

General Rule. The separate estate is not liable for debts or liabilities incurred by the wife either before or after her marriage (Hageman v. Vanderdoes, 15 Ariz. 312; McClure v. McMartin, 104 La. 496).

Necessaries. In Corbett v. Wade (Tex. Civ. App.), 124 SW. 889, action was brought to recover the reasonable value of necessaries furnished defendant's wife by a third party. Recovery was allowed, even though at the time the parties were living apart, it appearing that the separation was not due to the fault of the wife (Jones v. Davis [Ct. App. La.], 155 So. 269). The general rule is that the husband is liable for expenses incident to the last illness and burial of the wife (Riley v. Robbins, 1 Cal. [2d] 285).

Agency. In Hulsman v. Ireland, 205 Cal. 345, the wife operated a restaurant as a partner with one Ireland. The husband objected to her entering into the partnership, but accepted employment in the restaurant in a subordinate capacity. The wife used some community funds in the venture. It proved to be unsuccessful, and creditors sought to establish the individual liability of the husband. He was held liable even though it was found that he was not a partner, either actual or ostensible. The evidence established that the wife acted as the husband's agent (Brittain v. O'Banion [Tex. Civ. App.], 56 SW. [2d] 249).

COMMUNITY PROPERTY

Obligations Incurred by Husband and Wife Prior to Marriage.
The general rule is that the community property is liable for
obligations incurred by both husband and wife prior to marriage
(Van Maren v. Johnson, 15 Cal. 308). There are some statutory
variations to this rule. A different rule prevails in those states
where the community is considered to be a quasi-legal entity.
Under such a view the community can be held only for community obligations. In Stafford v. Stafford, 10 Wash. (2d) 649,
a divorce decree awarded alimony to the wife for the support
of herself and the minor son of the parties. Thereafter the husband remarried and acquired land with community funds. The
court held that since the judgment did not arise out of a community obligation, the community property could not be held
liable for its payment (Forsythe v. Paschal, 34 Ariz. 380).

Obligations Incurred by Wife After Marriage. Since management and control of community property is entrusted to the husband, such property is not to be held liable for the debts of
another. So community property is not normally liable for debts
of the wife incurred after marriage. In Adams v. Golson, 187 La.
363, plaintiff suffered injuries as a result of negligent operation
of an automobile by Mrs. Golson. The court held that the husband, Mr. Golson, as the head and master of the community,
could not be held liable for the torts of his wife committed out
of his presence, unless an agency relationship was established
(Smedberg v. Bevilockway, 7 Cal. App. [2d] 578). In those jurisdictions following the view that the community is a quasi-legal
entity, the community property may be held liable where it
appears that the wife incurred an obligation while acting for and
in behalf of the community. In Werker v. Knox, 197 Wash. 453,
the wife, while on a household errand, negligently parked her
car. Plaintiff suffered injuries as a result. Since the tort occurred
while the wife was engaged in a community enterprise, the community property was held to be liable.

Obligations Incurred by Husband After Marriage. The general rule is that the community property is liable for obligations
incurred by the husband after marriage. This rule is based on
the fact that he is entrusted with the management and control

of community property (32 Idaho 106). It is often provided by statute that the earnings of the wife, while constituting community property, are not liable for debts of the husband. In those states following the view that the community is a quasi-legal entity, the community property can be reached to satisfy obligations of the husband only where the obligation was incurred in connection with a community activity. In Bergman v. State, 187 Wash. 622, costs incident to a criminal prosecution were assessed against the husband. He conducted a fur business that constituted a community asset. He was convicted of the crime of arson, it being charged that he had feloniously set on fire the store building in which the fur business was conducted. The court held that the community property was not liable for the indebtedness, because the crime was not committed in connection with management of community property (See Tway v. Payne, 55 Ariz. 343).

DISSOLUTION OF COMMUNITY

DIVORCE

Separation Case. In Martin v. Martin, 17 S.W. (2d) 789 (Comm. of App. Texas.), husband and wife separated and the wife instituted this suit to have a receiver appointed to collect the husband's salary and turn over to her such portions thereof as were necessary for her support. This relief was denied. While a statute provided for the allowance of alimony pending suit for divorce, there was no statutory authorization for the relief claimed in this case where no divorce action was pending. In some states it is provided that an action for separate maintenance may be maintained without divorce.

Separation Agreements. In Cantrell v. Woods, 150 S.W. (2d) 838 (Tex. Civ. App.), the husband and wife orally agreed to permanently separate and to divide their community property. In conformity with the agreement the husband took possession of the land in question. The court held that the agreement was valid, following the view that an oral partition of land by concurrent owners will be sustained where the parties take possession of their respective portions. The husband and wife can partition their property upon permanent separation. According to the prevailing rule, husband and wife, upon separation, may enter into a property settlement. The validity of such an agreement will be determined by applying the general rule respecting contracts in general. There is authority that a reconciliation abrogates a separation agreement unless the contract contains an express provision to the contrary (Mundt v. Conn. Gen. Life Ins. Co., 35 Cal. App. [2d] 416).

Community Property. With some variations, the general rule is that the court, upon entering a decree of divorce, shall order such division of the community property as it deems just and right. In some states the statute provides that community property is to be divided equally, unless the decree is granted on the ground of adultery or extreme cruelty, when it may be awarded as the court deems just.

DEATH

Statutes. Some statutes confer the power of testamentary disposition with respect to some portion of the community property on both husband and wife. In the absence of such testamentary disposition some statutes provide that all community property is to be distributed to the surviving spouse; according to other statutes, half the community property belongs to the surviving children of the deceased spouse.

Source of Title Doctrine. In some states a special rule of inheritance is followed where the estate of the deceased was formerly the separate property of a predeceased spouse or was the community property of the deceased and a predeceased spouse. It is considered that while the estate of the deceased spouse is separate property, if that spouse dies intestate, without leaving a spouse surviving and without issue, the issue or parents of the predeceased spouse shall share in the estate.

In Underwood v. Carter, 51 S.W. (2d) 1061 (Tex. Civ. App.), the surviving husband and some, but not all, of the children of the marriage brought suit to cancel a deed executed by the husband for himself and as community survivor of his deceased wife. The court held that the children were not necessary parties, because the surviving husband had the right to convey the property to pay community debts. He having the right to convey, it followed that he had the right to maintain a suit in his own name to cancel the deed.

Community property is in effect in Arizona, California, Idaho, Louisiana, Nevada, New Mexico, Texas, Washington, Puerto Rico, the Philippine Islands, Mexico, and Quebec.

Sometimes a decision of the lower court is unsatisfactory because plaintiff or defendant feels that he did not receive justice or because there were gross errors in the trial. In that event appeal may be taken to the supreme court of the state if there are grounds for appeal and all requirements for appeal have been met.

At various times the supreme court hands down a ruling that makes a new change in the law and so makes a later case a precedent which may be followed in cases to be decided in the lower courts.

RECENT SUPREME COURT CASES DECISIONS

Two recent supreme-court cases in community property are as follows: Jeanne M. Bare, Plaintiff and Appellant v. Richard L. Bare, Defendant and Respondent 1967, 256 A C A 763; and See v. See, 64 Cal. 2d 778 1966.

The Bare v. Bare case follows, with the decisions made. The wife appealed from the interlocutory judgment, from the supplementary judgment, July 12, 1965, determining the community assets and separate assets of the parties, and from the court order dated October 6, 1965, denying fees and costs on appeal.

Jeanne and Richard Bare were married November 22, 1958. Husband managed the community funds except for wages, which wife handled. He maintained a single joint checking account and eight accounts for business in his name alone. Husband had gross earnings, separate and community, of $230,000. Adjusted community $90,765.88, excluding wife's earning. Court added 10,400 child support for total of $101,165.80, total gross community expenses $97,844.41 for net of $3,321.79, plus personal property, and awarded husband 55 per cent and wife 45 per cent. Expenditures were: home maintenance and payment $20,453.19, child support $14,712.57, one-two expenses of boat $11,064.35, divorce expenses $24,460.47. Husband had $23,125 cash and

$32,525.56 securities, personal expenses $20,000, total separate resources $75,670.56.

The supreme court held and decided as follows: A husband is not entitled to improve or enhance the value of his separate estate at the expense of the community, or to obtain from community funds without his wife's express consent reimbursement for community expenses he paid from separate funds.

A husband cannot sustain the burden of segregating assets he claims as separate property demonstrating that gross community income and throughout the marriage so offset by community expenditures that the community estate was substantially consumed, leaving only an insignificant balance at termination of the marriage.

The community has a *pro tanto* community-property interest in property purchased by one spouse before marriage, on which purchase payments were made during the marriage with community funds, in the ratio that payment on the purchase price with community funds bear to payment with separate funds (this is contrary to the rule in most community-property states, under which the community has only the right of reimbursement).

Where husband has used community property to increase his separate estate, the court must determine the increase in its equity from before and after marriage. The community is entitled to a minimum interest in the property as represented by the ratio of community investment to the total separate and community investment in the property. In the event the fair market value has increased disproportionately to the increase in equity, the wife is entitled to participate in that increment in a similar proportion.

A husband may not pay separate expenses with community funds and must reimburse the community if he does so. When he has used separate funds to pay communty expenses, even if no community funds were available, he cannot claim reimbursement without an agreement with his spouse but intentionally or not makes a gift to the community. Child support from previous marriage is chargeable to separate estate and to community.

The trial court abused discretion in denying her attorney's fees.

In See v. See, 64 Cal. 2d 778 (1966), plaintiff, Laurance A.

See, and cross-complainant, Elizabeth Lee See, appealed from an interlocutory judgment that granted each a divorce. Laurance attacked the finding that he was guilty of extreme cruelty, the granting of a divorce to Elizabeth, and the award to her of permanent alimony of $5,400 per month. Elizabeth attacked the finding that there was no community property at the time of the divorce.

The parties had been married since October 17, 1941, and they separated about May 10, 1962. Throughout the marriage they were residents of California, and Laurance was employed by a family-controlled corporation, See's Candies, Inc. He served for most of that period as president of its wholly owned subsidiary, See's Candy Shops, Inc. He received more than a million dollars in salaries from the two corporations in the twenty-one years of marriage.

The court held that the trial court can award alimony to wife when both parties are granted a divorce. Alimony may be awarded to either party even though a divorce is granted to both. The court further held:

The character of property as separate or community is determined at the time of acquisition.

If it is community property when acquired, it remains so throughout the marriage, unless the spouses agree to change its nature or the spouse charged with its management makes a gift of it to the other.

Property acquired by purchase during marriage is presumed to be community property, and the burden is on the spouse asserting its separate character to overcome the presumption.

The presumption applies when a husband purchases property during the marriage with funds from an undisclosed or disputed source, such as an account or funds in which he has commingled his separate funds with community funds.

XVIII. CRIMINAL LAW

DEFINITION OF CRIME

The Constitution of the United States and the Congress of the United States, given its authority by the Constitution, define what crimes are and what acts constitutes crimes. In our study of torts we found that a crime is a wrong, intentionally committed, which injures the entire public, and not just the individual, as does a tort, which affects only the injured party personally. Since the government defines what a crime is, that same government has the power to punish those who commit crimes and thus violate the Constitution and the laws passed by Congress. The state prosecutes every criminal in the name of the state. If Harry Lades commits a crime in Minnesota, the petition for the prosecution will read: State of Minnesota v. Harry Lades.

ILLUSTRATIONS

Suppose John does some act not declared a crime either by the Constitution or by any law which Congress has enacted up to that time. Even supposing the act a very vicious one, if prosecution is started against John, the court will hold that John cannot be convicted, because the act was not a crime when performed; and even if Congress passes a law, after the act is committed and before the trial is had, making the act a crime, John cannot be convicted.

Suppose John commits an act which at the time is defined as a crime. But after John has committed the act, and while he is being prosecuted, Congress repeals the law which defines John's act as a crime. The court will hold that the state cannot proceed further with its criminal prosecution, because the act which John committed, although a crime then, was not a crime any longer the moment Congress repealed the law. The case will be dismissed.

Suppose John has made up his mind to kill James but does not go any further. James learns of John's intention, and the state brings a criminal action against John. The court will hold that John did not commit a criminal act, because he did not execute his intention. In order that John be guilty of a crime, he must have criminally performed an act (or criminally neglected to perform an act). John would be responsible for the probable consequences of an act which he committed with criminal intent and which resulted in a crime, or of an act from which a crime naturally followed.

Persons are punished for crimes which they commit as examples to the public, and not to redress the injury committed against the individuals immediately affected. For example: Suppose John steals an automobile from James. James will have to bring suit for damages against John to recover the automobile or its equivalent in money. Because stealing is a crime in the United States, the state may bring a criminal prosecution against John.

Suppose John commits against a woman an act which is defined as a crime by federal law but commits it with the woman's consent. Suppose John is prosecuted. If he can prove that consent was given, he can use this as a defense.

Suppose John kills James. This act of crime consists of John's intent to do it and his actual doing it. To convict John of the crime, the act itself or its direct consequences must result in the killing of James; and associated with the act there must be criminal intent in John's mind.

Suppose John and James are officers actively engaged in management of a corporation. In the name of the corporation they perform an act defined as a crime by act of Congress. In days gone by, the officers of a corporation could not be held criminally liable for a crime committed by the corporation through its officers. But today the court will find John and James personally guilty, even though the criminal act was an act of the corporation and they performed and executed it as corporate officers.

Suppose John marries Genevieve and shortly afterward

Genevieve commits a crime. The court will hold that a married woman shall be held liable for torts and crimes committed by her, just the same as her husband would be if they were committed by him.

Suppose John takes a revolver, loaded and ready to fire, and nails it to a windowsill, pointing it directly toward James's breakfast table. He ties a string to the trigger and fastens the string to a board, which he places on Harry's lawn. In the morning while Harry is doing chores around his house, he sees the board and unknowingly picks it up for kindling a fire. The string attached to the board pulls the trigger of the revolver, which discharges and kills James. The court will hold that Harry cannot be prosecuted, because criminal intent on his part was lacking. Nor was Harry negligent; in picking up the board, he acted as any reasonable man would. So he may plead mistake of fact as a valid defense.

Suppose John is married to Gladys and they have a boy six years of age. The boy picks up a rifle and shoots a man walking by the house, killing him. The court will hold that a boy under seven years of age cannot be prosecuted for a crime. If a boy is between seven and fourteen, he can be held for a crime if he has the mental faculties to be able to distinguish between right and wrong. A boy past fourteen will simply be held responsible for all crimes he commits.

The courts say that if a man is insane, so as not to have full control of his mind and thus be able to distinguish between right and wrong, and he kills another, he will not be held responsible for the killing, because he is considered the same as an infant below the age of seven. The courts also say that if a man while under the influence of liquor kills another, he will be held responsible for his crime. If he pleads intoxication as a defense, the court will say that it was his own will that brought on the intoxication and therefore the defense is not permissible.

Suppose John, James, and Harry meet in a vacant house and plan to murder an entire family. John puts a loaded revolver into his pocket and starts down the street with James on their way to the house where they intend to commit the murder. Suppose Harry gave John the bullets for his revolver, and suppose Harry remains behind in the vacant house. James stands outside the family's residence to signal to John with a flashlight if anybody comes. John goes into the house and murders the family. In this case John, who commits the act, is a principal in the first degree, James is a principal in the second degree, and Harry is an accessory before the fact. Suppose that Paul harbors John in his cellar, away from the authorities, after the crime has been committed. The court will hold that Paul is an accessory after the fact.

If a criminal act originates, or is set in motion, in one state and takes effect in another, the latter state will have jurisdiction to try the crime. For example: Suppose John is standing near the southern line of the state of Minnesota. He takes his rifle and shoots James, killing him, while James is standing in the state of Iowa. A criminal action is brought against John by Minnesota. The court will hold that Minnesota does not have jurisdiction, but that Iowa, where the bullet took effect, has jurisdiction, and the laws of Iowa will govern in trying the criminal case. Suppose John is standing in the United States and shoots James, who is standing in Canada, just across the boundary line. The United States will not try the criminal; rather, the Dominion of Canada will have jurisdiction, because the bullet took effect in Canada, even though shot from the United States, and the trial will be conducted according to Canadian criminal procedure.

Suppose John kills James. This is called a homicide. A homicide may be justifiable, as when John kills in self-defense. But if John shoots James without justification and James dies within a year and one day from that date, this is called felonious homicide. Suppose John shoots James dead with malice aforethought. This is called murder. A shooting is called manslaughter if it is committed involuntarily; but both murder and manslaughter are homicides.

Suppose John unlawfully seduces a woman, without her consent. This is called rape, a crime against the person. Suppose John throws a stone and hits James intentionally, or suppose he unlawfully shoots a skyrocket along the main street of a city and the rocket hits a man crossing the street. This is called a battery. In order that a battery be committed, another person must be hit directly by the accused or else by some force set in motion by the accused.

Suppose in the nighttime John, intending to enter James's house, raises a window, reaches in, takes some valuables off a dresser, and returns home. Later a suit is brought against John for burglary. The court will hold that John is guilty, even though he stood outside the house, and never went inside, so long as he committed the act with his own hand or with an instrument. The court will also hold that John can be held for breaking in, even though he never went inside the house at all. If John just turned the doorknob with intent to commit a burglary, the court will hold that turning the knob was an act sufficient to constitute what is known as breaking and entering into a man's house, or habitation. In the United States this is a crime, and John would be held guilty of burglary, in a constructive sense, even if he simply turned the doorknob in an endeavor to break in, and finding the door locked, went away without taking anything. The statutes which define burglary say that it is an act which occurs in the night, with intent to commit a felony, against the dwelling place of another.

Suppose John goes over to James's farm and sets fire to James's house. John intends to burn all of the house, but only a small part of it burns before James puts the fire out. An action is brought against John for arson. The court will hold that John committed the crime of arson, because he went to James's house and set fire to it with the intention of burning it down, even though the bulk of the house was saved.

Suppose John, with felonious intent, takes James's automobile for his own use and keeps it against James's consent. This is called larceny.

Suppose John meets James coming down the street and with felonious intent points a revolver at him and compels him to hand over his pocketbook. Because of the violence which John used in taking James's property the court will hold that John committed robbery. In every robbery there must be violence used, or a threat of violence, whereas in larceny there may be none.

Suppose John is head bookkeeper for James and in the course of his employment takes $100 of James's money and uses it to pay some personal bills. The court will hold that John has committed the criminal act of embezzlement.

Suppose John takes a check given him for his salary and increases the amount of it by altering the figures. Or suppose he fills out a check and writes his employer's signature to it, intending to defraud. Either act is called the crime of forgery. Where John writes out a check and signs his employer's name, even if he is unsuccessful in passing the check, the court will nevertheless hold him guilty of forgery.

Suppose John steals a diamond ring in Aurora. He comes to Chicago, goes to a pawnbroker, tells him that he stole the diamond and sells it to him at a large discount. The owner of the diamond discovers it in the pawnbroker's window and brings suit against the broker for having received stolen goods. The court will hold that because the pawnbroker received the diamond while knowing that John had stolen it, he is guilty as an accessory to the theft.

Suppose a newspaper states in its columns that John stole a fur coat. The fact is that John did not steal the coat; and the editor of the paper cannot prove that he did. John brings an action against the editor. The court will hold that the editor has committed the crime of libel, for injuring John's credit and reputation. Libel is a breach of the peace.

Suppose John, a married man in Minnesota, marries another woman. He will be guilty of bigamy. Bigamy is a crime in all our states because it is against the public welfare to have more than one spouse.

Suppose John, a married man, unlawfully lives with another woman. John has committed adultery, a crime which affects the public welfare.

Suppose a bank clerk embezzles $1,000 from the bank. The clerk's father comes to the president of the bank and says, "Here, I will pay you a thousand dollars if you will agree not to have my son arrested for embezzlement." The court will hold that the banker and the father, if they enter into this agreement, are both criminally guilty of compounding a felony, because the agreement tends to obstruct the administration of public justice.

Suppose John goes from Kansas City to Omaha, then to the courthouse, and there offers to pay the city engineer $500 if he will use his influence to secure installation of a boiler for the city of Omaha to be purchased from John's firm. The court will hold that this is bribery, punishable as a crime because it tends to disrupt public administration and corrupt public officials.

Suppose John is suing James. Before John assumes the witness stand to testify, he takes an oath by raising his right hand and stating, "I will tell the truth, the whole truth, and nothing but the truth, so help me God." In violation of this oath John then knowingly and willingly makes false statements. The court will hold that John has committed perjury, a crime because perjurers tend to obstruct the public administration of justice and equity.

Suppose John goes into a courtroom, and while the case is proceeding, disregards the court's instructions, insults the court, etc. (When I say court, I mean the judge himself; these two words are used interchangeably among lawyers at the bar.) The court will hold that this is contempt of court, punishable by the court.

Suppose John commits a crime, and James sees him do it. James goes to the nearest justice of the peace. The justice listens to the evidence which James gives, and if satisfied with it, may write out and issue a warrant for John's arrest. This warrant is given to an officer of the law empowered to serve a warrant in a criminal case, usually the sheriff. As soon as John is discovered, the sheriff delivers the warrant to him in person. The moment John receives the warrant, willingly or unwillingly, he is under authority of the court. John reads the warrant; if he finds it regular on its face, he must not resist the officer. But if the warrant is irregular on its face, or is not a valid warrant, John has the power to resist the arresting sheriff.

A warrant may be used as a result of several procedures. As just stated, a warrant for John's arrest may be issued by a justice of the peace when the evidence is sufficient. Or a warrant may be issued for John's arrest after John has been indicted, or accused, by a grand jury. Or a warrant may be issued after the prosecuting attorney has filed an information. Every warrant should state why it is issued—whether by indictment, by information, or because someone presented evidence to a justice of the peace or other magistrate. It should contain the name of the party charged with a crime; it should also contain a discription of the party named. This description may be in the form of an affidavit, or it may be unwritten.

When John has accepted the warrant, and the warrant is regular in every way, he is then under authority of the court. He may be taken and placed in jail, under arrest, until the case comes up for trial, and he will remain in jail unless the court allows him to prepare an acceptable bond. After he has furnished bond, John will be released, until the case comes up for trial. Suppose John is arrested for a crime on an indictment. The indictment must be written; it must contain John's full name; it must make the criminal charge against John; and it must state the time and place of the crime. Usually a bill will have been presented to the grand jury by the prosecuting attorney or other qualified party. The grand jury takes this bill and analyzes the evidence tending to indicate that John is guilty. All twelve grand jurors vote either to indict or not to indict. If they vote to indict John, then the bill will be accepted, and the jury makes its report to the court and the foreman presents the indictment to the court. The judge himself takes the indictment and files it among his records with the clerk. A capias is then issued by which John may be commanded to be brought in, whereupon the court either permits him to be bailed or puts him into jail.

Suppose John is arrested, not on the basis of an indictment, but because the prosecuting attorney has filed a bill with the court accusing John of the crime. John will have been arrested by means of an information. The grand jury has nothing to do with it, because the prosecuting attorney has presented the information to the court under official oath. Then the sheriff goes and arrests John, after a warrant has been issued, just the same as if John had been indicted. John may also be arrested if a criminal complaint has been made against him in the form of an affidavit. The warrant for the arrest will be issued in the same way as before.

The Constitution provides that every person charged with a felony shall have the right and privilege of trial by jury. In the above case John is entitled to have a lawyer defend him. If he cannot afford to pay a lawyer, it is the duty of the court to appoint one for him. The court must permit every party accused of a criminal offense to give bail, except in capital cases, and has the privilege of naming the amount of bail. John may demand, and has the right, to read the indictment charging him with crime; and he is entitled to a copy of the indictment in order that he may prepare his case for trial. John may now, after he has read the indictment and furnished bail, enter a plea in abatement; or he may file a motion to quash the indictment; or he may file a demurrer to the indictment; or he may file a statement that he was tried for the same case once before; or he may plead guilty. If he decides to file a plea of abatement, he should do so as soon as possible, because a plea in abatement must be filed before a motion to quash the indictment; if he files a motion to quash first, he will not afterward be allowed to file a plea in abatement. Suppose John decides not to file a plea in abatement. The next plea, in order, would be a motion to quash the indictment; if he decides not to file a motion to quash, then all the other pleas in logical order, and John may file any of these which he may desire.

Suppose John's attorney discovers that the indictment is irregular, on the ground that some of the grand jurors were improperly impaneled, or that the indictment misstates John's initials. The attorney may then file a plea in abatement; such plea is based on the ground that there is some irregularity in the indictment, and not that the substance of the indictment is not valid.

Suppose John's attorney discovers that the substance of the indictment is wrong or invalid; he may then file a motion to quash the indictment. If the court decides that either the plea in abatement or the motion to quash has a proper foundation, then it may dismiss the indictment, and a new indictment will have to be issued before the prosecution can proceed further.

Suppose John's attorney files a demurrer. A demurrer to an indictment directs the court to examine the indictment to see for itself whether the subject matter contained therein is sufficient to constitute a crime. The accused should be very cautious in filing a demurrer, because if the court then finds that the indictment contains sufficient charges to sustain it, the court may immediately enter judgment against the accused, who will not be permitted to proceed further with trial of his case before that court.

Suppose John was previously tried for the same crime and acquitted. John's attorney will file a plea of former jeopardy, because every person has the constitutional right not to be twice put in jeopardy for the same crime. If the court sustains the plea, the indictment will be dismissed.

Suppose John enters a plea of not guilty, which denies all the allegations in the indictment. His attorney may then request that a bill of particulars be filed by the state, in order that the details of the indictment may be made more specific.

Suppose John enters a plea of guilty, which is an admission that he committed the crime charged in the indictment, information, criminal complaint, or summons. The court may then instruct the jury to bring in a verdict of guilty.

Suppose John, when indicted for the crime, finds the citizens of the community prejudiced against him, and he believes it is impossible to secure a fair and impartial jury from among them. John, through his attorney, may file a motion with the court asking for a change of venue, so that the case may be tried in some other community within the state.

Suppose that the judge before whom the case is to be tried is prejudiced. John's attorney may file a motion for a change of venue so that the case may be tried before some other judge. When a change of venue is requested, both attorney for the accused and attorney for the state file affidavits.

In every criminal case the state having jurisdiction prosecutes, in the name of the state, and attorney for the state prepares and conducts the case. Suppose John is unable to locate certain witnesses important to his defense within the time allowed before the case comes up for trial. John's attorney may file a motion for a continuance of the case. If a continuance is granted, the case is reset for some later date. Witnesses in behalf of defendant can be compelled to come into court and testify, whether they have received their witness fee in advance or not.

According to the Constitution, every party accused of a crime is guaranteed the right to have his case tried by a jury, or at his option, by a court. After all the preliminary pleas and motions have been filed, and the day set for trial has arrived, if the accused demands a trial by jury, then the attorneys in the case begin selection of a jury. The jury is selected in the following manner: A list of names is furnished the attorneys, taken from the roster of all jurors selected to serve on cases for that particular term of court. The attorneys proceed to make an examination of these jurors, until they have agreed on twelve jurors competent to sit and try the case. All these jurors are brought into the courtroom.

In selecting the twelve jurors, the attorneys for both sides ask such questions of each as: Are you a resident of the county in which this case is being tried? Are you prejudiced against the accused? Are you related to the defendant? To the attorney for the defendant? To the attorney for the state? To the wife of the accused? Each attorney is permitted a certain number of peremptory challenges, whereby he excludes certain jurors from serving on the case. No reasons for the challenges need be given.

The twelve jurors selected all rise, and the court swears them in, in a body. The jurors are instructed by the court that they are the sole judges of the evidence and testimony to be offered. The court instructs them not to talk about the case, either with any outside parties or among themselves, under penalty of the court. The prosecuting attorney then reads the indictment to the jury, and outlines what the state intends to prove. Next, attorney for the accused may outline to the jury what the defense will be. But he may wish to defer his opening statement and wait until attorney for the state has submitted the state's evidence against the accused. In their opening statements to the jury the attorneys should not argue the case but simply state the nature of their evidence, what they intend to offer by way of testimony, etc. These opening addresses are not to be considered evidence by the jury.

When attorney for the state has submitted all his testimony and evidence, then attorney for the accused has the privilege of either submitting the case to the jury at that time, without offering any evidence and testimony of his own, or making his opening statement to the jury and then introducing his evidence and testimony. When attorney for the accused has finished, attorney for the state may offer more evidence and testimony in behalf of the state, in rebuttal. All rebuttal testimony must be confined to that which was introduced in the former part of the case.

After the attorney for the state has introduced all his rebuttal testimony, attorney for the accused may make a motion asking that a verdict of not guilty be entered by the court. In the great majority of cases the court will overrule this motion because it would rather the jury assumed the responsibility of bringing in a verdict. If it happens that the State has absolutely, to the satisfaction of the judge, not made a sufficient case to support the allegations in the indictment, the court will sustain the motion and order the jury to bring in a verdict of not guilty.

After both sides have rested, attorney for the state argues his case before the jury. He reviews the evidence and testimony in an orderly way, so as to show it all in a connected form and in so clear and convincing a manner that the jury, to grasp and understand it. When he has finished, the attorney for the accused argues his case; according to the evidence and testimony and to the best of his ability, he tries to show the jury that his client is innocent and that the state has failed to prove its case.

The judge who sits in a criminal case has the power and authority to make certain rulings regarding the admissibility or inadmissibility of evidence introduced during the trial. He is the judge of the law involved in the case, while the jurors are the sole judges of the evidence. If, for instance, attorney for the accused tries to get some evidence into the record which attorney for the state thinks inadmissible, the latter will make an objection to the court. If the court sustains the objection, the evidence will be excluded. Where evidence is immaterial and irrelevant, attorney for the accused may then ask for an exception to the judge's ruling, the exception to be made part of the record of the case. In every case at law the questions asked by the attorneys and the answers given by the witnesses are taken down in shorthand by the court reporter, constituting what is known as the record of the case.

To convict a man indicted for killing another—that is, to prove that the indicted man is guilty—it must be established and proved, first of all, that the alleged victim is dead, that the death was criminally caused, and that beyond a reasonable doubt the accused actually killed him.

In the above case, after both sides have completed arguing the case before jurors and judge, the judge instructs the jury that they are the sole judges concerning evidence and testimony. He instructs the jury on the law applicable to the case. He instructs the jury to weigh all evidence and testimony and to take into consideration the actions and demeanor off all witnesses. Ordinarily the judge's instructions to the jury are written, and the attorneys for both sides may then assist the judge in preparing them. In some states the judge's instructions may be given orally, without having been written. In instructing the jury, the judge should be impartial, so as not to convey any of his own inclinations concerning the innocence or guilt of the accused. His instructions must not be considered evidence by the jurors, but are given only in order that they may understand the law in the case.

When the court has given its instructions to the jury, an officer of the court is given charge of the jury, to take them to the jury room and to keep them there until they agree on a verdict. When they have reached a verdict, the officer conducts them back to the courtroom, where the foreman reads the verdict aloud, in open court. All the jurors must be present when the verdict is read.

If the verdict is guilty, the party found guilty may put up a new bond for bail and within a reasonable time, file a motion for a new trial or a motion in arrest of judgment. If attorney for the accused finds that there is some newly discovered evidence, or that the judge misinstructed the jury, or that the jury was not properly selected, or that the judge excluded evidence that should have been admitted or admitted evidence that should have been excluded—if any of these things are discovered by attorney for the accused, he may file a motion for a new trial.

If attorney for the accused finds that the record shows that the state did not produce sufficient evidence to make a case against the accused, or that the grand jury which indicted the accused was improperly selected, or that the indictment was not presented in court, then he may file a motion in arrest of judgment.

If the court overrules the motions, it then sentences the accused.

Suppose the accused wishes to appeal from the district court to the appellate court. His attorney will file a writ of error, by having a transcript made of the shorthand record of the case made by the court reporter. When this transcript is made, an assignment of the errors must be attached to it or endorsed on it; and then this writ of error, composed of the transcript and the assignment of errors, is filed in the appellate court. After this filing the higher court may issue a scire facias, which is sent down to attorney for the state who prosecuted the case in the district court. Attorney for the state studies the writ of error and makes his answer to it. While the appellate court is considering the appeal, it may issue a supersedeas to delay execution of sentence passed. The accused may put up bail and thus be released from confinement until the appeal is heard.

If the appellate court sustains the district court, then the sentence of the district court will be imposed. If the appellate court reverses the district court, the accused will be released and judgment entered for defendant.

XIX. WILLS

DEFINITION

A will is a written instrument which does not take effect until the party who made it—the testator—has died. After his death all his property, personal and real, is distributed according to the terms of the will.

ILLUSTRATIONS AND LAW OF WILLS

Suppose John is an artist and has a valuable contract with James to paint a choice portrait. Suppose John wills this personal contract and all benefits under it to Harry, his son, who is also an artist. Suddenly while John is in the midst of painting the work, he dies. Harry claims this personal contract under the will of his father and proceeds to finish painting the picture. James objects, claiming that Harry has no authority. Harry brings suit against James. The court will hold that Harry cannot hold James to the contract, because contracts for personal work or services cannot be willed away.

The courts also hold that damage cases involving the person or the real property of the deceased cannot be willed away. The courts also hold that rights to a libel suit or a suit for seduction cannot be willed away. But the courts hold that if the testator has a valid right to secure certain personal or real property, this right to reclaim can be willed away.

JUDGMENT AGAINST PROPERTY CAN BE WILLED

A court will hold that if John has a claim against James's property of James or a judgment against it, the claim or the judgment can be willed away.

But suppose John agrees to marry Gladys, and then refuses to carry out his promise. Suppose Gladys attempts to will away her breach-of-promise suit against John. The court will hold that a contract for breach of marriage cannot be willed away.

The above cases are all construed according to the theory of common law.

Suppose John is married. He has a family of children. He has both real and personal property. He dies intestate—that is, without having made a will. The court would hold, according to common law, that all the real property descended to John's direct heirs. All the personal property descended to the next of kin.

Suppose Gladys, John's wife, had real and personal property in her own name when she married John. Suppose Gladys dies intestate. Under common-law theory the court would hold that John, had the right to administer Gladys's estate, and as administrator, after he had paid the funeral expenses, to keep all the balance of her estate. But under modern law, if Gladys dies intestate, most states will retain possession of all Gladys's personal property, and John will be permitted to retain a dower interest of one-third in all the real estate belonging to Gladys when she died. The two-thirds balance of Gladys's real property will go to her children. If she had no children, then the two-thirds will descend to her relatives—that is, to her mother and father; if her parents are both dead, then to her brothers and sisters; and if any of her brothers and sisters have died and left children, these children will receive whatever portion of the two-thirds their parents would have received if alive.

According to modern law, if the husband, John, has real and personal property and dies intestate, in most states the wife, Gladys, will be entitled to all John's personal property and will be permitted to retain a one-third dower interest in all John's real estate. The remaining two-thirds of the real estate will go to John's children. If John had no children, the two-thirds will descend to his relatives, in the same manner as outlined above for Gladys's relatives after her death.

In some states, however, statutes provide that instead of receiving all the personal property, the living spouse will receive one-third of the personal property of the spouse who dies intestate and one-third of the real estate. Both the one-third personal property and the one-third real property will be considered a dower interest, or estate, in the deceased spouse's estate. These rules apply if the deceased spouse leaves children or descendants. But if the spouse who dies intestate leaves no children or descendants, the surviving spouse, in most of these states, will receive one-half of the real property left by the deceased spouse, and the balance of the estate will escheat to the state. Since the laws of descent differ in the different states in some cases, the specific statutes applicable should be consulted.

Suppose John dies, leaving a will in which he gives certain real property to his wife, Gladys. The court will hold that Gladys may decide, at her option, to ignore the will and claim her one-third dower estate in all the real property which John had at the time of his death; or she may ignore her dower right and accept her portion of the real estate granted her according to the terms of the will.

The courts will allow the surviving wife, where a will has been made, the right to have certain property or money immediately upon the death of her husband, to maintain herself and any minor children. The courts hold that husband or wife will be permitted to retain the house in which they lived, if they owned it, as a homestead. Creditors of the deceased husband will not be permitted to attach the homestead for any debts which he owed them. The widow is privileged to retain the homestead, at least during her widowhood or during the children's minority, if there are children. Only after the widow remarries, or the children become of age, can the creditors attach the homestead.

A posthumous child—child born after the father's decease—inherits from the father in the same way as a child born before his death. An adopted child inherits in the same way as a natural child.

Suppose John makes a will in which he devises or bequeaths 160 acres of farm land to James. The court will hold that any natural person who has reached his majority may make a valid will. The court will hold that "will" in this sense refers not to the piece of paper on which the words are written but to the intent of the testator. A will is necessarily construed to carry out the actual intentions of the testator in distributing his property, whether personal or real. The court will further hold that a testator may devise or bequeath all his property, real and personal, in any way and for any purpose, which is lawful, he may choose, except that he cannot will away the dower right belonging to the spouse. The court will hold that a testator may dispose of his personal property by delivering it to the party whom he wishes to have it. If the testator is on the verge of dying when he delivers this personal property to the donee, his intended act is called a gift mortis causa. The donee, whether the personal property is a cow or a car, or a lease from year to year, or a stock certificate, or a note, or a mortgage, will have absolute title to it if the testator delivered it as a gift and provided the testator had testamentary capacity and intent.

The courts hold that a will must not be made as a joke. If it can be proven that the testator drew up the will as a joke, the courts will hold that there is no will. The courts also hold that a married woman, after she has reached her majority, may make a will. The courts also hold that if an insane person is sane enough at the time to know and appreciate what he is doing when he is drawing up his will, the will is valid.

If John is an old man, and while he is drawing up a will, one of his children or some outside party uses fraud in getting him to dispose of his property, or uses undue influence, so that the will does not really dispose of the property in the way the old man intended, the court will hold that the will is null and void. A testator must appreciate what he is doing and must be of sufficient mentality to intend to do certain things, and to know and distinguish what he is doing and to whom he is devising or bequeathing his property, at the time he makes the will; and fraud or duress must not be used.

The courts hold that an unwritten will, called a nuncupative will, is perfectly good for the purpose of disposing of personal property if witnesses hear what is said and see what is done at the time the will is made. Suppose John writes a will in his own handwriting, called a holographic will. To be valid, such a will must be written entirely by the testator. It may be signed by the testator himself, or a witness may write the testator's name if the testator gets so weak he cannot do it himself. The witness must sign in the presence of the testator. Ordinarily the will must be dated. The courts have held that in a holographic will the testator may sign at either the top or the bottom. The courts have held that where a holographic will is made, and besides the handwriting of the testator, the will contains typewritten parts, the entire will is invalid as a holographic will. Suppose the testator makes a written will but does not have it attested. The court will hold it to be a valid will but will enforce strict proofs of performance of all statutory requirements.

Today the great majority of wills are typewritten and formally attested, and then signed by the testator in the presence of witnesses, and a seal is attached. If the testator is too feeble to write his signature, another party may sign his name for him, in his presence and in the presence of a sufficient number of witnesses; and the witnesses sign the will. If all these conditions are carried out, the will is considered valid.

Suppose John begins his will: "I, John Adams, being of sound mind and memory, do make and execute this day . . . ." Most courts will hold that this is a sufficient signature; others, that the testator must sign his name at the bottom of the will. Therefore, to be perfectly sure and safe, the testator should sign at the bottom. While it is not absolutely essential to use a seal or to date the instrument or to name the place where the instrument is executed, yet it is advisable. Ordinarily the court requires two or three witnesses to be present to attest the signing of the will by the testator, and these witnesses must actually watch and see the testator write his signature, or have it written for him, and be present and actually hear what the testator wishes to have included in his will, or else be present and see the testator's signature acknowledged by the testator himself if the will has been drawn up, and the testator's signature written, by a third party. Some courts hold that the will should be published or read aloud in the presence of the witnesses, after it has been signed by the testator and the signature acknowledged by himself personally. The same courts hold that to be valid, the will must be signed by the testator in the presence of the two or three witnesses; and if an agent of the testator signs the testator's name for him, in the presence of the testator and in the presence of the witnesses, the testator must acknowledge his signature in the presence of the witnesses; and the will should be made and executed in the presence of the witnesses; and the will should be published or read aloud, either by the testator himself or by his agent, in the presence of the testator and in the presence of the witnesses. Lastly, the two or the three witnesses, as required by law, must sign the will. Then we have what is called a valid will.

Suppose John makes a will devising forty acres to James. John does not say, "To James, his heirs, and assigns," but instead simply says, "I hereby bequeath forty acres to James Adams." James dies before John dies. The court will hold that a will is absolutely of no legal effect until after the death of the testator; further, that James's wife or children, or descendants, cannot claim the forty acres when John dies, because John bequeathed the land to James alone, according to the wording of the will, and not to any of James's heirs or assigns. This forty acres willed to James is called a legacy or devise. It will have lapsed, because James died before it could take effect.

Suppose a person makes a will, marries afterward, and never makes a new will. The court will hold, in some states, that if a man or a woman makes a will and afterward marries, the marriage makes the will null and void. In some states the court will hold that if a man or woman makes a will before marriage and neglects to make a new will afterward, the will is valid, except when a child is born as a result of the marriage. This will make the will null and void because a testator who makes his will before he has a child cannot be presumed to have intended not to give his or her child anything in the will.

Suppose John makes a will and in it names James as the party to take charge of the estate and see that each person gets his due share according to the terms of the will. James is called an executor. If John neglects to name an executor in his will or the executor named dies, the court will appoint a party to take the affairs of the estate in charge; this party is called an administrator.

The moment the testator dies, the responsibilities, duties, and obligations of the executor begin. An administrator is not named in the will, and his responsibility, duties, and obligations begin, of course, only when the court has appointed him. The court that properly takes charge of the estate of the deceased, whether he died testate or intestate, is called a probate court. The probate court is part of the county court. If the deceased leaves a will, the will must be filed for probate in the probate court of jurisdiction. The court directs what shall be done in carrying out the testamentary intent of the executor. If the deceased does not leave a will, and the parties interested in the estate can divide it satisfactorily among themselves, the probate court simply acts in a ministerial capacity.

Suppose John dies and leaves a will in which he appoints James executor. Suppose John's relatives do not bury him. It then becomes James's duty as executor to bury John and to pay for the burial. When the estate is probated, the funeral expenses are deducted first from the estate, before any division of the estate is made among the parties named in the will.

Suppose John dies without leaving a will. All of John's real property will descend to the heirs, next of kin, and descendants, or escheat to the state. The wife, of course, if living, receives her dower out of all the real property held by John at his death.

The administrator appointed by the court may gather the rents and profits from the estate and divide them according to the terms of the will, or he may sell certain property according to the terms of the will and pay outstanding obligations as directed by the will. The administrator performs the same duties as an executor would in carrying out the instructions contained in the will itself and according to the interpretation of the probate court. All transactions by the executor or administrator must be done by means of an order issued by the probate court.

Suppose John dies, leaving a will that names James as a legatee to receive certain personal properties. Legatee here means a beneficiary of the will who is to receive only personal property. James will not be entitled to receive the property designated until the estate has gone through the due process of administration. If John at the time of his death owes several creditors, these creditors will not be permitted to receive money from any party except a duly qualified executor or administrator.

Suppose John makes a perfectly valid will, and dies. If he did not name an executor in the will, the court will appoint an administrator. The administrator should first get possession of the will and present it to the probate court of jurisdiction, within three months from the date of John's death. If a party named in the will refuses to give the will to the administrator, or tries to keep it away from him, the administrator may bring suit for damages against such party. In some states the administrator can bring suit for grand larceny. Some states provide that a will must be probated within three years from the death of the testator; others, within twenty years, otherwise an outside party may have title to the property of the estate by adverse possession. In equity and in justice to the parties named in the will as beneficiaries, the will should be probated as quickly as possible. Suppose John lives in Cook County and has his real estate in Henry County. Administràtion of the personal property will take place in Cook County; that is, the probate proceeding should be instituted by the administrator in the county where the testator lived and had his domicile just prior to his death. In the general course of events, probating the real estate covered in the will may also be instituted in the same court and at the same time as the personal property. However, real estate is often probated in the county where located.

Suppose John leaves a will. When the will comes up for probate, one of the parties named in it files a notice of contest, for the purpose of contesting the will. Notice will be sent out through the probate court to all interested parties, as well as to attesting witnesses, who are within the jurisdiction of the court. If any of these persons are without the jurisdiction of the court, and live in some foreign state, the court, through its agent, will have depositions taken of each absent witness and interested party. A deposition is a written legal instrument composed of questions put to and answers given by a witness or interested party, made under oath before a court, justice of the peace, or notary public. Notice of any deposition must be given by the probate court to the party contesting the will, so that he may have the privilege of cross-examining the witness or interested party, either himself, at the place where the deposition was taken, or though his attorney.

Suppose John makes a valid will and never cancels or annuls it. Suppose that after he dies and the executor or administrator comes to get the will, it cannot be found. The court will hold that if the interested parties to the will can prove to its satisfaction that a valid will was executed by John, and not annulled or canceled, and can prove what the contents of the will were, will is admissible to probate. Some courts hold that a lost or destroyed will must be proven by two witnesses and that it must also be proven that the will was lost or destroyed after the testator died, or that the will was lost or destroyed by fraud while the testator was still alive; otherwise the will cannot be admitted to probate.

Suppose John, who owns real property in several states and has his domicile in Minnesota, dies, leaving an uncanceled valid will. The executor or administrator of John's estate can then bring probate proceedings in Minnesota in the county where John lived and had his home, and the Minnesota court can probate that portion of the will having to do with real property located in Minnesota, and also the personal property within the court's jurisdiction. The Minnesota court cannot probate any part of the will which disposes of property in, say Iowa. To probate the portion of the will which disposes of real estate in Iowa, the Minnesota court will have an authenticated copy of the record of the probate procedure made there sent to the probate court in Iowa, in the county where the land is located. Then the Iowa court will probate that portion of the will which disposes of real estate located in Iowa. This same process is repeated in regard to real estate situated in other states. In all these cases the parties interested in the will must be duly notified of the probate proceedings by the court in the state where the real estate is located.

Suppose John has appointed a minor to act as sole executor of his estate. The court will hold that the minor is incapacitated to act as sole executor and will thereupon appoint a temporary executor, to act until the minor reaches his majority, when the minor will complete his duties of executor as directed by the will, under the direction and supervision of the court. In some states the courts will hold that married women, insane persons, dishonest persons, and highly immoral persons are not qualified to act as executors.

Suppose John does not name an executor in his will. Any interested party in the will may then make an application to the probate court to become administrator of the estate. If John leaves a widow, she has first right to be appointed administrator, in states where women can qualify as administrators. The administrator appointed by the probate court will be compelled to file a statutory bond, together with two sureties; the bond is set at twice the estimated value of the estate.

When the administrator has met all qualifications, he then proceeds to dispose of the personal property involved in the estate. After that a complete inventory is gotten up of all the property of the estate over which he has jurisdiction. After completing this inventory, the administrator has from fifteen days to six months during which to file it with the probate court. It is compulsory for the administrator to file the inventory, and the probate court may make him do it after the six months have expired. Should the administrator refuse, the court may bring suit against him on his bond or jail him for contempt. Should there happen to be no property to make an inventory of, it is the duty of the administrator to file an affidavit with the probate court so stating. Either the administrator must appraise the different properties of the estate, or the probate court has authority to appoint two or more disinterested parties to make the appraisal.

It is the duty of the administrator to run the properties to the best of his ability. He shall collect rents, defend the estate against suits, or bring suit, if necessary, to collect outstanding obligations due the estate. He should do this within a reasonable time, for the benefit of the parties interested in the estate. It is his duty to pay all beneficiaries any legacies due them and to distribute the various parcels of the estate according to the terms of the will.

All title to personal property vests immediately in the executor when the testator dies; title vests in the administrator when he has qualified, after having been appointed by the probate court. The executor or administrator must use ordinary care and reasonable diligence in the management of the estate, to protect the interested parties. In other words, he should use the same reasonable care and diligence as he would in managing his own estate. For instance, an administrator must keep all buildings insured, collect all rents, and keep all funds invested so as to provide both a reasonable return and ample security. If the administrator or executor willfully or with gross negligence invests the funds of the estate at a loss or mismanages the properties, the probate court will hold him liable on his bond for all damages caused the estate. The sureties who sign the bond of the executor or administrator, will be held liable to restore lost money to the estate. The executor or administrator will be promptly dismissed or discharged by the probate court. But if the executor or administrator has not been negligent in conducting the affairs of the estate, he will not be held liable on his bond for any losses sustained.

It is the duty of the executor or administrator to close up the affairs of the estate, under order of the probate court, as quickly and expeditiously as possible, unless the testator has provided in his will that the executor shall continue in office, managing the estate, indefinitely. When the executor or administrator first takes charge, he should, if necessary, sell all personal property to pay creditors or legacies. He must secure from the court an order before he can sell any property at all. Should he dispose of personal property, he must always sell it for cash; if he accepts credit instead of cash, he will be held liable on his bond for any loss sustained. The court will hold that he cannot buy any property which he sells for the estate, either directly or through an outside party, except where all interested parties to the estate consent.

For all these duties, responsibilities, liabilities, and obligations which the executor or administrator assumes, he is allowed by the probate court reasonable compensation. The court stipulates what his services are worth, unless the will provides what the executor's compensation shall be.

XX. EVIDENCE

WHAT IS A PETITION
OR BILL OF PARTICULARS?

In every case tried before a court a petition, or bill, is filed with the court, together with subsequent pleadings. These petitions, bills, and pleadings are all formal documents in writing, and their purpose and object is to reduce the facts at issue so as to focus attention on the material questions involved in the litigation. Evidence itself is either written or oral testimony in the form of facts, or alleged facts, intended to explain and clarify the material facts and issues in the case to the court or jury. It is the duty of the court or the jury to assist in determining what the issues of fact are, when the pleadings have been filed in court and when all evidence and testimony has been introduced, for the purpose of developing the different issues of fact, or alleged fact, contained in the pleadings. Evidence is introduced for the purpose of developing the issues of fact in favor of plaintiff or of defendant.

All evidence introduced in a lawsuit is for the purpose of proving or of disproving the facts stated in the pleadings.

We have two kinds of evidence: direct evidence and circumstantial evidence. Suppose John tells the court while he is under oath as a witness that he saw James shoot Harry. This testimony of John's is called direct evidence or testimony. Suppose a detective introduces in evidence in a criminal case a revolver whose magazine is loaded with cartridges, two of which have been discharged. Suppose Harry has been shot twice and this revolver shoots the same-size cartridges as those used in shooting Harry. Suppose James has the revolver in his hip pocket. The introduction of this revolver, and the testimony of the detective, that "I took this particular revolver from the person of James," is called circumstantial evidence, tending to prove that James shot Harry.

All evidence introduced in a lawsuit may be examined from

the viewpoint of its subject matter and of its form. Evidence is said to be relevant if it pertains to the subject matter of the facts at issue as contained in the pleadings. Evidence is competent if it is correct in form and pertains to the facts at issue, as alleged in the pleadings. Hearsay evidence is incompetent and therefore inadmissible, because when a witness gives hearsay testimony, that is, tells something which someone else told him regarding the facts at issue in the case, the court will hold, that the testimony of the party who told the witness would be the best evidence, because it would be direct evidence.

So far as possible, all evidence should be direct and have a bearing on the issues of the case; and evidence ought not to be prejudicial.

ILLUSTRATIONS AND LAW OF EVIDENCE

Suppose John confesses that he committed murder. This confession is purely hearsay; but if the confession is made of John's own free will and accord, without the use of duress or undue influence on the part of the officers in charge, the court will admit it, although as a general rule it will not admit testimony or evidence which is purely hearsay. A court will admit as evidence the handwriting of a party if the writing can be identified as such to the court's satisfaction. The deposition of a witness who is without the jurisdiction of the court will be admitted in evidence if it was taken under judicial sanction. The courts will also admit as competent evidence all public documents, and dying declarations, even though a dying declaration is purely hearsay evidence.

In the study of evidence we have what is known as the best-evidence rule. Suppose John writes a letter to James. John sends the original to James, and retains the carbon copy. The court will hold, according to the best-evidence rule, that the original copy should be introduced as evidence, if it can be found, in preference to the carbon copy.

Suppose John is trying a lawsuit against James, and James has a letter in John's handwriting. James refuses to give this letter to John, to be introduced by John as evidence in the case before the court. John may serve a notice against James to produce the letter in court, and the court will compel James to comply.

The courts hold that certified copies of all public records may be introduced as competent evidence in place of the original records, because constant handling of public records in court would soon destroy them.

We have a rule which provides that where evidence is written in form and the written instrument if offered, the court will not permit the parties to the instrument to alter or change it by the introduction of oral, or parol, evidence or testimony, provided the instrument is reasonably clear in stating the facts which it purports to contain. In other words, the parol-evidence rule provides that testimony may not be introduced in court to change or alter a written instrument if the instrument is reasonably clear on its face and is competent. The courts hold that in order to explain matters collateral to a written instrument or document, oral testimony may be introduced if not inconsistent with the written instrument or document itself. The courts also hold that parol evidence may be introduced to explain trade customs which pertain to the explanation of any written document. The courts also hold that oral testimony may be introduced to explain the intentions of two contracting parties where the contract between them, although written, is incomplete or unfinished, if such testimony is not inconsistent with the written instrument.

Suppose John makes a will which is ambiguous in its wording and consequently susceptible of two different interpretations. The court will hold that the parol-evidence rule may be overlooked, even though the instrument is a written one, and that oral testimony may be admitted to show what the testator actually meant.

Suppose John, an attorney, is examining a witness on the stand, before the court. The witness in giving his testimony will be permitted to state only facts. He will not be permitted to state his opinion on the case or any phase of it. Witnesses must state facts in their testimony, otherwise their testimony will be excluded as incompetent, because an opinion is not the best evidence, except in the case of expert testimony. If a physician, for example, gives his opinion in regard to certain medical facts of the case being tried, the court will admit such opinion in evidence, as competent, expert testimony.

In a criminal action a husband is not permitted to testify

against his wife, nor a wife against her husband. In civil suits—
suits on a contract, divorce suits, etc.—spouses are permitted to
testify against each other.

A witness can be compelled to come into court and give testimony, on the day fixed in a subpoena or summons served on him.
However, no witness can be called into court to incriminate himself by testifying against himself. If a witness fails to appear as
ordered, the court can have him arrested for contempt.

Suppose John is bringing a lawsuit against James and wishes
to have certain written documents produced in court, and a third
party refuses to bring them into court for John's use. The court
may then issue a subpoena duces tecum against the third party
compelling him to produce the document in court. If the third
party refuses to comply, the court can arrest him for contempt.

During the trial of every case each witness, before he testifies,
takes an oath. He raises his right hand at the request of the clerk
or officer of the court, is asked the following question, in the
form of an oath: "Do you solemnly swear that you will tell the
truth, the whole truth, and nothing but the truth, so help you
God?" The witness usually answers, "I will" or, "I do."

At its pleasure the court may exclude all witnesses from the
courtroom except the one who is testifying, so that the others
will not hear what the witness on the stand has to tell.

All civil suits are conducted according to the following order.
After all pleadings have been filed with the court, and the case
has been called for trial, and the court is ready to proceed, attorney for plaintiff presents in a brief opening statement the facts
which he will endeavor to prove. Then he calls his witnesses and
thus makes his complete, direct case. Next, attorney for defendant
briefly states the facts which he intends to prove. He then calls
his witnesses, and by means of the testimony makes his complete,
direct case. Now attorney for plaintiff calls his witnesses to give
testimony to rebut the evidence and testimony of the defense.
This is called the rebuttal part of the case. Next, attorney for
defendant calls the witnesses on his side and endeavors to rebut
the rebuttal testimony of plaintiff's witnesses. This part of the
trial procedure is called the surrebuttal. This concludes all the
evidence in the trial of a civil lawsuit. But before the case is
submitted to a court or jury for decision, attorney for plaintiff,
in an address before the court, reviews in a detailed way, and to

the best of his ability, all the testimony and evidence offered in the entire case which tends to prove his side, in order to secure a verdict or judgment for his client. Next, attorney for defendant, in his address, reviews all the testimony and evidence offered which tends to prove his side, in order to secure a verdict or judgment for his client. Finally the court instructs the jury on the law applying to the facts of the case. He then informs the jury that they are the sole judges of the evidence and testimony introduced, and directs them to retire and bring in a verdict according to written forms which he submits to them for the purpose. The jury's verdict is then read aloud in open court.

In the trial of a civil lawsuit, attorney for plaintiff introduces all the evidence he has that sustains the allegations made in his pleadings. In submitting this evidence, he must produce sufficient testimony to make out a prima facie case. If he does not, the court will at once dismiss the suit and render judgment in behalf of defendant. A prima facie case is one in which the evidence or testimony introduced by plaintiff is sufficient that if the case should then stop, plaintiff could secure a judgment.

Each attorney is entitled to cross-examine every witness whom the other side puts on the stand for direct examination.

The presiding judge regulates, and passes upon, all evidence in the case. For example: Attorney for plaintiff wishes to introduce in evidence a photograph of a wrecked automobile, to show the position of the automobile relative to the street corner. If the photograph is improper in its perspective, thus giving a misconception as to distances, relative positions, etc., attorney for defendant may object to its admission on the ground that it is incompetent evidence, and further that it is introduced for the purpose of deceiving the jurors. If the court agrees, it will sustain the objection, and plaintiff will not be permitted to use the photograph as evidence and thus will not be permitted to make it part of the record of the case. If attorney for plaintiff does not agree with the court's reasoning and still thinks the photograph ought to be introduced in evidence, he makes an exception to the court's ruling. This exception is made part of the record. Then, if the case is decided against plaintiff as it comes up for review on an appeal to a superior court, that court will analyze the exception as it appears in the record. If the superior court decides that the lower court acted properly in excluding the photograph, it will pass by the exception. If, on the other hand, it decides that the exception was properly made, it will make a notation in the record overruling the decision of the lower court on that particular exception. If the superior court finds that attorney for plaintiff is correct in a sufficient number of his exceptions, it will issue an order remanding the case to the lower court for a new trial, or else it may reverse the judgment of the lower court and enter a new judgment, for plaintiff. This ends the case if this higher court is the supreme court of the state, unless there is constitutional ground on which the case may be appealed to a United States federal court, for review there, as it was reviewed in the state supreme court.

Every witness in a civil suit may be examined in the following manner: First, questions are asked of him by the attorney who first puts him on the stand; this is called direct examination, or examination in chief, of the witness. Second, the witness is examined concerning his testimony by the opposite attorney; this is called cross-examination of the witness. Third, the first attorney may again examine the witness in regard to his testimony; this is called redirect examination of the witness.

An attorney examining a witness will not be permitted to ask leading questions. A leading question puts into the mouth of the witness the answer which the examining attorney desires. When a leading question is asked, the opposing attorney may object to the question in that form. Ordinarily the court will sustain the objection if the question as put really is leading. The witness asked the question will not be permitted to answer it until the court makes its ruling on the objection. If the court overrules the objection, the witness will be permitted to answer.

A witness, while being examined, is permitted to state only facts, and if the attorney examining him asks a question which calls for a conclusion, the opposing attorney may object.

When a witness is being cross-examined, the examining attorney may question the witness in detail on all facts testified to by the witness in direct examination. This cross-examination affords the attorney making it the opportunity to impeach the testimony of the witness given in direct. To impeach means to discredit, or to prove false what a witness has already testified to as being the truth.

Every attorney may re-examine his own witness, to counteract any testimony brought out on cross-examination which may be detrimental to his case.

If there is any conflict in the evidence given by two witnesses, the jury will have to decide which witness is telling the truth. The jury should take into consideration the demeanor of each witness while he is testifying. The jury are also the judges of the weight and sufficiency of evidence. All questions of law involved in the case must be decided by the court; also all questions of mixed law and fact.

In a civil case, when the jury brings in a verdict, if the judge concludes that the verdict is erroneous, that there has not been sufficient evidence produced by the party in whose favor judgment has been brought in to warrant such judgment, he is privileged to set the verdict aside. If he sets the verdict aside, he must also grant a new trial.

In criminal cases, if the jury brings in a verdict for defendant, and the court thinks the evidence produced by the state was beyond a reasonable doubt sufficient to convict, the court will nevertheless not be permitted to set the verdict aside—not even if that verdict is absolutely erroneous. This is so because the Constitution does not permit a party to be tried twice for the same crime.

XXI. CONSTITUTIONAL LAW

FEDERAL AND STATE

In the United States the supreme law of the land is the federal Constitution. The Constitution guarantees to every natural person certain fundamental personal, property, and political rights. All constitutional governments are granted by their constitutions certain constructive powers, rights, duties, and obligations, and are prohibited by their constitutions from exercising certain other powers and rights.

A study of the original American colonies, endowed with the spirit of freedom, takes us through one of the most interesting modern histories of governmental growth and development. The development of our American form of government dates from the settlement of Virginia. The governors of the colonies were granted certain powers by the crown of England, through what were called trading charters. These governors drew around themselves a legislative body, chosen from among the people of the colonies, to make laws necessary for their peculiar conditions on the new continent. We read of the early Indian wars, and of the English taxing the American colonies without giving them any representation in Parliament. We read of how England interfered with the foreign trade of the colonies. We read of the Stamp Act, of the Boston Tea Party. We read of the first great Continental Congress in 1774, which declared for American rights. Next, we read of the great battles of Lexington and Concord, and we read of a great Revolutionary War in 1775 between the mother country and her American colonies, separated by the great Atlantic Ocean. Later we read of how the Second Continental Congress convened, and taking charge, promoted and conducted a successful war against England. We read of the state governments being organized later, under the administration of the Second Continental Congress. And we read of how, in 1781, the Articles of Confederation were adopted, concentrating, or confederating, all the separate state powers into one large organic union of states. In 1776, we read, this famous Second Continental Congress adopted the Declaration of Independence, that Magna Charta of American political rights. We read of the eventual failure and downfall of the Articles of Confederation and the adoption of the federal Constitution. In 1786, we read, the great state of Virginia recommended that a commission meet at Philadelphia for the purpose of drawing up a constitution. According to this federal Constitution, we have three distinct and separate branches of government: (1) legislative; (2) executive; (3) judicial. These three constitute our central government. Immediately below the central government we have separate state governments. These state governments have separate constitutions of their own, not inconsistent with the federal Constitution. Each individual state of the Union has a separate form of government, divided into the same three distinct branches as the federal government: (1) legislative; (2) executive; (3) judicial. And as the President of the United States heads the executive department of the federal government, so the governor heads the executive department of a state.

The federal government is a government with limited powers, whereas the government of each separate state is a government of unlimited powers, except where the federal government prohibits it from exercising certain rights and where the constitution of the state restricts the powers and rights of the state government. Outside of these restrictions, the powers of a state government are unlimited.

As has been said, the Constitution of the United States gives and guarantees to every natural citizen certain political, religious, and civil rights. It prohibits state governments from making any laws which violate or in any way impair the private rights which the Constitution guarantees to the citizen. It further provides that no citizen shall be deprived of his personal liberty or any of his private rights without due process of law. Each state constitution has the same provision in regard to citizens of the state.

Every natural citizen of the United States is, first, a citizen of the United States. Then, he may be a citizen also of any individual state of the Union. So every American, under our constitutional government, may have two citizenships: first federal; second, state.

The Constitution provides that every citizen, male or female, shall have the right to vote after the age of twenty-one. It provides for freedom of speech, freedom of the press, the right to assemble, the right to petition, the right to bear arms. It provides for personal liberty and religious freedom. It provides that every man charged with a crime shall be granted the privilege of a judicial trial. It provides that no ex post facto laws can be passed by any legislature, federal or state. It provides that no man charged with crime can be compelled to incriminate himself by testifying against himself. It provides that all persons charged with crime shall have the privilege of being tried by a jury; and in all civil suits where the amount sued for is in excess of twenty dollars, the party sued may demand trial by jury. "Liberty" as used in the Constitution means the right of every citizen to enjoy all his faculties in a free and unrestricted way, so long as that way is lawful. Liberty also means the right to live and to pursue one's work wherever one may desire, so long as that work is lawful. The Constitution provides and guarantees equal protection of the law to all citizens. It provides for police power by which a government may regulate the conduct of individuals so as to preserve the public welfare; for example, under police power a government may enact laws regulating public health, public morals, public safety, public order, and public comfort. It provides that all taxes shall be levied for public purposes, shall be uniform and not disproportionate or confiscatory.

The Constitution provides that where the right of eminent domain is exercised, any private property so taken must be used for public purposes.

XXII. CONFLICT OF LAWS

DOMICILE DISTINGUISHED FROM RESIDENCE

Residence means physical presence with some degree of permanency; domicile connotes a place of permanent abode. The intent of the individual in question controls in determining the place of his domicile. One may have but one domicile at any time but have several places of residence.

In Texas v. Florida, 306 U.S. 398, the deceased had resided at various times in four different states, and each state claimed the right to levy an estate tax on intangibles. An original suit in the Texas Superior Court was instituted by Texas, in the nature of an interpleader, seeking that the court determine the issue as to domicile of the deceased at the time of his death. It was alleged that the tax claims of the four states plus the claims of the federal government would more than exceed the value of the estate (which was over $35,000,000). Thus the levy of such taxes would make impossible the payment of tax claims asserted by taxes. The court held that this case did not come within equity jurisdiction. So a Special master was appointed, who found that the domicile was in Massachusetts.

DOMICILE OF MARRIED WOMEN AND MINORS

The common rule is that the domicile of the wife is that of the husband. A wife's legal duty is to make her husband's home her home. (A contrary conclusion is expressed in Berlingieri v. Berlingieri, 372 Ill. 60.) However, where a wife does not desert her husband, she may acquire a separate domicile for the purpose of securing a divorce (Town of Watertown v. Greaves, 112 Fed. 183).

The common rule is that the domicile of an unemancipated legitimate child is the same as the father's. This is true unless custody of the child was awarded to the mother in divorce or separation proceedings. The domicile of an illegitimate child is the same as the mother's.

JUDGMENTS AND JURISDICTION
OF COURTS

1. Judgments: Article IV, Section 1, of the Constitution reads: "Full Faith and Credit shall be given each State to the public Acts, Records, and Judicial Proceedings of every other State. And the Congress may by general laws prescribe the manner in which such Acts, Records, and Proceedings shall be proved, and the effect thereof." A general rule is that a judgment is subject to collateral attack where it was secured as the result of fraud or where the court rendering the judgment was without jurisdiction over either the person of defendant or the subject matter of the litigation.

Appeal Case. In Paine v. Schenectady Insurance Co., 11 R.I. 411, Action was brought in Rhode Island for breach of contract. It was contended that the action could not be maintained because defendant had recovered a judgment against plaintiff in New York, where plaintiff had pleaded as a set-off the matters involved in this case. Plaintiff replied that there had been an appeal from the New York judgment. The court held that the New York judgment would be a bar to the present action. This conclusion was based on the ground that under New York law the judgment was in effect in spite of the appeal. Final disposition of the case was put off until the results of the appeal were determined.

Enforcement Case. In Lynde v. Lynde, 181 U.S. 183, Mrs. Lynde secured a New Jersey decree of $7,840 for back alimony and an award of future alimony at the rate of $80 a week. She then brought suit in New York for past due alimony, attorney fees, and $80 a week future alimony. She also requested an order for sequestration receivership and an injunction. The court

held that while a judgment such as this must be given full faith
and credit, this was true only with respect to a final judgment.
It was considered that since the order for payment of future
alimony was subject to the discretion of the Court of Chancery
of New Jersey, which might at any time alter it, there was no
final judgment as to that item. It was further held that the provision of the New Jersey decree for bond, sequestration, receiver,
and injunction, being in the nature of execution and not of judgment, could have no extraterritorial operation. In Barber v.
Barber, 323 U.S. 77, the wife secured a money judgment in North
Carolina for accrued alimony under a Connecticut separate-
maintenance decree. The decree was under a statute that gave
the court rendering the decree the right to modify the allowance at any time upon application of either party. This action
was instituted in Tennessee to enforce the North Carolina judgment. The court held that the judgment was entitled to full faith
and credit because sufficient finality was established. The rendering court did not have the right to modify the judgment as to
accrued payments. The same result was reached in Sistare v.
Sistare, 218 U.S. 1.

2. Jurisdiction: Jurisdiction means the power of a state to
create interests which under the principles of common law will
be recognized as valid in other states. A judgment where the
court did not have jurisdiction is void, even in the state where
rendered. The jurisdiction may arise either because there is jurisdiction over a person or because there is jurisdiction over property.

Jurisdiction over Property. In Pennoyer v. Neff, 95 U.S. 714,
action was brought to recover possession of land located in
Oregon. Plaintiff's title was based on a United States patent.
Defendant claimed title under a sheriff's deed, made on a sale of
land on execution of a judgment secured against plaintiff. The
validity of that judgment was questioned; although plaintiff
owned the land in Oregon, he was a non-resident of that state.
While plaintiff was not served personally with process, it was
claimed that substituted service was proper. The code of Oregon
authorized such service and declared the resultant judgment
valid to the extent that the non-resident owned property within
the state. The court held that the Oregon court was without jurisdiction and the judgment void. It was conceded that a state

might acquire jurisdiction to render a personal judgment to the extent that defendant owned the land or chattels within the state; but to make such a judgment valid the property must be attached as a preliminary step in the proceedings. By so attaching the property and bringing it before the court, the action became one of quasi in rem. A court might thus act through the thing over which it had jurisdiction. A personal judgment might then be rendered to the extent of the value of the property before the court. Any judgment in excess of that value was null and void.

Jurisdiction over Persons. In Millikin v. Meyer, 311 U.S. 457, the Colorado Supreme Court held that a Wyoming judgment against Meyer was null and void. When the Wyoming action was instituted, Meyer was domiciled in Wyoming. While there was no personal service on Meyer, there was substitute service in accord with a Wyoming statute that would make the judgment valid as against an absentee resident of the state. It was held that the Colorado court was required to give full faith and credit to the Wyoming judgment. Domicile in a state is alone sufficient to bring an absent defendant without its jurisdiction for the purpose of rendering a personal judgment. The authority of a state over one of its citizens is not terminated by the mere fact of his absence from the state.

A judgment against an absentee defendant who is domiciled within the state where jurisdiction is made to depend on substituted service is not valid if the local law does not provide for substituted service in such a case (69 Adv. Calif. App. 206).

In Blackmer v. United States, 284 U.S. 421, the petitioner, a citizen of the United States and a resident of Paris, France, was adjudged to be guilty of contempt of court. The contempt consisted in his failure to comply with the subpoenas served on him in Paris and requiring him to appear as a witness in behalf of the United States at a criminal trial pending in the Supreme Court of the District of Columbia. A fine resulted that was to be satisfied out of property seized in the United States. The procedure was in conformity with existing legislation, and the court sustained the penalty as imposed. The United States retains jurisdiction in personam over her absent citizens.

PERSONAL SERVICE. In Darrah v. Watson, 36 Iowa 116, an action was commenced in Virginia by personal service on defendant, who was domiciled in Pennsylvania and was only temporarily in Virginia. The court held that jurisdiction was acquired to render the judgment and it was entitled to full faith and credit under the federal Constitution.

CONSENT. Where a defendant has consented to the jurisdiction of a court, the judgment against him will be entitled to full faith and credit in other jurisdictions if the jurisdiction of the court was otherwise established (Feyerick v. Hubbard, KB Div. 71 L.J.K.B. 509). The consent as given must be strictly followed. In Grover v. Baker Sewing Co. v. Radcliffe, 137 U.S. 287, the consent was in the following form: ". . . authorizing any attorney of any court of record in the State of New York or any other state to confess judgment." The judgment was entered by a clerk of the court as was authorized by a Pennsylvania statute where the judgment was entered. The judgment so entered was not in accordance with the consent given and accordingly was not based on jurisdiction acquired over defendant. The general rule is that in the absence of statute authority one does not impliedly consent to submit to the jurisdiction of the state merely by the doing of an act within the state (Emanuel v. Symon, Ct. of App. 77 L.J.K.B. 180). Acts have been held to be constitutional that provide that one who performs certain acts within the state may be held accountable for such acts in the courts of the state.

Hess v. Pawloski, 274 U.S. 352, held that one driving a car within the state may be sued in the state court for injuries resulting from negligent driving. Such a statute as covers this must describe procedure that will conform with the concepts of due process. Wuchter v. Pizutti, 276 U.S. 13, held that a statute is unconstitutional where it does not require appropriate means of giving notice.

CORPORATIONS. Usually provision by statute is made that a foreign corporation doing business within the state thereby subjects itself to the jurisdiction of the state to the extent of the business so conducted. Jurisdiction is said to be based on consent, or it may be considered that the corporation is actually within the jurisdiction of the state.

APPEARANCE. In New York v. Texas, 137 U.S. 15, defendant leased land from the state of Texas. The lease provided that in any litigation thereunder the venue should be laid in Travis lit under the fed-

Ky. v. Exley, 64
ed into a contract
iff sought specific
the owner failed
Kentucky decree.
t, who purchased
ght this action in
the complainant
ntucky decree did

rth Carolina, 317
s of North Caro-
n their respective
ted service. They
d to live in North
. It was not ques-
micile in Nevada.
relied on the rule
62, that the state
a over the absent
omicile. The court
l to full faith and
not be sustained.
of the parties in
adequate for the
as a sovereign has
rimonial status of
he marriage status
urt overruled the
d repudiated the
ose a jurisdiction

ashua River Paper
contract between
vania corporation
. on the contract
hat the provision
to public policy

ought suit for non-payment
e was served on defendant
s domiciled. He appeared
iction of the court. While
ce which is solely to chal-
not a general appearance
urisdiction of the court, a
n Texas. Such a statute is
esult in denial of due pro-

od, 215 Ia. 979, action was
and made payable in that
ad in Minnesota. The court
on to render any judgment
of the mortgage on Min-
Co. v. Berry, 153 S.C. 496,
brough suit to specifically
and in South Carolina to
asis of substituted service.
as limited by a foreclosure
ere land is located within
o render a judgment with
ut personal service it does
rights (Combs v. Combs,

.S.) 148, plaintiff brought
a citizen of Kentucky, to
Ohio. It was held that the
could render a decree that
even though the land was

tiff wife secured a decree
ourt also awarded to her
nd failed to comply with
to the wife; so a commis-
l a purported conveyance.
gs in Nebraska to establish
held that the Washington
r a judgment that would
aska land and that such

judgment was not entitled to full faith and cre
eral Constitution.

In Redwood Investment Co. of Stithton,
Calif. 455, the owners of California land ente
in Kentucky to sell the land to plaintiff. Plain
performance of the contract in Kentucky, bu
to convey the land in accordance with the
Thereafter the land was conveyed to defenda
with notice of plaintiff's equity. Plaintiff bro
California to quiet title. The court held tha
stated a good cause of action, because the Ke
not operate to fix the equities of the parties.

Divorce Case. In Williams v. State of N
U.S. 287, Williams and Mrs. Hendrix, resider
lina, went to Nevada and secured divorces fro
spouses. The divorces were based on substit
then married each other in Nevada and return
Carolina, where they were convicted of bigam
tioned that they had established a bona fide d
In seeking to sustain the conviction the state
declared in Haddock v. Haddock, 210 U.S.
granting the divorce did not have jurisdictio
spouse, it not being the state of matrimonial d
held that Nevada divorce decrees were entitle
credit and that the convictions involved coul
The court followed the view that the domicil
Nevada created a relationship to the state
numerous exercises of state power. Each state
a rightful and legitimate concern in the ma
persons domiciled in the state, and may alter
of those domiciled in the state. Thus the c
earlier decision of Haddock v. Haddock, a
theory that only the innocent spouse may ch
for the purpose of securing a divorce.

Limitations on Exercise of Jurisdiction. In N
Co. v. Hammermill Paper Co., 223 Mass. 8, a
a Massachusetts corporation and a Pennsyl
provided that no action could be maintaine
other than in Pennsylvania. The court held
could not be enforced because it was contrar

as an attempt to place a limitation on the powers of a court. In some states a statute provides that the court, in its discretion, may refuse to exercise jurisdiction over designated litigation. This is sometimes true in tort actions between non-residents where the tort arose outside the state. This is not unconstitutional, because discrimination is not on the basis of citizenship but on the basis of residence. The restriction would be applicable to citizens of the state as well as to citizens of other states. Torts.

LAW GOVERNING LIABILITY. The law of the place where the wrong was committed fixes the tort liability of the parties as a general rule (223 Mass. 8). If a defendant is not liable according to the lex loci delicti, he may not be held elsewhere (Alabama Great Southern R.R. Co. v. Carroll).

If a defendant is liable according to the lex loci delicti, he should be held liable elsewhere. In Gray v. Gray 87 N.H. 82, husband and wife were domiciled in New Hampshire. Plaintiff wife suffered personal injuries as a result of defendant husband's negligence. The alleged wrong occurred in Maine, where a wife could not sue her husband for personal injuries. The court held that since recovery was denied according to the lex loci delicti, an action could not be maintained elsewhere (Alabama Great Southern R.R. Co. v. Carroll).

MARRIAGE CASE. In Buckeye v. Buckeye, 203 Wis. 248, plaintiff claimed the right to recover damages for personal injuries sustained by her while a passenger in defendant's automobile. The accident occurred in Illinois, but plaintiff was a resident of Wisconsin. After commencement of the action but prior to the trial, plaintiff married defendant. Recovery was denied on the ground that under the law of Illinois the marriage had the effect of extinguishing the action's cause. The law of the place where the wrong occurred was controlling as to the effect of subsequent marriage on the right to maintain the action.

AGENCY. In Venuto v. Robinson, 118 Fed. (2d) 679, actions were brought to recover damages arising out of an automobile collision in New Jersey. It was claimed that the driver of a truck involved in the collision was defendant's agent. The contract of employment was made in North Carolina. The court held that the nature of the relationship between the parties was to be governed by the law of New Jersey rather than of North Carolina.

STATUTORY LIABILITY. In many states statutes provide that the owner of an automobile is liable for injuries resulting from its operation in the state in cases where it is being operated with the owner's consent. This liability will attach even though the owner is not domiciled within the state with his consent (Young v. Masci, 289 U.S. 253).

WRONGFUL DEATH STATUTES

Nature of Statutes. They provide for (1) survival of the cause of action that arose in favor of the deceased; (2) a new cause of action in favor of the heirs or the estate of the deceased. It seems that where a cause of action arises under either type of statute the right should be enforceable elsewhere. In Rose v. Phillips Packing Co. Inc. (Dist. Ct. U.S. D. Md.), 21 Fed. Supp. 485, the administratrix of the estate of the deceased, appointed in Virginia, brought the action. It was contended that she was without capacity to sue other than in the state where she was appointed. The court held, however, that she could maintain the action as a trustee.

Purpose of Statutes. The purpose of most of the wrongful-death statutes is to provide compensation for the loss suffered by the estate or the heirs of the deceased person. In a few states its purpose is to punish the wrongful doer. Because it is penal in nature, it could be contended that it cannot be enforced other than in the state where the wrong occurred. However, it has been held that such a statute is not a penal statute in the strict sense and that enforcement is proper even though the wrong happened elsewhere (Louchs v. Standard Oil Co. of N.Y., 224 N.Y. 99).

WORKMEN'S COMPENSATION STATUTES

According to the general rule, benefits under the workmen's compensation act of the state where an injury occurs may be claimed by or on behalf of the injured employee. It is generally true that benefits may be claimed under the act of the state where the contract of employment was made. Compensation awarded in one state will bar a second recovery in another state (Magnolia Petroleum Co. v. Hunt).

In Bradford Electric Light Co. v. Clapper, 286 U.S. 145, the contract of employment was entered into in Vermont. The Vermont statute provided that the remedy available under it was to be the exclusive remedy in the event of injuries outside the state. The employee suffered injuries in New Hampshire that resulted in his death. The court held that the Vermont act was entitled to full faith and credit under the federal Constitution and that remedies could not be had under the New Hampshire act.

CONTRACTS

Capacity. Generally the law of the place of contracting determines the capacity of the parties. In University of Chicago v. Dater, 277 Mich. 658, a married woman living in Michigan executed a mortgage on Illinois land. Under Michigan law, she did not thereby incur any personal liability on the indebtedness, because of lack of capacity. The mortgagee sued on the indebtedness in Michigan, seeking to establish personal liability, which was possible under Illinois law. The trust mortgage and notes had been sent by mail from Chicago to Michigan for signature of the mortgagor, and defendant signed the papers in Michigan. The check covering the amount of the loan was payable in Illinois. The court held that the law of the place where the contract was made determined the capacity of defendant with respect to the obligation and that the contract was made in Michigan. But even assuming that the law of the place of performance determined the capacity of the parties, under Illinois law the law of Michigan would be controlling (Burr v. Becker, 264 Ill. 230). It was determined that because the contract was made in Michigan, there would be no personal liability on defendant.

Corporations. In general the law of the place of incorporation determines the capacity of a corporation to contract. However, the extent to which a corporation may rely on the defense of ultra vires depends on the law of contracting.

General Rule. The general rule is that the law of the place of contracting determines the validity of a contract. Some authorities support the view that the law of the place of performance governs; others, that validity is determined by the law intended by the parties. For instance, in Green v. Northwestern Trust Co., 128 Minn. 30, a contract for the loan of money was consummated in Minnesota. It involved a purchase-money mortgage on Montana land. An interest provision was usurious under Minnesota law but valid under Montana law. The validity of the interest provision was questioned in Minnesota. The court held that Montana law would be applied in order to sustain validity of the contract. While the parties to the contract did not express any intention in the matter, the court followed the view that there was a strong presumption that the parties intended to contract with reference to the law of the state where the transaction was valid.

NEGOTIABLE INSTRUMENTS. In the case of negotiable instruments, the general rule is that the law of the place of performance governs as to negotiability. The law of the place where an instrument is negotiated governs the rights and liabilities of the parties to the negotiation (United States v. Guaranty Trust Co., 293 U.S. 340).

PERFORMANCE. The general rule is that as to matters of performance, the law of the place of performance governs (Louis-Dreyfus v. Paterson Steamships Ltd. [C.C.A. 2nd], 43 Fed. [2d] 824).

PENAL LAWS

Penal Law Defined. Generally one state will not lend its assistance to enforcement of the penal laws of another state. The rule is not limited to cases where a fine is levied because of an offense against the state; it may include awards made payable to individuals as well (Adams v. Fitchburg R.R. Co., 67 Vt. 670). In Huntington v. Attrill, 146 U.S. 657, the court stated the test as follows: "The question whether a statute of one state, which in some aspects may be called penal, is a penal law in the international sense, so that it cannot be enforced in the courts of another state, depends upon the question whether its purpose is to punish an offense against the public justice of the state, or to afford a private remedy to a person injured by the wrongful act."

APPLICATION TO SPECIFIC CASES

In Derrickson v. Smith, 27 N.J. Law 166, a New York statute required corporations to make annual reports and provided that upon failure to make such reports, the trustees of the corporation were to be jointly and severally liable for all debts of the company then existing and those incurred prior to compliance. Action was brought in New Jersey to recover under the provisions of this statute. It was claimed that liability was based on contract. Recovery was denied on the ground that the statute was penal in nature. There was no original liability in this case. Liability arose from failure to comply with certain conditions.

Usury Case. In Blaine v. Curtis, 59 Vt. 120, under a New Hampshire statute one found guilty of usury forfeited three times the amount of interest to the person aggrieved. Enforcement was denied in Vermont on the ground that the statute was penal in nature.

Civil Death Case. In Panko v. Endicott Johnson Corp., 124 Mo. 178, plaintiff, a resident of Pennsylvania, brought an action in federal district court in New York on the ground of diversity of citizenship, claiming damages for personal injuries resulting from alleged negligence of defendant in New York. Prior to the accident plaintiff had been convicted of murder in Florida. It was contended that plaintiff could not maintain the action because of Section 511 of the Penal Laws of New York, which provides: "A person sentenced to imprisonment for life is thereafter deemed civilly dead." There is no similar statute in Florida. The court held that plaintiff could maintain the action because the New York statute did not have extraterritorial operation.

SUBSTANCE V. PROCEDURE

In many cases, whether a particular issue is to be determined by the law of the place where the cause of action arose or by the law of the forum is of controlling importance. If the issue is one of substance, the law of the place where the cause of action arose is applied. If the issue is one of procedure, the law of the forum is applied. If the issue is one of substance, then the law of the place where the cause of action arose is applied.

What may be considered a matter of procedure for some purposes may be considered a matter of substance for other purposes. It is not always possible to draw a clear-cut distinction between matters of substance and matters of procedure.

The general rule is that questions of "substance" or "procedure" are determined by the conflict-of-laws rule of the forum.

APPLICATION TO SPECIFIC SITUATIONS

Remedy Case. In Ruhe v. Buck, 124 Mo. 178, a contractual obligation was incurred in Dakota and attachment proceedings were instituted through an action in Missouri. The court held that the right to proceed by attachment depended on the law of Missouri. It was a matter of procedure and not of substantive law. In Saunders v. American Express Co., 71 N.J. 270, an action was brought in New Jersey against a partner on an obligation that arose in New York. A New York statute provided that a partnership could be sued in the firm name, and further provided that before an action could be brought against an individual partner, an action had to be brought against the partnership in the firm name. The court held that the procedure was governed by the New Jersey law and under that law it was not necessary to proceed first against the partnership. As a matter of substantive law, governed by the New York law, defendant was liable for the entire indebtedness.

Statute of Frauds. Whether the statute of frauds is considered "substantive" or "procedure" depends somewhat on the wording of the statute itself. The English statute of frauds, section four, provides: ". . . no action shall be brought on any of the contracts specified . . . unless there is a proper note or memorandum in writing." This language indicates procedure. Even if a contract cannot be enforced in the state where made, it may be enforceable according to the law of the forum. Section 17 uses different language and provides that a contract not complying with the required formalities shall not be allowed to be good. This language indicates that the statute is a matter of substance. Unless a contract is in writing as required by the law of the place where made, it is not enforceable elsewhere. The purpose of both sections is the same. In Marie v. Garrison, 13 Abb. N.C. 210, a Missouri contract was the basis of plaintiff's New York action. Defendant relied on the New York statute of frauds. The court held that the New York statute pertained to substantive law and not procedure, so that it had no application to the Missouri contract.

Statute of Limitations. Generally the statute of limitations is declaratory of procedural rights. So if a cause of action is not barred by the local statute of limitations, recovery will be allowed (McElmoyle v. Cohen 13 Pet. [U.S.] 312). Sometimes a statute creating a right prescribes the time within which an action must be brought to enforce the right. Where a statute is subject to such a construction it is held that the limitation period goes to the right and not merely to the remedy (Davis v. Mills, 194 U.S. 451).

Burden of Proof. The general rule is that the law of the forum governs as to the burden of proof.

FEDERAL COURTS

In Erie R.R. Co. v. Tompkins, 304 U.S. 64, Tompkins, a citizen of Pennsylvania, was injured in that state by one of defendant's trains. Claiming negligence, he brought suit in the federal court for southern New York to recover damages. Federal jurisdiction was proper because of diversity of citizenship. It was contended by defendant that recovery should be denied because of the Pennsylvania rule that would make plaintiff a trespasser under the circumstances. Plaintiff contended that the railroad's duty and liability should be determined in the federal courts as a matter of general law. This view was supported by the decision in Swift v. Tyson, 16 Pet. 1; in that case it was held that the federal court exercising jurisdiction in diversity-of-citizenship cases need not, in matters of general jurisprudence, apply the unwritten law of the state as declared by its highest court; that it is free to exercise an independent judgment as to what the common law of the state is, or should be. The court construed that

Section 34 of the Judiciary Act of 1789 required the federal courts to follow only the statutory law of a state and not the common law as interpreted by the highest courts of the state. The court held, however, that such a construction was erroneous and thus overruled Swift v. Tyson. Under the view adopted by the court the Pennsylvania law was controlling. Underlying the decision is a consideration of policy that it is undesirable to have the outcome of litigation substantially affected by the mere fact that there exists diversity of citizenship that enables a litigant to secure federal jurisdiction.

In Sampson v. Channell, 110 F. (2d) 754, while traveling in Maine, a car driven by defendant's testator collided with a car driven by plaintiff, who sought to recover damages. The action was instituted in the federal district court of Massachusetts. There was an issue as to contributory negligence. According to the Massachusetts rule, the burden of proof as to contributory negligence was on defendant. According to the Maine rule, the burden was on plaintiff to show affirmatively that no want of ordinary care on his part contributed to the injury. Thus the issue was raised whether the federal court must follow the state rule as to burden of proof. The court stated it would be an oversimplification to say that the case turned on whether burden of proof was a matter of substance or of procedure, because there were no clear-cut categories. It is also pointed out that the greater the likelihood there was that litigation would come out one way in the federal court and another way in the state court if the federal court failed to apply a particular local rule, the stronger the urge would be to classify the rule as more a mere matter of procedure than of substantive law falling within the mandate of the rule declared in Erie R.R. Co. v. Tompkins. Under Rule 8 (c) of the Federal Rules of Civil Procedure, it is indicated that contributory negligence is an "affirmative defense," thus implying that the burden is on defendant. This was only a rule of pleading, so the conclusion might still be reached that the burden of proof was on plaintiff. The court concluded that the issue as to the burden of proof should be considered a matter of substance and not a matter of procedure. Only by such a conclusion would it be possible to avoid the conclusion that the outcome of litigation was made to depend on the choice of tribunal in diversity-of-citizenship cases. The question was then raised whether the court should apply the rule of Maine, where the injury occurred, or the rule of Massachusetts, where the action was brought. It was concluded that the law should be applied as it would be if the action had been instituted in the state court. If the action had been instituted in the Massachusetts court, that court would have applied its own rule as to contributory negligence, because the state rule is that it is a matter of procedure. Thus the court went to the fullest extent to further the policy declared in Erie R.R. Co. v. Tompkins. It was first held that the issue as to the burden of proof in contributory negligence is not one of procedure in the sense that the federal rule might be applied. It was then held that the rule of the state where the action was brought should be applied regardless of the fact that locally the burden of proof might be considered procedural in nature. In Cities Service Oil Co. v. Dunlap, 308 U.S. 208, it was held that the state law is to be applied as to the burden of proof where one claims an interest in land on the theory that he is a bona fide purchaser for value without notice.

RECENT COURT DECISIONS

Some of the recent decisions coming down in the field of conflict of laws present an interest-oriented approach which leads to the law of the state of dominant interest. The new approach indicates purpose more important than place and causes more important than location. So some of the decisions in conflict-of-laws cases to be decided in the future may have the center-of-gravity approach. Several cases in conflict of laws that have been decided recently are being mentioned here.

In Kuchinic v. McCory, 22 A 2d 897 (Pa. 1966), four residents of Pennsylvania had flown in a private plane to a football game in Miami on New Year's Day. When they were returning home, the plane crashed in Georgia, and three passengers and the pilot were killed. Claim was made that the accident was due to the inexperienced pilot's flying in bad weather. The passengers brought an action against the pilot's estate, claiming negligence. The law of Georgia was assumed to be the law that would apply, as the law of damages were better than that of Pennsylvania. Gross negligence had to be shown to prove liability under the law of Georgia. Georgia had a plane statute, but Pennsylvania did not have any statute concerning airplane deaths and accidents. Proof of simple negligence was sufficient under the law of Pennsylvania. At the trial the jury brought in a verdict for defense, saying there was no gross negligence. The case was appealed to the Supreme Court. The result was the granting of a new trial, at which the law of Pennsylvania was followed. The place-of-crash theory gave way to the center-of-gravity-and-interest theory, because the flight had started in Pennsylvania and was to end in Pennsylvania. Decedents were from Pennsylvania, as well as their heirs, beneficiaries, and dependents.

In Griffith v. United Airlines, 416 Pa. 1 203 A 2d 796, the law of the place formerly applied was overruled. The center-of-gravity theory became the law of Pennsylvania. This theory holds that the law of the state with the greatest interest in the outcome of the proceeding governs the case. In the Griffith case the court applied the Pennsylvania Wrongful Death and Survivor's Act and refused to apply the Colorado statute that denied recovery in death actions except for damages suffered until death. So the Griffith holding was made part of the appeal of the Kuchinic v. McCrory, 22 A 2nd 897 Pa., case.

The idea began with Kilberg v. Northeast Airlines Inc., 9 N.Y. 2d 34 (1961), where the New York Court of Appeals refused to follow a Massachusetts death statute that limited recovery in a lawsuit by a New York resident against the airline. Pearson v. Northeast Airlines, Inc., 307 F. 2d 131 (22d Cir.), followed the Kilberg case. The decisions in the Pearson and Kilberg cases were so rendered because it was against New York State public policy to apply the death statute that limited the amount of damages.

This theory may be used in extraterritorial application of statutes. In Smith v. Driscoll Hotel, Inc., 249 Minn. 376, two Minnesota residents met with an accident in Wisconsin. The men had been drinking strong liquor excessively, and so the dramshop statute of the state was applied, even though the accident happened outside the state and in a state that did not have a dramshop statute.

Where an accident happens in a state that has a very short statute of limitations and the case is tried in a state with a longer statute of limitations, the court may apply the longer of the two statutes.

XXIII. JUDGMENTS

A judgment is the decision or conclusion arrived at by a court after hearing all the evidence and testimony in a lawsuit presented before a judge.

A judgment is invalid if the court which renders it does not have jurisdiction over the person or the property involved in the lawsuit.

All judgments are either final or interlocutory. A final judgment completely disposes of the case, and there is no appeal to a superior court.

Suppose Adam sues Arthur in tort because Arthur hit him with his fist. If Adam receives a judgment against Arthur, the judgment will be against Arthur personally, and will be called a judgment in personam. Suppose Adam brings a suit of attachment against a carload of beef. If Adam is given a judgment, the judgment will be directed against the commodity; it will be a judgment in rem.

After a judgment has been entered, the party receiving it may execute it against the person of the other party or else against property belonging to that party, according as the judgment is in personam or in rem. Every judgment draws interest from the date it is rendered until it is paid. The statute of limitations runs against judgments, the same as against any other contracts, formal or informal.

Interlocutory judgments are such as are given in the middle of a cause upon some plea, proceeding, or default which is only intermediate, and does not finally determine or complete the suit. Any judgment leaving something to be done by the court before the rights of the parties are determined, and not putting an end to the action in which it is entered, is interlocutory. Such is a judgment for plaintiff on a plea of abatement, which merely decides that the cause must proceed and defendant put in a better plea. But in the ordinary sense, interlocutory judgments are those incomplete judgments whereby the right of plaintiff is indeed established but the quantum of damages sustained by him is not ascertained. This can be the case only where plaintiff recovers.

XXIV. ATTACHMENTS, GARNISHMENTS AND EXECUTIONS

Once a judgment has been secured, the party favored may have the court of jurisdiction issue an execution on the judgment for the purpose of forcing collection on it. A judgment would be of no value if it could not be enforced and collected. Executions, attachments, and garnishments are all proceedings, issued by a court of competent jurisdiction, by which a judgment may be collected.

The property belonging to the party against whom an attachment is issued is brought into custody of the court. After the property has been attached, so that the court has possession of it, the court may order it to be given over to the proper party, or to be held until its status has been determined by a court of proper jurisdiction.

Garnishment is a process issued against some third party who has in his possession money belonging to defendant in the case. In the process of garnishment the court orders the third party to hold this money until the court instructs him whom to pay it to. If plaintiff wins the case, the court will order this third party, called the garnishee, to pay the money to plaintiff. If plaintiff loses, the court will order the garnishee to pay to defendant.

A process of attachment can be issued when the suit is first begun or at any time before judgment is given, while one of execution is issued only after a judgment has been given. An execution process issued prior to judgment is void.

After a judgment has been issued by a court of competent jurisdiction, the same court will be the only court that can issue

Survey of American Law

any process for collecting the judgment, unless the original records of the case have been removed to some other court. An attachment process can be issued only by the court in which the action is actually pending. Before an attachment process will be issued by a court, an affidavit must be filed. This affidavit may be made and executed by any party acting in behalf of the creditor and having personal knowledge of the facts involved in the case. An affidavit is given under oath, and is signed by the affiant and by the officer who administers the oath. It should be entitled in the court and cause of action in which and for which it is issued, if the affidavit for attachment is made while the suit is still pending.

The following are the different parts of a judicial process:

(1) Venue: State of Illinois } ss.
Cook County

(2) Title as to the Court: In the District Court of Cook County, Illinois.

(3) Title as to Cause: John Jones, Plaintiff
vs.
Elmer Emerson, Defendant }

(4) Style: In the name of the people of the State of Illinois, etc.

(5) Address: To the Sheriff of Cook County, Greetings, etc.

(6) Body: This part of the judicial process directs or commands what is to be done, and when, where, and how it is to be done.

(7) Testate: Witness, the Honorable Elmer Holmgren, District Judge, at the City of Chicago, Cook County, this 24th day of January, A.D. 1968.

(8) Signature of Clerk of Court: Harold Hanson, clerk of said court, by Arnold Ames, Deputy.

(9) Seal of the Court: The court seal should be placed at the left of the clerk's signature.

(10) Endorsement: Johnson and Maxwell, attorneys for plaintiff.

A process of execution issued by a court will be good only within that court's jurisdiction, whether it is county or state. A county court cannot issue a valid execution process outside the limits of the county. In the same way, if a state court issues a process of execution against the property of a party living in another state, the process will be null and void. Courts have held that the process of execution issued by a court is of no validity the moment the jurisdictional bounds of the court issuing the execution have been passed and an invasion made into the territory or jurisdiction of some other court.

XXV. PRACTICE

All actions concerning real estate must be brought in the county where the real estate is located. Such actions are called real actions.

All actions for money damages where the subject matter of the action is personal injury, personal property, or chattels may be brought in any county where defendant can be located and process served on him. Such actions are called transitory.

A lawsuit, under modern code-pleading procedure, is said to have begun when plaintiff has filed his petition and subpoenas have been taken out, and the constable or sheriff has served, or made a reasonable attempt to serve, the process on defendant and witnesses.

Every court has jurisdiction over all property within the state or county in which the court is located. If it is a state court, it will have jurisdiction over all property within the state; if it is a county court, it will have jurisdiction over all property located within the county.

Every court can compel a witness to appear in court on a particular day, at a specified hour, by serving process on him through a constable or sheriff. If the witness fails to appear as specified, the court can have him arrested for contempt. The process is made out by the clerk of the court, and a copy of it must be left with each witness served. If the witness lives in another state, process may be issued against him by publishing notice of service in a newspaper in the county where the court presides, for the statutory period.

After the pleadings have been filed in a case and all processes served on parties to the case, the case comes up for trial. The jury is impaneled and sworn; then the attorney for each side makes an opening statement to the jury. Then the plaintiff's attorney introduces all evidence and testimony in behalf of his client and the defendant's attorney offers all his evidence and testimony in behalf of his client. When all the evidence is in, the attorneys may file any motions which they desire. After the court has passed on these motions, both attorneys argue the case before the jury and court. The court instructs the members of the jury who then retire to the jury room until they reach or agree on a verdict. They return to the courtroom, and in open court the foreman of the jury reads the verdict in the presence of all the jurors. This verdict is then recorded and made a part of the court records. The attorney whose case is lost may make a motion for a new trial. If the court denies a new trial an appeal may be taken to the superior or the appellate court. When judgment has been entered according to the verdict of the jury, the party receiving the judgment may execute it, and attachment or garnishment proceedings may be instituted against the defeated party, or against the defeated party's property, so that the judgment may be collected.

INDEX

by act of fault of consignor,
233
arising from nature of goods,
234, 235
by public authority, 235
by fire, 232, 233
by public enemy, 233
of passengers, 238 ff.
receipt, 231
rights and duties, 239, 240
right to refuse goods, 229, 230
when liability begins, 230, 231
terminates, 241
Common stock, 276
Community property, 377 ff.
Compensation, of agent, 191, 192
of a partner, 253
Complaint, xxvii
Compound interest, 146
Compromise with creditors, 24, 25
Concealment in life insurance, 292,
293
Condition, in contract, 64
in contract of sale, 93 ff.
Conditional contract, filing of, 94,
95
of sale, 93 ff.
Conflict of laws, 434 ff.
Consideration, compromise, 24, 25
contracts under seal, 4, 5
in executed contract, 20, 21
in executory contract, 20
extension of time, 25
for gift, 21
good, 25
moral obligation, 25
must be legal, 25, 26
must be possible, 26
must be present or future, 26,
27
payment of smaller amount, 22-
24
promise may be sufficient, 22
settlement to avoid litigation,
24
valuable, 21, 22
Constitutional law, xxi, 431 ff.
Contract, against public policy, 39,
40

assignment of rights under, 43-
45
consideration, 20 ff.
defined, 3
discharge of, 52 ff.
of drunkard, 13, 14
entire and divisible, 63, 64
executed, 3, 4
executory, 3, 4
express, 5, 6
filing conditional, 94, 95
formal, 4, 5
implied, 5, 6
of infants, 7 ff.
of insane person, 12 ff.
made on Sunday, 38
of married women, 14, 15
necessary conditions of, 3
not to be performed within one
year, 49, 50
object must not be illegal, 36,
37
operation of, 42 ff.
oral, 5
parties, acquiring rights under,
42, 43
necessary, 6
in restraint of trade, 40-42
of sale, 90-93
in writing, 93
simple, 4, 5
subject matter, 36 ff.
uberrima fides, 31, 32
under seal, 4, 5
of wager void, 38
waiver or rescission of, 52
written, 5
Copartnership, *see* Partnership
Corporate, name, 268
seal, 266, 268
Corporation, 265 ff.
bylaws, 268
common and preferred stock,
276
directors, 278, 279
dissolution, 272-275
dividends, 276
formation of, 269
implied powers, 270-272

Survey of American Law

ELMER C. JOHNSON, J.D., Ph.D.

Lawyers, teachers, students and laymen who find a broad knowledge of legal practices to be of value, have long felt the need for a systematic gathering of the fundamentals of law into one book. This volume fills that need. For the lawyer it is a handy reference work; for the layman it provides legal first aid. Teachers in schools of law will find it a comprehensive, well-organized textbook. At the same time the book will serve as an introduction to the study of law for college seniors and as a text for law school students in their first year of study.

The author of this comprehensive book has been teaching and practicing law for many years. After his Preface, and Introduction that traces the origins of American law, he begins a thoroughgoing discussion of twenty-five legal subjects. The result of much research and study, the main subjects contain judicial court decisions upon which American law is based, with the name of the case and the citation.

Dr. Johnson's subjects are: Contracts, Quasi-Contracts, Sales of Personal Property, Negotiable Instruments, Suretyship and Guaranty, Agency, Bailments, Partnership, Corporations, Insurance, Real Property, Chattel Mortgages, Real Estate Mortgages, Trusts, Torts, Domestic Relations, Community Property, Criminal Law, Wills, Evidence, Constitutional Law, Conflict of Laws, Judgment, Attachment-Garnishment-Execution, and Practice.

Addressing the following remarks to the layman, the author writes, "Knowledge of the law builds respect for law and order. Once you know your rights and duties as a citizen, you will have a guide to legal first